Motorbooks International

POWERPRO SERIES

HOW TO
REBUILD
YOUR
ENGINE

DATE DUE

Ben Watson

"This book is dedicated to Ben and Gladys Watson who funded my automotive education and volunteered the family car for experiments and experience."

First published in 1993 by Motorbooks International Publishers & Wholesalers, PO Box 2, 729 Prospect Avenue, Osceola, WI 54020 USA

Motorbooks International is a certified trademark, registered with the United States Patent Office

The information in this book is true and complete to the best of our knowledge. All recommendations are made without any guarantee on the part of the author or Publisher, who also disclaim any liability incurred in connection with the use of this data or specific details

We recognize that some words, model names and designations, for example, mentioned herein are the property of the trademark holder. We use them for identification purposes only. This is not an official publication

Motorbooks International books are also available at discounts in bulk quantity for industrial or sales-promotional use. For details write to Special Sales Manager at the Publisher's address

Library of Congress Cataloging-in-Publication Data
Watson, Ben. 1953
    How to rebuild your engine / Ben Watson.
    p.   cm.—(Motorbooks International powerpro series)
    Includes index.
    ISBN 0-87938-762-9
    1. Automobiles—Motors—Maintenance and repair.   I. Title.   II. Series.
TL210.W35   1993
629.25'04'0288—dc20   93-13647

On the front cover: An example of how smart a properly rebuilt engine can look is this 1966 425hp 426 Hemi. The owner is Bill Jacobsen of Silver Dollar Classic Cars, Odessa, Florida; the engine was rebuilt by Silver Dollar's Joe Johnson. *Mike Mueller*

Printed in the United States of America

Contents

Introduction

During the 1960s, one of the more "manly" hobbies was building cars. With the advent of emission control systems during the 1970s and 1980s, many hobbyists abandoned working on cars and rebuilding engines in favor of more mundane pursuits such as trading stocks and bonds.

Folks, let's get real for a moment. How could the mere acquisition of personal wealth compare with the satisfaction of building bits of iron and aluminum into a flaming, screaming powerhouse—or at least an economical powerplant for a little commuter car? Few experiences in the life of a man or woman could possibly compare to the sense of wonder experienced when a few hundred pounds of metal, crafted by one's own hands, breathe to life.

I rebuilt my first engine while I was still in high school. A friend owned a 1959 MGA. On his way to classes, the engine developed a knocking noise. That evening, he called me over to his house to ask my opinion on what should be done. I do not recall exactly how I answered him, but I am reasonably sure it was something to the effect of, "Turn up the radio." Bill insisted that we tear the engine apart. We enlisted the assistance of another high school friend, one who had earned the moniker Boy.

A couple of days later, at the agreed time, I arrived at Bill's garage in full dress grubbies. A short time later, Boy arrived dressed in white pants, a white shirt, a white belt, and white shoes. In fact, he looked like a refugee from a Pat Boone look-alike contest. Realizing, much to our dismay, that some people just do not have a burning desire to disassemble and reassemble metal, we sent Boy after a box of "oil clearance" or something, and began to remove the engine.

What is it about British engineers? Do they own stock in bolt companies? When one bolt will do the job, why do they use three? After what must have been several hours of removing nuts and bolts, Bill and I were finally ready to remove the engine from the car.

Bill searched through the garage and located an old block and tackle. Tying the block and tackle to one of the rafters of the garage, we began to hoist the engine from the car. Unfortunately, we could not raise the engine high enough to clear the front of the car, not to mention the fact that we had not calculated the difficulty in moving the garage rafter in order to swing the engine away from the car and onto the ground. Minutes later, Bill and I found ourselves flat on our back, with the front tires of the car flattened, pushing on the front bumper with our feet to roll the car out from under the engine.

Since both of us were neophytes at engine rebuilding, and since Bill wrote the book on doing things by the book, we followed the instruction manual implicitly during the disassembly process–that is, until we tried to remove the flywheel. The section on removing the flywheel said that it was first necessary to remove the rear main bearing cap. Cool; we turned to the section on removing the rear main bearing cap. This section indicated that it was first necessary to remove the flywheel. We offered the book as a burned offering to Synchro, the ancient pagan god of all things both frustrating and automotive.

After a first experience like this, how could I resist becoming a professional automobile mechanic? (By the way, the engine had a broken crankshaft. It had broken in such a way that the two halves mated and meshed. The engine ran fine, except for what I felt was an insignificant noise. I guess turning the radio up was not really an adequate long-term fix.)

Engine Rebuilding Basics

1

This book is about rebuilding the internal-combustion four-stroke gasoline piston engine. One of the most serious and financially devastating things that can happen to an automobile is a serious engine problem. Today, a major engine failure can result in thousands of dollars in repair bills. Although a repair shop is justified in these charges, you can save hundreds of dollars by rebuilding the engine yourself.

Professional mechanics often joke about the guy who comes into the shop and announces that he used to work on his own cars, but he just does not have time since they started putting all this pollution control stuff on these engines. The implication here is that the fellow feels he can no longer do an adequate job. When it comes right down to it, it is likely that the consumer *can* do an adequate job. In fact, the consumer may do a job superior in quality to that of the professional. In spite of all the professional's skills and experience, the consumer has something the professional seldom has: time. Time is what is really needed to do the superior job. The professional is always racing against the flat-rate manual.

Major Components
Pistons and Rings

The piston forms the lower end of the combustion chamber and transfers the power released during combustion to the crankshaft by way of the connecting rod. Pistons come in several styles. The styles can be divided by skirt design, by piston head design, by manufacturing process, and by metallurgy.

The rings fit around the top of the piston. They form an arc slightly larger than the piston. When the ends of the arc meet inside the cylinder, a seal is formed, and this seal keeps the combustion gases out of the crankcase and the crankcase oil out of the combustion chamber.

Skirt Designs

Two basic skirt designs are used for pistons. Older pistons in slower-running engines have full

Any automobile worthy of preserving is worthy of an engine rebuild. Worthy might mean the car is irreplaceable like this Tucker, it might mean you see no sense in replacing an essentially solid machine with a $25,000 chunk of aluminum and plastic, or it might mean you want to be the only person on the block with a fire-breathing Vega.

Although the things bolted onto the outside of 1990s engines make them seem significantly more sophisticated, they really differ little in complexity from this Model A engine.

skirts. The full skirt increases the reciprocating mass, which increases the inertial drag and reciprocating mass of the engine.

When crankshafts acquired counterweights and engine speeds increased beyond the level produced in a lawn mower, pistons developed partial skirts. The partial skirt decreased the weight of the piston and provided clearance for the counterweights. Almost all modern engines use a partial-skirt piston. The reduced reciprocating mass of the partial-skirt piston allows an increased maximum number of revolutions per minute (rpm).

Head Design

Standard pistons normally have a flat top. Many high-performance engines, especially ones that have been modified for racing, utilize a piston with a domed or high-rise head. In many cases, installing these "pop-up" dome pistons is of no benefit, as they impede the propagation of the flame front through the combustion chamber. As the piston comes up on the compression stroke, the pop-up dome fills a portion of the combustion chamber in the cylinder head. This feature increases the compression ratio. Although the increase in the compression ratio improves the potential power output of the engine, it also tends to increase the combustion temperatures. When the combustion temperature rises above 2,500 degrees Fahrenheit, oxygen and nitrogen combine in the combustion chamber to form oxides of nitrogen. These emission gases are among those most closely controlled by the federal government. When you decide to rebuild your engine, consider whether the pistons you

This European engine designed during World War I shows most of the characteristics of a modern engine. It is a low-rpm engine that features an external valvetrain and oil pump. Engines of the 1990s look more complicated, but most have no more parts than this museum piece.

Although thought by many to be a fairly modern development, the V-8 dates from the 1930s. This engine features removable cylinder banks and a flathead design. Note that the valves are in the cylinder bank adjacent to the cylinders. This engine would be far more complicated to rebuild than most 1990s engines.

Since the beginning of time, parents have taught their children the skills of "adulthood." In today's economy and society, this rite of passage has suffered much. Engine rebuilding can be a good family activity—especially if the engine is not needed to go buy the groceries this week. Contrary to what this picture illustrates, my daughter participates more in this rite than my son.

choose are legal for your intended use.

Manufacturing Process

The pistons can be either cast or forged. Forged pistons are stronger and more precisely manufactured and more expensive. For these reasons, they are normally reserved for high-performance, high-power engines.

Metallurgy

Back when the hot car at Indy was the Miller, pistons for consumer cars were made of cast iron. Cast-iron pistons represented an enormous reciprocating mass. This mass robbed the engine of precious power and top rpm.

The 1950s and 1960s saw the introduction of aluminum pistons into the technology of the mass-produced automobile engine. This allowed higher maximum rpm and less parasitic loss of power to the reciprocating movement of the piston mass.

Piston Design

The typical piston is not round like the cylinder. It is an ellipse, with the long axis, called the thrust axis, perpendicular to the short axis, called the wrist pin axis. This piston design is called a cam grind and allows for the thermal expansion of the piston along the wrist pin axis. Additionally, the cam grind allows for compression of the thrust axis of the piston during the power stroke. When measurements of the piston are being taken during the disassembly process, the cam grind needs to be accounted for.

Connecting Rods

The job of the connecting rods is to connect the power generated by the explosion of the air and fuel in the combustion chamber, above the pistons, to the crankshaft.

Manufacturing Process

Like the pistons, the connecting rods can be either cast or forged. Forged pistons are stronger and more precisely manufactured; therefore, they are normally reserved for performance engines.

Metallurgy

Connecting rods for consumer cars are made of cast iron. These rods represent an enormous reciprocating mass. This mass robs the engine of precious power and top rpm. Racing engines and other high-performance engines use aluminum connecting rods.

The 1950s and 1960s saw the introduction of aluminum connecting rods on performance engines. This allowed higher maximum rpm and less parasitic loss of power to the reciprocating movement of the connecting rod mass.

Connecting Rod Design

Each connecting rod has a big end and a small end. The small end fits into the piston where the power is transferred from the piston to the connecting rod by a wrist pin. The wrist pin may be pressed into the rod and floating in the piston, it may be pressed into the piston and floating in the rod end, or it may be full floating, meaning that it is floating in both the piston and the connecting rod.

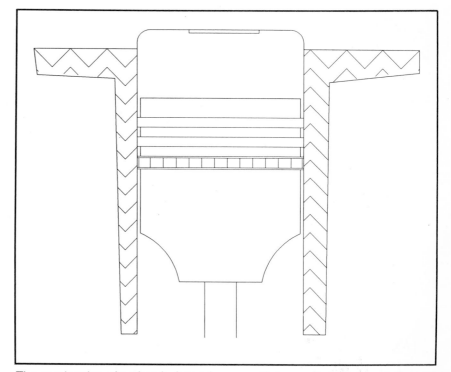

The combustion chamber is formed by the top of the piston, the bottom of the cylinder head, and the cylinder walls. In this closed chamber, the explosive equivalent of more than 32 sticks of dynamite is ignited each hour. Precision and strength are required to make the engine durable.

The two common styles of piston skirts are the full skirt, right, and the partial skirt, left. All other things being equal—metallurgy, mass—the full-skirt piston is stronger. This extra strength comes at the cost of a greater reciprocating mass, which affects the maximum rpm and the rate at which the rpm of the engine can change.

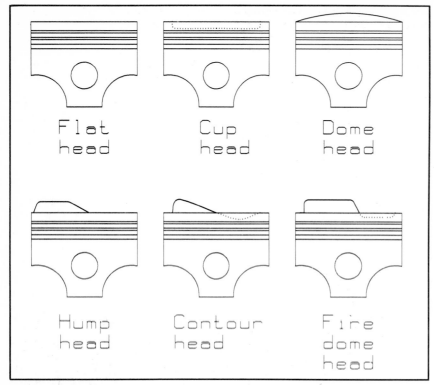

The head of the piston is available in several different designs. Each design exists to solve a specific problem. For most engine rebuilds, the flathead piston is the right one to use. The domed pistons are very popular among high-performance addicts.

The dome, however, affects the flow of the flame front and increases the compression ratio. High-compression engines do not generally run very well on the standard pump gas available to the average consumer in the 1990s.

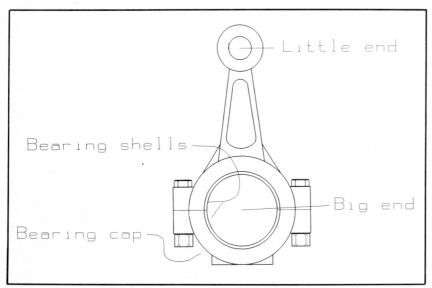

The connecting rod transfers the vertical forces released by the explosions in the combustion chambers, to the crankshaft. Although these rods must be tough, they should transfer as little of their own inertial weight to

the crankshaft as possible. Simply, they need to be light and tough. This combination is easy to optimize; the level of optimization increases as the purchase price of the rods increases.

The big end of the connecting rod connects to the crankshaft. Around the inside of the big end is a replaceable bearing shell. Owing to the enormous stress exerted on these bearing shells, they are among the engine components most prone to failure.

Crankshaft

The power created by the engine is conveyed to the transmission through the crankshaft. It could be said that the crankshaft converts the vertical action of the pistons in the cylinder to the rotational action required to move the car down the road.

The crankshaft is either forged or cast, from a variety of alloys. Although the forged crankshaft is usually stronger, it is also expensive. The cast crank is more than adequate for most non-racing uses.

After casting or forging, the bearing surfaces are machined and are then fine ground and polished. Modern crankshafts feature counterweights that balance them against the weight of the pistons and connecting rods. Further balancing is accomplished by shaving and drilling the counterweights.

Cylinder Head

The cylinder head has several functions. It contains the combustion chamber and provides a path for the intake air-fuel charge from the intake manifold to the combustion chamber. Additionally, the head provides a path for the exhaust gases to pass from the combustion chambers to the exhaust manifold. This path is opened and closed by the valves. Since World War II, these valves have been located in the cylinder head.

Valves and Valvetrain

The valves control the flow of intake and exhaust gases to and from the combustion chamber. The intake valve opens every other time the piston makes a downward stroke, to pull fuel and air into the combustion chamber. The exhaust valve opens on every other upward stroke of the piston, to allow the burned air-fuel charge, or exhaust gases, to be pushed from the combustion chamber.

Most engines have only two valves for each cylinder: one intake and one exhaust. In an effort to improve the flow of intake and exhaust gases through the combustion chamber, many late-model engines will use two or even more intake or exhaust valves, or both, for each cylinder. Although on the surface, this might seem to make the engine more complicated, it really only means more parts, not more complexity.

Camshaft

The camshaft consists of a series of egg-shaped lobes responsible for opening and closing the intake and exhaust valves. In most domestic engines, it is located inside the engine block. The connection between the camshaft and the valve is accomplished with lifters and pushrods.

Many import engines and late-model domestic engines place the camshaft over the top of the valves. The camshaft more or less directly opens the valves. In these engines, the only parts between the camshaft and the valve are a rocker and a follower. Many engines omit even the rocker. This eliminates the need for lifters and pushrods. Eliminating the lifters and pushrods reduces the number of components in the engine that are prone to wear. Additionally, higher rpm are possible because eliminating the pushrods eliminates the potential negative effects that might be caused by their flexing.

Camshaft-Valvetrain Configurations

When Chuck Yeager broke the sound barrier in 1947, humans were driving around with flatheads under the hood. In a flathead configuration, the valves are located in the block. During the 1950s, a major innovation found its way into mass production: the overhead valve engine. Moving the valves to the cylinder head meant better flow of the intake and exhaust gases through the combustion chamber.

About the time disco music began to become popular in the mid-1970s, U.S. manufacturers began to move the camshaft from its nice, safe position in the middle of the engine to its more aggressive position on top of the cylinder head. This configuration, which had already been popular on European engines for many years, is known as the overhead cam. Some more radical engine designs use separate overhead-mounted camshafts for the intake and exhaust valves. This

design is called the dual overhead cam. For domestic engines, a good example of this engine design is the Ford Super High Output (SHO) engine.

Timing Gears, Chains, and Belts

Gears, sprockets, chains, and belts are, and have been, used to keep the crankshaft and the camshaft synchronized. Although these are important components in any engine, their catastrophic failure is far more serious in some engines than in others.

If the open valves have negative clearance with the piston at top

dead center, and if the timing gear/chain/belt system fails to maintain proper synchronization of the cam and the crank–such as might occur when the timing belt or chain breaks–severe damage can occur. As the pistons contact the valves, the valves are bent. If you are lucky, that is all the damage that will be done. If you are not lucky, the failure of a timing belt or chain can destroy the cylinder head, the valves, the pistons, and possibly the engine block.

A word to the wise: A $50 timing belt and a few hours' work or labor charges are a lot less costly

The crankshaft converts the vertical forces transferred through the connecting rods from the combustion chambers, into rotating forces. The mass of a 4,000 pound (lb) car, or even a 16,000lb truck, is transferred through a piece of metal barely 4in in diameter.

The cylinder head–this one is sitting on a partially disassembled engine block–is the path for the combustible gases to enter the combustion chamber. Each cylinder has two valves.

than a new engine. If your owner's manual suggests the replacement of the timing belt at a certain mileage interval, change it at that interval.

[1]The Four Strokes

The modern automotive gasoline engine is a four-stroke engine. The four strokes are called intake, compression, power, and exhaust. Although these words have long been used to explain the operation of the internal-combustion four-stroke engine, I prefer the far more descriptive terms used by a Canadian associate. I have modified his terms a little to make them printable: *suck*, *squeeze*, *boom*, and *belch*.

Intake (Suck)

At the beginning of the intake stroke, the intake valve opens. Synchronized to the opening of the intake valve, the piston starts one of its downward strokes. The downward movement of the piston creates a low-pressure area in the cylinder. Air and fuel rush into the cylinder through the open intake valve. At the bottom of the piston travel during the intake stroke, the cylinder is charged with air and fuel. Rarely does the cylinder fill to atmospheric pressure with the air-fuel charge. The volumetric percentage of air at atmospheric pressure in the combustion chamber in relation to the volumetric size of the combustion chamber is called volumetric efficiency.

Compression (Squeeze)

At the bottom of the piston travel during the intake stroke, the intake valve closes. The piston travels past bottom dead center and begins one of its upward strokes. With both the intake and exhaust valves closed, the upward movement of the piston begins to compress the charge in the cylinder. As the charge is compressed, the temperature of the charge rises. This process is known as adiabatic heating. Adiabatic heating is essential for proper combustion of the air-fuel charge. During the compression stroke, temperatures will rise several hundred degrees Fahrenheit.

The opening of the valves is accomplished on most domestic engines with pushrods and rocker arms. Although, as seen in an earlier photos of the World War I vintage engine this is a very old method, it remains very functional.

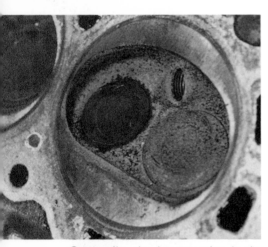

Generally, the larger valve is the intake valve. The intake valve opens to allow the air and fuel to enter the combustion chamber. The smaller valve, called the exhaust valve, opens to allow the gases to leave after the combustion process is completed.

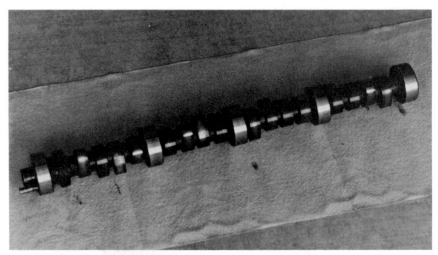

The camshaft is driven by and synchronized to the crankshaft. The cam lobes move lifters up and down, the lifters move pushrods, and the pushrods pivot the rocker arms to open the valves. In general, the higher the lift of the cam lobes, the greater the amount of air that atmospheric pressure can force into the cylinder, and the longer the duration, the more time that atmospheric pressure has to push the air into the cylinder.

Power (Boom)

As the piston approaches the top of the compression stroke, the ignition system fires the spark plug. The firing of the spark plug begins the burn of the air-fuel charge. Momentum carries the piston over top dead center as the igniting, heating air-fuel charge begins to expand. As the burning air-fuel charge expands, it drives the piston downward. The power being released by the expanding gases is transferred from the top of the piston to the crankshaft by the connecting rod.

[2]Exhaust (Belch)

As the piston swings past bottom dead center, the exhaust valve opens. The piston starts its upward journey, pushing remains of the burned air-fuel charge out of the cylinder through the exhaust valve. As the piston approaches top dead center, the intake valve begins to open, readying the cylinder for the next engine cycle.

Note: The intake valve opens before the exhaust valve closes on most modern engines. This is known as valve overlap. This accomplishes a couple of things: First, the flow of the exhaust gases out of the combustion chamber creates a low pressure that helps the air-fuel charge enter the combustion chamber. Second, as the piston starts its trip down on the intake stroke and the exhaust valve is still open, some of the exhaust gases are drawn back into the combustion chamber. Since the exhaust gases have a very low content of oxygen and fuel, the gases that are drawn back into the combustion chamber contribute nothing to the combustion process. However, they absorb heat during combustion, lowering the combustion temperature. Keeping the temperature in the combustion chamber below 2,500 degrees Fahrenheit reduces dramatically the production of environmentally hazardous oxides of nitrogen.

Lubrication

The condition of the lubrication system is critical to the proper life of the engine. To rebuild the engine without paying proper attention to the components that protect it from the excessive wear of poor lubrication is like performing lung cancer surgery without making sure the

Although pushrod engines have been around a long time, and although they are very dependable, new priorities and requirements for automobile engines are slowly seeing them replaced.

patient stops smoking three packs a day.

Oil Pump

The main component of the lubrication system is the oil pump. The oil pump generally consists of a set of intermeshing gears contained in a housing and driven either directly or indirectly by the camshaft. Most oil pumps are located deep in the interior of the engine. Some late-model engine designs place the oil pump outside the engine.

Replacement of the oil pump should occur every time the cam, the rod, or the main bearings are replaced. When testing oil pressure on a troubled engine, keep in mind that pumps only provide volume. A pump with reduced volume may provide adequate pressure at the point where the pressure is tested, but the volume may be insufficient to lubricate the engine properly.

The overhead cam engine was perfected during the 1920s. The elimination of the pushrods provides better control of the valves and less inertial drag within the engine. Although widely used on European and Japanese engines since the 1970s, this design only began to become dominant on U.S.-designed engines as the mid-1990s approached.

Even if the oil pressure tests good before an overhaul, play it safe and replace the oil pump.

Some companies market high-volume oil pumps. These can improve oil pressure as the engine ages. However, they are not beneficial enough to justify a great deal of extra expense unless the engine is to be used for racing.

Pump Screen

The oil pump pickup runs from the oil pump to near the bottom of the oil pan. Across the bottom of the pickup is a screen. The purpose of this screen is to keep large chunks and foreign objects out of the oil pump. Over years of operation and poor maintenance, carbon is built up in the oil. Slowly, some of the carbon adheres to the screen, restricting flow through the screen. Because the oil pump pushes the oil much better than it pulls it out of the sump, a little restriction in this screen can have a big effect on the output volume of the pump.

Screen Bypass Valve

A screen bypass valve is used on many applications. It is designed to open when the screen becomes restricted. Unfortunately, bypassing the screen allows large chunks and foreign objects in the oil to pass through the oil pump.

6Pressure Relief Valve

The oil pump is equipped with a pressure relief valve. Particularly when the engine is new or freshly rebuilt, the oil pressure tends to be excessive when the engine is cold. High oil pressure causes the pressure relief valve to open. If the pressure relief valve is stuck or inoperative, oil pressure can be excessively high.

Several years ago, I overhauled an engine for a customer. He paid his bill, took his car, and drove only a few blocks when he heard a muffled pop and smoke started pouring out from under the hood. The oil pressure had been so high that it blew the oil filter off. Since then, I have always tested the oil pressure with a mechanical pressure gauge after completing an overhaul.

Oil Types

Oil types are described in several different ways:

Engine type (normally aspirated spark ignition, normally aspirated diesel, turbocharged spark ignition, turbocharged diesel)

Load usage

Operating temperatures (sump temperatures)

Amount of combustion residue (blowby) generated

Oil capacity

Intended oil change intervals

Type of oil cooling

SAE Viscosity Ratings

Society of Automotive Engineers (SAE) viscosity ratings are intended only to indicate the viscosity of the oil; they do not indicate

The timing chain connects and synchronizes the camshaft and the crankshaft. The chain shown here is a common design. Performance timing chains are roller chains. Many expensive European engines have used roller chains as standard equipment for decades. The larger gear is the cam gear; the smaller is the crank gear. The off-center, circular hub on the larger gear is the fuel pump drive. This drive is missing on most fuel-injected engines, as they use an electric fuel pump.

Many overhead cam engines use a chain to link the cam to the crank, but most use a belt. Use and age tend to weaken the rubber sprockets of the belt, condemning it to eventual failure. A stripped timing belt can cause serious damage to the pistons and valvetrain if it fails at a high engine speed—and on some engines, even at idle. Replace the timing belt every 50,000 miles.

the quality of the oil. The higher the SAE rating number, the more viscous, or thicker, the oil. Generally speaking, if it is winter, or in cold climates, you will want to use a low-viscosity oil. In the summertime, or in warm climates, use a high-viscosity oil.

Multigrade Ratings

Multigrade oils have been used for decades to satisfy the needs of both cold weather operation and hot weather operation. These oils cover three or more viscosity grades.

API Gradings

The American Petroleum Institute (API) grading system goes from SA to SG. This system is based on the types of additives in the oil. SA oil is pure mineral oil and should only be used in the lightest-duty applications. The higher the second alpha digit (the letter in the grading code), the greater the ability of the oil to protect engines.

Note: When choosing which oil you are going to use in your engine, remember that oil is always less expensive than metal.

Cooling System

A mistake commonly made, even among professional mechanics, is spending several hundreds or even thousands of dollars rebuilding an engine, and ignoring the cooling system. This is a very serious mistake. Even when the problem that initiated the rebuild is obviously poor lubrication, its cause may be poor cooling of the engine block. Every engine rebuild should be accompanied by a thorough inspection of the radiator, hoses, and coolant passages in the engine. Since many of today's radiators feature lateral rather than vertical coolant flow, it is virtually impossible to check the condition of the radiator core visually.

When dozens of hours and hundreds of dollars are being spent to recondition an engine, it is only logical to spend a few extra hours and hundred dollars or so to ensure that your work will not be ruined by overheating.

Coolant and Its Additives

In 1977, I bought an old house in Fort Worth, Texas. In the garage, I found a text called *Automobile Engines* with a copyright date of 1945. In those days,

antifreeze came in three major categories: alcohol, glycerin, and Eveready Prestone.

Alcohol was the least expensive but had the disadvantage of having a lower boiling temperature than water. Any time the engine approached what would be considered operating temperature on today's engines, the alcohol would boil away. This made the use of alcohol as a summer coolant impractical, not to mention combustible.

Radiator glycerin had a boiling point higher than water, making it practical in both winter and summer. The primary disadvantages were a high price and a failure to offer protection quite as good against winter freeze-up as alcohol provided.

Eveready Prestone was the predecessor to modern antifreeze coolant. The primary ingredient in modern antifreeze coolant is ethylene glycol. The boiling point of ethylene glycol is 330 degrees Fahrenheit, it is noncorrosive, has no significant odor, and in a 40-60 glycol-water mixture, it can protect against freeze-up at temperatures

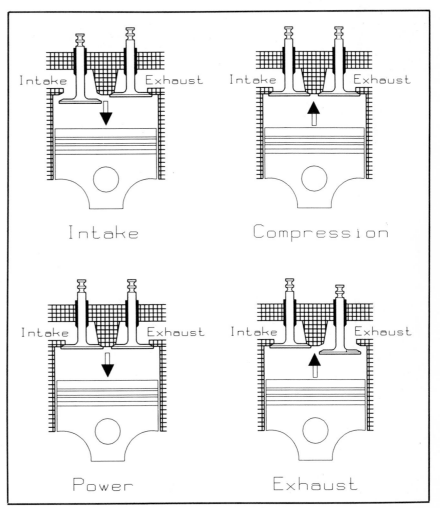

The four-cycle spark ignition gasoline engine is the most common engine used to power the automobile and light-duty trucks. The four cycles are the intake cycle, where air and fuel enter the combustion chamber through the open intake valve; the compression cycle, where the air-fuel charge in the combustion chambers is compressed, which increases the temperature and the density of the charge; the power stroke, where the ignited and expanding gases drive the piston downward; and the exhaust stroke, where the rising piston pushes the exhaust gases out of the combustion chamber through the open exhaust valve.

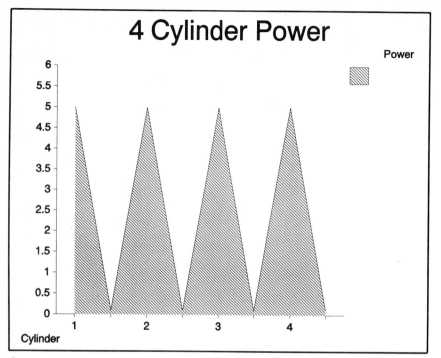

4 Cylinder Power

A small number of cylinders destines an engine to rough operation. A four-cylinder engine provides power through the crankshaft only once every 180 degrees of rotation. With the power pulses are pulses of equal size when no power is delivered through the crankshaft. Inherently, a four-cylinder engine will run rough. In spite of this, Fiat, in the 1920s, built a 15-liter four-cylinder engine–which, at 915 cubic inches, was three times the size of the popular Chevy 305.

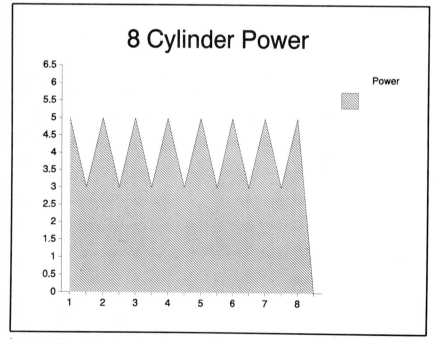

8 Cylinder Power

In an eight-cylinder engine, power is delivered through the crankshaft every 90 degrees of rotation. At no time is no power at all being transferred through the crankshaft. This means that an eight-cylinder will run smoother than a four-cylinder or a six-cylinder.

as low as -65 degrees Fahrenheit. Various additives are added by manufacturers to inhibit leaking, rust, and restrictive scale.

Ethylene glycol is a hazardous waste well known for its ability to do severe kidney and brain damage. Consumption of as little as 1/2 cup can cause irreversible damage or may be fatal. Check with your local department of ecology to determine the proper way to dispose of antifreeze coolant waste.

Look in the future for ethylene glycol to be replaced by a less hazardous chemical. Two of the chemicals being discussed are propylene glycol and polyethylene glycol. Although these sound like virtually the same chemical as ethylene glycol, they are not as toxic. In fact, polyethylene glycol is an ingredient in popular soft drinks.

Radiator

The radiator is a heat exchanger made of copper or aluminum. Older radiator cores consist of copper tubes separated by corrugated fins. The tubes and fins dissipate the heat of the coolant to the air passing through the radiator. These radiators have copper tanks located at each end of the core. Back when my dad was trying to teach me how to release a clutch without leaving the universal joints in the gutter, the tanks were located on the top and bottom of the radiator. This was called a vertical flow radiator.

The oil pump is as important to an engine as the heart is to a human being. A failure of the oil pump means a reduction in the volume of oil available to the lubricated surfaces of the engine. Reduce the oil volume enough, and the engine will fail.

Most radiators in the 1990s are of the cross-flow design. In the cross-flow design, the tanks are located on the left and right sides of the radiator.

Many modern radiators consist of aluminum core tanks made of polyamide with glass fiber reinforcement. One distinct advantage of the polyamide tanks for the manufacturer is that the mounting brackets can be cast as part of the tank. This reduces a vehicle's production cost. Some of the German imports were among the first to use this design. In the early days of these "plastic tank" radiators, we had a lot of leaking problems. To this day, I have a prejudice against them. In spite of this, like many technologies, they have been improved over the years, and they seem to be quite dependable in the 1990s.

Transmission Oil Cooler

Most cars equipped with an automatic transmission have a transmission oil cooler in the radiator. Sometimes, oil from the transmission cooler can leak into the radiator. This oil can sometimes be misinterpreted as a blown head gasket or an intake manifold problem.

Hoses

Water hoses are the part of the cooling system that the car owner has the greatest ability to monitor. Good-quality hoses can be expensive but are worth every penny. Over the years, I have used the corrugated, so-called universal radiator hoses. But engine compartments of the 1990s are so tight and the angles that the hoses have to be twisted so sharp, I recommend that you pop for an extra few bucks and buy the molded hoses. To be frank, when I told my customers, "Of course it's as good as a molded hose, and cheaper," what I really meant was, "I can't get the right hose for your car."

Many automotive fleet users replace the standard black rubber radiator and heater hoses with green silicone hoses. These hoses are most commonly found on emergency equipment applications. Although they are more expensive, they are also much more durable.

Years ago, I bought a Pinto that nearly cost me my marriage. One mild north central Texas after-

Failure to change the oil frequently will allow deposits to build up on the filtering screen of the oil pickup. A dirty filter screen will reduce oil flow through the pickup.

noon–the temperature was only in the low hundreds–I blew a lower radiator hose. The coolant dumped out of the cooling system so fast that I did not even notice. Fortunately, I had a scapegoat for my inattention: a corrugated universal hose. Although these hoses are useful for emergency repairs, they are not nearly as dependable as the preformed hoses.

Hose Clamps

There is no such thing as a used hose clamp. A new $0.50 clamp can mean the difference between a successful, long-lasting overhaul and a $1,000 box full of new, but junk, parts.

Radiator Cap

You can buy a new one for about five bucks, so it cannot be

This oil was drained from a car belonging to a government fleet in Alaska. Routine oil changes will prevent most major engine failures. The oil cannot be changed too often. Oil is always less expensive than metal.

The water jacket carries coolant around the cylinders. The coolant absorbs the heat from the cylinders and transports the heat to the radiator. If the engine block and the cylinder heads were made of a material capable of handling large changes in temperature, a coolant and the water jacket would not be necessary. Poor maintenance of the cooling system can cause deposits to build up in the water jacket and reduces the volume of coolant available to the cylinders.

The thermostat regulates the temperature of the coolant. In many climates, it is standard procedure to remove the thermostat. It is thought that this will allow the engine to run cooler. The reality is that in many cases, removing the thermostat will allow the coolant to move through the radiator too quickly. The coolant never has an adequate opportunity to give up its heat to the air passing through the radiator, and the result is that the engine runs hotter rather than cooler.

important, right? Wrong! The radiator cap is both the pressure regulator and the pressure relief valve for the cooling system. If it does not hold a high enough pressure, coolant loss and overheating can result. If it does not properly relieve pressure, the tanks can blow off the radiator.

Water Pump

The water pump is responsible for ensuring that the coolant moves through the cylinder head and block to remove potentially damaging heat. Further, it moves the heat-saturated coolant through the hoses to the radiator where the heat can be dissipated to the air passing through the radiator. Although the water pump is normally driven by belts on the front of the engine, the Saab engine drives it with the camshaft.

Thermostat

The thermostat prevents coolant from passing through the radiator, until the engine reaches operating temperature. It is then responsible for ensuring that the coolant temperature does not drop below the operating temperature.

It is common practice in places like Guam to remove the thermostat entirely. Although this may seem like an incredible feat of wisdom for a warm climate, in reality, removing the thermostat may allow the coolant to pass through the radiator so fast that the radiator does not have a chance to cool it. Removing the thermostat can actually cause overheating.

The thermostat is a temperature-controlled valve. As the temperature of the coolant behind it rises, the thermostat opens, allowing the coolant to pass into the radiator. If the thermostat fails to open, the engine will overheat.

Replace the thermostat any time major work is done on the engine.

Water Jacket

The water jacket is the system of passageways cast into the cylinder head and block, through which the coolant passes.

2

Symptoms and Diagnosis

Rebuilding modern engines is not nearly as complicated or as different from rebuilding engines of the 1960s as you might think. This and subsequent chapters will guide you through the entire process.

Symptoms

When do you need to rebuild an engine? Answering this question may be the most difficult part of the rebuilding process. An engine may need to be rebuilt for many reasons, including the following:

Low oil pressure
Main bearing noise
Connecting rod noise
Noisy valves
Worn camshafts
Low compression
Smoking
Oil bypassing the rings
Oil bypassing the valve guides
Oil loss
Leaks
Desire for better performance
Desire for more power
Desire for better fuel economy
Just the fun of it

Low Oil Pressure

Low oil pressure can manifest itself in several ways. If the car is equipped with an oil pressure gauge, the most obvious evidence of low oil pressure will be low readings on the gauge. But, before condemning large, expensive pieces of iron and bearing material, check a few things.

Confirm that the oil pressure gauge is reading accurately. Most oil pressure gauges installed on the assembly line are electric instead of mechanical. These gauges are notorious for being inaccurate. Confirm that the problem is really low oil pressure by removing the oil pressure sending unit and installing a mechanical oil pressure gauge in the same port. If your personal toolbox does not include a mechanical oil pressure gauge, one can be rented from almost any store that rents tools or any of the better auto supply stores in town.

The amount of oil pressure you should expect will vary with the temperature of the oil. The temperature of the oil will vary with the temperature of the engine. It is likely that when you perform this test, the engine will be cold. Cold oil will inherently provide a higher

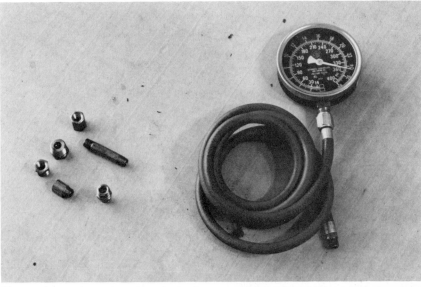

Never depend on the electrical oil pressure gauge during the diagnostic process. Invest in a mechanical gauge when testing the oil pressure.

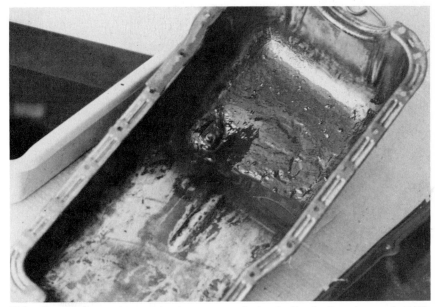

This oil pan shows the result of too-few oil changes over the years. The sludge in the bottom is nearly 1/2in thick.

17

Defective main bearings can cause reduced oil pressure or even a loud knocking noise. The sound will be a high-frequency dull "whanking." Main bearing replacement will be part of every engine rebuild.

oil pressure than warm oil. This is even true when multi-viscosity oils are being used.

Once the mechanical oil pressure gauge is connected to the port where the oil pressure sending unit had been connected, start the engine. Immediately after the engine is started and before actual-ly checking the oil pressure, inspect the fittings where the gauge has been installed, to confirm there are no leaks. Even minor leaks on some gauges can cause the gauge to read inaccurately. If you find no leaks, observe the oil pressure and compare the readings with those in the chart below.

Causes That May Not Require Overhaul

The oil pressure might be low for several reasons that would not require the engine to be over-hauled. Among these are the following:

Low oil level
Restricted oil filter
Thin or diluted oil
An oil pump relief valve that's stuck open
Damaged oil pump suction tube

Low Oil Level

Checking the oil level is essential before making a trip to the rental yard to rent an engine hoist. When the oil level is low, it is difficult for the oil pump suction tube to take in a sufficient volume of oil to maintain pressure in the engine lubrication system. Low oil pressure under these circumstances is of little concern compared with the severe damage that low oil pressure is doing to the engine. Probably the biggest favor you could ever do for your engine is to check the oil level on a weekly basis, adding oil as needed.

Restricted Oil Filter

The simplest, and most embarrassing, reason for low oil pressure is a restricted oil filter. Unfortunately, there is no way to say gracefully that this is usually a result of neglect or sabotage. If the oil has not been changed for some time in a vehicle suffering from low oil pressure, change the oil and replace the filter.

Thin or Diluted Oil

The idea of purchasing oil that is too thin—is of too low a viscosity—is rather silly. If you are using oil that has been purchased for the purpose of lubricating automobile engines, it is almost impossible to get one that all by itself could cause low oil pressure. Some might disagree with this statement on the basis that using a thicker, higher-viscosity oil will cause the oil pressure to be higher. That is often true. However, if the engine lubrication system, oil pump, and bearings are in good condition, even a low-viscosity oil should yield an oil pressure within proper specifications.

Diluted oil is another matter. Oil can become diluted in several ways. Probably the most common way is through not being changed often enough. As the engine is used, especially after a cold start-up, some of the combustion gases bypass the rings and end up in the crankcase. These gases carry quantities of unburned gasoline. The unburned gasoline dilutes the engine oil. This diluted engine oil can cause low oil pressure. What may be even more critical about this is that the unburned gasoline combining with moisture in the crankcase can form acid that can damage bearings and bearing surfaces long before the low oil pressure caused by the dilution damages the engine.

Another way engine oil can become diluted is with coolant. If a head gasket begins to leak, or if a cylinder head or block becomes cracked, coolant could leak into the combustion chamber or the crankcase or both, and dilute the oil.

Although defective cam bearings seldom inspire the rebuilding of an engine, they can cause a severe loss of oil pressure. They seldom suffer severe catastrophic failure, so many professional technicians do not replace them during a rebuild. This is a mistake. Excessive cam bearing clearance can cause a loss of oil pressure, which will reduce the life of a freshly rebuilt engine.

Although low oil pressure due to oil dilution can be fixed by simply changing the oil, a question that has to be asked is, Does the engine need major work done because a defect caused the oil to become diluted? Another question that needs to be asked is, What amount of damage has been done as a result of the oil dilution? Simply changing the oil may increase the oil pressure, but damage has been done to the engine, and that damage needs to be repaired before a catastrophic failure occurs.

Stuck-Open Relief Valve in the Oil Pump

All engines are equipped with a pressure relief valve in the oil pump. The purpose of the valve is to limit oil pressure within a range that will prevent the oil filter from being turned into a fragmentation grenade. Occasionally, the pressure relief valve will stick open, allowing oil pumped by the oil pump to be bypassed back to the oil pan. This fault can be very difficult to distinguish from a need to completely rebuild the engine.

If time is not critical, remove the oil pan and install a new oil pump. Although it might be possible to repair the pressure relief valve, it does not make much sense to remove the oil pan and make a "maybe" repair just to save a few dollars.

Damaged Oil Pump Suction Tube

When the oil pump is removed during the procedure for installing a new pump, inspect the oil pump suction tube for possible damage. If the tube is cracked or loose, the oil pump will not be able to draw oil from the oil pan. This will result in low oil pressure. Before replacing the pump, confirm that the suction tube is in good condition.

Causes That Require Overhaul

The oil pressure might be low for several reasons that would require the engine to be overhauled. If you decide to rebuild the engine based on low oil pressure, pay particular attention to

Main bearing and main journal condition

Rod bearing and rod journal condition

Camshaft bearing and camshaft journal clearance

Timing chain or gear oiler condition

Oil gallery plug condition and oil gallery condition

Main Bearing and Main Journal Condition

When the crankshaft's main bearings or main bearing journals or both suffer from severe wear, the clearance between the bearing and the journal increases. The increase in the clearance allows oil to escape easily from the space between the bearing and the journal. The escaping oil causes the oil pressure to decrease. The only repair for this problem is machining or replacing the crankshaft and replacing the bearings.

Rod Bearing and Rod Journal Condition

Like the main bearings and main bearing journals, the rod bearings and rod bearing journals can cause a loss of oil pressure if the clearance between them increases dramatically. A significant increase in the clearance allows oil to escape easily from the space between the bearing and the journal. The escaping oil causes the oil pressure to decrease. The only repair for this problem is machining or replacing the crankshaft and replacing the bearings.

Camshaft Bearing and Camshaft Journal Clearance

Often overlooked by the inexperienced, excessive cam journal-to-cam bearing clearance can cause the same low oil pressure as excessive rod bearing or main bearing clearance. When I first entered the auto repair business, I repaired engines under the direction of older, more experienced mechanics. These mechanics encouraged me to believe that because the cam bearings were not subjected to the same stresses as the rod and main bearings, they did not require anything more than a casual visual inspection. Nothing could be further from the truth. With the design of most overhead valve engines, the cam bearings are virtually impossible to replace without completely tearing down the engine. To rebuild the engine and not carefully check the cam bearings and journals risks an overhauled engine that still suffers from low oil pressure. Be sure to check the cam bearings and journals carefully.

Timing Chain or Gear Oiler Condition

Some engines, such as the old B18 and B20 Volvo engines, use a

Defective connecting rod bearings cause a thudding noise higher in pitch than the thud created by the main bearings but lower in frequency. The thud of a rod bearing occurs only when the spark plug fires the mixture in the combustion chamber. The thud of a main bearing occurs each time any of the spark plugs fire.

Some engines chronically suffer from camshaft failure. Sometimes, this is due to improper metallurgy choices by the engineers. Often, camshaft failures are a result of poor maintenance or inferior lubricants.

directional spray pressure oiler to improve the durability of the gears or chain. If the spout for this oiler has been damaged or broken off, it will cause a reduction in oil pressure.

Oil Gallery Plug and Oil Gallery Condition

If the oil galleries are restricted with sludge owing to inadequate maintenance, or if the end plugs of the galleries are leaking, the engine will suffer from low oil pressure. While overhauling the engine, send the block and heads to a machine shop and have them hot-tanked. This will ensure that these oil gallery passages are clean and can flow oil freely.

Main Bearing Noise

Not only will excessive bearing clearance cause low oil pressure, but the low oil pressure is usually accompanied by a knocking noise. This noise is a high-pitched, high-frequency sound from deep within the block. The term *high-pitched* relates to the musical note quality of the knocking noise. The term *high-frequency* relates to the number of knocks occurring during an engine cycle. If the frequency seems to be about the same as that of the spark plugs firing, the main bearings will require attention.

Some engines use a fiber cam gear driven by a metal crankshaft gear. When the timing gears of these engines get worn, they may knock with a pitch and frequency very similar to those of main bearings. A lot of time and frustrating effort can be saved by having an oil sample analyzed. Most auto supply stores can either send your oil sample for analysis or direct you toward a company that performs oil analysis. The oil analysis will tell you the amount of bearing and crankshaft material present in the oil. If the quantity of these materials is high, then an engine overhaul is indicated. If the quantity of these materials is low, then the problem may be something as easy and inexpensive to remedy as worn timing gears.

Note: Many professional technicians, including myself, may claim an ability to distinguish between worn timing gears and main bearing noises. The frequency of error in this type of educated guess is quite high. Actually, any reasonable degree of accuracy in such evaluations takes a lot of familiarity with the engine in question.

Connecting Rod Noise

Connecting rod noise can sound a lot like main bearing noise. Its pitch can vary from higher than that of a main bearing noise, to lower. The key difference is a lower frequency. This is because the rod in question, unlike the main bearing, is only subjected to high pressures when its cylinder fires. The frequency of the rod noise will be one knock in each engine cycle. This is because the cylinder with the defective rod only fires once in each engine cycle.

The problem with analyzing bearing noises by sound is that unless you are very familiar with the engine you are working on, you will have to say to yourself, "Is that bearing noise a higher or lower pitch, a higher or lower frequency, than the one I am not hearing that would be coming from the other component if it were bad?"

Noisy Valves

Many engines have manually adjusted valves. On these engines, the valve noise can often be eliminated by adjusting the valves. Even for engines with hydraulic lifters or lash compensators, noisy valves do not always require the engine to be thoroughly rebuilt. An old wives' tale says that doing major valve work will cause a failure in the sealing ability of the piston rings. Like many old wives' tales, this one contains an element of truth. When the sealing ability of the valves increases, the combustion chamber pressures rise closer to what they were when the engine was new. The piston rings are no longer new. They begin to bypass compression. The result is that the valve job appears to have caused the rings to go bad. The reality is that the rings have now replaced the valves as the weakest link in the chain.

The bottom line on all of this is that if an engine has enough wear to justify a valve grind, it probably has enough to justify a complete overhaul. This is a rather bold statement, and at times, an overhaul will not be necessary, such as when a rocker arm has failed owing to a manufacturing defect.

Worn Camshafts

Some engines, from some production years, have chronic problems with wear of the camshaft lobes. Before making a decision about whether worn cam lobes warrant a complete overhaul or simply replacement of the camshaft and lifters, consult a local machine shop. If the engine type in question has a reputation for cam lobe failure, then it is probably advisable simply to replace the camshaft. On the other hand, if the engine type in question has no history of failure, then the failed camshaft lobe may be indicative of other hidden problems; rebuild the engine.

Low Compression

Gradually, as an engine wears and deteriorates, the ability of each cylinder to seal and build pressure decreases. This can be attributed to several factors. First, the valves do not seal as well as they did when the engine was new. Over thousands of miles, the rings do not seal as tightly as when the engine was new. Over thousands of miles, the cylinders become slightly oval shaped, and the rings do not seal as well as they used to. When an engine gets into this condition, it is "tired."

Low compression on a single cylinder will usually be the result of one of two defects. One is a burned, bent, or poorly seated valve. The other is a blown head gasket. The best way to distinguish between these two defects is with a cylinder leakage tester. The proper technique for performing this test is covered later in this chapter, under "Initial Tests."

Low compression on a single cylinder is usually the result of the catastrophic failure of a single component. Many years ago, I did something that a professional mechanic should never do. I agreed to rebuild the engine in a Volkswagen (VW) van. I made two mistakes here, actually. My first mistake was to invoke Murphy's fourteenth law, thirty-second corollary, which states that if you are going to be unsuccessful in a major repair job, it will be on a friend's car. My second mistake was allowing my friend to talk me into using inexpensive (inferior) parts. Within 2,000 miles, a valve seat in the left cylinder head dropped out of place. This catastrophic failure caused low compression in a single cylinder but had the potential of doing severe damage to the entire engine. The morals of this little tale are as follows:

1. Never use inferior-quality parts.

2. Be sure to check carefully for additional damage when doing a patch job. A catastrophic failure of a single component can cause damage to other components. It can also

be indicative of other soon-to-occur failures.

3. Never work on a friend's car.

Oil Leaks

Relatively new engines should not require a major overhaul just because a little oil is dripping on the garage floor. However, older engines can have so many oil leaks that the only practical and logical way to repair them all is to remove the engine and reseal it. Once a person has gone to the trouble of removing the engine from the car and tearing down the engine to reseal it, it is only reasonable that the engine be overhauled.

Oil Burning

Two failures cause an engine to burn an excessive amount of oil: oil bypassing the rings and oil bypassing the valve guides. Each failure has its own symptoms and cures.

Oil Bypassing the Rings

The most common symptom associated with rings that are worn and allowing oil to bypass is blue smoke on acceleration. Before condemning the rings, however–and condemning yourself to a couple of weeks of knuckle-busting, backstraining pleasure–check a few other things.

If the pressure in the crankcase is too high, it can force oil past the rings into the combustion chambers. If the crankcase pressure is too low, the oil can be pulled into the intake. When either of these happens, the oil is burned when the air-fuel charge is ignited. Although the symptoms are identical to those for worn rings, this problem is relatively easy to repair.

Since the 1960s, automotive gasoline engines have been equipped with a positive crankcase ventilation (PCV) system. The purpose of this system is to capture the hydrocarbon gases that have "blown by" the rings and escaped the combustion chamber, and pull them back into the combustion chambers for a second chance to be burned. When the PCV vent becomes restricted, the pressure in the crankcase begins to drop. The drop in pressure is a result of intake manifold vacuum pulling gases out of the crankcase without the air in the crankcase being replaced through the PCV vent. The result is that as the pressure drops, the intake pulls an ever-increasing amount of oil through

the PCV system. If the PCV valve itself is restricted, the crankcase pressure builds and oil is pulled past the oil control rings during the intake stroke.

Another cause of oil burning that is characteristically similar to oil bypassing the rings is a stuck or sludged oil ring. This presents exactly the same problem as worn rings, but for a different reason. A stuck ring can often be liberated with the use of a high-detergent oil. Also, many oil additives can clean up the rings. Ask your local experienced auto parts person which product to use.

Oil Bypassing the Valve Guides

If blue smoke is coming from the tailpipe while the engine is decelerating, it is likely to be a result of worn valve guides. During deceleration, the pressure in the intake manifold decreases dramatically and the vacuum increases. The higher vacuum causes the empty combustion chamber to seek vacuum from anywhere. Excessive clearance between the valve stem and the guide allows the combustion chamber vacuum to draw air from the top of the cylinder head, beneath the valve cover. This air is saturated with oil. The oil is drawn in with the air and burned in the combustion chamber.

The problem of oil bypassing the valve guides is easily cured without a complete overhaul of the engine. However, the piston rings, crank bearing, rod bearings, camshaft, and cam bearings probably have just as many miles on them as the valve guides. You need to consider if you are trying just to patch a symptom or to make the engine usable for several tens of thousands of miles.

Desire for Better Performance

Better performance may be measured as increased power or improved fuel economy or both.

Desire to Increase Power

I cannot think of a better reason to rebuild an engine than to increase power. During the 1960s, doing so was a very popular hobby. Beginning in the 1970s, however, emission control regulations restricted this hobby to those who could afford to own a car that could never be used on the street. Especially in states such as California, little could be done to an engine without violating those regulations. As we began our journey through the 1990s, more and more performance part manufacturers were building performance components that were legal in forty-nine states and even California.

Desire for Better Fuel Economy

During the 1970s, a desire for fuel economy improvements replaced a lust for the ultimate fire-breathing metal monster as the main reason for the average enthusiast to rebuild an engine. It may be because I grew up during the generation of factory land rockets, but I cannot think of a more boring reason to rebuild an engine. Still, any excuse is better than none.

Just the Fun of It

Actually, this chapter, up to this point, has just been a list of justifications to give a wife, a husband, or a parent in order to spend time in the garage, spend a few hundred bucks, and have some fun.

Initial Tests

Noise Identification

It is not necessary to identify precisely which component in the engine is responsible for a noise; your goal is simply to determine whether the failure of a major engine component could be causing the sound you hear. If the knocking component is a major engine component, then it does not matter which one it is; the repair is the same in every case: an engine rebuild.

Home mechanics use three tools to identify the possible source of a knock in the engine: plug wires, a stethoscope, and a rubber hose.

Plug Wires

With the engine idling, disconnect each of the plug wires, and reconnect them in turn. If the intensity of the knocking sound changes when one of the plug wires is disconnected, a rod bearing is

causing the knock. If the sound does not change significantly, the knock is probably the result of a bad main bearing or something simpler. Do not forget to think about things such as the timing gears and valve adjustment.

Stethoscope

A mechanic's stethoscope has the ability to pinpoint noises in the engine. Place the tip of the stethoscope against the block or the cylinder head at the location of the suspect component. Once the sound is detected through the stethoscope, move the instrument around until the sound is the most intense. The component located closest to the point where the most intense sound is detected is most likely at fault. Keep in mind, however, that sound can telegraph from one point to another through metal.

Rubber Hose

If you do not have access to a mechanic's stethoscope, use a piece of heater hose. It does not work as well as a stethoscope, but it does work.

Smoke Analysis

Three significant smoke colors are used in engine diagnosis: black, white, and blue.

Black

Black or dark brown smoke is usually associated with an engine that is running rich. Although engine conditions can affect the air-fuel ratio, especially on fuel-injected engines, rebuilding the engine is on the bottom of the list of things to do to eliminate the smoke. Refer to reference materials on repairing fuel injection or carburetor systems for more information.

White

White smoke has two common sources: transmission fluid and antifreeze. If the car is equipped with an automatic transmission, look for a vacuum modulator. You will find the vacuum modulator located toward the back of the transmission, next to the output shaft housing. It is easy to recognize because a vacuum hose goes into it. Remove the vacuum hose, and inspect for transmission fluid in the hose. If you see transmission fluid in the hose, replace the vacuum modulator; this is the most likely source of the white smoke.

If you see no transmission fluid in the vacuum hose or if the car is not equipped with an automatic

The vacuum gauge is a handy tool in diagnosing valvetrain and camshaft problems. Either of these types of failure will cause manifold pressure fluctuations that can be seen as needle fluctuations on the gauge. However, manifold pressure fluctuations *can be caused by everything from ignition problems to holes in pistons. A vacuum gauge should be used only to confirm that a problem exists, not to pinpoint the location of that problem.*

transmission or does not have a vacuum modulator, the most likely source of the white smoke is a blown head gasket, a cracked cylinder head, or a cracked block. These conditions can be confirmed with a compression test or, better yet, a cylinder leakage test. See chapter 3 or the section titled "Compression Testing" later in this chapter for more about how to use a cylinder leakage tester.

It is relatively easy to determine whether white smoke is burned transmission fluid or burned antifreeze. The antifreeze has a distinct sweet odor, whereas the transmission fluid just smells smoky.

Blue

Blue smoke indicates that engine oil is being burned. Note when the smoke is coming from the exhaust. As mentioned earlier in this chapter, if the smoke occurs during acceleration, look to the piston rings as its source. If it occurs during deceleration, look to the valve guides.

PCV System Testing

Crankcase pressure can affect whether or not the intake vacuum will pull engine oil into the intake manifold. Test the PCV system before tearing an engine apart to repair a smoking problem.

You can choose from two valid ways to test the PCV system. One option is to replace the PCV valve and inspect the vent hose for restriction. A more scientific option is to make a trip to an auto parts store that sells tools. It will sell a PCV tester, which is installed over the PCV vent hose to determine if the crankcase pressure is in the proper range. Of course, if the pressure is incorrect, you will have to replace the PCV valve and inspect the vent hose for restriction.

Vacuum Gauge Testing

Using a vacuum gauge is a simple way to begin distinguishing low compression problems as a result of ring or head gasket problems from low compression as a result of valve problems. With the engine idling, connect a vacuum gauge to the intake manifold. If the needle oscillates violently, some of the valves are not sealing properly. Low compression as a result of ring or head gasket problems will also cause the needle to oscillate, just not as much.

Distinguishing between various causes of low compression with a vacuum gauge takes a lot of experience and is largely subjective. Two other, superior methods are compression testing and cylinder leakage testing.

Compression Testing

Compression testing is one of the best ways to determine if an engine needs to be rebuilt. Begin the test by removing all the spark plugs. Connect a screw-in-type compression gauge to cylinder number one. (The cheap compression gauges that are held in place by the technician tend to be very inaccurate.) Crank the engine until twelve puffs have been heard. Observe the gauge. Repeat the procedure for each of the cylinders.

If the compression for any of the cylinders is considerably different than that for the average of the rest, repeat the test. When you repeat the test, squirt about a teaspoon of oil into each cylinder before testing it. This is called a wet compression test.

If the compression on all cylinders is extremely low, the camshaft is likely out of phase with the crankshaft. Replace the timing gear and chain or the belt.

If the compression is low on only one or two cylinders and does not rise when the wet compression test is done, the affected cylinders are suffering from valve problems. If the compression on the affected cylinders does rise during the wet test, the affected cylinders have ring problems.

Only the ring problems demand a complete overhaul of the engine. Keep in mind, however, that the valve or timing system problem may indicate future problems.

Cylinder Leakage Testing

The cylinder leakage test is superior to the compression test, although its goals are the same. It also requires more equipment. With the piston at top dead center during a compression stroke, connect the cylinder leakage tester to cylinder number one. Measure the percentage of leakage. Additionally, use a piece of heater hose with one end held to your ear to determine where the leakage is. Stick the open end of the heater hose in the open bore of the fuel injection throttle assembly or carburetor. If a great deal of air is escaping through here, you have an intake valve problem. Now stick the open end of the hose in the exhaust. If a great deal of air is escaping, you have a bad exhaust valve. Observe the radiator coolant. If a lot of bubbles are in the coolant, you have a blown head gasket, a cracked head, or a cracked block.

For more information about how to do cylinder leakage tests, refer to chapter 3.

Oil Analysis

Of all the different ways one could determine if an engine needs major work, oil analysis is by far the most accurate. Contact your local parts house. Most auto supply stores can either send your oil sample for analysis or direct you toward a company that performs oil analysis. The oil analysis will tell you the amount of bearing and crankshaft material present in the oil. If the quantity of these materials is high, then an engine overhaul is indicated. This procedure will cost a few dollars–usually fewer than twenty–but could save you hundreds, and many hours of labor.

Summary

Rebuilding your engine can be a fun, cost-effective way of adding years to the life of your car or truck. Do not be intimidated by the apparent complexity under the hood. The subsequent chapters of this book will guide you through the entire process.

Tools

Three times a year, men lay plastic on the counter of a retail jewelry store: Christmas, their wife's birthday, and their anniversary. As they do so, they are thinking, "Why am I buying this? It serves no practical purpose, it is horribly expensive, and she will probably only wear it once." Men need to realize that jewelry replaces the ritual body painting and scarring of primitive cultures. Women use it to demonstrate their independence and uniqueness.

Three times a year, women lay plastic on the counter of a retail hardware store: Christmas, their husband's birthday, and their anniversary. As they do so, they are thinking, "Why am I buying this? It

serves no practical purpose, it is horribly expensive, and he will probably only use it once." Women need to realize that tools replace the weapons of the hunt in primitive cultures. The film *Mr. Mom* hit the nail on the head when Michael Keaton demonstrated his manliness to Martin Mull by firing up a chain saw in the living room.

A number of specialized and common tools are needed or are handy for engine rebuilding.

Compression Tester

The compression tester is a pressure gauge with a check valve. When installed in a spark plug hole, it is able to record and display the amount of pressure created in the cylinder as the engine is cranked.

To get ready to run a compression test, remove all the spark plugs, disconnect the primary power supply to the ignition coil, and block the throttle wide open. Install the compression gauge in the number one spark plug hole.

Crank the engine twelve revolutions. Listen to and count the puffing noises. Record the compression reading. Now, move to the number two cylinder. Repeat the process on each of the cylinders.

When you are done, compare the compression readings. If the reading from any of the cylinders is considerably different than the average reading from the rest, repeat the test. When you repeat the test, squirt about a teaspoon of oil into each cylinder before testing it. This is called a wet compression test.

Cylinder Leakage Tester

The cylinder leakage test is superior to the compression test, although its goals are the same. It also requires more equipment. With the piston at top dead center during a compression stroke, connect the cylinder leakage tester to cylinder number one. Measure the percentage of leakage. Additionally, use a piece of heater hose, with one end held to your ear, to determine

The compression gauge is an essential tool in troubleshooting engine problems that cause the engine to run rough. Low compression can result in a low power output from the offending cylinder, and that can cause rough engine operation.

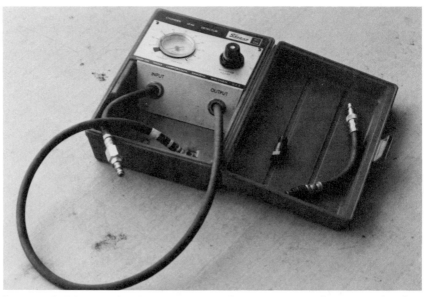

Some technicians prefer the cylinder leakage test to the compression test. This cylinder leakage tester shows

the percentage of compression lost from the cylinder tested.

where the leakage is. Stick the open end of the heater hose in the open bore of the fuel injection throttle assembly or the carburetor. If a great deal of air is escaping through here, you have an intake valve problem. Then, stick the open end of the hose in the exhaust. If a great deal of air is escaping, you have a bad exhaust valve. Observe the radiator coolant. If a lot of bubbles are in the coolant, you have a blown head gasket, a cracked head, or a cracked block.

Next, remove the oil filler cap. Place the open end of the heater hose in the oil filler neck or the valve cover opening. If you hear excessive air, the rings are allowing the air to bypass. Now, place the open end of the hose over the spark plug holes of the adjacent cylinders. If you hear a significant amount of air from one of the adjacent cylinders, then the engine has a blown head gasket between the cylinder being tested and the cylinder where the air is heard.

You will hear the sound of air leaking in all the places discussed above. It will only be significant when the cylinder leakage indicated is excessive. The difficult part of the cylinder leakage test is determining how much leakage is too

much. Opinions differ on this topic as much as they do on the Kennedy assassination. Manufacturers such as Honda say that more than 5 percent leakage is too much. Some professional technicians feel that 15 percent is acceptable. The truth of what is acceptable lies somewhere in between. Being realistic, consid-

er that you have gone to the trouble of performing the cylinder leakage test because the engine has an obvious problem. Generally speaking, the types of problems that would be caused by a 5 to 10 percent leakage would not be noticed. You are looking for a problem resulting from cylinder leakage

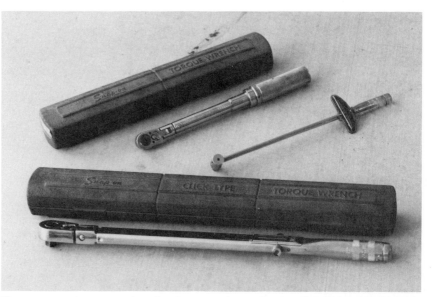

Torque wrenches range in price from about $20 to several hundred dollars. Opinions vary on which is better, the beam type or the click type. Properly used, either one works well.

One of the trickiest simple jobs is installing the piston rings. Rings break when they are stretched too far during installation. These piston ring installation pliers make the job easier and less expensive.

A piston ring compressor is necessary to install the pistons into the cylinder when the rings are fitted on the pistons. When no tension is on the rings, they are slightly larger than the cylinder; compressing the rings allows the pistons to slide easily into the cylinder when tapped with the butt of a hammer handle.

that is probably greater than 15 percent.

Oil Pressure Gauge

The oil pressure gauge is a mechanical gauge that screws into one of the oil galleries in the engine block. When the engine is started, the oil pressure should rise to the proper specification or higher.

Piston Ring Pliers

One tricky operation of rebuilding an engine is to remove and install the brittle piston rings without breaking them. Although the rings can easily be spread far enough to go over the piston head and slip into the piston ring grooves, they can also easily be spread far enough to break. The piston ring pliers do not eliminate the possibility of breaking the piston rings, but they do decrease it.

Torque Wrench

The most essential tool for rebuilding engines is the torque wrench. All bolts and other fasteners stretch when they are tightened. If they are tightened too much, their threads will strip or they will shear. If they are not tightened enough, the bolt will loosen. Spare no expense when you purchase a torque wrench.

Two types of torque wrenches are available: the beam type and the click type. The beam type uses a pointer that indicates the amount of torque on a scale attached to a flexible bar. As torque is applied to the bolt, the flexible bar bends. The amount of bending in the bar indicates the amount of torque being applied to the bolt. The beam torque wrench was the industry standard for decades, and in highly skilled hands is still an adequate tool. Its biggest weakness is its low consistency of accuracy, even in the most skilled hands.

The click torque wrench is far more accurate, especially for the occasional user. The desired torque is dialed in. When the prescribed torque is reached, a click is heard and felt, telling the user to stop

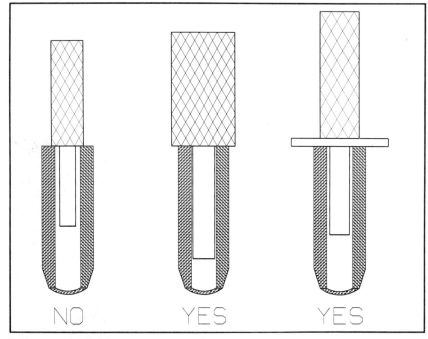

Drifts are available to remove and install valve guides on cylinder heads where the guides are removable. Since the inner diameter of valve guides varies greatly from one application to another, be sure to choose the appropriate diameter for the application being worked on. If a large-enough drift is not available, a thick washer can be used to spread the load of the drift on the valve guide.

Although a little on the brutal side, bits are available for an air chisel to change removable valve guides.

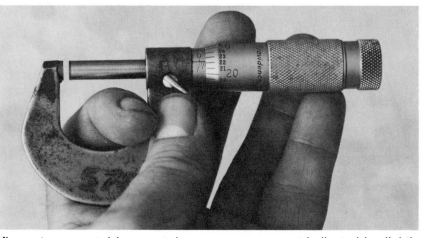

Micrometers are precision measuring instruments. This is a 0in-to-1in micrometer. The current setting or measurement indicated is slightly more than 0.047in.

tightening the bolt. This torque wrench features a high degree of accuracy. Although it can cost dozens of times more than its beam counterpart, it can be money well spent. One incorrectly torqued bolt can result in your having completely to redo a rebuild, and this is both expensive and time-consuming.

Piston Ring Compressor

After the rings have been installed on the pistons, you still face the challenge of slipping the pistons into the cylinders even though the rings do not fit. Each ring is shaped so that it is larger than the cylinder in order to maintain a firm contact between the ring and the cylinder wall. A gap in the ring allows it to be squeezed together so that it will fit in the cylinder. The open ends of the ring must be squeezed together in order to get the pistons into the cylinder. This is the job of the piston ring compressor.

Although most engines can use any piston ring compressor, some engines require a special compressor. With most domestic and foreign engines, the pistons go in from the top. A few engines like the old VW air-cooled engines require that the pistons be installed from the bottom. On these applications, the connecting rod is attached to the crankshaft before it is installed into the cylinder. A standard ring compressor could not be removed once the piston is installed. Although there are ways around this problem, a special ring compressor is available—one designed to come apart for easy removal.

Valve Guide Drift

Some cylinder heads have valve guides that are pressed into place. Although it is advisable to have these guides replaced by a qualified machinist during a valve grind, you can replace them yourself with a special set of drifts. These drifts have not only a surface for pressing the guide into place, but an undercut area that fits into the guide to prevent it from collapsing on itself.

Any time the valve guides are replaced, a valve grind should be performed. For this reason, unless you plan on doing the valve grind yourself, just let the machinist replace the guides.

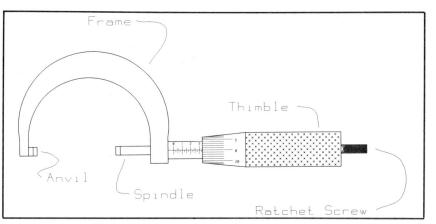

To measure an object with a micrometer, place it between the anvil and the spindle. Then, rotate the thimble to make the spindle snug against the object. A ratchet screw is provided on some micrometers. Use this screw to provide the proper tension against the object to be measured.

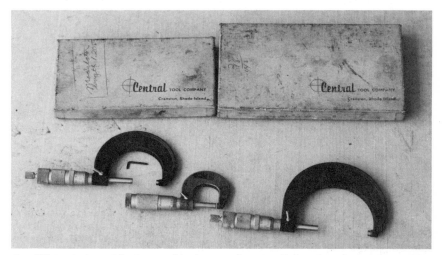

As different-size objects need to be measured in an engine, different-size micrometers are available. A good set of micrometers should include at least a 0in-to-1in micrometer, a 1in-to-2in micrometer, a 1in-to-3in micrometer, and a 3in-to-4in micrometer.

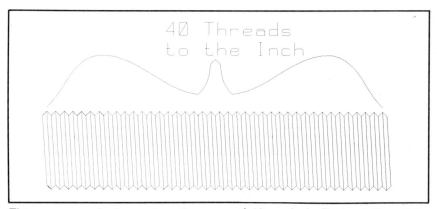

The accuracy of micrometers does not rely on a secret formula. The thimble rides on threads with a pitch of 40 per inch. Each rotation of the thimble moves the spindle 0.025in.

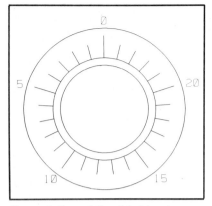

One rotation of the thimble changes the gap between the spindle and the anvil by 0.025in.

Outside Micrometer

An automobile engine is made up of dozens of closely machined parts. The measurement of these parts requires precision to 0.001 inch (in). The micrometer provides this level of accuracy. A basic set consists of a 0in-to-1in micrometer, a 1in-to-2in micrometer, a 2in-to-3in micrometer, and a 3in-to-4in micrometer. Working with large engines, big-block, and truck engines may require a 4in-to-5in or larger micrometer.

A precision instrument, the micrometer should be handled with extreme care. The micrometer is a very simple device in spite of its high level of accuracy. The basic parts are the spindle, the thimble, the anvil, and the barrel. The spindle is threaded at a standard of forty threads per inch. Rotating the thimble moves the spindle 0.025in. On the standard micrometer are twenty-five graduations around the thimble. This configuration allows an accuracy of 0.001in. The barrel of the micrometer is marked off in 0.025in units. A numerical marking appears every four marks. The numerical marking, therefore, indicates a movement of 0.01in.

To use a micrometer, place its anvil and spindle against opposite ends of the object to be measured. Rotate the thimble until the spindle makes firm but not heavy contact with the object. Read the highest numerical marking visible on the barrel. This will indicate the nearest 0.01in. Counting the barrel markings beyond the visible numerical mark will indicate the nearest 0.025in. Observe the twenty-five marks on the thimble and how they align with a line on the barrel; this will indicate the measurement to the nearest 0.001in.

A quality micrometer should be treated as the precision instrument it is. Overtightening when taking measurements can stretch the

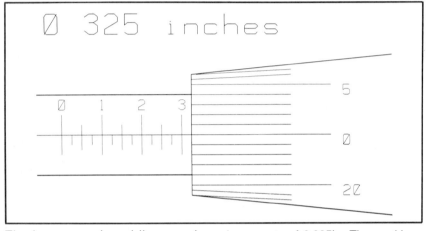

The longer numbered lines mark increments of 0.1in, the slightly shorter lines represent increments of 0.05in, and the shortest lines indicate increments of 0.025in. The markings on the thimble are in increments of 0.001in. This micrometer is set to [(3)(0.1in)] + 0.025in, or 0.325in.

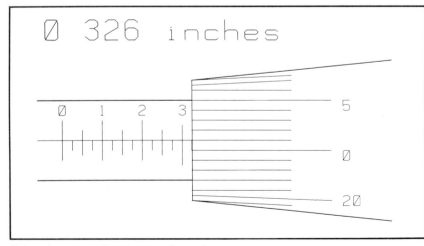

This micrometer has been adjusted to [(3)(0.1in)] + 0.025in + 0.01in, or 0.326in.

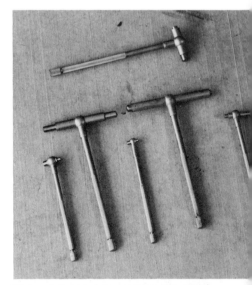

These telescoping gauges are used to measure inside diameters. Expand the gauge by rotating the knob on the end. When the correct diameter is achieved, measure the distance of the telescoping plungers with a micrometer.

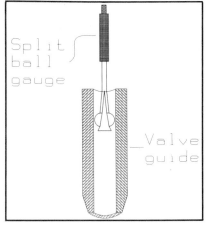

The split ball gauge works a lot like the telescoping gauge but is used on small bores and diameters like those of a valve guide.

Feeler gauges are used to measure gaps and clearances. Here, a technician checks the clearance between the rocker arm and the tip of the valve stem.

frame, decreasing the accuracy of the micrometer. Often, this can be remedied by adjusting the instrument using a gauge block. Dropping the micrometer can damage it beyond adjustment. Top technicians are therefore not inclined to lend you their micrometers.

Inside Micrometer

The inside micrometer works just like the outside micrometer; however, its design allows it to be used to measure the inside of a bore.

Split Ball Gauges

When the cylinder or bore is smaller than 2in, the inside micrometer cannot be used. To measure extremely small bores requires the use of split ball gauges. Inserted into the bore of something like a valve guide, the split ball can be adjusted to the diameter of the guide. When the ball is removed from the bore, a

The dial indicator is used to measure minute movement. In this case, it is being used to measure the protrusion of a piston beyond the deck of the block.

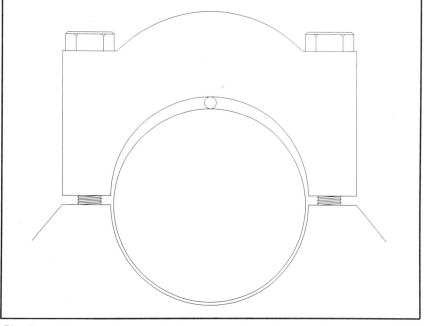

Plastigage is a precision round piece of soft plastic. When placed between a bearing journal and the bearing surface, it is used to measure the oil clearance

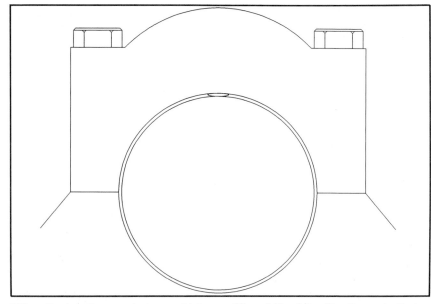

When the bearing cap is torqued into place, the Plastigage is flattened.

The width of the Plastigage indicates the oil clearance.

requires a little skill. Extend the measuring instrument until it makes firm but gentle contact with the surfaces being measured. Gently move the measuring device back and forth to ensure firm contact, so that it will give the proper measurement.

Dial Indicator

The dial indicator consists of a precision gauge, usually marked in thousandths of an inch, which is moved by a plunger. When clamped or mounted firmly to a block or a cylinder head, it can be used to measure the amount of front-to-rear movement or end play in the camshaft or crankshaft. Not limited to this job, the dial indicator can be used to measure minute movement in virtually any component. Additional jobs for this device include checking the flatness and run-out of rotating objects like the flywheel.

Feeler Gauges

Feeler gauges are thin strips of steel or brass machined to very

standard micrometer can be used to measure the size of the split. This will be the diameter of the guide.

Telescoping Gauges

Telescoping gauges are available in sizes up to several inches. They consist of spring-loaded rods that make contact with the sides of

the cylinder or bearing bore to be measured. When these rods are removed, the length of the telescoping rods can be measured with a standard micrometer to determine accurately the bore diameter.

Note: Using outside micrometers, inside micrometers, split ball gauges, and telescoping gauges

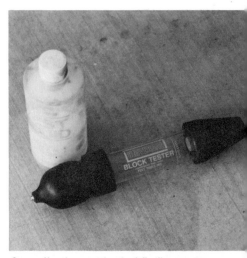

One effective method of finding combustion leaks into the cooling system is to use the chemical block tester. A blue liquid is poured into a clear plastic tube. The rubber-ended tube is then placed over the open neck of the radiator. A rubber vacuum bulb is squeezed to draw air from the top of the radiator into the clear plastic tube. If combustion gases are in the coolant, the blue liquid will turn yellowish green. Combustion gases in the coolant might indicate a blown gasket, a cracked head, or a cracked cylinder block.

The cooling system tester can be used to test for leaks in the cooling system or to test the relief pressure of the radiator cap. When the head gasket is blown or when the water jacket has large external cracks, this tester can be used to pressurize the cooling system and find the leaks.

close tolerances. They are used to measure the gaps between components. Piston ring side clearance, crankshaft thrust clearance, and valve lash are among the gaps that can be measured with feeler gauges.

Plastigage

Plastigage is made of thin strips of plastic and is used to measure the rod and main bearing clearances. Remove the bearing cap, and tear off a piece of Plastigage approximately the length of the bearing width. Place the strip of Plastigage on the bearing journal, then install and torque the bearing cap. Remove the bearing cap, and compare the compressed width of the Plastigage to the scale on the package. The compressed width indicates the oil clearance between the journal and the bearing.

Tachometer

The tachometer is used to measure engine rpm. Although this tool is not essential for the actual rebuilding process, it is essential for adjusting the curb idle speed during the final tuning process.

Timing Light

Like the tachometer, the timing light is a tune-up instrument, not an engine rebuild necessity.

The timing light is used to synchronize the primary ignition system to the position of the crankshaft.

Radiator Pressure Tester

The primary task of the radiator pressure tester is to locate leaks in the cooling system. When installed on the radiator neck, it pressurizes the cooling system, and

coolant will seep or leak out. An added benefit is that the tester is able to locate a leaking external head gasket and leaking freeze plugs.

Chemical Block Tester

Filled with a blue fluid and inserted into the filler neck of the radiator, the chemical block tester

Valve spring compressors are helpful in removing the valve springs during the disassembly of the cylinder heads. A valve spring compressor is absolutely necessary for the reassembly of the cylinder heads.

The cylinder hone is used to break the glaze that forms as the pistons travel up and down in the cylinders. The glaze inhibits new rings from breaking in quickly.

Grinders and wire wheels are used to clean parts and trim metal from where it should not be. Unfortunately, the wire wheel is often overused, damaging parts.

Even though arbor presses are basic and "low-tech," they can be very handy for pressing wrist pins into pistons. They offer excellent control and ease of use.

As the engine runs, over a period of years, metal is moved from the walls of the cylinder to the top of the cylinder. A ridge is formed around the top of the cylinder. This ridge can make the pistons difficult to remove and can damage the new rings when a rebuilt engine is started. The ridge reamer is used to remove this ridge during the early stages of disassembly.

extracts some of the vapor in the radiator. If hydrocarbons are present in the vapors, the blue fluid will turn yellowish green. The presence of hydrocarbons in the radiator vapors indicates leakage from the combustion chamber into the radiator. This leakage could be a result of a blown head gasket, a cracked cylinder, or a cracked cylinder head.

Cylinder Hone

The cylinder hone is used to break the glaze that forms on the cylinder walls. If this glaze were left in place, freshly installed piston rings would not seat properly. The result would be high oil consumption and reduced cylinder performance. The hone consists of abrasive stones mounted on a shaft. When this shaft is locked into a drill, the stones scrape the glaze off the cylinder walls.

Proper use of the cylinder hone involves moving it up and down in the cylinder very rapidly as the drill is running. The rapid up-and-down movement causes a crosshatching on the cylinder walls. The crosshatching accelerates the break-in of the new rings.

Two common types of hones are available. One is the classic hone, which features three or four flat stones held against the walls of the cylinder by spring tension.

A good tachometer and dwell meter are necessary for both the troubleshooting of problems and the tune-up procedure following a rebuild.

Another type is the berry-ball hone, which has dozens of small abrasive stones held against the cylinder walls by spring steel wires. Both hones are very effective, but I recommend the berry-ball hone for the amateur or occasional rebuilder.

Timing Wheel

The timing wheel is used to make precision adjustments in camshaft timing for performance.

Valve Spring Compressor

The valve spring compressor looks like a large C-clamp with a set of hooks on one end to cradle the valve spring. When this device is tightened, the valve spring is compressed, which allows the valve keepers to be removed. Although this tool is not absolutely necessary during the disassembly process, it is indispensable during the reassembly process.

Some overhead cam engines have the valves recessed in the head. These engines require special valve spring compressors.

Ridge Reamer

The ridge reamer is used to remove the ridge that builds at the top of the cylinder walls. This ridge forms during thousands of miles of operation as the rings move tiny bits of metal up the cylinder walls, depositing them at the top of the cylinder in a formation like the terminal moraine of a glacier.

Valve Adjusting Clips

Valve adjusting clips are spring steel clips that fit over the end of the rocker and pushrod on overhead valve engines. Overhead valve engines equipped with hydraulic lifters must have the valves adjusted with the engine running. If these clips are not used, this procedure is very messy.

CC Gauge

The CC (cubic centimeter) gauge is known to chemists as a graduated burette. A burette is a glass tube marked in milliliters. At the bottom of the tube is a petcock. When the burette is filled with mineral oil and the oil is slowly drained through the petcock into the combustion chambers of the cylinder head, it is possible to measure the volume of each combustion chamber. When you are blueprinting an engine, an equal volume for each combustion chamber is critical to achieving equal power from each of the cylinders.

Common Hand Tools

Make sure you have a set of combination wrenches ranging in size from 1/4in to 1in; a 3/8in- and 1/2in-drive SAE socket, ratchet, and extension set; and miscellaneous screwdrivers, pry bars, and hammers. If the engine is in a foreign car, you will need metric wrenches and sockets. If it is in a late-model domestic vehicle, you will need to have both SAE and metric wrenches and sockets.

A variety of scrapers are needed to clean old gaskets off the mating surfaces of components. Be sure always to use great care when scraping off old gaskets. Scrapers are sharp and can cause severe cuts.

Something as simple as a trash bag is an important part of the rebuild. Use it to seal out damaging dust and dirt between work sessions.

Fasteners

Bolts

Sizing Bolts

Bolts are measured by the maximum diameter of the threads and the distance from the bottom side of the head of the bolt to the end of the bolt. The number of threads per inch or millimeter determines the pitch of the threads. On an American engine, bolts typically have two thread pitches: coarse and fine. The finer the pitch, the more threads per inch, and therefore the greater the holding power of the bolt.

Four sizing standards are used: Unified Screw Thread (UST), International Standardization Organization (ISO) metric, pipe, and Whitworth. Within the UST standard are Unified Course (UNC) and Unified Fine (UNF). These are the standards used for decades on American-built cars. The UNC standard refers to coarse-thread bolts, and the UNF refers to fine-thread bolts.

Metric bolts designated with the letter *M* followed by the bolt diameter have a coarse thread. An example would be a bolt designated M8. This would be a coarse-thread 8-millimeter (mm) bolt. Bolts designated with the letter *M* followed by the bolt diameter, then a multiplication sign (x) followed by a number, have a fine thread. An example would be a bolt designated M10x1.25. This would be a 10mm bolt with a pitch of 1.25 threads per millimeter.

Pipe thread is indicated by the letter *G* preceding the pipe size. Only one pitch is available for each diameter.

People who work on older English-built cars are likely to run into Whitworth measurements. These are British pipe thread measurements. They are designated by the letter *R* followed by the pipe size, for externally threaded parts such as bolts; *Rp* indicates internal threading. For example, R1/4 is a 1/4in external pipe thread, and Rp1 is a 1in internal pipe thread.

Metallurgy

Bolts are made from cast iron, steel, malleable iron, aluminum and magnesium, and a variety of exotic metals. Steel bolts can be electroplated with zinc or cadmium. These platings help to reduce corrosion.

The art of torquing fasteners, theorem 1: Tighten a bolt until the head breaks off, then back it off a quarter turn.

Grades and Types

The primary fasteners used in the assembly of engines are nuts and bolts. Anyone undertaking major surgery on a vehicular powerplant needs to be aware that a bolt is not just a bolt. These fasteners come in several grades and types based on strength and corrosion resistance.

A bolt has only three major parts: these are the head (the part where the wrench goes), the shoulder, and the threads.

Based on strength, two measuring standards are used: the SAE and the ISO. Each organization has specifications and standards for

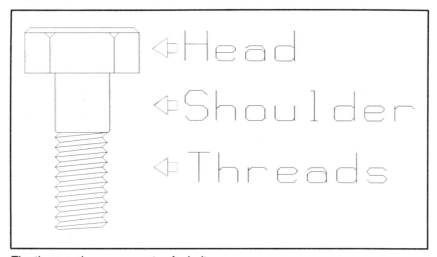

The three major components of a bolt are the head, the shoulder, and the threads.

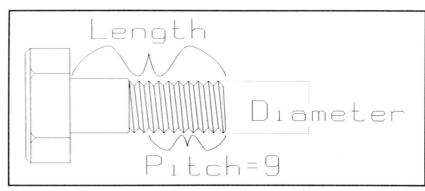

Bolts are measured by length, diameter, and pitch.

tensile strength, yield point, ultimate strength, and proof pounds-per-square-inch (psi) load.

To picture tensile strength, imagine holding the bolt by its head and attaching weights to the end of it. The tensile strength is the projected weight at which the bolt would break.

The yield point refers to the stress point at which the bolt can no longer return to its original shape. A good comparison would be to the elasticity of a pair of men's briefs. As long as the wearer of these briefs remains svelte, the elastic in the briefs retains its ability to return to approximately its original size. If, however, several months of waistline increases are followed by a sudden waistline reduction, the elastic will likely retain the more corpulent shape.

The ultimate load strength is the approximate point at which the bolt snaps. As a rule of thumb, this tends to be about 10 percent more stress than the yield point.

The proof psi load is the stress point that is considered to be the bolt's typical long-term load value. I used to own a 1965 VW Beetle with a 1200cc engine. Downhill with a tail wind, it would achieve 90 miles per hour (mph). Little if any injury was done to the engine during this short span of maximum stress. However, if I had driven this car flat out for several hours, extreme damage to the engine would have been done. By driving the VW at the safe and sane speed of 55mph for its entire life (yeah, right), I put less stress on the engine, and therefore, it lasted much longer.

Bolts are typically tightened to about 90 percent of their proof psi load. Torque specifications are in pounds-feet (lb-ft), however, not in pounds per square inch.

SAE Grades

By SAE standards, four types of bolts are identified according to strength: grades 2, 5, 7, and 8.

SAE Grade 2 Mild Steel Bolts

Often referred to as hardware bolts, SAE grade 2 mild steel fasteners have the lowest strength qualities of any bolts found in use on the automotive engine. Their tensile strength ranges from 60,000psi of cross section to 74,000psi of cross section. The proof load of these bolts is between 33,000psi and 55,000psi. A typical

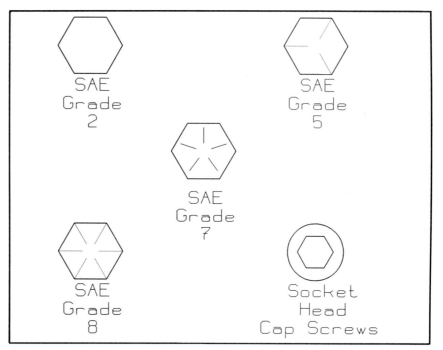

The head of a bolt tells what grade the bolt is. In American sizing, a plain head indicates a grade 2 soft hardware bolt, three lines radiating from the center denote a grade 5 bolt, five lines designate a grade 7 bolt, and six lines mark a grade 8 bolt.

In metric sizing, the number to the left of the period indicates the diameter of the bolt and the number to the right of the period represents the strength of the bolt. The larger the right-hand number, the stronger the bolt.

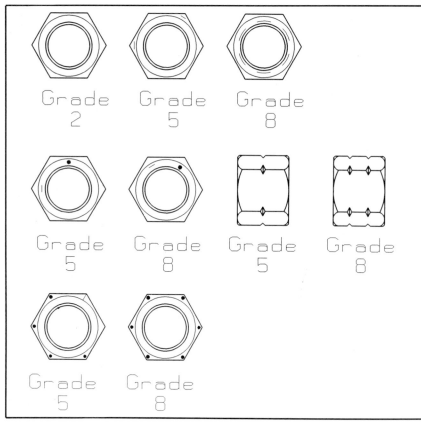

American nuts have marks to indicate their strength. The most common mistake made by even professional technicians is to use a grade 8 bolt and a grade 2 nut to fasten parts together. Always select a nut suitable to the job being done by the fastener.

torque spec for a 1/2in grade 2 bolt is 59lb-ft. These bolts are recognized by a lack of radial lines on the top of the head.

SAE Grade 5 Bolts

SAE grade 5 bolts are found where greater torque values and an increased need to maintain a torque are required. Their tensile strength, at 105,000psi to 120,000psi, is nearly twice that of the grade 2 bolt. Their proof load is 74,000psi to 85,000psi. A typical torque spec for a 1/2in grade 5 bolt is 90lb-ft. These bolts will have three radial lines around the head.

SAE Grade 7 Bolts

The SAE grade 7 bolt is commonly used in engines. Although it has a relatively high tensile strength, it is considerably less expensive than the grade 8 bolt. The grade 7 bolt can be recognized by five radial lines around the top of the head.

SAE Grade 8 Bolts

When great strength is required, SAE grade 8 bolts are used. The tensile strength of grade 8 bolts is 150,000psi, and their proof load is 120,000psi. A typical torque spec for a 1/2in grade 8 bolt is 128lb-ft.

Socket-Head Cap Screws

When maximum strength is required, socket-head cap screws are available. These are designed with a tensile strength of 160,000psi and a proof load of 136,000psi. A typical torque spec for a 1/2in socket-head screw is 145lb-ft. These bolts have six radial

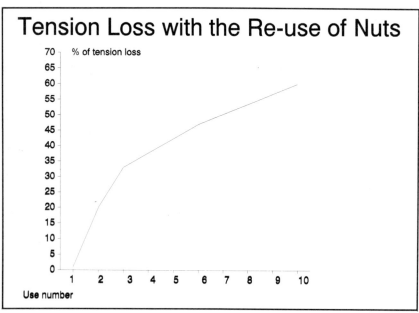

The reuse of nuts is a common practice in the auto repair industry. However, nuts lose much of their strength during the first use. When disassem-
bling the engine, keep a tally of the sizes and quality of the nuts, and replace the nuts when reassembling the engine.

Studs stretch when nuts are tightened on them. It is tempting not to replace the studs because they are not usually removed during disassembly.

lines around the head. Engineers are strange beasts. In this instance a bolt type is known as a "cap screw," therefore both terms—bolt and screw—are correct and used appropriately.

The art of torquing fasteners, theorem 1, corollary 1: The more expensive the component into which you are tightening the bolt, the greater the probability of stripping the threads out of that component.

ISO Property Classes

The ISO rates metric bolts. ISO ratings include tensile strength and proof load. The tensile strength is measured in kilograms per square millimeter (kg/mm^2).

If the tensile strength of a bolt is $40kg/mm^2$, a small 4 will appear to the left of a period (.) on the head of the bolt. An 8 to the left of the period means the tensile strength is $80kg/mm^2$. Obviously, the higher the number, the stronger the bolt.

The number to the right of the period is ten times the ratio of the minimum yield point to the minimum tensile strength. It should suffice to say, the bigger the number, the stronger.

Those who are hung-up on the use of American standard and want some way of approximating the ISO to the SAE can use the following chart:

SAE Grade	ISO Property Class
Grade 2	5.8
Grade 5	8.8
Grade 7	9.8
Grade 8	10.9

Nuts

Like bolts, nuts are also graded by their strength. I have seen professional technicians spend a great deal of time locating the correct bolt for a given use, then mate it with any nut that is handy and fits. Common sense dictates that the nut must be as important as the bolt; reality dictates the use of a new nut during assembly. I realize that every shop, whether business or personal, has a shrine of used nuts and bolts that is cherished

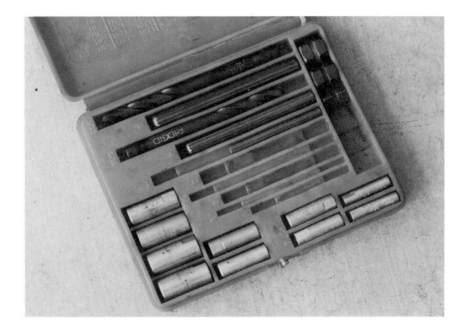

One vital tool of the auto repair industry is a broken-bolt or -stud removal tool. Several different types are available. To remove a broken fastener, a hole must be drilled in it, the removal tool placed in the hole, and the broken fastener threaded out. Note the removed fastener on the removal tool, center.

To reduce the likelihood of bolts breaking the next time they are removed, use a tap to clean all the threads when cleaning the parts or during the reassembly process.

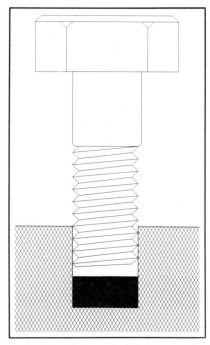

A damaged threaded hole may be repaired in many ways: retapping the hole, installing inserts, and creating liquid threads. To use liquid threads, first drill the hole to the outside thread diameter, pour the liquid thread material into the hole, and coat the bolt with the release compound provided with the liquid thread kit.

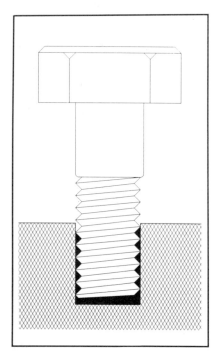

Next, gently screw the thread into the hole containing the liquid thread material.

beyond a spouse. Nevertheless, when rebuilding an engine, you would like it to last at least as long as its first incarnation. Use new nuts, and preferably new nuts and bolts.

Nuts should be replaced because they conform to the threads of the bolt. In doing so, they lose a little of their holding ability.

Washers

Washers come in several varieties, each with a different purpose. There are wave washers, split ring washers, and star washers that are used to hold tension against the threads of a bolt or nut to prevent the bolt or nut from loosening. These are often referred to by the generic name *lock washers*.

Two types of flat washers are available: through-hardened and case-hardened. The through-hardened flat washer is used to spread the load of a tightened bolt out across a flat surface. The case-hardened washer does the same; however, the core of the washer is soft and compresses under a load that would allow the bolt or nut to loosen. About 30,000psi of clamping force is lost for every 0.001in the washer compresses. When selecting washers for use with a bolt or nut that has a torque specification, always use a through-hardened washer.

Studs

Studs are used in place of bolts in many places. A stud is threaded at both ends. Carburetors and fuel injection throttle bodies are often attached with studs. A few engines, such as the one found in early 1970s Saabs and in the Triumph TR-7, use studs to hold the cylinder head in place. These studs should be replaced each time the head is removed. You probably would not need to be told this if you were working on one of these heads. The disadvantage of using studs to hold the head in place is that they often corrode in place, making it extremely difficult to remove the cylinder head. In fact, I have often had to use a Porta-Power to remove a TR-7 head; this usually damages the head severely.

Studs should only be removed with a stud removal tool. Several tool companies market these.

Broken-Bolt Removal

The art of torquing fasteners, theorem 1, corollary 2: The likelihood of breaking a bolt is directly proportional to the difficulty in accessing the broken bolt.

Using a Broken-Bolt Removal Tool

There are as many different types of broken-bolt removal tools as there are surfboards on Oahu. All removal tools require drilling a hole in the center of the bolt, inserting the removal tool, and screwing the bolt out—before attempting to remove the bolt by applying oil around the threads. The removal tool is made of very strong but brittle metal. If the threads of the bolt are seized in the component, your first warning may be when the removal tool breaks. This will be an experience you will never forget. The risk of this can be reduced by using the largest-possible removal tool. Most broken-bolt removal tools are harder than the drill bits you own. However, drilling may be your only alternative if the removal tool breaks.

Drilling the Bolt Out

The alternative to using a broken-bolt removal tool is to drill the bolt out. Drilling can be used in two ways. One way is to provide stress relief. Drilling a large enough hole in the bolt relieves the tension of the bolt threads against the hole threads. Often, this, along with the largest possible removal tool,

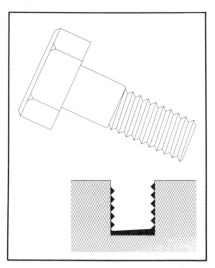

After the liquid threads have had time to harden, remove the bolt. You are now ready to use the new threads.

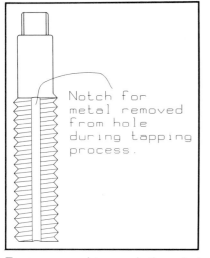

Notch for metal removed from hole during tapping process.

Taps are used to repair threaded holes. They are also handy to clean a threaded hole prior to reassembly.

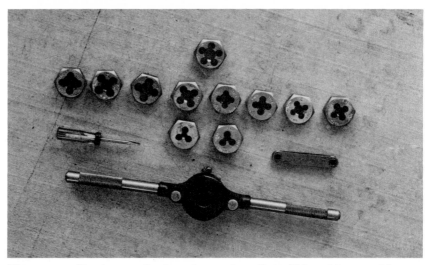

Dies are used to clean up the threads on bolts and studs. Purchase good-quality dies, and they can last a very long time. This set is over 20 years old and has had very heavy use.

loosens the broken bolt sufficiently for removal.

If drilling does not sufficiently loosen the bolt for easy removal, use increasingly larger-sized drill bits to enlarge the hole in the bolt until the threads can barely be seen. With a chisel, curl what is left of the bolt in on itself for removal.

Torching the Bolt Out

If all else fails, you can use what the industry calls a blue-tipped wrench: an oxyacetylene torch. However, if you are not skilled with a torch to the extent that you can weld two drops of water together, pay an expert to do it.

Thread Inserts

The art of torquing fasteners, theorem 1, corollary 3: The likelihood of stripping a threaded hole increases as the degree of difficulty in even seeing that hole increases.

Several brands of threaded inserts are used to replace damaged or stripped threads. The kits for installing the inserts include a drill bit, a tap, a threaded insert installer, and threaded inserts.

Drill the hole oversize with the bit supplied in the kit. Tap the hole, and screw the insert in. Properly installed, these inserts have all the strength of the original threads.

Liquid Threads

The art of torquing fasteners, theorem 1, corollary 4: What works

great for everyone else will never work for you when it really needs to.

One of the newer disaster relief products could be called liquid threads. An epoxy glue is squirted into the damaged hole. A special releasing agent is then spread over the threads of the bolt. The bolt is screwed into the hole, and the epoxy is allowed to dry. After several hours, the bolt is removed. New epoxy threads are now where the damaged metal threads were. As the above corollary states, however, when you really need this stuff to work...

Taps and the Art of Tapping

A better solution than using liquid threads, and in many cases than installing an insert, is to drill and tap the hole. This is only an option if the situation permits a larger bolt to be used.

Begin by drilling the hole in question until all the old threads are removed. Be sure the hole being drilled is perpendicular to the mating surface, or at the same angle as the original hole. A chart is provided in the Appendix to help you choose the correct size drill bit for this task.

Lubricate the tap you have chosen, with the appropriate type of lubricant for the type of material you are attempting to tap (see the chart in the Appendix). Slowly screw the tap into the hole a half

turn, then remove the tap. Clean any metal shavings from the hole, then restart the tap. Repeat this process slowly and patiently until the hole is fully tapped.

Dies

A die is a relatively useless piece of equipment. Actually, for every time I have used a tap, I have used dies several times. Nevertheless, a die is useless in the sense that if when the threads of a bolt or stud have been damaged to a point where a die is necessary to make a repair, the fastener should be replaced. Occasionally there will be a bolt or stud that cannot be replaced. This could be because it is unavailable or an integral part of the unit. At times like this, a die is essential.

To use a die, place it over the end of the bolt or stud. Rotate the die a half turn, and back it off. As with the tap, this helps to clean the metal shavings out of the new threads. Repeat this process until the bolt or stud is satisfactorily repaired.

Pipe Plugs

Threaded pipe plug holes are used primarily in the water jacket, for fittings to channel water through the heater core, and in the intake manifold, for vacuum sources. On a given engine application, if these sources are not being used, these threaded holes will be plugged with a threaded plug.

Lubrication

5

The lubrication system of the modern gasoline engine consists of a semi-pressurized oiling system. Most of the moving parts in the engine receive lubrication under pressure from the oil pump, but for many components, the lubricating is handled by little more than gravity.

I have heard it argued that oil does not deteriorate or break down, that the only deterioration is in the additives. I suppose if the filtration system were more ideal, if the environment the engine were being operated in were ideal, and if no combustion gases leaked past the pistons and rings, this would be true.

Poor maintenance is the most common cause of engine damage. This damage does not occur suddenly in most cases. Slowly, oil volume passing through the engine is reduced. This reduction occurs as the oil pump gears wear, as the screen on the oil pickup becomes restricted with sludge. Long before the reduced oil volume causes a pressure problem, it causes another problem. The main bearing, rod bearings, and cam bearings are usually the first components to oil. These components will probably receive an adequate, though not ideal, amount of oil. Camshaft

lobes, lifters, pushrods, and rocker arms oil last. The pistons, cylinder walls, and valve guides oil only with residual oil splashing or dripping from other parts. Since a little oil is lost during each oiling stage, reduced oil volume can cause reduced oiling and excessive wear in the last components to oil.

It is no accident that parts like the cam lobes, pushrods, and rocker arms were chosen to oil after the main bearings and rod bearings. As soon as the main bearings and rod bearings lose oil, they begin to make noise. I once had an apprentice who rebuilt a VW Rabbit engine. Unlike many engines, this one had a hole in only one of the rod bearing shells to allow oil from the inside of the crankshaft to feed to the bearing-journal surface. My apprentice installed the bearing shell incorrectly. Immediately upon starting of the engine, a severe rod knock was heard. We shut the engine off, pulled the oil pan, and found no damage to the bearing surfaces. We put the bearing shells in their correct position, and there was no problem. The point is, when the main and rod bearings suffer a catastrophic and sudden loss of oil pressure, the engine makes a lot of noise all of a sudden. Sometimes, little or no damage occurs. A grad-

ual loss of volume is more insidious. Slow oil starvation causes silent wear and silent destruction.

Frequent oil changes reduce the likelihood of sludging, which increases the likelihood of long engine life.

Oil Pan

The oil pan acts as a reservoir and in most engines, the only cooler the oil will have. Although for most domestic passenger car engines it will hold 4 quarts (qt) to 5qt, I have worked on applications with a capacity of 12qt.

Most oil pans are made of stamped steel. Some applications are made from cast aluminum or even plastic.

An oil pan is shaped to ensure that as lateral and longitudinal G forces change, the oil will stay near the oil pump pickup. On some engines, it will have an odd shape—a bubble or an indentation—in the side. This apparent deformity has been engineered into the oil pan to reduce engine noise.

Oil Types

The purpose of the oil is to provide a cushion or film of oil molecules between pieces of metal that are in relative movement. This layer separating the metal surfaces prevents the extreme friction that would result if those surfaces came in direct contact.

Oil types are described in several different ways. The decision of what type of oil to use should be based on several factors, including:

Engine type (normally aspirated spark ignition, normally aspirated diesel, turbocharged spark ignition, turbocharged diesel)

Load usage

Operating temperatures (sump temperatures)

Amount of combustion residue (blowby) generated

Oil capacity

Intended oil change intervals

Type of oil cooling

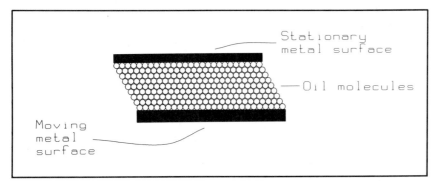

Oil forms a film between two metal surfaces that are moving with respect to one another. The oil film prevents direct contact between the compo- nents, and prevents the extreme heat of friction, which would cause component failure.

SAE Ratings

SAE viscosity ratings are intended only to indicate the viscosity of the oil. They do not indicate the quality of the oil. The higher the SAE rating number, the more viscous, or thicker, the oil. Generally speaking, if it is winter, or in cold climates, you will want to use a low-viscosity oil. In the summertime, or in warm climates, use a high-viscosity oil. As the engine wears, the bearing clearances increase and the oil pressure drops. A temporary bandage for this can be provided by using an oil with a higher viscosity rating.

SAE 5wt

SAE 5 weight (wt) is an extremely thin oil recommended only for cold weather and very light load applications. The low viscosity provides for the oil to be thin at cold temperatures. At extreme sub-zero temperatures, 5wt can allow for free movement of the internal engine parts, which can make the engine easier to start. Since viscosity tends to decrease as the oil heats up, an oil this thin can be too thin to provide proper lubrication when the engine warms up.

SAE 10wt

Also extremely thin, SAE 10wt provides slightly better protection than SAE 5wt for a warm engine.

SAE 20wt

For most applications, SAE 20wt is the low-viscosity practical oil, especially in cold climates for passenger cars or light-duty trucks.

SAE 30wt

SAE 30wt is a good all-around choice for most North American climates. It is thin enough to provide easy cold weather starting–assuming, of course, that you do not spend your winters in Minot, North Dakota–yet thick enough to provide good protection.

SAE 40wt

An oil with a 40wt viscosity tends to cause difficult starting when the engine is cold. The thick oil impedes the rotation of the engine during a cold start. Of course, it might not be impractical if you spend your summers in Yuma, Arizona.

Multigrade Ratings

Multigrade oils have been used for decades to satisfy the needs of both cold weather operation and hot weather operation. These oils cover three or more viscosity

The oil pump is usually a gear pump mounted inside the oil pan.

grades. The multi-viscosity nature of these oils is accomplished by viscosity index enhancers. The viscosity index relates to an oil's ability to alter its viscosity according to the engine's needs as its temperature increases. A 10W-40 oil would have approximately the same viscosity as 10wt oil at 0 degrees Fahrenheit and as 40wt oil at 212 degrees Fahrenheit. The W following the 10 indicates that the viscosity test was done at 0 degrees Fahrenheit; the number following the hyphen gives the viscosity at 212 degrees Fahrenheit.

Viscosity index enhancers often consist of oil soluble polymers. Oil containing them should be replaced at manufacturers' suggested intervals, as these enhancers tend to be unstable and to break down, allowing the oil to thin out at higher temperatures.

API Gradings

API grading goes from SA to SG. This system is based on the types of additives in the oil. SA oil is pure mineral oil and should only be used in the lightest-duty applications. The higher the second letter of the grading, the greater the ability of the oil to protect engines.

Synthetic Oils

Synthetic oils have received exaggerated good press and exaggerated bad press. The fact is that they have excellent low-tempera-

ture characteristics and a better viscosity index than mineral oils. This does not make them a miracle solution to engine wear problems—just good. Their major disadvantage is their expense. A good-quality mineral oil with additives appropriate to the engine is more than adequate and considerably less expensive.

The Best Choice

Over the years, I have been asked what is the best brand of oil. My usual reply is, "The brand your father used." All name brand oils meet standards appropriate for their use.

Oil Pump

Generally, the oil pump is a gear pump located in the oil pan. Suspended from the bottom of the block, its pickup extends to near the bottom of the oil pan. Here, the oil pump picks up engine oil. Over the end of the pickup is a screen. This screen prevents large particles, nuts, bolts, washers, and other chunks from making their way to the oil pump. This screen can become coated with residual carbon deposits that result from infrequent oil changes. The residue can limit the ability of the oil pump to pick up the oil at its source.

After being picked up from the oil pan, the oil is carried through the gear teeth of the oil pump. The

The oil pump picks up oil from the bottom of the pan through the oil pickup tube and screen. A restriction in the screen or a hole in the pickup tube can severely reduce the volume of oil provided to the oil pump and therefore to the rest of the engine.

oil pump's responsibility is to supply the engine with an adequate volume of oil. Oil pressure is determined by the restrictions created by the small clearances between the lubricated surfaces. Should the oil clearances get larger, as a result of wear or damage, the amount of restriction decreases and the oil pressure drops.

Low oil pressure can also result from a lack of volume. Low oil volume can be caused by restrictions in the pickup screen, wear in the oil pump, or restrictions in the oil filter or oil galleries. The low oil pressure that results from low volume causes excessive wear in the bearing-to-journal and other metal-to-metal surfaces. This wear results in lower pressure. What works best to avoid this scenario is regular maintenance.

The oil pump is also equipped with a pressure relief valve. On new engines or engines with just a little wear, the potential oil pressure is much higher than components such as the oil filter can handle. Too much oil pressure can blow the oil filter off the engine. The pressure relief valve limits the oil pressure by diverting some of the oil back to the inlet side of the pump.

Typical Oiling Path

Once the oil leaves the oil pump, it passes through the oil filter on its way to the main oil gallery. From the main oil gallery, it is then distributed to the camshaft and lifter. On a pushrod engine, the oil is carried through the pushrods to the rocker arms and the upper valvetrain. A second oil path, parallel to the one feeding the upper valvetrain, carries the oil to the main bearings of the crankshaft. Oil is then forced through galleries in the crankshaft to the rod bearings. The timing chain on most North American engines is splash oiled. Some applications spray a pressurized stream of oil on the timing chain and gears. Overhead cam engines that use a timing belt do not oil the belt.

Air Filter

Several years ago, I taught a technician upgrading class at a large Marine base. The students related a story about a training session on maintaining tactical vehicles. Apparently, this session had been done in a desert environment. During the training, the vehicles were test driven with the air filters not installed. The result was the need to rebuild the engines. The short test drive allowed enough sand to enter the cylinders to do severe damage to the engine.

This little anecdote illustrates that the air filter is an important part of the lubrication system. Just as the oil filter removes contaminants from the oil, the air filter helps keep those contaminants from getting in the oil in the first place. As part of the routine maintenance on an engine, the air filter should be replaced. On throttle body—injected and carbureted engines—the little paper gasket between the air cleaner and the top of the carburetor or throttle body is not a throwaway item. This gasket is an essential part of protecting the cylinders from fine-particle damage.

How much damage? When I was in trade school, the instructor told me that two aspirins worth of grit can instantly cause the same amount of wear as 75,000 miles of clean driving.

Cooling System

6

The engine pushes the car down the road by converting heat energy into rotary motion. Each gallon of gasoline contains about 114,396 British thermal units (Btu) of heat energy. Most of this energy is wasted—not used actually to push the car down the road. Thirty-three percent, about 37,751Btu, is carried away as heat energy in the exhaust gases. Friction accounts for 3 percent, or 3,432Btu, of the wasted energy. The rotation of the water pump and fan consumes another 3 percent. Pulling the air for combustion into the cylinders and the exhaust gases out of the cylinders takes another 4 percent, or 4,576Btu. About 27 percent, or 30,886Btu, makes it out the end of the crankshaft. This means that the cooling system must dissipate 30 percent, or 34,319Btu, of the heat energy in each gallon of gasoline.

Should the heat intended to be dissipated by the cooling system be retained by the engine, severe damage may occur. The metals used in the gasoline internal-combustion engine tend to warp and deteriorate when subjected to high temperatures.

Coolant

The primary ingredient in modern antifreeze coolant is ethylene glycol. The boiling point of ethylene glycol is 330 degrees Fahrenheit. Ethylene glycol is noncorrosive, has no significant odor, and in a 40%–60% glycol-water mix can protect against freeze-up at temperatures as low as -65 degrees Fahrenheit. Various additives are added by manufacturers to inhibit leaking, rust, and restrictive scale.

Ethylene glycol is a hazardous waste well known for its ability to do severe kidney and brain damage. Consumption of as little as 1/2 cup can cause irreversible damage or may be fatal. Check with your local department of ecology or waste disposal to determine the proper way to dispose of antifreeze coolant waste.

Look in the future for ethylene glycol to be replaced by a less hazardous chemical. Two of the chemicals being discussed are propylene glycol and polyethylene glycol. These sound like virtually the same chemical being used today, but they are not as toxic. In fact, polyethylene glycol is an ingredient in popular soft drinks.

Radiator

The radiator is the principle heat exchanger in the cooling system of water-cooled engines. As the engine runs the water pump forces the coolant solution through the hoses in and out of the radiator. In the radiator the coolant passes through tubes where the heat is dissipated to fins that pass between the tubes.

An important part of every engine rebuild should be to have the radiator cleaned and pressure tested. It makes little sense to put several hundred, or even thousand, dollars at risk to save a few dozen. Since removing the radiator is one of the first tasks involved in the removal of the engine, the last thing that should be done on the first day of the engine rebuild project is to drop the radiator off at the nearest radiator shop.

If the radiator is plastic and aluminum there is little that most radiator repair shops can do to cure them of leaks. Even though there have been several techniques developed in the last few years to effectively clean and reseal these radiators, they are not always effective. Talk to the man at the local radiator shop, he can offer valuable input regarding his abilities with these radiators. (Remember while talking to him that these guys frequently work with lead, this might serve to explain why he may not remember your conversation when it comes time to settle the bill.) If the vehicle is equipped with one of these radiators you should probably add a new radiator to your parts list.

Transmission Oil Cooler

After draining the radiator inspect the coolant for reddish/brown oil. The presence of this oil indicates the metal separating the engine cooling section of the radiator from the transmission cooler. If there is even a suspicion of transmission fluid in the coolant, replace or repair the radiator. Transmission fluid in the coolant will do very little damage to the engine, however coolant in the transmission could add a transmission to the list of parts you need to get this vehicle back on the road.

Hoses

Do not even think about not replacing the hoses. When I first began teaching, a student who worked for a large retail chain failed to replace a marginal hose. The student had replaced a head gasket and felt that he would do the owner of the car a favor. Not replacing the hose saved almost $25 on a $450 bill. The customer picked up the car and within hours blew the hose in a mountain pass. The cost of this savings was a new cylinder head, a new timing belt, all the labor and the mechanic's job.

Hose Clamps

Unknown to many is the 11th commandment, there is no such thing as a used hose clamp. A new $0.50 clamp can mean the difference between a successful, long-lasting overhaul and a $1,000 box full of new, but junk, parts.

Radiator Cap

You can buy a new one for about five bucks, so it cannot be important, right? Wrong! The radiator cap is both the pressure regulator and the pressure relief valve for the cooling system. I was still young in the business when a man came in with the top tank of his radiator peeled open like a clam.

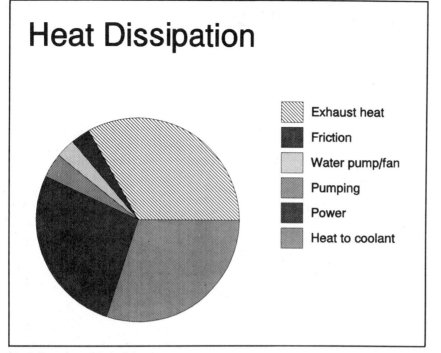

Heat Dissipation

Exhaust heat
Friction
Water pump/fan
Pumping
Power
Heat to coolant

Less than one-third of the heat energy created by the combustion process actually makes it out of the back end of the crankshaft. Most of the heat energy is lost in the exhaust and transferred to the coolant.

Upon interrogation we found that the radiator cap had been leaking. Concerned about his engine he jammed the pressure relief function of the cap to keep to coolant in the system. The pressure finally built to the point where the upper tank blew off. If the radiator cap does not hold a high enough pressure, coolant loss and overheating can result. If it does not properly relieve pressure, the tanks can blow off the radiator.

Water Pump

The water pump is responsible for ensuring that the coolant moves through the cylinder head and block to remove potentially damaging heat. Back in the days before the rumble seat the coolant was circulated through the water jacket by simple convection. The warmer water was slightly lighter and tended to rise to the top of the water jacket. The cooler water was heavier and tended to gravitate toward the bottom. The result of this relative displacement was the tendency for the water to move from the top of the engine into the top of the radiator, through the radiator and out the bottom of the radiator, cooler, and back into the bottom of the water jacket. Modern engines use a water pump to force the coolant through the radiator. Although the water pump is normally driven by belts on the front of the engine, the Saab engine drives it with the camshaft and the Quad 4 engine drives it with the timing chain.

Thermostat

The thermostat prevents coolant from passing through the radiator, until the engine reaches operating temperature. It is then responsible for ensuring that the coolant temperature does not drop below the operating temperature.

The thermostat is a temperature-controlled valve. As the temperature of the coolant behind it rises, the thermostat opens, allowing the coolant to pass into the radiator. If the thermostat fails to open, the engine will overheat.

Replace the thermostat any time major work is done on the engine. It may be tempting to use a lower temperature thermostat to allow the engine to run cooler. While there is little doubt that a lower operating temperature is kinder to many of the metal components, on older cars it causes an increase in exhaust emissions. The emission increase is due to a less efficient burn in the combustion chamber. A less efficient burn results in creation of more corrosive hydrocarbon particulates. These can be abrasive and can contribute to the production of damaging sulfuric acid. On newer cars the absence of a thermostat can keep the temperature of the engine from rising to the point where the computer can enter closed loop. The result is driveability problems and poor fuel economy. (NOTE: Hypertech Corporation markets a "Power Thermostat." This is simply a 160F thermostat that prevents the computer and keeps the timing curve in the additional advance warm up mode and the warm up enrichment curve.)

Water Jacket

The water jacket is the system of passageways cast into the cylinder head and block, through which the coolant passes. Over the years the engine's water passageways have probably been the beneficiary of a wide variety of deposits. Consult your local machinist to determine the best method of eliminating these deposits.

7

The Getting-Ready-to-Rebuild-Checklist

It was a joyous day when Barney and his neighbor John removed the engine from Barney's classic Mustang for rebuilding. Two years and a marriage later, the Mustang is back on the road.

A disastrous scenario like this can be avoided with proper preparation. Begin by making a list of the parts you are likely to need. Some parts are needed in every rebuild. If the engine you are overhauling is unusual–a Lamborghini or an Elva–seek out your parts sources well in advance. Even what would seem like a common engine can have unusual variations that are hard to find parts for.

When I was in trade school, my lab partner and I were given a Dodge 225 slant six in a Dart to rebuild. Even at the tender young age I was back then, I thought acquiring parts for such a common engine would be no problem. As we started to remove the engine, our lack of experience kept us from seeing that it was a rare aluminum 225. My partner and I spent virtually the entire semester just trying to get the parts. The moral of this story is, Know what you need, and know where you can get it before you start.

Most parts houses are very cooperative when it comes to letting customers return unused engine rebuild parts. It is strongly recommended that you have all the parts you know you are likely to need sitting on the workbench before you begin removing the engine. Below is a list of these parts.

Antifreeze
Assembly lube
Camshaft (almost always needed)
Camshaft bearings
Clutch disc (if manual transmission is used)
Clutch pressure plate (if manual transmission is used)
Distributor cap and rotor (unless distributorless ignition is used)
Freeze plugs
Gasket sealer
Head bolts or nuts (as applicable)

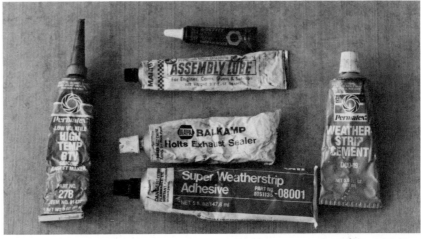

A variety of tubed products are necessary to reassemble an engine. These products should be purchased carefully to ensure that they are appropriate to the engine being rebuilt.

Ignition module, or points and condenser
Lifters (must be replaced if the camshaft is replaced)

Lower end gasket set
Main bearing cap bolts
Main bearings
Oil

Clear RTV silicone has been used for decades to help seal valve cover, timing cover, and oil pan gaskets. If the engine is equipped with an oxygen sensor, this type of silicone can prove fatal to the oxygen sensor.

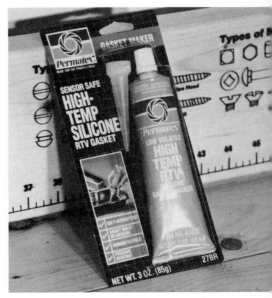

Fortunately, the manufacturers of sealing compounds make silicone sealers that will not damage the oxygen sensor. These are referred to as "low-volatile" silicones.

Removing gaskets during disassembly and measuring can be a time-consuming and frustrating process. Spray gasket removers make it easier. In the absence of such compounds, paint remover works quite well.

Oil filter
Oil pump
Pilot bearing (if manual transmission is used)
Piston rings
Plastigage
Rod bearings
Rod bolts and nuts
Spark plugs
Spark plug wires
Thermostat and gasket
Timing chain
Timing gears

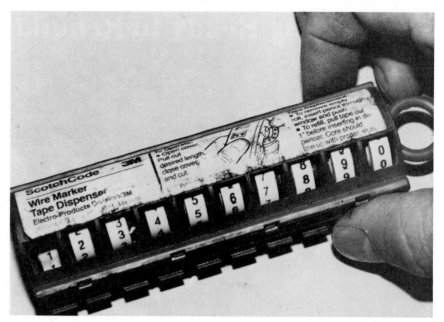

When the wires and vacuum hoses are removed from the engine, they tend to turn into a mass of spaghetti. These numbered tapes are available to help keep them organized and charted for easy installation after the rebuild.

Upper end gasket set

In addition to these parts, make sure you have the tools you will need, a good supply of rags, and cleaning solvents.

The subject of cleaning solvents is of extreme concern. Solvents such as gasoline, naphtha, and kerosene have been responsible for tragic fires. It is a relatively small and wise investment to call up a commercial supplier of cleaning solvents. The supplier will not only provide a safe cleaner, but also pick it up and take it away when you are done. Under current hazardous waste regulations, disposing of the used solvent may be very difficult. The commercial solvent suppliers handle the disposal as part of their service.

Probably the most important thing to organize at the outset is time. A quality overhaul can take time and patience that marriages and jobs sometimes don't have to spare. Before deciding on a date to begin the project, check for important conflicts, including the birthdays of children, of your spouse, and of significant relatives. Do not forget about anniversaries and the truly important dates in life–those of the Indy 500 race, the Super Bowl, and must-sees on the new fall TV schedule. As silly and trivial as this may sound, careful attention to a starting date can keep a project car that you planned to work on for a couple of efficient weekends from becoming a permanent fixture in your garage.

8

Removal and Disassembly

Allegedly found on the wall of a chariot repair shop in ancient Pompeii: *Nolore id cogere capre malleum majorum* (Don't force it; get a bigger hammer).

Safety

Disassembly can be a dangerous experience. Wear goggles, gloves, and long sleeves as much as possible.

Most easy-to-acquire cleaning solvents are more at home in a Molotov cocktail than in a repair shop. Take the time to be safe: spend the money for a commercial cleaning solvent.

When removing the engine, rent an engine hoist. The block-and-tackle-over-a-beam method may put life and limb at severe risk.

Although traditional in some circles, the consumption of alcoholic beverages and engine rebuilding do not mix.

Removal

Begin by opening a can of your favorite soda, then sit back in a lawn chair and watch your teenagers remove the engine.

If you have the misfortune of being without teenagers, begin by opening a can of your favorite soda, then disconnect and remove the battery. Place the front of the car on good jack stands. In 1985, I had a young mechanic wannabe working for me. He had put a Toyota Celica on four cheap, stamped steel jack stands. After several minutes of strenuous wrenching, lifting, and twisting, he rolled out from under the car just as all four jack stands collapsed, leaving the Celica flat on the floor. Only fate and seconds in time saved him from certain death.

Drain the coolant, the power steering fluid, the engine oil, and the aforementioned can of soda.

Now comes the most frustrating part of the removal process: remove the bolts or nuts or studs that hold the exhaust down-pipe or -pipes to the exhaust manifold.

Jack stands will be necessary to let you get under the car during the engine removal procedure. Never get under a car without first setting it on jack stands. How much should you pay for a set of jack stands? How much is your life worth?

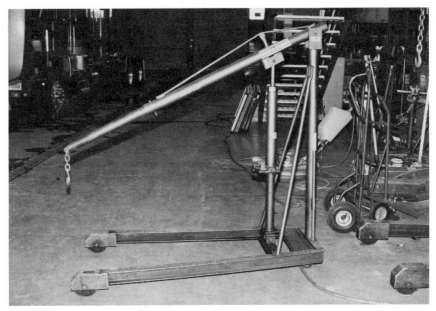

A good engine hoist is indispensable for removing the engine. It is tempting to throw a block and tackle over a rafter to save a few bucks, but this is not only unsafe, it also does not work very well.

Few things are more frustrating than rolling an engine back and forth across the floor to work on it. This

Ford 3-liter SHO engine is mounted on a quality engine stand.

engine bolts that are accessible from underneath. If the car has an automatic transmission, remove the bolts that couple the torque converter to the flex plate. Failure to take out these bolts will cause the torque converter to be removed from the transmission when the engine is pulled from the car. Although this will probably not harm either the transmission or the torque converter, it will make a real mess of your garage floor as a quart or two of transmission fluid pours out of the converter. Even if the transmission fluid is drained, there will still be a quart or two in the converter.

Remove the nuts or bolts that hold the motor mounts to the frame. Many standard transmission applications have the clutch lever secured to a ball stud mounted on the side of the block. If the application you are working on is set up this way, remove the ball stud. Roll forward on your creeper, open the radiator petcock, and drain the coolant into a drain pan. As you watch the usually light green fluid pour into the pan, contemplate this latest addition to your new collection of hazardous waste. Remove and plug the cooling lines for the automatic transmission, if the car is so equipped. When the radiator has dripped its last,

Drain the fluids from the engine before disassembling. Responsible citizenship requires that these fluids be captured and disposed of properly. Besides, engine fluids can damage lawns and garage floors.

Spray large quantities of penetrating oil on these fasteners. Assume from the outset that these bolts or nuts or studs are going to break when you try to remove them.

Once the down-pipe or -pipes are released, move them to the side. Remove all the transmission-to-

Begin the disassembly procedure by removing the rocker arms. A common type of rocker arm is these cast-

steel rockers mounted on individual studs.

48

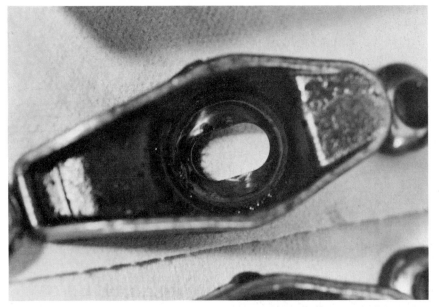

Inspect carefully the pivot surfaces of the rocker arms. If you have any doubt about the condition of a rocker arm, replace it. If several of the rocker arms are badly worn, replace all the rockers.

Check the pivot ball on individual stud-mounted rockers. If it is badly worn, replace both the ball and the rocker. Never replace the ball without replacing the rocker, and never replace the rocker without replacing the ball.

close the petcock and remove the lower radiator hose.

Now, move to the top of the engine. Remove the upper radiator hose and the transmission bolts accessible from the top. Disconnect the throttle linkage, and tie it out of the way. Most cars and trucks have an air conditioner. Guess what: another hazardous waste. The Freon contained in the air conditioning system has been linked to depletion of ozone in the upper atmosphere. Carefully remove the compressor from the engine and tie it to the inner fenderwell, without disconnecting the hoses.

Remove the radiator, and take it to the radiator shop. Rebuilding the engine and not having the radiator at least rodded and sealed is as silly as rebuilding the engine and reusing the original oil filter.

Tie the air conditioner condenser out of the way, and you are ready to remove the engine. Install the engine lifting cradle that came with the engine hoist. Connect the hook from the engine hoist, and lift the engine from the vehicle.

Disassembly and Inspection

Begin by mounting the engine on an engine rebuild stand. If you do not have one, rent, borrow, or buy one. Although you probably drained the oil and the coolant from the engine prior to its removal from the car, you should be aware that a gang of elves has the job of putting fluids back into engines just prior to disassembly. In other words, no matter how well you drain the fluids, some residual will always remain.

One important part of disassembling an engine is to do so with your eyes open. As a shop manager and owner, I found this emphasis to be lacking in even the best professional technicians. Carefully inspect each component as it is removed from the engine. Disassembly is the time to clean and measure parts.

A typical teardown procedure begins with the valve cover and ends with the crankshaft. The exact sequence of disassembly and procedure you use on the engine you are rebuilding will vary with the engine's design.

Remove the Valve Cover

Begin the disassembly by removing the valve cover. Inspect the valve cover for cracks, damage, and warpage. If necessary, start a list of additional parts needed, with a new valve cover.

Inspect the Rocker Arms

Remove the rocker arms or the rocker arm assembly. Overhead valve engines have three common rocker arm designs.

Rocker Design 1

The first rocker design is a stamped steel rocker arm that mounts on studs protruding vertically from the cylinder head. The rocker arm is held in place by a nut. To facilitate rocking, the nut has a rounded bottom. This is called a ball nut.

When removing rocker arms of this design, check them for cracks in the area where the ball nut makes contact. In spite of their low cost, these rocker arms have few failures. The most common failure is when one of the nuts allows the tension created by the valve spring and the pushrod to force its way through the floor of the rocker arm. The second-most-common failure is when the pushrod is forced through the end of the rocker arm. Inspect this mating surface equally well. Wear can also occur on the machined surface where the rocker makes contact with the end of the valve stem.

Even a pro occasionally misses a deteriorated rocker arm. If you have any doubt about the condition of the rocker arms, add them to your list of things to buy.

Rocker Design 2

The second rocker arm design has a shaft that runs from one end

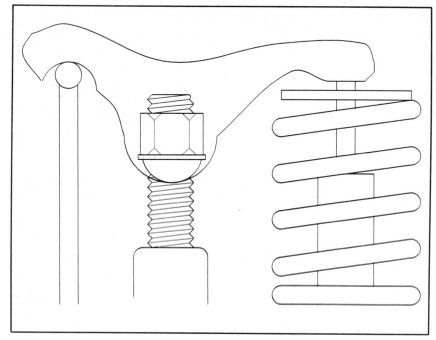

Replacing the stud on an individual stud-mounted rocker will reduce the number of valve adjustment prob-

any signs of wear, replace the shaft and all the rockers. Also inspect the surface where the rocker contacts the top of the valve stem. If the shaft is in good condition, replace only the defective rocker. If more than one-third of the rockers show significant wear on any of the wear surfaces, replace all the rockers and the shaft.

Rocker Design 3

The third rocker arm design is much like the second. A single shaft supports and provides the pivot point for all the rockers. Unlike the second design, however, the third features a rocker with no actual bearing. This stamped steel rocker has a machined area that pivots on the shaft.

Check the surface that mates with the shaft for evidence of wear. Inspect the shaft. Make sure the pushrod cup is in good condition, as well as the rocker arm surface that comes in contact with the valve stem. If the shaft shows evidence of wear, replace the shaft and all the rockers. If the shaft is in good condition, replace only the worn rockers.

Remove the Pushrods

Find a piece of cardboard, and punch two holes for each cylinder in

lems experienced in the life of the rebuilt engine.

of the cylinder head to the other. This design features a cast rocker, and an oiled bearing surface between the rocker arm and a shaft. The rocking surface of this type of rocker arm is pressure lubricated, and therefore, this arm tends to be more dependable than the ball nut-mounted arm.

During disassembly, inspect both the bearing surface of the

rocker arm and the area of the shaft where that bearing surface mates. If either the shaft or any of the rocker bearing surfaces shows

Cast rocker arms that ride on a shaft that runs the length of the cylinder head can wear the shaft or the surface through which the shaft passes. Inspect these surfaces carefully.

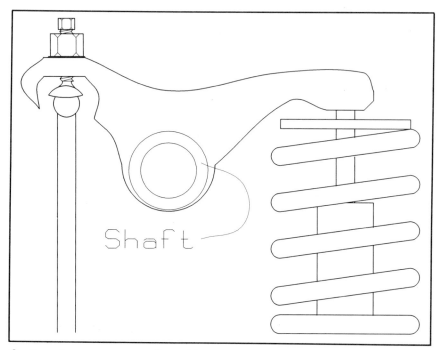

Cast rocker arms are adjustable whether they are used with hydraulic or solid mechanical lifters.

it. Remove the pushrods from the engine, and push them through the cardboard, noting which cylinder each is from and whether it is exhaust or intake. After all the pushrods are removed, lay a clean piece of glass on a flat surface. One at a time, roll the pushrods across the glass. Any that do not roll easily are bent and should be replaced.

Remove the Lifters

If the engine is a V-6 or a V-8, remove the intake manifold. Remember that if the cylinder heads on these engines are to be resurfaced, it may be necessary to machine the intake manifold. Failure to machine the manifold surface that mates to the cylinder head may result in vacuum leaks.

Remove the lifters from the block. If the lifters are to be reused, they must be kept in order. A small box, just big enough for the lifters to fit in two rows for V-6 and V-8 applications or a single row for inline applications, would be a perfect solution. Label the box Left, Right, Front, and Back. During an overhaul, do not replace the camshaft without replacing the lifters, and do not replace the lifters without replacing the camshaft.

Remove the Overhead Camshaft

Overhead cam engines come in two common designs with respect to the actuating of the valves. In the first design, the camshaft sits to the side and applies pressure to the rocker arms, which open and close the valves. In the second design, the camshaft sits immediately above the valves and opens and closes them by means of a cup and shim.

Rocker Arm-Style Overhead Camshaft

On many overhead cam engines, it will be necessary to remove the timing cover and the timing chain before removing the camshaft. Draw a diagram of the alignment of the timing chain and gears before removing the chain. In the rocker arm-design overhead cam valvetrain, the camshaft is placed to the side of the valves. A rocker arm is supported by a ball-tipped stud on one end and by the end of the valve stem on the other. The cam contacts a flat place on the rocker arm. The downward pressure of the cam against the rocker

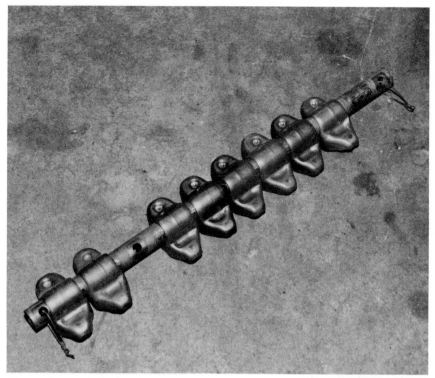

These stamped steel rocker arms are not adjustable. Their common shaft bolts to the head. After several years of operation, the shaft can wear and the valves will become noisy. During a rebuild, both the rockers and the shaft should be replaced.

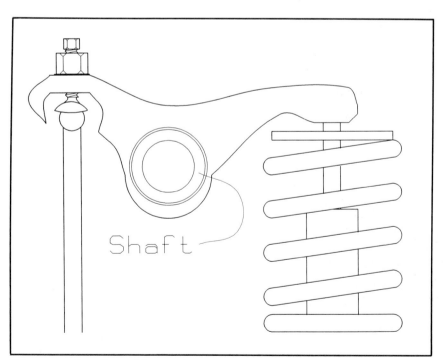

When cast adjustable rockers become worn owing to constant movement on the shaft, they should be replaced. If the engine is rare, or if for some other reason the replacement of these rockers will cost a prohibitive amount of money or is impossible, a machinist can install bushing inserts.

Inspect the rocker arm surface that comes in contact with the top of the valve. If the rocker shows wear like that on the one in this photograph, replace it.

pivots the rocker on the ball stud, forcing the valve open.

When removing the rocker arm-style overhead camshaft, inspect the machined surface on which the cam rides, for evidence of wear and pitting. In many engine designs, these machined surfaces are lubricated very poorly. Also check the ball cup surface that mates to the ball stud. Wear on the machined surface that mates to the valve stem is also common. It is a fairly safe bet that you will find enough damage to warrant replacing these rockers. Take this opportunity to inspect the camshaft lobes carefully for wear, rust, pitting, and other damage.

Shim-and-Cup-Style Overhead Camshaft

With the shim-and-cup overhead cam configuration, a cup fits over the end of the valve, which is recessed in the head. An adjustment shim fits in the top of the cup. As the cam rotates, it presses on the adjustment shim, which forces the cup downward, opening the valve.

Remove the camshaft and inspect it. Remove and inspect each of the valve shims. In most situations, these shims will appear to be reusable; if yours do, set them aside

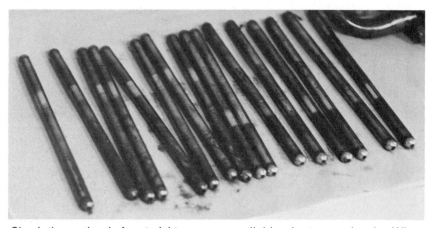

Check the pushrods for straightness. Place them one at a time on a piece of glass or a similar flat surface, and roll them. A bent pushrod will not roll smoothly. If the head or the block deck is resurfaced, it might be necessary to replace the pushrods with available shorter pushrods. When removed from the engine, the pushrods should be kept in order. If they are to be reused, they should be mated with the rocker and lifter to which they have grown accustomed.

The lifters ride on top of the camshaft and serve as a link between the camshaft and the rocker arms. Sludge and years of wear may make them difficult to remove from the engine. Rotating the cam and the crankshaft will make them more accessible for removal. Note: Do not try to remove the camshaft before the lifters are removed.

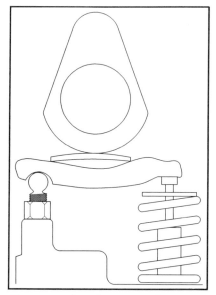

Many overhead cam engines use rocker arms. For these applications, an additional surface that needs to be checked is the machined surface that mates to the camshaft. Wear on this surface can cause noisy valves.

to be reused during reassembly. Note that the chances of the same shim fitting in the same place for reassembly are pretty slim.

Inspect the sides of the cup for damage. Check for damage where the cup slides into the head. Make sure the cup moves smoothly in the head. If it does not, tell the machinist when you have the valve work done on the head.

Remove the Valve Keepers

Although, as previously implied, some valve removal techniques do not require a valve spring compressor, safety demands the use of one. Compress the valve spring with the compressor. Carefully remove the valve keepers, and put them in a safe place. It is a little-known fact of engine rebuilding that an extraterrestrial race from the planet Zaphod uses valve keepers as a nutritional source. Being a generous race, they take only one valve keeper from every engine rebuilt in the galaxy. Protect your valve keepers.

Inspect the Valve Springs

Look for broken or cracked valve springs. Set them on a flat surface side by side. All the intake springs and all the exhaust springs should be the same height. If they are not, replace them.

Professionally, I have seldom replaced the valve springs during an engine rebuild. However, several years ago, the boss's father's boat broke down in British Columbia. One of the employees volunteered to drive the father's Cadillac to bring parts and make the repairs. On the way, the Cadillac overheated severely. Upon returning, the car had a severe misfire on two cylinders. Over $100 worth of ignition parts and a couple of days of frustration later, we discovered that the overheating had weakened the valve springs. As a trainer on the use of automotive diagnostic oscilloscopes, I have often seen scope patterns that indicate weak valve springs on engines with no perceivable driveability problem. Do not assume that your valve springs are in good condition; have a machine shop test them or replace them.

Remove the Valves

In a piece of cardboard, punch as many holes as you have valves. Number the holes corresponding to

Removing the camshaft without damaging the lobes can be very tricky. Here, a piece of all-thread is used to provide the leverage needed to remove the camshaft without causing damage.

the cylinders. Remove each valve, inspecting it for wear on the valve stem and burning around the margin. Add to your parts list any valves that need to be replaced.

Many technicians may argue the necessity of keeping the valves organized in the cardboard, but at the very least, it reduces the possibility of their being damaged by being dropped.

Inspect and Measure the Valve Guides

Measuring the valve guides now will help you more effectively coordinate the work your machinist will do for you. Use a split ball gauge to measure the diameter at the top, just below the edge, at the bottom, and in the middle.

If the valve guides are worn, the machinist will have several options for you. First, if the guides are removable, they can be replaced. In fact, if you have a spirit more daring than that of the average mortal, you can procure a set of valve guide drifts and a press, and replace them yourself.

Second, if the guides are a cast part of the head, they can be either knurled or sleeved. Knurling the valve guides involves a tool that pulls metal toward the center of the guide. The next step is to machine precisely a new diameter in the guide.

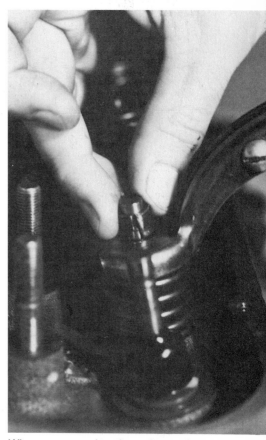

When compressing the valve spring to remove the valves, guard the valve keepers carefully. As the spring compresses, the keeper can come loose suddenly and fly across the shop.

When the valve springs are removed, check them for squareness. Warped or distorted springs should be replaced. This spring is in good condition. If the engine has been overheated, the springs should also be checked for tension.

Sleeving the guide involves drilling the guide larger and pressing in a metal sleeve. This technique is time-consuming and has largely been replaced by the methods mentioned above.

Check the Head for Warpage

After removing the valves from the head, take a few minutes to clean the old gasket material from the head surface that mates with the block deck. Now is the time to check for warpage. Place a machined straight-edge on the machined head surface. Using a feeler gauge, check for clearance between the head and the straight-edge. Now, lay the straight-edge diagonally across the head and check for twist.

Inspect the Head for Cracks

Carefully inspect the cylinder head for any evidence of cracking or damage. Begin with the assumption that the head is cracked. If you cannot see any cracks, then you can be sure the cracks are hidden. To prove that the head is not cracked, have it pressure tested.

Homer's law: You will never see the crack that causes a problem.

Cracked heads can sometimes be repaired; ask your machinist.

Inspect the Block Deck

Inspect the block surface that mates with the cylinder head. Look for cracks and warpage, just as you did on the cylinder head. Since the block is the component onto which all other parts are mounted, definitely plan on having it pressure tested.

Mark the Pistons

With a center punch, gently tap dots corresponding to the cylinder number into the top of each piston. This will ensure that if no major cylinder work is done and the pistons are reused, they are returned to their proper home.

Remove the Freeze Plugs

At this point, knock the freeze plugs out of the engine. Expect coolant to gush all over whatever dry places remain on your garage floor.

Remove the Oil Pan

Rotate the block upside-down, and remove the oil pan. It will in all likelihood be stuck. After the bolts or nuts are removed, tap gently on the sides of the pan with a soft mallet. This will not loosen the pan for removal; it is just a ceremony of vain hope that professional mechanics perform before driving a chisel between the block and the pan. The chisel technique has several adverse possibilities. First, if either the pan or the block is aluminum, the chisel technique has a good possibility of breaking it. Second, if the pan is stamped steel, the chisel technique will warp it. A

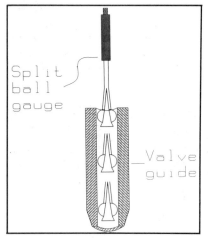

Measure the valve guides at three places from top to bottom. If a guide is too large or tapered, oil can bypass—especially during deceleration—and result in blue smoke.

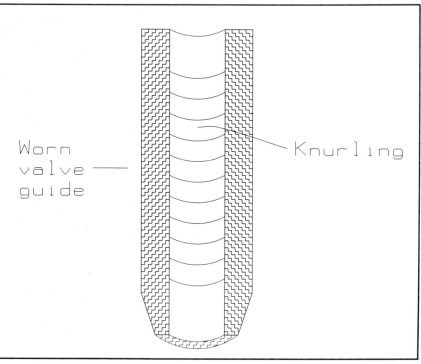

Several viable solutions are available for worn valve guides. Knurling is a popular fix that is both inexpensive and effective.

warped pan may leak after reassembly.

Mark the Rod and Main Bearing Caps

With the oil pan removed, use a center punch to mark each of the rod and main bearing caps. Tap a single dot on cap one, two dots on cap two, and so on. This reduces the possibility of mixing up the caps during cleaning, and saves time during reassembly. Mismatching the bearing caps on either the rods or the mains can result in a seized crankshaft after reassembly and possibly severe damage to the crankshaft, the rods, and the block after only a few minutes of running.

Also mark the front of each cap and each rod. A rod installed backwards can increase wear on the piston and the rings and might even make a noise.

Remove the Timing Gear/ Chain Cover, Timing Chain, Camshaft and Crankshaft Gears

Remove the timing gear/chain cover. Remove the chain and the gears. A gear puller will probably be necessary. On most applications, the cam and crank gears are not press fit, but they are extremely snug. If an appropriate puller cannot be located, gentle prying with a couple of pry bars may let you slide the gear off the shaft. Remember, screwdrivers are not designed for this purpose.

The cam gear, the crank gear, and the chain will eventually end up in a landfill, but save them for now to ensure that the new ones are correct.

Remove the Oil Pump

Remove, but do not bother to inspect, the oil pump; this is one component you will definitely replace. Not replacing the oil pump would be like taking a shower in a raincoat; it would defeat the whole purpose of the job. If the rebuild is being done for performance purposes, and the oil pump was recently replaced, however, then it may be acceptable not to replace the pump.

Remove the Pistons

With a ridge reamer, remove the ridge that has formed through thousands of miles of operation. This makes removal of the pistons easy, and failure to remove the ridge before installing new rings

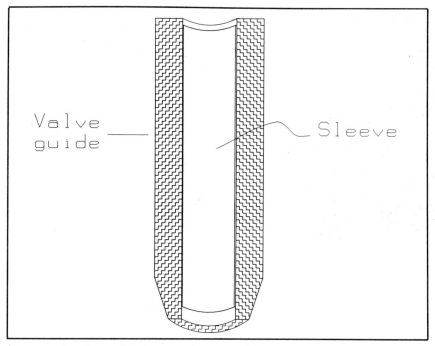

In some situations, sleeving may be the only practical solution to worn guides. Discuss guide repair options and prices with your machinist.

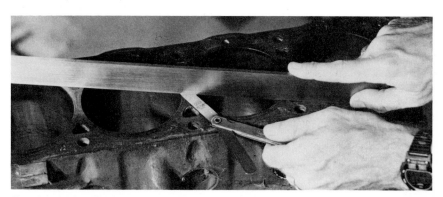

To check the flatness of the block deck, a machined straight-edge—not a metal yardstick from the local hardware store—is laid on the deck. A feeler gauge is used to find gaps between the straight-edge and the block. The procedure is the same for checking the flatness of the head.

Part of an overhaul must be the replacement of the freeze plugs. To remove the freeze plugs, drive one edge of them into the block or head and pull them out with a pair of pliers.

As the engine is disassembled, be sure that both the main and rod bearing caps are marked for front and back and for location. This is the number three main bearing cap, third from the front, and the arrow points toward the front of the engine.

will result in damage to the new rings. Push the pistons out of the block. If you plan on reusing either a piston or a rod, it would be better for you to catch the piece than for the floor to catch it. Inspect the cylinders for cracks and scarring.

Remove the Crankshaft and the Main Bearings

Remove the flywheel or the automatic transmission flex plate

A new timing chain will be tight when installed. This loose chain allows the cam timing to be retarded. Retarded cam timing can have a significant effect on the performance of the engine.

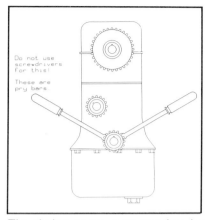

The timing gears may need to be removed with gear pullers. Sometimes, the trick of using pry bars may speed their removal.

from the crankshaft. Loosen and remove the rod bearing caps. As the rod bearing caps are removed, push the pistons and rods down the cylinder until the top of each piston is flush with the block deck. Loosen and remove the main bearing caps. Inspect the bearings and the crankshaft bearing surfaces for damage. Although the bearings will not be reused, damage to them can indicate problems with the crankshaft.

Lift the crankshaft from the block. Inspect the upper half of the main bearings. Remove the main bearing shells from the block and the caps.

Remove the Freeze Plugs

Place a long punch at the inner edge of one of the freeze plugs in the side of the block. Drive the edge of the freeze plug into the block; be careful not to drive the entire freeze plug into the block. With a pair of angle-head pliers, pry the freeze plug out of the block's water jacket. Repeat this procedure for each freeze plug. The block is now stripped and ready for cleaning and machining.

Cleanup

Several options are available for cleaning the engine parts. At this point, in the old days, we would pack all the parts off to the local car wash, where we would wash the oil and dirt down the drain. In this day of environmental awareness and regulation, we real-

In a "dishwasher" for car parts, hot water and a solvent are sprayed at the parts as they rotate on a turntable. Machines like this do a great job of cleaning parts.

ize that washing the oil into the sewer system is wrong.

Another option is to toss the parts one at a time into a solvent tank you have rented. This is a slow and not-very-thorough method.

The best option is to take the engine parts to the local machine shop and pay it a few dollars to clean them thoroughly. Many modern machine shops not only have hot tanks and steam cleaners, but also have spray-type hot tanks. These tanks clean the parts thoroughly, leaving no residual oil film or scale. The added benefit is that the machine shop will have to dispose of the hazardous and toxic materials. For a few dollars more, it will even perform the next step—measurement—for you. But why should you pay the shop to have the fun?

9

Measuring

The engine rebuilding task that requires the most skill is measuring. Clean off the workbench and lay out a machined straightedge, feeler gauges, micrometers, telescoping gauges, split ball gauges, and a dial indicator. As you complete each measurement and calculation, enter it in a "Disassembly Measurements" chart like the one at the end of this chapter.

Block and Cylinders Measurements

The one component of the engine that is most liable to cause the whole project to be shelved or postponed is the block. Before taking the time to measure the block, carefully inspect the cylinder bores for cracks and grooving. Look over the outside of the block for evidence of cracks and damage. Then measure the cylinders.

In each cylinder, take three measurements:

1. The cylinder bore at a right angle to the centerline of the engine, just below the ridge. This is called the centerline top measurement.

2. The cylinder bore along the centerline of the engine, just below the ridge. This is called the 90-degrees-to-centerline measurement.

3. The cylinder bore at a right angle to the centerline of the engine, near the bottom of the piston stroke. This is called the centerline bottom measurement.

Two results are derived from these measurements:

• Taper = Measurement 1 - measurement 3
• Out-of-round = Measurement 1 - measurement 2

In general, the maximum specification for out-of-round is 0.005in, and the maximum specification for taper is 0.01in. Although these figures are a good rule of thumb, in the Appendix, you will find specifications for the specific application you are rebuilding.

Main Bearing Bore Alignment

If the cylinder measurements are within specs, check the main bearing bore alignment. Remove the engine block from the engine stand; having the block in the stand during this measurement can distort the block and affect the accuracy of the readings. Place the machined straightedge in the main bearing saddle of the block. Use a feeler gauge to check for clearance between the straightedge and each of the bearing saddles. The clearance should be less than 0.0015in.

Block Deck Warpage

With a flat file, clean the burrs and old gasket material off the block deck surface. Place the straightedge on the block surface that mates with the cylinder head. Using a feeler gauge, check this surface for warpage. Three measurements are advisable: two at an angle across the deck and one parallel to the longitudinal centerline of the block.

It is very uncommon for the block to be warped. Cylinder heads warp far more often. The clearance measured with the feeler gauge should be less than 0.002in.

The telescoping gauge is used to measure the bores of such things as cylinders.

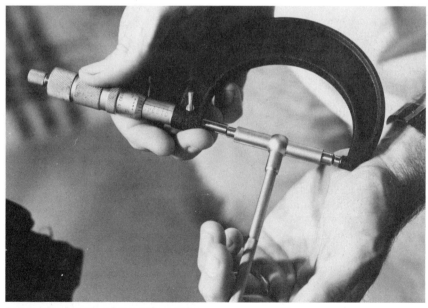

Later, the length of the telescoping gauge will be measured to determine the diameter of the cylinder.

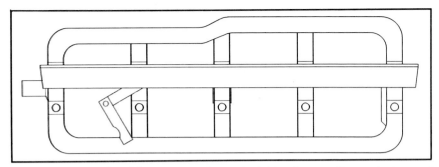

If the main journal saddles are out of alignment, the crankshaft can bind, robbing power. Check the alignment of the saddles by placing a machined straight-edge on the main journal saddles of the block. Use a feeler gauge to find gaps between the straight-edge and the block.

At this point, make a list of your measurements as follows:
Cylinder taper:
Cylinder out-of-round:
Main bearing bore alignment:
Block deck warpage:

Checking for Head Warpage

Pick up the cylinder heads and place them on the bench. Check the head surface with the straightedge. Constantly changing temperatures make head warpage a common occurrence. Check for flatness along the longitudinal centerline of the block as well as diagonally. For short cylinder heads, such as those on V-8s and four-cylinders, the maximum allowable clearance between the straightedge and the head is 0.004in. For long cylinder heads on inline six-cylinder engines, the maximum allowable clearance is 0.006in. Carefully measure along the length of the cylinder head. No more than 0.003in of warpage should be present in any 6in length of the head.

If the cylinder head in question is made of aluminum, inspect the area around the water ports of the head. If you find evidence of corrosion, the cylinder head must be resurfaced even if it is flat.

Camshaft Journal Alignment

If the engine is an overhead cam, the straightness of the top of the cylinder head is as important as the straightness of the bottom. If the cylinder head has cam journals with little bearing caps resembling the main bearing caps of a block, remove the caps and check cam journal alignment the same way you tested main bearing bore alignment. That technique is difficult or impossible to use when the overhead cam journals are one-piece in design. For these applications, slide the camshaft into place and rotate it by hand. Since the most important consideration regarding the straightness of the top of the cylinder head is whether the cam will be put in a bind, this rather crude test is normally adequate.

If the cam journals are not true, after the block mating surface of the cylinder head is machined flat, the cam journals will need to be align bored.

Measuring the Valve Guides

The valve guides are measured using split ball gauges. Slip the gauge into the guide. Since the guides are prone to both general top-to-bottom wear and tapering, measure the guide at the top, in the middle, and at the bottom. The maximum allowable diameter is 0.003in greater than the diameter of the new valve. The maximum allowable taper is 0.003in.

If the valve guides are worn or tapered, you have a couple of alternatives. First, the valve guides may be replaceable. Replacing the valve guides would amount simply to pressing the old guides out and the new ones in. Second, for applications where the guides are part of the head, or non-replaceable, the options are knurling or sleeving the guide.

Sleeving the guide is an awkward, time-consuming, and expensive option. The procedure involves boring out the existing guide and pressing in a sleeve or insert. Much more efficient and even more effective is knurling the guide.

Knurling involves using a special tool to pull metal from the worn guide toward the center. This reduces the inside diameter of the valve guide to less than the diame-

Before align boring cam journals

After align boring cam journals

If the bottom of the cylinder head is warped, the top of the head is likely also warped. On many overhead cam engines, this means the journals in which the camshaft rides may be out of alignment. Misaligned cam journals can cause the camshaft to bind, damaging timing belts and stretching timing chains.

ter of the valve stem. A precision ream is then used to size the guide for the valve. Although this may sound like a flaky repair, in reality, it is an excellent way to repair the guides. Knurling leaves behind parallel grooves perpendicular to the centerline of the guide. These grooves help to control oil slipping down the guide to be burned in the combustion chamber.

A symptom of bad valve guides is puffs of smoke in the face of the competition you just passed as you decelerate into the next turn.

Valve Stems

Since the valve stem is always made of a much harder metal or alloy than the guide, it will seldom wear significantly. To confirm that little wear has occurred, use a 0in-to-1in micrometer to measure each valve stem at three points: near the top, in the middle, and near the bottom.

     Head warpage:
     Head topside warpage:
     Valve guides:
       Diameter:
       Taper:
     Valve stem:

Valve Springs

A complete check of the valve springs will include testing their tension; this requires special equipment and needs to be done by a machine shop. The tension of each spring should be within 5 percent to 10 percent of the factory spec, and there should be no more than a 10lb difference between them. If you do not have access to a spring tester and you are in doubt about the condition of your valve springs, replace the springs. Assurance is always less expensive than doubt.

A quick and dirty test of the springs is a squareness-and-free length test. Use the piece of glass you used earlier to check the pushrods, and an accurate steel rule—a square would be best. Measure the springs one at a time. Rotate each spring as it sits on the glass. You should find less than a 1/16in variation in the height of each spring as it is rotated, and less than a 10 percent variation in free length between the springs.

The most common cause of variation in free length or squareness is overheating. Since all the springs were subjected to the same

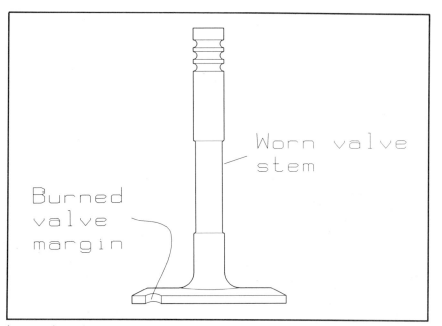

Inspect the valves carefully. Look for burned valve margins and worn stems. Look for evidence of wear in the grooves where the valve keepers are installed. Replace a valve if any of these areas looks defective or even marginal.

overheating conditions, if any of the springs shows squareness or free height problems, replace all the springs.

Measuring the Crankshaft

The measurements that need to be made on the crankshaft are end play, rod journal out-of-round, rod journal taper, main journal out-of-round, and main journal taper. End play is the clearance between the thrust surfaces of the crankshaft and the thrust surfaces of the main bearings. We find a bit of a Catch-22 concerning the measurement of crankshaft end play. The easiest and best way to test end play is to check the amount of fore-and-aft movement in the crankshaft with the crank bolted into the block. This means that the checking of end play needs to be done with new main bearings installed. You should not buy new main bearings until you know what bearings need to be purchased as a result of any machine work that needs to be done. Of course, if any machining needs to be done and the thrust surfaces need attention, then the thrust surfaces should be repaired at the same time, so you will not know what bearing to use to check

the thrust surface until the machining is done.

Are you confused yet? Let me try to straighten it out. Inspect carefully the thrust surfaces of the

This valve spring has been warped and must be replaced. The warping may indicate that the spring tension has changed owing to age or heat.

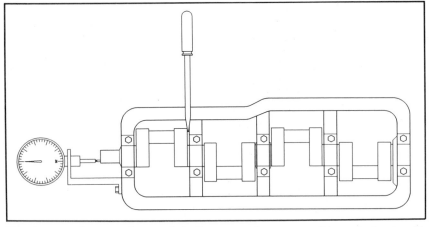

The thrust surfaces on the crankshaft along with the thrust surfaces on one of the main bearings limit the crankshaft end play. The most accurate way to measure this end play is with a dial indicator. This reading should be taken with the new main bearings installed.

main bearings. These are identified as a flange that hangs over the side of the main bearing saddle on one of the main bearings; some older engines use a separate thrust bearing that looks like this flange but is detached from any main bearing. If the bearings show signs of wear, and if the main journals are going to need machining, have the thrust surfaces checked or repaired by your machinist. If you see no excessive wear on the thrust bearing surfaces, the thrust surfaces of the crankshaft are probably acceptable.

After you have completed this inspection and any needed repairs have been made to the crankshaft during the machining phase of the overhaul, you will need to check the end play with the crankshaft reinstalled and bolted and torqued into the block.

Check the diameter of each rod journal and main journal, with a micrometer at one end of the journal (measurement A). Then, rotate the micrometer 90 degrees and check it again (measurement B). Take these measurements again at the other end of each journal (measurements C and D). The difference between measurements A and B, or C and D is the out-of-round of the journal. Out-of-round wear should be less than 0.0005in. If any journals show greater wear, the crankshaft will have to be machined. If only the main bearing journals exhibit excessive wear, only the main journals will need to be machined. If only the rod bearing journals exhibit excessive wear, only the rod journals will need to be machined. In fact, after you show the measurements to your machinist, he or she may advise you to machine the rod and main journals to different undersizes.

The taper on each journal is the difference between measurements A and C, or B and D. The maximum allowable tolerance for taper is 0.0005in.

Regrinding the Crank

When the machine shop grinds the crank to 0.01in undersize, it means that 0.005in of metal has been removed from around the journal. Because 0.005in of metal has been removed from both sides of the crank, the total amount removed equals 0.01in.

Most machine shops do not have crank grinding capability. If you confirm that your crank will need to be ground, and the machinist you have chosen to use does not have this capability, the machinist will need to send the crank to another machine shop. This is common practice and should not deter you from using this machinist. Crank grinding equipment is very expensive, and is an investment that's difficult for a small machine shop to realize a return on. However, you may want to deliver the crank to your machinist a few days before the rest of the components you will be taking in. This will allow for turnaround time, and you will be able to pick up all your machined parts at the same time.

End play:

Rod journal first diameter measurement:

Rod journal second diameter measurement:

Rod journal out-of-round:

Rod journal taper:

Although less accurate than the dial indicator, a feeler gauge can also be used to measure end play. Inspect the thrust surfaces for smoothness before checking end play with either device. If the surfaces are not smooth, they must be repaired regardless of the end play.

Main journal out-of-round:
Main journal taper:

Measuring the Pistons

If any serious damage occurred to the cylinders, do not bother to measure the pistons, because you are going to replace them. If you have determined that the cylinders will need to be rebored, do not bother to measure the pistons, because you are going to replace them. If the cylinders are in good condition, the pistons are probably in good condition.

Piston measurements include size, clearance, and taper. Since the important part of the inspection of pistons is visual, actual measurement of the pistons is to confirm their apparent good condition.

Measure the size of each piston 3/4in below the centerline of the piston perpendicular to the wrist pin. Compare this reading with the factory specifications for the engine you are rebuilding.

To measure piston clearance, subtract the piston size from the diameter of the cylinder. The clearance for pistons to be reused should always be less than 0.0035in. If the clearance is excessive, ask your machinist whether you should have the pistons knurled. Knurling raises the metal on the skirt of the piston, to reduce the piston-to-cylinder wall clearance.

To find the piston taper, measure the diameter of the piston just below the oil ring and at the bottom of the skirt. The difference between these measurements is the taper. Taper should not exceed 0.01in.

Measuring the Camshaft

Since the camshaft is a major wear item in the engine, it really does not need to be measured, it only needs to be replaced—and do not forget to replace the lifter with the camshaft as well. If curiosity is more important than time, however, begin with a thorough visual inspection of the cam lobes. If any of them show evidence of pitting or appear to have a shape or wear pattern different from that of the rest, replace the camshaft. Additionally, check each lobe for the correct wear pattern. The wear pattern should be centered on the lobe, wide at the nose (pointy end) of the lobe, and narrow toward the heel (rounded end). At no point around the lobe

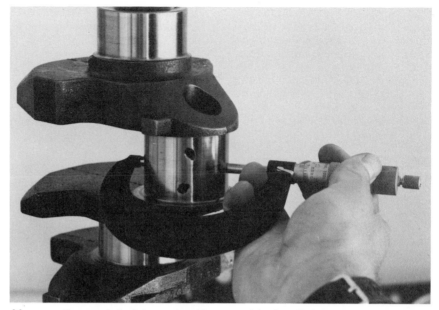

Measure the crankshaft journals with a micrometer. Although this rod journal looks all right, it is tapered and must be reground.

should the wear pattern extend to the edges of the lobe.

Many overhead camshafts have oil galleries to provide lubrication between the cam and the follower. On engines with these camshafts in particular, but also on engines with in-block cams, the condition of the camshaft gives you the best evidence concerning the effectiveness of your preventive maintenance program. Although camshaft failures can occur at any time as a result of manufacturing defects, a failed camshaft is a good indicator of maintenance problems. If your cam shows evidence of excessive wear, consider decreasing the interval between oil changes, or changing oils.

In a side-view cross section, the camshaft lobes are tapered

The proper technique is critical when using a micrometer. The anvil and the spindle should fit snugly around the surface being measured. The mic is not a C-clamp, however; tightening it too much will distort the frame and render the micrometer and the readings useless.

0.0007in to 0.002in. When they are mated with the usually convex lifter face, this taper causes the lifter to rotate as the cam revolves. This action spreads out the forces generated by the interaction of the camshaft and the lifter. Since these forces can exceed 100,000psi, rotating the lifter greatly reduces wear.

The taper on the lobe makes accurate measurement of the cam lobes difficult. Also, cam specs are among the most difficult engine measurement specifications to obtain. Rather than killing a day at the parts house and library looking for them, you can spend your time on another procedure that is almost as good as following the specs. Use a micrometer to measure and record the tallest and the broadest areas on each lobe. Make these measurements carefully, at exactly the same places on each lobe, to reduce the potential inaccuracy of taking readings at different points on the taper. Compare the readings of all the lobes. The measurements in each set—tallest and broadest—should be within 0.002in of one another.

This covers the measurements that need to be done prior to purchasing your parts and machine work. They should make it possible to order your parts. Keep your measuring tools handy, however; you will have more measuring to do during reassembly.

Parts Needed

Record how many of each listed part you need as a result of your measurements.

Block	[Y][N]
Pistons	
None needed	[ ]
0.01 over	[ ]
0.02 over	[ ]
0.03 over	[ ]
Rod bearings	
0.01 over	[ ]
0.02 over	[ ]
0.03 over	[ ]
Main bearings	
0.01 over	[ ]
0.02 over	[ ]
0.03 over	[ ]

Disassembly Measurements

Photocopy the following chart, and use it to record your measurement data:

Cylinder measurements:

Cylinder Number	Centerline Top	Centerline Bottom	90 degrees to Centerline	Taper*	Out-of-round•

*Taper = column one - column two
•Out-of-round = column one - column three

Main bearing bore alignment:
Block deck warpage:
Head warpage:
Head top-side warpage:
Camshaft journal alignment:
Valve guides:
        Diameter:
        Taper:
Valve stem measurements:

Valve Number	Near the Top	In the Middle	Near the Bottom

Valve springs:
Valve spring tension:
Valve spring height:

End play:
Rod journal first diameter measurement:
Rod journal second diameter measurement:
Main journal first diameter:
Main journal second diameter:
Journal measurement A:
Journal measurement B:
Journal measurement C:
Journal measurement D:
Rod journal out-of-round:
Main journal out-of-round:
Rod journal taper:
Main journal taper:
Piston specs:

Cylinder Number	Piston Size	Cylinder Diameter	Clearance	Taper

Valve spring specs:

	Intake		Exhaust	
Cylinder #	SpringTension	SpringHeight	SpringTension	SpringHeight
#1				
#2				
#3				
#4				
#5				
#6				
#7				
#8				

Crank journal specs:

	Measurement 1	Measurement 2	Out-of-round	Taper
Rod 1				
Rod 2				
Rod 3				
Rod 4				
Rod 5				
Rod 6				
Rod 7				
Rod 8				
Main 1				
Main 2				
Main 3				
Main 4				
Main 5				
Main 6				
Main 7				

Machining Operations

10

One of this book's goals is to guide you through the engine rebuild process so you can save money over what it would cost to have all the work done by a shop. However, there are some procedures that require the equipment and expertise of a professional shop, particularly a machine shop. In this chapter we'll cover several rebuild steps that–unless you're a machine shop owner–will require you to farm some work out to a qualified and trustworthy machine shop.

Don't fool yourself into believing your visual inspections or simple tests of components are always thorough enough. Instead, swallow the fact that a high-quality rebuild will require some machine shop expenses. Considering the thorough inspections, testing, and machining these shops specialize in, the benefits to your engine will be worth every penny.

Among the procedures covered here are: pressure testing, magnetic crack inspection, dye crack testing, cylinder head reconditioning, cylinder block reconditioning, crankshaft operations, camshaft operations, connecting rod operations, and piston operations.

Pressure Testing

Perhaps the most important operation that can be done by the machine shop is testing the integrity of the water jacket in the block and the head.

Most machine shops are equipped to do pressure testing. To begin the pressure test, all the water ports in the head or the block are plugged. Air or water is forced into the cylinder head or the block. If air is being used, soapy water is sprayed on the surfaces in question. If the component has a leak, air bubbles will be seen.

Aluminum blocks and heads sometimes become porous. When this occurs, coolant will seep through the metal when pressurized. Should your machinist find this situation, she or he can some-

This is not a torture device found in the dungeon of some medieval European castle; it is used to pressure test cylinder heads and blocks for cracks in the water jacket.

Cracks can be elusive, but a common place to find them is between two holes or ports in a flat surface.

This crack was located using a dye method.

times seal the component with a resin. Like so many other things in rebuilding an engine, however, because of the amount of work required to repair mistakes or the results of bad judgment, a porous head should just be replaced.

Magnetic Crack Inspection

Magnetic crack inspection only works on ferrous metals, as it depends on the dispersion of the magnetic field through the metal. The principle is similar to that of the famous high school physics experiment that illustrates magnetic flux fields. In that experiment, a magnet is placed under a sheet of paper and iron filings are sprinkled over it. As the iron filings fall, they line up along the magnetic fields of flux. In magnetic crack inspection, the same basic technique is used.

Iron filings are sprinkled on the head. A large electromagnet is then held a fixed distance above the head. Cracks in the cylinder head create distortions in the magnetic field that affect the alignment of the iron filings.

Dye Crack Testing

Have you ever gone into one of those roadside diners along Route 66 in northern Arizona? Few people know that all the cracked coffee cups in the universe are transported there by supreme forces beyond our comprehension. If you examine one of the cracks in one of these cups, you will find residue from the coffee of customers who sipped a little java while waiting for the bus to take them off to World War II. This is the principle of dye crack testing.

A penetrating dye is sprayed on the surface of the item being tested. After it is allowed to soak in and dry, a cleaner is used to remove it from the surface. Like coffee stains in the crack of a cup, the dye will remain in the cracks of the component being tested. The dye method is especially effective on nonferrous metals such as aluminum and magnesium.

Cylinder Head Reconditioning
Head Resurfacing

Of the machining operations done during an engine rebuild, cylinder head resurfacing may be the most common. Constant changes of temperature coupled with inadequate maintenance such as routine retorquing of heads, or incorrect retorquing of heads, result in warpage.

Resurfacing the head involves milling off several thousandths of an inch of metal. In effect, this removes the high spots, making the head flat again.

Several things must be taken into account when the head is resurfaced. If the engine is an overhead cam design, removing several thousandths of an inch of metal will cause the camshaft to be closer to the crankshaft. This can affect the tension or amount of slack in the timing chain or belt. Additionally, a warped bottom of the head may indicate that the top of the head is warped. If the top of the head is warped, the cam bearing alignment may be off. Misaligned cam bear-

The crack in this cylinder was likely caused by overheating. If overlooked, coolant seeping through this small crack could have caused the rebuild to fail and the engine to be a water pump instead of a powerplant.

This machine is used to resurface the cylinder head. Warped heads can cause improper sealing of the head gasket.

ings can bind, damage, and even break the camshaft.

Solutions? First, realize that taking a link out of the timing chain to shorten it is not the answer. Within one or two revolutions of the crankshaft, the camshaft would be far enough out of phase to bend every valve in the head. As you read this, you are probably thinking, "Oh, come on, no one would actually do that." Well, I once witnessed a professional technician in a hurry to finish a job do that very thing. He knew better; he just was not thinking. Think.

For many applications, automatic chain and belt adjusters will take up a great deal of slack. When too much metal has to be removed, the slack can be corrected by shimming the cam bearing towers. This assumes that the application you are working on has removable cam towers. The shims you will need can be obtained through your machinist or in some cases through the appropriate dealer. For applications where the cam towers are not

removable, your machinist might be able to line bore the cam journals of the towers and install oversize cam bearings. Some head designs do not lend themselves to this solution either, and will simply have to be replaced.

Straightening the head may be another solution that eliminates many of the problems addressed above. The technology for this procedure is not available everywhere, and its success seems to vary a great deal with the skill and knowledge of the technician. The process involves bolting the head to a machined flat plate and heating it to a high temperature. Although this may seem simple enough to do in your oven at home, overheating the head can soften the metal or make it brittle, whereas not applying enough heat will be ineffective. Better to replace the head.

Misaligned cam bearings can be corrected by the same procedure used for tightening the chain or belt. Your machinist should be able to line bore the cam journals of the

towers off center and install oversize cam bearings.

If the engine is a V-design, both cylinder heads should be machined the same amount. Since resurfacing the cylinder head alters the size of the combustion chamber and affects the compression ratio, machining the heads differently will create unequal power and performance characteristics from each side of the engine. Additionally, removing metal from the heads can affect the interference angle between the intake manifold and its mating surface on the cylinder head. No more than 0.024in should

If the bottom of the head was distorted, the top of the head is probably also distorted and the cam journals are misaligned. A simple way to check cam journal alignment is to insert the camshaft and turn it. If the camshaft turns freely, the alignment is probably okay; if it does not turn freely, have the cam journals line bored.

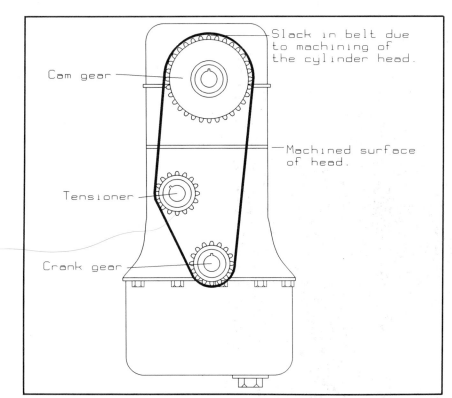

Overhead cam engines use a long chain or belt to synchronize the cam and the crankshaft. When the bottom of the head is resurfaced, it makes the distance between the cam gear and the crank gear smaller, and this makes the chain or belt looser. Although the tensioner can compensate for some of this additional slack, its ability is limited.

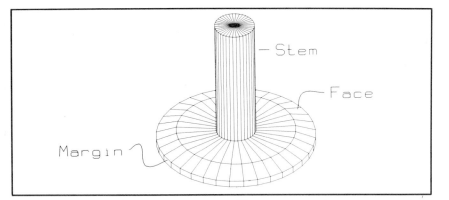

The stem of the valve is the shaft that slips through the cylinder head. The face of the valve is the machined surface that mates with the valve seat.

The margin is the narrow surface perpendicular to the bottom of the valve.

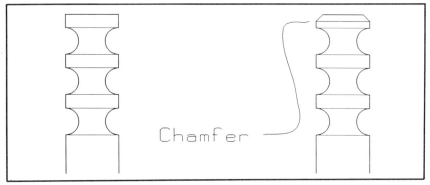

When using most valve grinding machines, the first step is to chamfer the valve tip. This ensures that the valve will be centered and will align properly when it is in the chuck of the valve grinder.

A valve grinding machine is a very expensive piece of equipment, but absolutely necessary for doing a proper valve grind. At several thousand dollars for one of these machines, the average hobbyist will probably prefer to pay a machinist to grind the valves.

be removed from these heads. If a head is badly warped, your machinist will need to machine the mating surface of the cylinder head with the intake manifold. Not doing so creates several potential problems:

1. The ports of the intake manifold may not line up properly, which can cause air leaks (often and incorrectly referred to as vacuum leaks), oil leaks, and coolant leaks.

2. Since the rocker arm shaft or studs are closer to the camshaft, the rockers may bottom out the valve springs.

Note: This problem is not unique to the V-4s, V-6s, and V-8s; it can happen on any overhead valve-design pushrod engine.

3. Removing metal from the mating surface of the head and block increases the compression ratio. Increasing the compression ratio increases the potential for detonation or pinging. Imagine that after inhabiting that precious corner of the garage where the spouse or other domestic cohabitant usually parks his or her car, after having spent $1,000 or more in the pursuit of excellence of repair, you find that the boss can hear you accelerate up the hill over five blocks away when you are late for work. The oil companies are shifting their emphasis away from antiknock additives and toward emission control additives. Make every effort to retain the same compression ratio unless you are willing or desire to take some extraordinary steps to prevent spark knock. Raising the compression ratio may require the use of the most expensive gasoline available or the habitual use of a spark prevention additive.

The simplest solution to the problem is to use a specially designed shim or a thicker head gasket. Fel-Pro Gaskets makes 0.02in shims available for several engines. Fel-Pro and other gasket companies also make head gaskets in various thicknesses. Check into these options with your local parts house, and consult with your machinist. This solution solves all the potential problems.

Another option: If shims or thicker gaskets are not an option for the application you are working on, follow the formula for determining how to machine the intake manifold to match freshly resurfaced cylinder heads. (See chart added at the end of this chapter.) Doing so still leaves the problem of shorter pushrods being required. For people who were born with a Hurst shifter T-handle in their right hand and are impressed with flame-breathing monster iron, they do make shorter pushrods.

Valve Guide Knurling

Although it is recommended that valve guide knurling be done by an experienced individual, kits can be purchased at a reasonable price to do it yourself.

Knurling the valve guides involves using a special tool to pull metal from the worn guide toward the center. This reduces the inside diameter of the valve guide to less than the diameter of the valve stem. A precision ream is then used to size the guide for the valve. Although this may sound like a flaky repair, in reality, it is an excellent way to repair the guides. Knurling leaves behind parallel grooves perpendicular to the centerline of the guide. These grooves help to control oil slipping down the guide to be burned in the combustion chamber.

If the guides are not replaceable, knurling makes good sense in a repair. However, many cylinder heads are designed with removable and replaceable guides. If the guides are removable, then replacement is the better option.

Valve Guide Replacement

Replacing the valve guides is a much easier operation than it might at first seem. The only special tools required are an appropriate valve guide drift and a press or a hammer. Slip the drift into the old guide, and gently tap the guide out with a hammer. When the old guides are removed, install the new guides by tapping them into place. The diameter of the step of the valve guide drift must be larger than the outside diameter of the guide. This is usually not a problem with drifts designed for this purpose. If the diameter of the drift is too small, it will damage the new guide.

Valve Face Resurfacing

Valve face resurfacing requires a valve grinding machine. At several thousand dollars, this machine is probably an unreasonable purchase for just one or two engine rebuilds.

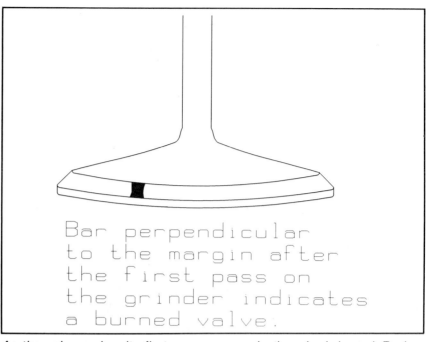

As the valve makes its first pass across the grinding stone, if a narrow band appears perpendicular to the margin, the valve is burned. Replace it.

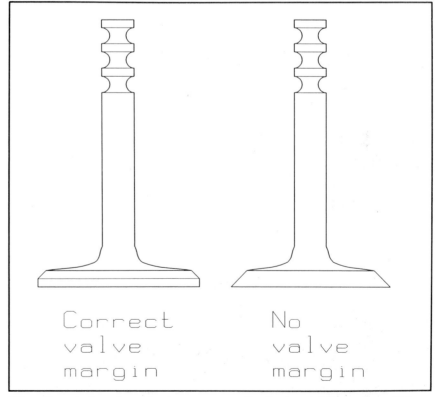

When the grinding of a valve is completed, it should have a narrow margin. The valve without a margin, right, is subject to damage from heat. The sharp edge will not dissipate heat effectively, and the valve will burn after a short period of use. If resurfacing the face of the valve eliminates the margin, replace the valve.

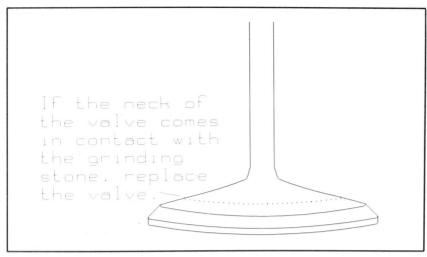

If the neck of the valve comes in contact with the grinding stone, replace the valve.

If the grinding stone scribes the neck of the valve accidentally while the valve's face is being resurfaced, replace the valve.

The valve is held in the arbor and rotated at a relatively low speed. A grinding stone is also rotated at a relatively low speed. As a cooling oil is poured on the valve face, the arbor assembly is moved across the stone. An adjustment wheel determines how much contact is between the valve and the grinding stone. Metal is slowly removed from the face of the valve until it looks smooth and even all the way around.

Any valve that shows a narrow band perpendicular to the valve margin during the first couple of passes is burned and should be replaced. If, when the face is smooth and even, an inspection of the margin reveals a sharp edge instead of a margin, the valve should be replaced. Some machinists will cut a new margin on the valve. For a few dollars, it is better to have a valve that can be trusted for 150,000 miles rather than one that has already been run 150,000 miles. Based on that statement, you may be tempted to replace all the valves. That is not a bad idea, but valves can be bent and damaged during transportation and storage. Even new valves should be refaced.

After each of the valves is refaced, the stem tips should be ground smooth. If a tip is badly worn, grinding it smooth will remove its hardened surface. This

Valve face resurfacing is a procedure that requires skill and practice. Your machinist should always resurface the valve faces and grind the valve seats.

Resurfacing the valve face usually begins with chamfering the valve tip. This increases the accuracy of centering when the valve is chucked up in the arbor of the valve grinder. The next step is inserting the valve in the arbor of the grinder and adjusting the arbor head to the correct angle. The face angle for most applications is 45 degrees.

Many kinds of valve seat resurfacing machines are on the market. This type is both easy to use and relatively inexpensive.

Although formerly a male rite of passage, valve lapping is a wholly inadequate method of grinding a valve.

hardening is only a few thousandths of an inch thick. If in doubt about having passed through the hardening when grinding the tip, replace the valve.

If the valve neck accidentally comes in contact with the grinding stone, replace the valve. This has likely weakened the valve in a critical area. Reusing the valve may cause it to break off the stem and become stuck in the piston in the future. Although this can generate some unusual sculptures, it is hardly worth the trouble.

Note: Some applications use valves filled with metallic sodium. If enough metal is removed to expose the sodium to atmospheric moisture, it will burst into flame. Grinding these valves is extremely dangerous. It is recommended that either these valves be replaced instead of ground or the grinding be left to professional, experienced machinists. If you are going to grind the valves yourself and you are possibly working with sodium-filled valves, contact your local fire department before you start, for tips on how to extinguish the fire.

[2]Valve Seat Resurfacing

Because the valve seat must be concentric to the guide, all valve guide repairs must be made before the valve seats are ground. Valve grinding comes in three major categories.

Lapping

Back in the days of duck tails, white socks, and cuffs in your blue jeans, you might have found Billy Joe down at the town drive-in grinding his valves with a suction cup on a stick, to impress the girls and lesser males. This method is known as lapping the valves. A spot of valve grinding or valve lapping compound is dabbed on the valve seat. This compound is an abrasive grit suspended in a lubricant. When the valve is placed on the seat and rotated back and forth rapidly, the valve imperfections and the seat imperfections are theoretically matched. The reality is that matched imperfections are still just imperfections. Lapping also does not correct incorrect valve seat width.

Valve lapping was never an effective method of ensuring a proper seal between the valve and the seat. In the days of the Model T, it was often done when the carbon

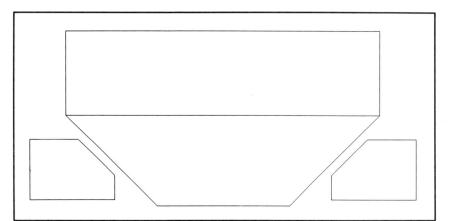

The valve seat should be ground to a 45-degree angle. Some manufacturers recommend a 44-degree angle. After the seat is ground, the valve that will be used in it should be placed in position. The seat should contact the valve on the midpoint of the valve face.

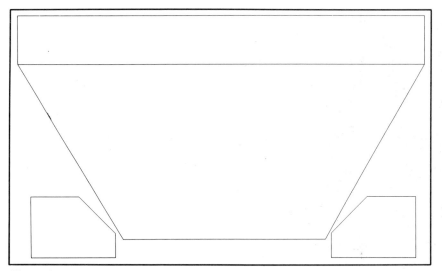

The valve seat is narrowed (contact with the valve face is lowered) from the bottom up with a 60-degree grinding stone.

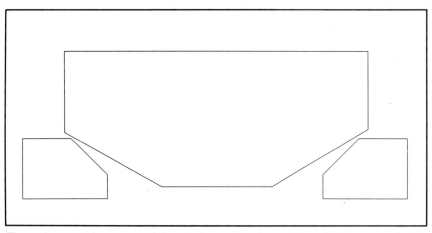

The valve seat is narrowed (contact with the valve face is raised) from the top down with a 30-degree grinding stone.

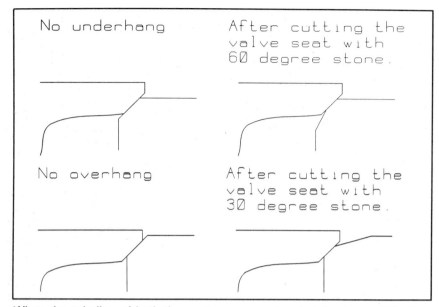

No underhang

No overhang

After cutting the valve seat with 60 degree stone.

After cutting the valve seat with 30 degree stone.

When the grinding of both the seat and the valve face is complete, the valve seat should contact the valve face in the middle of the face, with a narrow band at the top and the bottom of the face where no contact is made.

was scraped from the cylinder head. Even in those days, it was an unsatisfactory method of grinding the valves.

Although lapping valves is valid when minor repairs are required, during an engine overhaul, it is a wholly inadequate technique.

Stone Grinding

The second method of grinding the valve seats requires a stone grinder. Generally, three stones are needed. The first stone, usually ground to a 45-degree angle, determines the seat angle. The second stone, usually ground to a 60-degree angle, narrows the seat from the bottom up. The third stone, usually ground to a 30-degree angle, narrows the seat from the top down. The correct seat width is important in the proper transfer of heat from the valve to the valve seat to the cylinder head. When no specifications are available, the intake valve seat width should be no more than 0.0625in and the exhaust seat width must be no less than 0.078in.

To begin the stone grinding procedure, insert a machined pilot into the valve guide from the combustion chamber side. This pilot ensures that the centerline of the grinding stone is perpendicular to the ground surface of the valve seat. Next, slip the grinding stone holder over the pilot. Then, lower a driver (a large electric motor resembling a drill) onto the stone holder. Power the driver briefly, and remove it from the stone holder while it is still spinning. Take extreme care not to allow the weight of the driver to rest on the stone holder at any time. The weight of the driver can seriously affect the quality of the grind as well as cause excess wear on the grinding stones.

After the initial 45-degree grind is made, try the valve to be used in that seat. Place a spot of Prussian blue on the valve face. Slip the valve into the guide. Using a lapping stick, rotate the valve against the seat at least twice. Remove the valve, and inspect the face of the valve. The Prussian blue should form a stripe roughly centered in the face of the valve. If the stripe is high on the valve, use a 30-degree stone on the seat to lower the contact point between the valve and the seat. If the stripe is too low, use a 60-degree stone on the seat to raise the contact point. If the contact stripe is too wide, use both a 30-degree stone and a 60-degree stone to narrow the stripe. If the contact stripe is too narrow, use a 45-degree stone to widen it.

Many manufacturers and machinists will recommend grinding the seats to 44 degrees. The valve faces are usually ground to 45 degrees. This provides an interference angle of 1 degree. This slight,

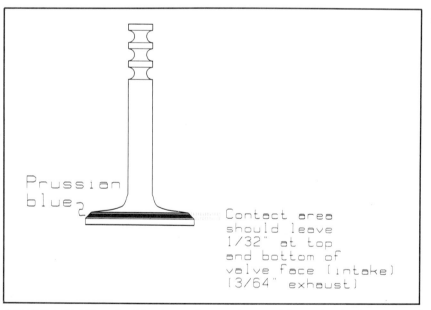

Prussian blue

Contact area should leave 1/32" at top and bottom of valve face (intake) (3/64" exhaust)

A "paint" called Prussian blue is used to mark the contact point between the valve face and the seat. A small drop of the paint is placed on the valve, and the valve is then rotated against the seat surface. This leaves an image of the contact area on the face of the valve.

deliberate mismatch of angles is intended to help the valves seat. After as few as 100 miles, the interference angle disappears.

Performance Grinding

Performance valve grind is one of my favorite marketing terms. What if you do not buy the performance grind? Does the engine run slower and safer?

All valve grinds should be performance grinds. If the machinist insists there is a difference between a "standard" and "performance" grind, do not argue, just pay the few dollars extra for the performance grind. Some shops, when doing a "standard grind," will hit the seat with only a 45-degree stone. This fails to ensure proper seat contact width or depth.

Camshaft Bearing Journal Realignment

When the cylinder head has been warped on the bottom, it has probably also been warped on the top. This is a minor problem for engines that are not overhead cam. For overhead cam engines, however, it can cause a misalignment of the cam bearing towers. Misalignment can cause binding of the camshaft, which can cause the cam to break or the timing belt or chain to break.

Note: If you have had chronic problems with the timing belt breaking or stripping, it is a fairly safe bet that the cam towers are misaligned.

The machinist has an easy cure for cam tower misalignment. She or he will bolt the cam towers in place, line bore them, and then install bearing inserts. The procedure is the same for applications where the cam towers are part of the head.

Cylinder Block Reconditioning

Line Boring

Line boring corrects for misalignment of the crankshaft journals in the block. Extreme heating and cooling of the engine block can cause warping. Even a slight misalignment of 0.0015in can cause a power loss and premature failure of the main bearings, and possibly break the crankshaft. The block should be line bored any time the engine is being rebuilt as a result of a broken crankshaft.

This device stone resurfacer is used to ensure that the stones used for grinding the seats have the proper angle and smoothness to do the job properly.

Line boring equipment is very large and very expensive. Many machine shops will opt to sublet this operation.

When a block is line bored, it is placed in a boring machine and small amounts of metal are removed. As the metal is removed, the main journals are aligned. If too much metal is removed, the crankshaft is moved too far up in the block; this alters the compression ratio and slackens the timing chain. Even if the engine has a tim-

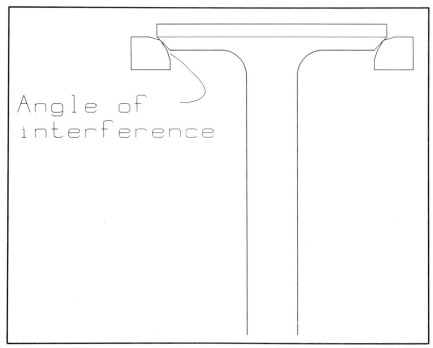

Some manufacturers recommend a 1-degree-or-so angle of interference between the valve face and the seat. It is felt that this helps these two surfaces to mate more quickly and more effectively.

A completed cylinder head is a work of art. This head has been thoroughly cleaned and resurfaced, and the seat ground.

Even though lapping is not considered an adequate method of resurfacing the valve, a final step of the valve grind should be to place a little valve lapping compound on the valve and lap the valve in.

ing chain tensioner to compensate for the slack chain, cam timing will still be retarded. If the cam timing is controlled through meshing gears, special gears will have to be purchased, as the tooth penetration of a stock gear will be too deep. Excessive penetration can cause premature wear. Ask your machinist whether or not to replace the block.

Deck height is described as how far the block deck surface extends above the top of the piston, and defined as the distance from the centerline of the main bearing bore to the top of the block surface that mates with the head. Deck height is an important consideration when having the block line bored. If the deck height is inadequate, damage can occur to the pistons and severely affect compres-

sion ratios. Machining operations that affect deck height are line boring and block decking.

When the block needs to be decked, clean out the trunk, get someone to help put the engine block into the trunk and head for the machine shop. The machinist will use a milling machine or a grinder to true the mating surface of the block with the cylinder head. This is a relatively rare operation. The most common cause of the block warping is overheating. Severe overheating can cause changes in the metallurgy of the block. If the engine has been overheated or otherwise damaged to the extent that it needs to be decked there is probably sufficient other damage to warrant discarding the block.

Cylinder Boring

Damaged cylinders must be repaired before the block can be reused. If the problem is excessive taper or out-of-round, this can be repaired by reboring the cylinders. Since the procedure alters the diameter of the cylinder, and since changing the diameter affects the combustion chamber volume, the rebored diameters of the cylinders must all be equal.

Often, cylinders are rebored to increase performance. This increases engine displacement. A classic

Ford 302 "punched" 0.03in over becomes a 306. At the same time, the compression ratio rises slightly.

Boring the cylinders also removes metal from the cylinder walls that is an essential part in the dissipation of heat. Engines with cylinder walls that are too thin can run hot.

Before discussing with your machinist how much you are going to have the cylinders bored, check the sizes of replacement pistons that are available. Typical replacement sizes are 0.02in, 0.03in, 0.04in, and sometimes 0.06in oversize. The most common rebore is 0.03in oversize.

Cylinder Welding

If the cylinder wall is cracked, the machinist may be able to weld the crack, then bore the cylinders. This may sound a little peculiar, but it works quite well when replacement blocks are expensive or rare. Those possessing the skills required to weld cylinders are rare, however, and better alternatives often exist. Show the crack to your machinist and get an opinion.

Cylinder Sleeving

Sleeving the cylinder is a far more common and generally better alternative than welding the cylinder. For this operation, the machinist will bore the cylinder slightly smaller than the outside diameter of the sleeve being used for the repair. This provides for an interference fit. The industry standard is to bore the cylinder 0.0005in smaller per inch of bore. If the engine has a 4in bore, the cylinder is therefore bored four times 0.0005in, or 0.002in, smaller than the outside diameter of the sleeve.

For the sleeve to be installed, the block has to be heated to about 200 degrees Fahrenheit while the sleeve is chilled in a bucket of dry ice and kerosene. Locking compound is applied to the top and bottom of the sleeve, which is then pressed in place. As the temperatures begin to equalize, the sleeve will become harder to install. The machinist has to work fast.

Honing

Honing the cylinders is an operation that can be done by anyone. An engine cylinder hone can be purchased for as little as $20. As the engine is run, over the years, the old piston rings polish, or glaze, the walls of the cylinders. Honing removes and breaks up this glaze, and allows the rings an abrasive surface to help them seat.

The correct honing technique will produce a crosshatch pattern on the cylinder walls. To begin, place the hone in a low-speed electric or air-powered drill motor.

Note: To produce a 45-degree crosshatch with an air-powered drill motor rotating at 20,000rpm, your arm must be capable of reciprocating about 330 times per second. So, if you are not a special government project with a $6 million price tag, make sure you use a low-drill speed.

Hold the drill and hone vertically, and move it in and out in slow, even movements. Continue the process until you see conspicuous 45-degree crosshatch marks in each cylinder.

Camshaft Bearing Replacement

On many overhead cam engines, replacing the cam bearings is a very easy operation, similar to replacing rod bearings. Most overhead valve engines, however, have the rod bearings pressed into the block. Replacing these bearings is an easy operation with the right tools; unfortunately, most of us do not have the cash resources to pur-

Boring the block requires a large and expensive machine that very few machine shops own. When you are selecting a machine shop to patronize, it will help to expedite the machining process if the shop has a cylinder boring machine and a crank grinding machine.

This Honda CVCC block shows what a sleeve would look like installed in a cylinder. The block shown here is aluminum with a steel cylinder sleeve, a common design for aluminum blocks.

chase a tool costing several hundred dollars, for occasional use.

Cam bearings suffer little from chronic wear problems. In many domestic engines, they are installed into the block rough. After installation, they are machined to the proper tolerances. This works well at

This illustrates what can happen if the block is both line bored and decked. This properly installed piston has a negative clearance with the block deck of over 0.05in. Every time the pistons in this application came to top dead center, they hit the head. The rods had to flex for the engine to run. The compression ratio for this engine, as assembled, was 18.67:1!

the factory, but these rough bearings are not readily available after the factory. The problem is that on these engines, little attention is paid to machining accurately the cam journals of the block. When the new cam bearings are installed, they may be crushed slightly, as a result. The machinist will cut the proper oil clearance on the camshaft journals. When you have the cam bearings installed, be sure to give the machinist the camshaft you are going to use.

Your machinist will remove the old bearings with a special drift. The new cam bearings are installed with a driver designed specifically for that purpose. The cam bearings are held in place with rubber O-rings, a cone centers the driver, and the bearings are forced into place.

Thrust Journal Repairs

The thrust journal is the main journal that controls the end play of the crankshaft. Many factors can cause damage to the thrust journals. Several years ago, I had a customer with an A-14 Datsun engine in a 310 model. The engine was overhauled, and the clutch was replaced. Within weeks, the car was back with nearly 1/4in of end play. The rebuilt clutch we had installed was applying so much thrust that it destroyed the thrust journals. Several years later, there was a similar experience with a ballooning torque converter on a Dodge van.

In each of these examples, the damage was on the crankshaft and bearing surfaces. If the block had been damaged, it would have been

After the cylinders are bored, they must be honed. Even though the boring machine generally leaves a relatively smooth surface, if the cylinders are not honed, excessive wear will result. This honing machine turns an otherwise-tedious job into an easy job.

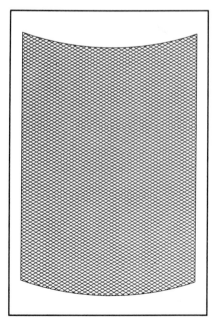

After the cylinders are honed, they should have a crosshatch pattern. The cylinders must be honed during a rebuild even if they were not bored. As the pistons travel up and down in the cylinders for several years, they form a glaze on the cylinder walls. The glaze inhibits the new rings from breaking in quickly.

replaced. A welding repair for this type of damage should only be done when the block is irreplaceable, say from a 1932 Hudson.

Cracked Block Repairs

Cracked blocks are common in some applications, climates, and uses. They are rare in others. If the block is cracked, several repair methods are available to you–welding and sealing with threaded plugs among them.

Welding the block is a highly specialized art; most machinists recommend replacement. If the block is a rare application, ask your machinist to recommend someone who is qualified locally to do the welding.

Sealing the crack with threaded plugs works very well when the crack is small and replacement or welding of the block is out of the question. In this technique, the crack is stop drilled, meaning that a series of large holes is drilled along the length of the crack. Special threaded plugs are then screwed into the holes. When these are turned in as far as they will go, they are cut off and ground flush with the block surface.

Consult your machinist for advice on repairing cracked blocks.

Crankshaft Operations
Crankshaft Polishing

Even when the crankshaft has such minor wear and damage that no major machine work needs to be done, it should still be polished. Even crankshafts that appear to be perfectly smooth have microscopic burrs that can cause damage to a new bearing. Industry specifications dictate that the crank journals should be polished to a smoothness of 5 to 10 microinches. Visual inspection of the crank journals to determine their need to be polished is wholly inadequate. The human eye has an ability to see objects as small as 10 microns, or 394 microinches. The smallest object you can see is therefore about forty times larger than the minimum industry standard for smoothness.

Several methods are available for checking the smoothness of the crankshaft. The crudest method, and the method used by virtually every professional mechanic is to run a fingernail across the journal.

Although this method can find gross damage to the crankshaft that cannot be detected with the eye, it is extremely inaccurate. The "high-tech" method is to use a profilometer. This is an electromechanical device that is sixty-two times more accurate than your fingernail.

The bottom line is to have the crankshaft polished with each engine rebuild. Polishing should also be done after the crankshaft has been machined.

Crankshaft Regrinding

When the crankshaft has been damaged owing to spun bearings or extreme wear, it will need to be machined. Be sure to confirm the availability of undersize bearings. Common sizes for undersize bearings are 0.01in, 0.02in, and 0.03in. If you are working on an import application, it is especially important to check availability, as the bearings on foreign units do not always run in the standard sizes.

When the crankshaft is machined to 0.02in, the machinist will mount it in a lathe designed exclusively for that purpose. The machinist will then set the lathe to remove 0.01in of metal from each journal of the crankshaft. Since the same amount of metal is removed all the way around, the crank will end up being 0.02in undersize.

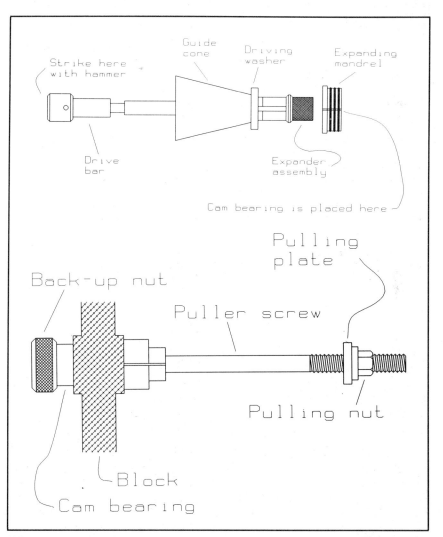

When cam bearings are replaced, they must be pressed into the block. The proper equipment has no substitute. Two options for this task are the cam bearing driver, top, and the cam bearing press, bottom. Either works well and can usually be rented, but your machinist could complete the job while you are looking up rental companies in the Yellow Pages.

Even a crankshaft that looks and feels smooth can have microscopic burrs. These burrs can cause premature deterioration of the bearings and result in premature failure of the rebuild. The machinist will polish the crankshaft after grinding it; even a crankshaft that does not need grinding should be polished.

This crank grinding machine represents a major investment for a machine shop. The use of the machine requires a high level of expertise. Machining cranks is not inexpensive. The lowest quote you get may be from a machinist who does not take time or is not confident of his or her work.

After machining the crankshaft, the machinist will then use an attachment for the lathe to polish it.

Crankshaft Welding

When a crankshaft is badly damaged, it is common practice to add metal to the crank journals before grinding. Although this is not an acceptable repair for a cracked or broken crankshaft, it works quite well for damaged journals.

Crankshaft Hardness Testing

Crank hardness tests include the Rockwell test, the Brinell test, and the Vickers test. The Rockwell test uses a diamond point or steel ball against a flat surface of the specimen. A small load creates an initial indentation, which will hold the penetrant in position. Next, a heavy load is applied for at least 30 seconds. The penetration depth is then measured; it is typically only 1.2 to 3.4 microns. The readings will be in units of measure called the Rockwell hardness coefficient (HRC). The steel used in roller bearings is greater than or equal to 60HRC. The main advantage of this hardness-measuring system is its simplicity, mass production capability, and relatively low cost. Its main disadvantage is the fragility of the equipment.

The Brinell hardness test is used on materials of low to medium hardness. Although usually not applicable to crankshafts, it is applicable to lead and zinc components and to crankshaft bearings. In this procedure, a specified load is applied to a flat surface of the test sample. The load is applied through a test ball that is held in place for at least 15 seconds. Two diameters of the resulting dimple are taken at right angles to one another. A formula is then used to convert these measurements to the Brinell hardness (HB) scale. The hardness of engine bearings varies at around 30HB. The advantage of this method is that the test sample need not be finely machined.

The Vickers test has the widest range of usage. A square, diamond-shaped, very hard and very sharp pyramid is used to indent the surface of the specimen. After measurements of the indentation are taken, a formula is used to determine the Vickers hardness (HV).

The Vickers hardness of case-hardened steel is 700HV.

The hardness of a soft crankshaft can be improved by a process called nitriding. This process increases the nitrogen content of the surface layer of the crankshaft. Generally, nitriding can only be performed on components that have been previously hardened. Nitriding a component that has not been previously hardened can result in warpage. When the metal is heated to 932 to 1,076 degrees Fahrenheit, nitrogen comes to the surface layer, and this can produce a layer several millimeters thick with a rating of 700HV to over 1,200HV.

Most crankshafts for stock application rely on a hardening technique known as work hardening. Work hardening occurs as the crankshaft spins in normal operating conditions. The nickel content of the crank comes to the surface, creating a hard shell on the bearing journal. On a crank that has been not reground, simply polished, the nickel will give the journals a yellow hue.

Crankshaft Shot-peening

The most common method of strengthening the crankshaft is shot-peening. After the journals are masked to protect them, high-velocity shot is targeted at the other areas of the crank. Particular attention is paid to the fillet or radius areas of the main journals. The impact of the shot relieves stress in the metal that could cause microscopic cracks that could later lead to a broken crankshaft.

Thrust Surface Repairs

The thrust surfaces of the crankshaft ride against the thrust surfaces of the main bearings. Heavy-duty clutches, torque converter problems, and normal wear and tear can cause damage to the thrust bearing surfaces and eventually to the crankshaft. Should the end play be excessive or the thrust surfaces of the crankshaft show evidence of damage, the surface can be welded and then machined.

Camshaft Operations

For most people, regrinding the camshaft is a waste of time and money. Replacement camshafts are readily available for applications dating from the 1950s. Rare engines and special-purpose uses

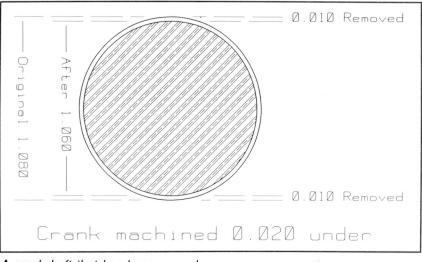

A crankshaft that has been ground 0.02in under has had 0.01in removed all the way around.

might justify asking a machinist to prepare your camshaft.

Connecting Rod Operations

Big End Repairs

The big end of the crankshaft connecting rod can become stretched or machined oversize by spun rod bearings. Like so many other things, connecting rods are usually expendable and should simply be replaced. If the rod is rare, a machinist can machine the mating surfaces of the rod and the rod bearing cap. This makes the big end hole smaller top to bottom, but about the same diameter side to side. To adjust for this distortion, the machinist will now machine the proper diameter in the rod's big end.

Straightening

Even minor twists and bends in the connecting rods can cause significant abnormal wear in the

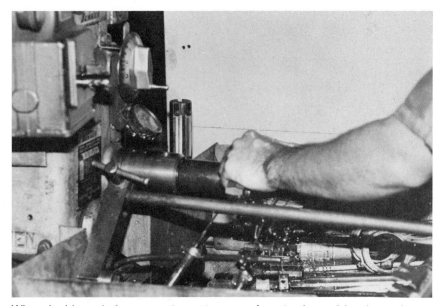

When the big end of a connecting rod becomes damaged, it can usually be repaired. The bearing cap mating surface to the rod is trimmed, and then the hole in the big end is made round again on a machine like this.

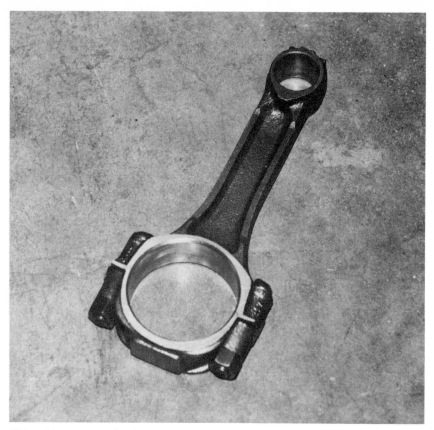

For most street applications, a rebuilt connecting rod is just as good as a new connecting rod. Usually, a busy machine shop will have rebuilt rods on the shelf waiting for you, or it can rebuild yours.

If the crankshaft is to be stored outside the engine for an extended period of time, it should be hung. Laying the crankshaft on its side can cause it to warp. Most machine shops will employ a rack such as the one shown here to store their crankshafts.

piston. Replace any piston rod that shows evidence of being bent or twisted. If the engine came to a sudden stop—thereby inspiring you to spend your weekends rebuilding it for a month or two—have your machinist check the rods for straightness. Sudden engine stopping can result from a hydraulic condition such as when a cylinder fills suddenly with coolant, or from a mechanical problem such as when a piston and valve attempt to occupy the same space.

Piston Operations

Knurling the pistons is another one of those "cheap fixes" for a problem that should actually demand replacement of the pistons. Knurling can only be used to compensate for worn piston skirts. Knurling may be appropriate in some cases, but generally, if in doubt, replace the pistons in question. You have better things to do than rebuild this engine again next year.

If you choose to have the pistons knurled, scrape the knurling with an old wrist pin before you install them. This ensures that the rough edges of the knurling have been removed.

Machine Shop Check List

Pressure testing
Magnetic crack inspection
Dye crack testing
Cylinder head reconditioning
    Head resurfacing
    Valve guide knurling
    Valve guide replacement
    Valve face resurfacing
    Valve seat resurfacing
        Lapping
        Stone grinding
        Performance grinding
Camshaft bearing journal realignment
Cylinder block reconditioning
    Line boring
    Cylinder boring
    Cylinder welding
    Cylinder sleeving
    Deck height
    Honing
    Camshaft bearing replacement
    Thrust journal repairs
    Cracked block repairs
Crankshaft operations
    Crankshaft polishing
    Crankshaft regrinding
    Crankshaft welding

Formula: For intake manifold resurfacing to compensate for head resurfacing.

The number in the first column represents the angle of the "V" formed by the mating surfaces of the cylinder head and the intake manifold.

5 Amount removed from head and deck surface x 1.1 = Amount to be removed from the mating surface between the head and intake manifold.

10 Amount removed from head and deck surface x 1.2 = Amount to be removed from the mating surface between the head and intake manifold.

15 Amount removed from head and deck surface x 1.4 = Amount to be removed from the mating surface between the head and intake manifold.

20 Amount removed from head and deck surface x 1.7 = Amount to be removed from the mating surface between the head and intake manifold.

25 Amount removed from head and deck surface x 2.0 = Amount to be removed from the mating surface between the head and intake manifold.

30 Amount removed from head and deck surface x 3.0 = Amount to be removed from the mating sur-

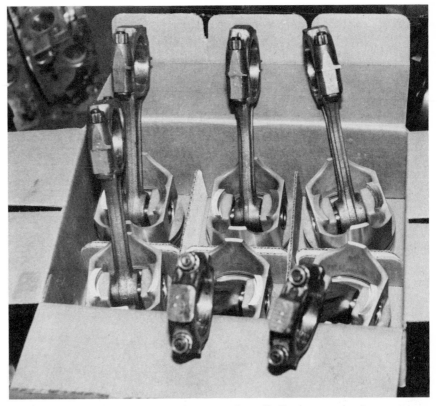

If your machinist is to do any work on either the pistons or the connecting rods, allow her or him to remove or install the rods. Some rods install on full-floating wrist pins; for these, the connecting rod is easy to remove and install. Some connecting rods are mounted on semi-floating wrist pins; for these, the wrist pins must be pressed into either the piston or the connecting rod.

face between the head and intake manifold.

35 Amount removed from head and deck surface x 4.0 = Amount to be removed from the mating surface between the head and intake manifold.

40 Amount removed from head and deck surface x 8.0 = Amount to be removed from the mating surface between the head and intake manifold.

Amount removed from head and deck surface x 1.71= Amount to be removed from the mating surface between the cylinder block and the intake manifold.

11

Reassembly

Well, you probably thought you were done with the tedium of measurements. All the parts are back from the machine shop, and you are ready to reassemble. Sorry; it is time to get those micrometers, dial indicators, and feeler gauges back out. Confirming the many measurements as the new parts are installed is part of the reassembly process.

Install the Main Bearings

Turn the block upside-down. Clean the main bearing saddles thoroughly with a light solvent. The oil clearances of the main bearings will be less than 0.002in. Even a small piece of sand could distort the bearing or bind the crankshaft.

This block has been cleaned, decked, bored, honed, and line bored.

Place the main bearing shells in the saddles. Be careful to note two things: first, install the main bearing with the thrust surface on the correct saddle, and second, if only half the bearing shells have an oil supply hole in them, be sure the hole lines up with the oil gallery port. Take it from experience: the engine will make a very annoying knocking sound if the oil cannot get through the bearing to the crank journal.

With the bearing shells properly laid in the saddle, smear assembly lube across the bearing surface. Carefully lay the crankshaft in the block.

Lay a short piece of Plastigage on each crank journal. Clean the main bearing caps to remove grit, and place the bearing shells in them. Install the main bearing caps, and torque them to the proper specification. Remove the bearing caps, and use the Plastigage packaging to measure its width on the journal. Typical bearing clearances for passenger-car and light-duty truck engines are 0.0015in to

0.002in. If the bearing clearance is incorrect, you must have measured your crank diameter incorrectly, you have the wrong bearings, or a mistake was made in the machining process. Remove the bearing shell from the bearing cap. On the back side of the shell, near one end, should be a small marking indicating the undersize of the bearing (e.g., .010 for 0.01in undersize). Be sure this marking coincides with the marking the machinist stamped on the crankshaft near one of the main journals. If they match, mic (measure with your micrometer) the crank; it was probably machined to a size other than that indicated.

If the Plastigage shows the oil clearance to be correct, apply assembly lube and install the main bearing caps and torque them to the proper specification. Some people like to remove the Plastigage before installing the bearing caps, but it is not really necessary.

After all the main bearings are torqued, check the crankshaft end play. Install a dial indicator on the

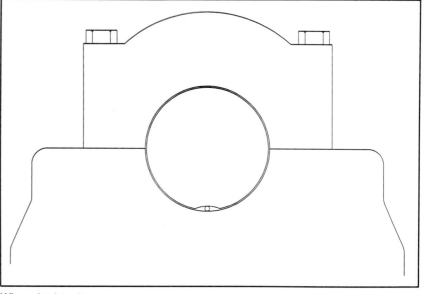

When the bearing cap is torqued into place, the Plastigage is flattened.

The width of the Plastigage indicates the oil clearance.

block to detect movement in the crankshaft. Using a pry bar, gently force the crank as far back in the block as possible. Adjust the dial indicator to 0, and pry the crank as far forward as possible. The dial indicator will show crankshaft end play. Although allowable end play differs from one application to another, a general rule of thumb is that it should be 0.003in to 0.008in. If the end play is incorrect, the crankshaft thrust surfaces will need to be repaired.

If you do not have access to a dial indicator, an alternative, though slightly less accurate method, is to use a feeler gauge. Pry the crankshaft all the way to the rear, and place the largest feeler gauge blade possible between the crank thrust surface and the main bearing thrust surface.

Install the Connecting Rods to the Pistons

With the main bearing caps torqued in place, it is now time to install the rods into the pistons. It is critical to make sure the piston and rod are mated properly. Each has a front and a back to it. Normally, the top of the piston will have a notch indicating how the piston is oriented to the front of the

engine (notch to the front). The rods should have been marked during disassembly. If new rods are being used, refer to the instruction sheet in the box. If the rods were purchased from a machine shop, ask the machinist. .

The wrist pin is installed into the piston and rod in one of two ways: full floating or semifloating.

Full Floating

Installing the pistons onto the rods in the full-floating wrist pin

design is easy. The wrist pin slides through both the piston and the rod with pressure applied by even the frailest thumbs.

Semifloating

The semifloating wrist pin is more of a problem. The wrist pin either slides through the piston and presses into the rod or presses into the piston and slides through the rod. Either alternative offers a perfect opportunity for the rebuilder to damage the piston. The safest route

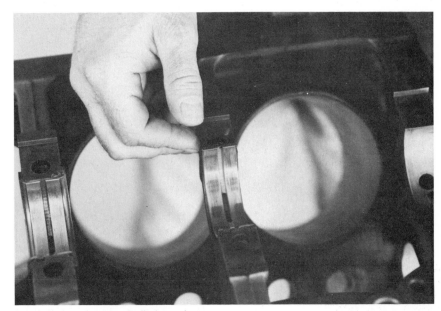

Slide all the bearing shells into place.

Clean the crankshaft saddles in the block. Even minute particles between the saddle and the bearing shells can cause the crankshaft to bind and the bearing surfaces to wear prematurely.

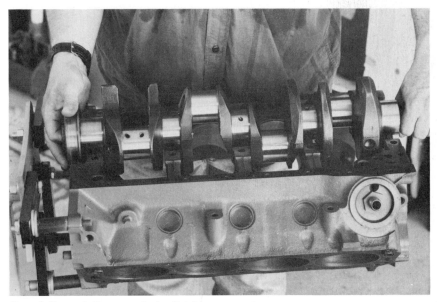

Carefully set the crankshaft into place.

Place a piece of Plastigage on each of the main bearing journals. Install the main bearing caps, and torque them to the proper spec.

is to have a machine shop install semifloating wrist pins.

If you want to try your luck, you can make a press tool to facilitate the pressing of wrist pins in semifloating applications. Using a piece of hardwood, carve a cradle the diameter of the piston. This will support the piston evenly as the wrist pin is pressed into place. This cradle can also be purchased commercially. Still, allowing the machinist to install the wrist pins on semifloating applications may be the best answer.

Ring End Gap

Place each of the piston rings to be used in the cylinder in which it is to be used. With a feeler gauge, measure the gap between the ends of the ring, and compare it to the specifications for this application. If the ring end gap is incorrect, you have the wrong rings or the cylinders have been bored or honed incorrectly.

Install the Rings

If you have not done so already, be sure the ring grooves are clean and clear of debris and carbon. A special tool called a ring groove cleaner is sold for this purpose. However, those who have good health insurance and a first aid kit can use a broken ring to scrape the carbon from the grooves. Extreme caution should be exercised when using a broken ring to clean the grooves. The broken ring is sharp and can leave nasty cuts. Wear gloves.

With the ring grooves clean, install the new rings on the pistons. Stagger the rings before installing the pistons into the cylinder. This will provide for a better seal during the early stages of running the engine. The rings are usually identified as top, middle, and oil control by the papers covering them in the box. Also, a mark on the two compression rings will indicate which way is up. This mark may be a dot, a bar, or even a corporate logo. In a few instances, the rings may be unmarked; instructions will come in the box.

Two techniques are available for the actual installation of the rings. The first is to start one end of the ring in the correct groove. Rotate the ring around the center of the piston, and it will practically fall into place. Plan on breaking an occasional ring using this technique. The second technique is to use piston ring installation pliers, which can be purchased for only a few dollars at most auto parts stores. Using these pliers virtually eliminates the possibility of breaking rings.

Install the Pistons

With the rod installed in the piston and the rings in place, put a piston ring compressor around the rings. You may find that no piston ring compressor really works well, so good luck. With the ring compressor in place, protect the crank journal and the rod bolts from one another with a couple of pieces of

Remove the bearing caps, and compare the width of the Plastigage with the marks on the Plastigage package. The oil clearance on this journal is 0.002in.

rubber hose. Long pieces of rubber hose can even help guide the connecting rod into its proper position on the crankshaft. Gently lower the piston into position. With a small, soft mallet, tap the edges of the piston ring compressor to ensure that it is firmly seated against the deck of the block. Tap the piston into position with firm application of the blunt end of the mallet. If the piston is stopped by a ring slipping from between the ring compressor and the block, start again.

After installing the first piston, Plastigage the journal. Use the same method described for Plastigaging the main bearings. If the oil clearance on the first rod journal is correct, proceed to the next piston.

Repeat this process until all the pistons are installed. It may be a little obsessive-compulsive, but it is a good idea to Plastigage each rod journal before proceeding to the next piston.

After the pistons are installed and the connecting rods are torqued, check the connecting rod side clearance for each rod. Hold the connecting rod as far to one side as possible. Measure the side clearance using a feeler gauge. Verify the acceptable range of clearances with the specifications. Typical side clearances are 0.01in to 0.02in. If the side clearance is outside the specified range for this application, replace the connecting rod. If the side clearance is still incorrect, the crankshaft has a problem.

Install the Oil Pump

If the oil pump mounts in the oil pan, it should be installed at this point. Many applications mount the oil pump outside the engine—for instance, as part of the timing cover; on these, the pump should be installed later.

Remove the oil pump cover and pack a little light grease into it. This will help to prime the pump for initial start-up. Torque the cover plate back on, to the proper spec. Many overhead valve applications use a shaft turned by the gears of the distributor to drive the oil pump. If your engine is configured in this manner, now is the time to install this shaft. Be sure to inspect the shaft for twisting and warping; these could foreshadow future problems. Install the oil pump.

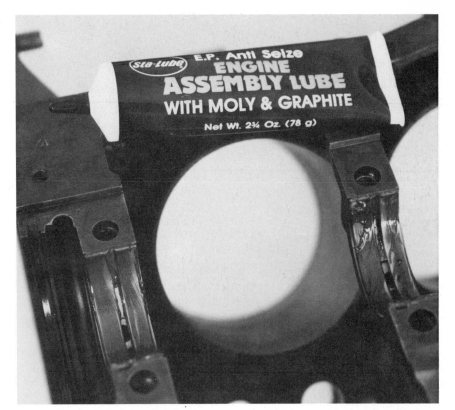

After the main bearings have been Plastigaged, it is time to install the crankshaft. Liberally apply engine assembly lube to the block side of the bearing shell and the cap side. Set the crankshaft back in the saddle, and install the bearing caps.

Torque the main bearing caps.

After the main bearing caps have been torqued into place, the crankshaft should still turn freely. If it does not, grit may have accumulated between the bearing saddle and the main bearing shell or between the main bearing shell and the journal, or the block may need to be line bored.

Install the Camshaft

The camshaft on an overhead cam engine is installed when the head is assembled. On an overhead valve engine, it is installed into the block, and that should be done at this time.

Installing an overhead valve camshaft is a lot like pushing a rope uphill. The part you can hold onto is too short to be able to support it while you thread it through the journals. The answer to this is a camshaft installation tool. This can be purchased, or made from a piece of all-thread that matches the center bolt hole of the camshaft.

Lube the cam lobes and bearings with high-pressure assembly lube. Be sure you use high-pressure lube; forces at the cam lobes can exceed 100,000psi. Using the all-thread to shift the center of gravity and as a handle, install the crankshaft. Take care to ensure that the cam lobes do not damage the cam bearings.

Install the Timing Gears

On the overhead cam engine, the timing gears are not usually installed until the cylinder head is installed. On the overhead valve engine, the timing gears should be installed now.

Typically, you will find marks, usually dots, on both the cam gear and the crank gear. These dots normally line up opposite one another and as close together as possible. This industry standard varies somewhat, and the factory service manual for an engine should be consulted when in doubt.

If the engine uses a chain to drive the camshaft, the gear can be placed in the chain; the crank gear started first; and then the crank gear, the cam gear, and the chain

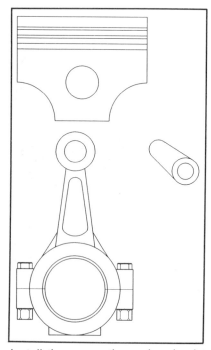

Install the connecting rod and wrist pin into the piston. Be sure the front of the rod and the front of the piston line up properly.

Full-floating wrist pins can be installed by simply pressing them into the piston with a thumb.

all slid into place together. Usually, only gentle persuasion from a soft hammer is necessary to position the gears. In many cases, the larger gear (the cam gear) has nylon teeth. These teeth can be damaged by a hammer; be careful.

Where meshed timing gears are used with no chain, the cam gear is usually fiber. Part of the factory tool kit with these applications is a fiber gear puller and installer. Removing the gear from the engine was no problem because you did not care about its condition; installing the new gear requires the use of this special installer. The center of the cam gear where it mates with the camshaft is usually metal. Drive the gear into place using a round, hollow driver on the metal

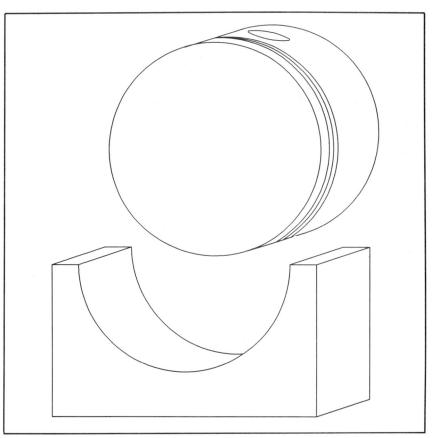

A cradle is used when semi-floating wrist pins are pressed into the pistons and rods.

Installing semi-floating wrist pins requires a press.

The piston ring gap is checked by placing the ring into the cylinder and measuring the gap with a feeler gauge. It is important that the plane of the top of the ring be parallel to the plane of the block deck. Performance rings often come with no gap or a negative gap. These rings must be gapped by filing their ends with a special grinder.

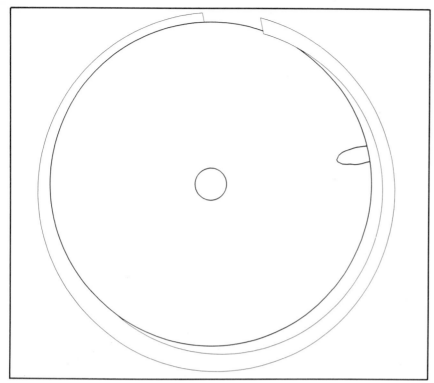

The piston ring can be installed using piston ring pliers. Ring installation can be performed by rolling the ring into the groove.

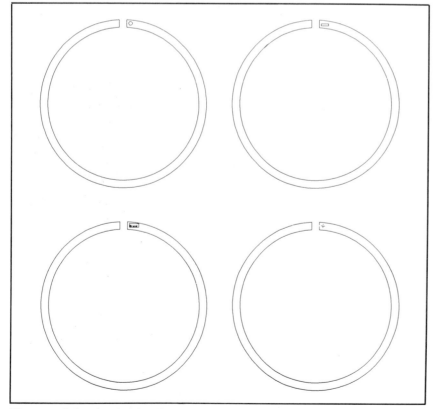

The top of the ring is identified by a mark. If no mark is stamped into the top of the ring, read the instructions that came with the rings.

area. As the cam gear slides into place on the shaft, be sure the cam can rotate freely. Should the gear bind, it can damage the teeth as it slides into place.

Note: Engines like the Volvo B20 overhead valve four-cylinder have a "freeze-plug" at the back of the gallery, for the camshaft. If the cam gear is driven on too hard, this plug will pop out of position. Normally, oil will not begin to leak immediately; it will wait until several weeks after the engine installation to pour out. Of course, it will wait until you are late to a wedding at which you are supposed to be the best man or maid of honor. Use care, and inspect this plug thoroughly.

Reassemble the Cylinder Head

Probably, when you got the cylinder head back from the machinist, the valve seals, the valves, and the springs had been installed. If not, begin by sliding the valves into place.

Now, install the valve seals. Some valve seals snap onto the valve guide and are held in place through friction. These are popular on domestic engines. Another type is the umbrella type. These just slip onto the valve stem, forming an umbrella over the top of the valve guide. Umbrella seals are very popular on domestic engines. Do not think that new valve seals will cure oil burning resulting from worn valve guides; valve guide repairs are all that will accomplish this.

Most engine rebuild gasket kits or valve seal kits come with a little Mylar sheath that fits snugly over the end of the valve stem to protect the seal as it is slid over the stem. Failure to use this can result in the seal being cut and oil being burned.

With the valves and the valve seals in place, install the valve springs, retainers, and keepers. The valve spring compressor you used to take the head apart needs to be used again to reassemble it.

If the engine is an overhead cam design, install the camshaft now. Some applications use bucket-shim cam followers. These should be installed after checking the cam for free rotation and removing the cam. The installed followers will bind the camshaft, preventing it from rotating freely. If the cam does not rotate freely before the followers are installed, it will be necessary to have the cam journals line bored, as described in chapter 10.

With the free camshaft rotation confirmed, remove the camshaft if necessary to install the cam followers. For most applications that use a rocker-type follower, the rockers will slip into place when the valve is partially depressed. Many professionals line up the rockers and drive them into position with a hammer. Although this may not do any obvious damage to the rockers, the cam lobes, or the rocker supports, it can damage the hardening and cause premature component failure.

Install the Cylinder Head

Cylinder head installation is the part of reassembling the engine that requires the best technique and care. Be sure both the head and the block mating surfaces are clean. Place the head gasket on the block deck. Look carefully to ensure that the proper side is up. Head gaskets are not always marked for correct installation. The ports in the water jacket and the ports in any oil gallery ports between the cylinder head and the block should line up through the head gasket. As stated on the packaging for an aftermarket head gasket I once purchased for a Japanese car, "Do not smear sealers and all sorts of other things on this gasket." If the head is properly machined and flat, sealers are not needed. If the head is not properly machined or flat, it should be repaired or replaced.

If the cylinder head was resurfaced on the bottom, the combustion chamber volume has been reduced. This will have raised the compression ratio. If the engine has a 4in bore, removing 0.03in from a head will decrease the combustion chamber volume by 0.4cc. This will raise the compression ratio by only about 0.5 percent. However, if you are building a relatively high-compression engine that you plan to feed pump gas, you may want to consider using a thicker-than-stock head gasket or, if available, a shim.

Place the cylinder head gently on the head gasket. Be careful not to allow one of the edges of the head to dent or otherwise damage the head gasket. Many head gasket failures are a result of damage to

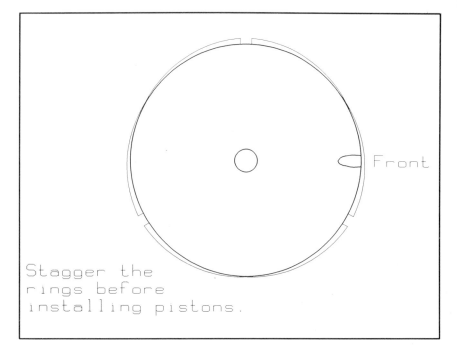

Before installing the piston into the cylinder, the ring gaps should be staggered at 12 o'clock, four o'clock, and eight o'clock. Further, if the oil control ring is a three-piece ring, the upper and lower rings should be staggered.

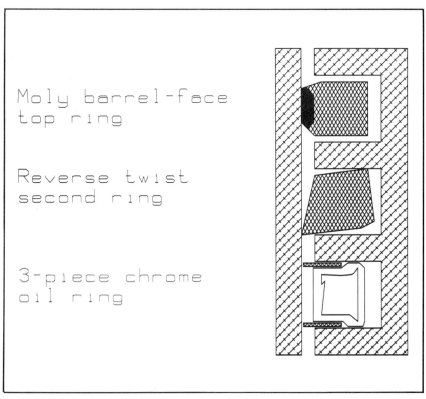

On a three-ring piston, the two top rings seal compression in the combustion chamber. The third, or bottom, ring keeps oil that is splashed by the crankshaft onto the cylinder wall, from ending up in the combustion chamber to be burned.

To check the ring side clearance, slip a feeler gauge between the ring and the side of the piston. The largest feeler gauge blade that will fit without being forced is the side clearance.

If you were careful to mark the connecting rods before removing the pistons from the engine, then you will know the proper direction of installation and be able easily to install the bearing caps.

the head gasket when the head is installed.

Now comes the most critical part of the head installation process: torquing. In general, cylinder heads are torqued from the center to the ends, in steps. This prevents warping the head. Some heads are torqued to an angle rather than the more common pounds-feet specification. The most notable of these is the Volvo V-6 engine. If possible, consult the factory service manual for the proper torque spec. If no service manual is available, it is usually acceptable to begin with the centermost bolt, torque it to 25 percent of the spec, go to the bolt next-closest to the center, and begin tightening the bolts in an hourglass pattern, crisscrossing the head until all are torqued to 25 percent of the spec. Repeat this process at 50 percent of the torque spec, then 75 percent, and finally 100 percent. On applications with aluminum heads, it will be a good idea to retorque the head after the engine has been run for a few hours and allowed to cool.

Adjust Overhead Camshaft Timing

During the mid-1970s, I worked at a Lotus dealership in Texas. A mechanic who was old enough to know better installed the cylinder head on a dual overhead cam Lotus engine. Curiosity got the better of his judgment, and he cranked the engine over before installing the timing chain. His motive was to confirm that the engine turned over smoothly. At several points, the engine bound up and was difficult to turn over. With more leverage, he was able eventually to get the engine to rotate smoothly. This, of course, was after he bent the valves that had been interfering with the pistons.

The moral of the story is that after the cylinder heads are installed, never attempt to rotate the crank until the timing belt or timing chain is installed. This is especially important on overhead cam and dual overhead cam engines, but also applies on overhead valve engines.

If the engine is an overhead cam design, now is the time to adjust the cam timing and install the timing chain or belt. If a timing belt is used, be aware that many versions are designed with a front side and a back side. These belts should only be installed one way. Consult the factory service manual for details.

Install the Valvetrain

Install the lifters. Do not use new lifters on an old camshaft, and do not install a new camshaft without new lifters. Put a little assembly lube on the sides and especially on the bottom. The lifters should fall into place with only the slightest pressure.

Set the pushrods through the heads and into the lifters. Install the rocker arms.

Adjust the Valves

Almost all of today's engines have hydraulic lifters or hydraulic valve compensators. These will probably require readjustment after a few minutes of running. Whether the lifters are hydraulic or not, they should be adjusted at this point.

Overhead Valve Engines
Mechanical Lifters

Mechanical lifters are generally adjusted to a hot specification, which can be found on the Environmental Protection Agency (EPA) sticker located under the hood. If no cold specification is given, adjust the valves to 0.002in tighter than the hot specification.

Rotate the crankshaft, and observe the lifters on the cylinder that is a companion to the one you are going to adjust. When one of the lifters on the companion cylinder stops moving down and the other lifter starts moving up, the valves on your cylinder are ready to adjust. The companion cylinder is the one that is opposite in the firing order. Check the factory service manual for the firing order to the engine you are working on. Some typical firing orders are as follows:

Inline Engines

4-cylinder	1-3-4-2 or
	1-2-4-3
5-cylinder	1-2-4-5-3
6-cylinder	1-5-3-6-2-4 or
	1-2-4-6-5-3 or
	1-4-2-6-5-3 or
	1-4-5-6-3-2
8-cylinder	1-6-2-5-8-3-7-4 or
	1-3-6-8-4-2-7-5 or
	1-4-7-3-8-5-2-6 or
	1-3-2-5-8-6-7-4

Rubber hoses placed over the rod bolts will prevent the rod bolts from damaging the crankshaft during installation. Using rubber hoses 6in long will help to guide the connecting rods into place without having otherwise to guide the rods over the risk of damaging the crankshaft.

The ring compressor will hold the rings tightly in place while the piston is tapped into the cylinder. Often, the oil control ring will slip out from under the ring compressor and keep the piston from sliding into the cylinder. Do not force the piston into the cylinder when this happens; remove the piston, reset the ring compressor, and start again. Note: Tapping the edges of the ring compressor firmly against the block deck with a hammer reduces the tendency of the oil control ring to slip out.

Check the rod side clearance with a feeler gauge placed between the connecting rod and the crankshaft.

Torque the connecting rods carefully; remember, the big end of the connecting rod is moving several thousand feet per minute at high engine speeds.

V-engines

4-cylinder	1-3-2-4
6-cylinder	1-2-5-6-4-3 or
	1-4-5-6-2-3
8-cylinder	1-6-3-5-4-7-2-8 **or**
	1-5-4-8-6-3-7-2 **or**
	1-8-3-6-4-5-2-7

Pancake Engines

| 4-cylinder | 1-4-3-2 |

To find the companion cylinder easily, divide the cylinders at the midpoint. The first cylinder of the first half is the companion to the first cylinder of the second half. The second cylinder on the first half is the companion to the second cylinder on the second half. And so on. In the V-8 engines with the firing order 1-5-4-8-6-3-7-2, cylinders one and six are companion cylinders, and so are five and three, four and seven, and eight and two.

With the lifters of the companion cylinder rocking, insert the correct-thickness feeler gauge between the rocker arm and the top of the valve stem. Tighten the rocker arm against the feeler gauge until the gauge slides snugly in and out with a slight resistance. Repeat this process for each of the cylinders.

Hydraulic Lifters

The preliminary process of adjusting the valves is the same for overhead valve engines with hydraulic lifters as it is with mechanical lifters. Final adjustment of the lifter, however, must be made with the engine running. New lifters, or even old hydraulic lifters that have bled down during the rebuilding or cleaning process, will compress easily as the rocker is adjusted. This would allow the valve to open too far after the engine is started and the lifters pump up. Damage may occur when the valves are in overlap on the transition between the exhaust and intake strokes. For a moment, the intake and exhaust valves are both open as the piston is approaching the top of its stroke; should the lifters be adjusted too tight, after they pump up, they may meet the piston. Generally speaking, it is devastating to an engine to have two metal objects attempting to occupy the same space at the same time. To ensure that the lifters will not cause damage to the valves once the engine is started, be careful not to depress the lifters as the valves are being adjusted.

Overhead Camshaft Engines

In many cases, the machinist will have made a preliminary adjustment of the valves when the valve grind was performed. Be sure to ask about this when you pick up the cylinder head.

Different overhead cam configurations will require different techniques for adjustment. The three most common configurations are rocker arm, shim-on-top-of-follower bucket, and shim-under-follower bucket.

The adjustment procedure for the rocker arm design is exactly the same as for the overhead valve engines. Rotate the crankshaft until the valves of the companion cylinder are in overlap. Notice that the heels of the cam lobes on the cylinder you are adjusting are both in contact with the rocker. Adjust the valves with the adjusting screws at the ends of the rockers.

For applications with the shim located on top of the follower bucket, a special tool is required to change the shim. This tool slips between the camshaft and the follower, depressing the follower and valve spring as it is levered downward. Measure the clearance for each valve. If the valve clearance is incorrect, remove the old shim using the special tool, and replace it with a shim that is of the correct thickness. These shims are easy to get from the dealer and are even available on the aftermarket. Their thickness is usually incremented in tenths of a millimeter. In many cases, the old shim may be difficult to remove from the follower. Although a special pair of pliers resembling a snap ring pliers can be purchased, a pick generally works just as well.

The third design places the shims under the bucket. Replacing this type of shim requires removal of the camshaft. The easiest way to adjust valves with this design is to check the adjustment of all the valves, determine how much of a change needs to be made on each, remove the camshaft only once, and replace all the shims at once. As you reinstall the camshaft after replacing the shims, make sure the valve timing is correct.

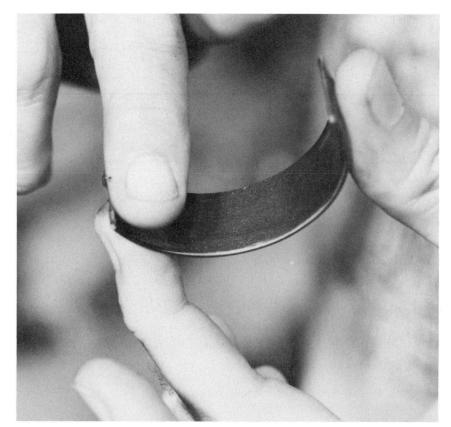

After checking the oil clearance with Plastigage, coat each bearing shell liberally with assembly lube before installing.

Make sure the oil pump is free of moisture, then pack the pump with a light grease to prime it. Priming the pump ensures that oil will be picked up and pumped as quickly as possible.

Before installing the camshaft, coat it generously with assembly lube. The mating surface between the cam and the lifters is subject to a force of thousands of pounds per square foot; if the assembly lube is the wrong type, it will displace as the engine is being cranked for start-up, and damage will occur.

Prime and Install the Oil Pump

Remove the cover plate on the oil pump. Pack light grease between the gears of the pump. This will prime the pump and get oil to the bearing surfaces as quickly as possible on initial start-up.

Install the Oil Pan and the Valve Covers

The only thing that is not obvious about installing the oil pan and valve covers is gasket dimples. Gasket dimples occur as the oil pan or valve cover is bolted into place. The stamped steel units tend to dimple as they are torqued. Check for this, and repair it by peening from the back side before installing.

Install the Intake Manifold

Set the intake manifold gaskets in place. If this is a V-engine, the gaskets may not want to stay in place as the manifold is set into position. A light film of grease on the gasket surfaces will solve this problem. Torque the manifold in a decreasing hourglass-shaped pattern, starting at the outer ends. Torque in 25 percent, 50 percent, 75 percent, and 100 percent stages, just as with the cylinder heads.

Do not try to install the camshaft by "bouncing" it into the block.

Installing the camshaft without damaging the lobes can be very tricky. Here, a piece of all-thread is used to provide the leverage needed to remove the camshaft without causing damage.

Most gasket kits for engine rebuilds come with umbrella-type valve stem seals. Better seals are available at additional cost, but if the valve guides are in good condition or have been properly repaired, the additional expense is not required.

In most cases, the cam timing is correct when the mark on the cam gear is opposite the mark on the crank gear. This is not true on all engines; if your engine lacks these marks and you failed to note the position of the cam timing during disassembly, consult the factory service manual for proper alignment.

Install the Distributor

Installing the distributor may be the trickiest part of the reassembly process. Set the crankshaft to top-dead-center number one compression. Drop the distributor into place so that when it is in the seated position, the rotor points to the number one position on the distributor cap. Although this does not ensure that the ignition timing is correct for driving the car, it gets the timing close enough to get the engine started. The gear at the bottom of the distributor has a helical

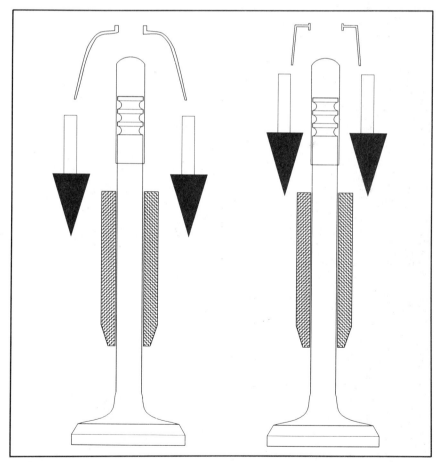

That small Mylar tube, sealed at one end, that came with the gasket set for engine overhaul actually has a purpose. Place it over the valve stem to protect the valve stem seal as it is being installed.

Be sure to install any valve spring shims that may have been removed during disassembly, back onto the valves from which they were removed.

cut. When the distributor slides into position, the distributor shaft will rotate the equivalent of about two teeth. Therefore, the teeth of the distributor gear should be aligned about two teeth out of phase as you begin to drop it into position.

Install the Exhaust Manifolds

It is a good idea to make sure the exhaust manifolds are flat and true before installing them. Many applications depend on a machine fit between the exhaust manifold and the head, rather than using a gasket. Torque the manifold in place from the ends to the center, in stages.

Install the Flywheel or Flex Plate

Use new bolts to install the flywheel or flex plate. Use a torque wrench.

This Honda CVCC head is ready to be installed on the block. Note the precombustion chamber located next to the spark plug hole. This chamber has its own intake valve. Several import manufacturers used this prechamber technology in the late 1970s and the early 1980s.

If the lifter bores have been cleaned properly, the lifter should slide into place with virtually no resistance.

Reassembly Measurements

Main bearing oil clearance:
Plastigage rod journals:
Plastigage main journals:
Crankshaft end play:
Piston ring end gap:
Rod journal oil clearance:
Camshaft end play
Rod side clearance:
Timing gear backlash

Procedures

Install the main bearings
Honing the cylinders
Install the camshaft
Installing the crankshaft
Aligning the timing gears and chain
Install the pistons on the connecting rods
    Full floating
    Semifloating
Install the rings
Install the pistons
Install the oil pump
Install the camshaft
Install the timing gears
Reassemble the cylinder head
Installing the valve seals, types
Install the cylinder head
Install the valvetrain
Adjust the valves
    Overhead valve engines
        Mechanical lifters
        Hydraulic lifters
    Overhead camshaft engines
Prime and install the oil pump

Some head gaskets will look almost identical when they are rightside-up and upside-down. This gasket is marked Front. When this word is visible and toward the front of the engine, the gasket is installed properly.

Always replace all the freeze plugs as part of an overhaul. Recently, kits like this have made the job of getting all the right freeze plugs easier.

Set the head into place gently; dropping it on the head gasket can damage the gasket, resulting in premature failure.

95

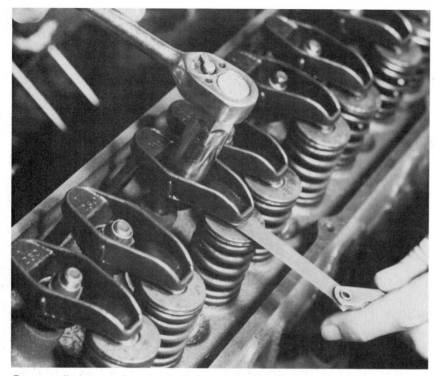

Install the oil pan and the valve covers
Install the intake manifold
Install the distributor
Install the exhaust manifolds
Install the flywheel or flex plate

Do a preliminary adjustment of the valve while the engine is still on the stand. No matter what type of lifters the engine has, the valves will have to be adjusted again once the engine is started.

A common mistake made on an engine rebuild is to forget to install the distributor drive shaft. It is much easier to install the distributor drive shaft before the oil pump, the oil pan, and the engine have been installed.

Engine Installation

12

The engine rebuilding process can be a dangerous experience. Wear goggles, gloves, and long sleeves as much as possible. Most of the easy-to-acquire cleaning solvents are more at home in a Molotov cocktail than in a repair shop. Take the time to be safe, spend the money for a commercial cleaning solvent. When installing the engine rent an engine hoist; the block and tackle over a beam method may put life and limb at severe risk. Although traditional in some circles, the consumption of alcoholic beverages and engine rebuilding do not mix.

Install the Rebuilt Engine

Go back to the tool rental store, wherever you got the engine hoist for disassembly, and bring the hoist back to the car. Place the front of the car on good jack stands. Install the engine lifting cradle that came with the engine hoist. Connect the hook from the engine hoist, and prepare to lift the engine. With the engine still on the ground, install and torque the flywheel or flex plate.

If the vehicle has a standard transmission, install the clutch at this time, using a clutch alignment tool. Universal clutch alignment tools can be purchased for $30 to $40, or an alignment tool for your particular application can be bought for as little as $5.

With the flex plate, the flywheel, and the clutch installed, raise the engine and move it over the engine compartment. Slowly lower the engine into the engine compartment, aligning the flywheel with the transmission input shaft if the car has a standard transmission or the flex plate with the torque converter if it has an automatic.

Install all the transmission-to-engine bolts that are accessible from underneath. If the car has an automatic transmission, make sure the torque converter is fully seated, and install the bolts that couple the torque converter to the flex plate. If

This is a completed Ford 3-liter SHO. The rebuilder has installed as many of the peripheral parts as possible.

Once the engine is installed, it is a matter of minutes until the initial start-up.

the torque converter slid forward during the installation process, be very careful when seating it back into position. Some transmissions contain a Torrington bearing that can slip out of position and be damaged if the torque converter is forced back into position. If the torque converter does not slip easily into the full seated position, call a local, reputable transmission repair shop and ask for advice.

Install the nuts or bolts that hold the motor mounts to the frame. Many standard transmission applications have the clutch lever secured to a ball stud mounted on the side of the block. If the application you are working on is set up this way, install the ball stud. Roll forward on your creeper, open the radiator petcock, and drain the coolant into a drain pan. Install the cooling lines for the automatic transmission, if the car is so equipped. Make sure the petcock of the radiator is closed, and install the lower radiator hose.

Install the exhaust down-pipe to the exhaust manifold. This is a good place to use a rust inhibitor and an anti-seize compound on the studs before installing the nuts. Doing so will help prevent a repeat of the frustration you went through when you were trying to remove these nuts.

Now, move to the top of the engine. Install the upper radiator hose and the transmission bolts accessible from the top. Connect the throttle linkage. If the car is so equipped, install the air conditioner compressor. Since you did not disconnect the air conditioner hoses when you removed the engine, the air conditioner will not need to be serviced.

If the engine is carbureted and the carburetor was not removed during the engine rebuild process, remove the carburetor and replace the gasket between the carburetor and the intake. Rebuilding an engine without rebuilding the carburetor is destined to fail to glean the maximum potential of the work that was done.

If the engine is fuel injected, replace the throttle body gaskets and the fuel injector seals. The engine rebuild gasket set quite likely contained neither of these. A vacuum leak caused by an old seal or gasket can result in the engine running either rich or lean, depending on the leak's location and proximity to the oxygen sensor.

Install the Distributor

If you were careful to end your valve adjustment procedure with the number one piston at top-dead-center compression, then simply drop the distributor into place so that when it is in the seated position, the rotor points to the number one position on the distributor cap. Although this does not ensure that the ignition timing is correct for driving the car, it gets the timing close enough to get the engine started. The gear at the bottom of the distributor has a helical cut. When the distributor slides into position, the distributor shaft will rotate the equivalent of about two teeth. Therefore, the teeth of the distributor gear should be aligned about two teeth out of phase as you begin to drop it into position.

Make sure the oil drain plug is tight and the oil filter is installed. If you have not done so already, install the oil filter. Make sure the radiator petcock is closed and all the radiator hoses, the bypass hose, and the heater hoses are connected. Reconnect any power steering lines that were disconnected when the engine was removed.

Add Fluids

Put in the engine oil, the antifreeze coolant and water, and the power steering fluid. Be sure to confirm the correct amount of engine oil with the vehicle owner manual or the paperwork that came with any replacement oil pan you may have installed.

It has been said that engine break-in oil needs to be thin, with a low viscosity. Thin oil is able to be lifted easily by the oil pump and moved to the new critical engine parts. It is also said that engine break-in oil needs to be thick to protect the new critical engine parts. The best oil to use is the oil you will use during the rest of the life of the vehicle. The most important issue concerning the engine oil is to make sure the engine does not overheat during the critical first few minutes after initial start-up. Overheating at any time thins the oil, reducing its ability to form a

If the vehicle is equipped with a standard transmission, it is necessary to align the clutch disc as the pressure plate is installed. The black clutch alignment tools are dedicated to a specific application, whereas the light-colored set is universal.

98

barrier between the bearing surfaces and the cam-to-lifter surfaces.

On many import and some domestic applications, the cooling system can develop air pockets behind the thermostat. When the engine is started, these air pockets can prevent the hot coolant from coming into contact with the thermostat, so that the thermostat never opens. As a result, severe engine damage can occur within minutes of initial engine start-up. Many of the engines for which this is the most common problem have a valve to release the trapped air.

Whether the power steering pump was removed from the vehicle or left connected, with the hoses simply tied to the side when the engine was removed, considerable fluid was likely lost. Fill the power steering fluid reservoir to the correct level. Be sure to check it again after the engine has run for several minutes. As the pump runs and begins to circulate fluid, the level in the pump reservoir will drop.

These are the fluids critical to the starting of the engine. Do not forget that the fluid level of the transmission and of the differential should also be checked before driving the vehicle.

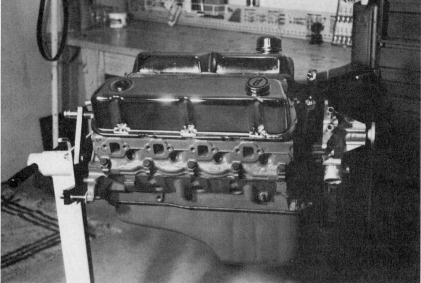

A couple of weeks and a few hundred dollars turned a filthy boat anchor into gleaming muscle iron ready for the road.

99

Initial Start-up

13

The most critical moments in the life of any freshly rebuilt engine are the first few moments of operation. Preparation makes the difference between a gentle introduction to renewed life and a more damaging one. Several things are obvious concerning starting the engine: oil should be in the engine, coolant should be in the engine, and the timing should be at least approximated. Several other less obvious things are critical.

Preparation

After the engine is installed, confirm that the oil is at the proper level. Consult the owner's manual for the proper specification. If you have chosen to use a nonstock oil pan, read carefully the specification for that pan.

If the camshaft has been replaced, it is recommended the engine be started on a high idle for several minutes. The battery should be fully charged, and the ignition timing as close as is humanly possible.

When the engine is started and run for an initial 20-minute "run-in," more than 130gal of deadly carbon monoxide gas will likely be produced. This is enough, under the right conditions, to kill hundreds of people. Make sure the shop area you are working in is well ventilated, and make sure no people are occupying the second floor, above your workshop. Make sure the windows in any area above the workshop are open, to ventilate that space fully even if it is not occupied. Carbon monoxide is an insidious gas, able to sneak into closed-up areas and linger for hours, or even days. This initial run-in time is especially dangerous if your workshop is an attached garage.

Start-up

At this point, the freshly rebuilt engine is ready for starting. Connect a timing light, a tachometer, and an oil pressure gauge. If the engine has hydraulic lifters, remove the valve covers before starting it. Most better auto parts stores carry spring metal clips that fit over the rocker arms to deflect oil while the engine is running and the valves are being adjusted. Failure to use these clips will result in unusual patterns in the paint of the front fenders and psychedelic patterns on the ceiling of the shop.

Pick up the can of starting fluid that the insecure side of your personality persuaded you to purchase, and hide it. Using excessive amounts of starting fluid on any engine can do severe damage. Starting fluid is even more potentially damaging when the engine is freshly rebuilt. Prime the fuel system. The best way to do this on carbureted engines is by cranking the engine with the spark plugs out. On electronic fuel-injected engines, cycle the ignition switch on and off a few times.

Note: Pouring gasoline into the intake to start the engine is on an intellectual par with juggling vials of nitroglycerin.

Crank the engine and listen for signs of life.

If the engine pops or backfires through either the intake or the exhaust, the timing is off. However, a couple of small pops in the intake may just indicate that the first few drops of fuel are being picked up by the cylinders. Persuade your assistant to move the distributor back and forth while you crank the engine. The engine should start. If the engine fails to start, or runs too poorly to justify keeping it running after it does start, refer to chapter 14.

Run-in

Once the engine starts, raise its speed immediately to 1500rpm to 2000rpm. Stabilize the engine speed. The camshaft and the lifters will wear into one another better if the engine is not allowed to idle during the first 20 minutes of its

One dread of both the amateur engine rebuilder and the professional is reconnecting all lines, wires, and hoses during installation. Numbering, mapping, and even photographing the engine compartment as the engine is removed turned this nightmare into only a hassle.

new life. For most engine applications, the camshaft receives considerably less oil at idle speeds; the rpm should be kept high to keep the cam and lifters well lubricated. Also, do not rev the engine up and down during the first 20 minutes. Not maintaining a relatively steady engine speed puts unnecessary stress on new parts, tight tolerances, and unmatched surfaces. Be sure, during this 20-minute run-in period, to watch the oil pressure and the engine temperature. If either shows abnormal readings, slowly bring the engine to a momentary idle, shut the engine off, and repair the cause of the problem.

During this initial run-in period, set the timing. Although it will have to be readjusted at the proper engine speed after the engine is brought to an idle, setting the approximate timing now will help to reduce the tendency of the engine to overheat. Watch carefully for oil leaks, coolant leaks, power steering leaks, and transmission fluid leaks.

Idle

After the 20-minute run-in, allow the engine to return slowly to an idle, idle it only long enough to adjust the initial timing, adjust the dwell if the distributor is an older point-condenser Delco, and set the idle speed. If the car is equipped with hydraulic lifters, adjust the valves now with the engine running.

Adjusting the valves on engines with hydraulic lifters is easy. Tighten each valve until the engine begins to misfire. Loosen the valve slowly until the misfire just stops. The valve is properly adjusted.

Shut the engine off, and prepare for the first test drive.

Test Drive

Now you are ready to test drive!

Start with a very short drive—once around the block. Since the car has not been driven for several days or months, listen carefully for unusual noises, and monitor the temperature and oil pressure gauges constantly. For safety, it would be best to take a copilot while you drive. If a gauge goes out of the normal range, shut off the engine immediately and find the source of the problem.

Note: Do not test drive the car until all parts have been installed and all systems are operable to the best of your knowledge. Remember the story about the "shade tree" mechanic who, after rebuilding his air-cooled VW engine, decided to drive the car around the block a few times to make sure everything was working properly, before going to the trouble of installing the "tin." The tin is the cooling system for the air-cooled engine. By the time he got the car back to his garage, rebuilding the engine the first time had become just practice for what he had to do now.

After you drive around the block, it is time to do the first post-invasive assessment of the powertrain's vital signs. Disconnect the timing light and the tachometer. If possible, position the oil pressure gauge where it can be seen with the engine running. If the hose on the gauge is too short, remove the gauge, verify that the oil pressure warning light is working, and watch the gauge closely during the test drive.

Now, drive the car around the block several times. During this second test drive, the likelihood of a primary ignition wire falling off, or worse, to leave you stranded is directly proportional to the distance you are from home base. Stay close.

Upon returning to home base, inspect the wiring harness, including the secondary ignition wires. Check the oil level, inspect for oil leaks, and repair as necessary. Check the coolant level, inspect for coolant leaks, and repair as necessary. If the engine is equipped with mechanical lifters or cam followers with or without hydraulic compensation, readjust the valves now.

With the initial test drive done, with the loose hoses, drain plugs, and oil pan bolts tightened, the vehicle is now ready to put into service for a couple of weeks. The drivers should be aware of the recent overhaul and drive the vehicle with open eyes on the instruments and warning lights, and open ears on unusual noises.

The 600- to 1,000-Mile Service

At somewhere between 600 and 1,000 miles, the car should return to the shop. Allow the engine to cool completely, preferably overnight. Loosen and retorque the head bolts, and readjust the valves, using the appropriate technique. Change the oil and the oil filter. Check the tightness of all the belts and hoses. Check the oil level in the transmission.

If these items check out, and if no coolant or oil is dripping on the ground, accept the applause of your family and take your spouse to dinner in celebration.

14

Troubleshooting

If the engine failed to start or does not run right once started, check the basics first. This is especially true if the engine is fuel injected or computer controlled. Computer control has a tendency to divert even the best technicians from the basics.

Check the fuel supply. Look into the carburetor as you move the throttle from the closed position to the wide-open position. The accelerator pump should spray fuel.

If the engine is fuel injected, check the fuel pressure. If the fuel pressure is okay, use a mechanic's stethoscope (or a heater hose held to the ear) to see if the injector is receiving pulses from the computer.

Check the ignition timing. Remove the distributor, bring the number one piston to top-dead-center compression, check the rotor and point or pickup coil alignment, and reinstall the distributor.

Check the firing order; make sure you begin numbering from the number one position on the distributor cap.

Although you may be confident about the cam timing, remove one of the valve covers. Rotate the crankshaft until the rockers or the cam lobe of the number one cylinder or its companion cylinder is at exactly overlap. The timing marks on the crankshaft should indicate top dead center. If they do not, blame your helper and tear down the engine enough to reset the valve timing.

If all else fails, use the more detailed troubleshooting information that follows.

Troubleshooting–Symptoms

No Start

No-start problems are probably the easiest to troubleshoot. Three things are required to get the engine started: fuel, air, and spark. Confirm that air, fuel, and spark are available to the engine.

Check for Air

Connect a vacuum gauge to the intake manifold, and crank the engine with the throttle closed. If the gauge reads 2in or 3in of vacuum or more, that should be enough vacuum to get the engine started. A failure to read vacuum could mean that the engine is cranking too slow. Connect a tachometer to the negative terminal of the coil and crank the engine. If the cranking speed is less than 150rpm, recharge the battery and try again tomorrow. If the engine still cranks slow, check for free crankshaft rotation: does the crank turn freely by hand? If the engine rotates freely and the battery is charged, replace the starter.

If the engine cranking speed is adequate and yet there is still not enough vacuum, you must have set up the cam timing incorrectly. Confirm this, and correct the error.

Check for Fuel

For carbureted applications, checking for fuel is easy. With the ignition switch off, pump the accelerator several times while watching the venturis of the carburetor. Fuel from the accelerator pump should squirt down the venturis. If it does not, remove the fuel line from the carburetor and run a hose from the line into an approved fuel receptacle. Have someone crank the engine, and observe the end of the line. If fuel pumps, the carburetor needs repair. If fuel does not pump, check for fuel line restrictions between the tank and the pump. If the fuel lines are in good condition, replace the fuel pump.

Checking for fuel delivery on throttle body—injected engines is easy. While someone cranks the

Before making the first attempt to start the engine, connect a tach-dwell meter; a timing light; and if the car is fuel injected, a fuel pressure gauge. If the engine fails to start, you will already have the basic diagnostic tools hooked up. If the engine starts, you will be ready to fine-tune for the first test drive.

engine, observe the tip of the injectors; they should be spraying fuel into the throttle bore. If the injectors do not spray, use a mechanic's stethoscope to see if the injectors are clicking. If they are, then either the vehicle is out of fuel or the fuel pump is inoperative. Confirm that fuel is in the tank. Check the fuses and the power leads to the fuel pump, with the engine cranking.

Note: The fuel pump of a fuel-injected car receives no power if the engine is not being cranked.

If the pump is receiving power and has a good ground, replace the fuel pump.

On multipoint fuel-injected engines, checking for fuel to the engine is a little more difficult. Install a fuel pressure gauge to confirm that fuel is available to the injectors. Confirm that fuel is in the tank. Check the fuses and the power leads to the fuel pump with the engine cranking. If the pump is receiving power and has a good ground, replace the fuel pump. If the fuel pressure is about right–30psi to 45psi for most multipoint applications–use a mechanic's stethoscope to see if the injectors are clicking. If the engine has fuel pressure and the injectors are clicking, the no-start problem is not related to the injection system.

Check for Spark

To check for spark, you can disconnect one of the spark plug wires and perform the Ben Franklin test. Hand the plug wire to your nephew, and crank the engine. If he begins to jump around, then you know you have good spark. However, if you like your nephew or fear reprisal from his parents, insert a screwdriver into the plug wire and hold the screwdriver about 1/4in from the engine block or cylinder head. Have someone crank the engine, and observe the spark. If you see a good, crisp blue spark, replace the spark plugs. If the spark is not a good, crisp blue, move on to the next step.

Remove the coil wire from the distributor cap, and hold it 1/4in from ground. Crank the engine. If the spark is a good, crisp blue, replace the distributor cap and rotor. Keep in mind that the problem could be a defective set of plug wires. The reason I do not suggest their replacement at this point is that it is very unlikely all the plug

If the engine fails to start, check for fuel. If the car is carbureted, work the accelerator to see if the accelerator pump squirts into the carburetor bores. If the car is equipped with TBI, have someone crank the engine while you watch for spray from the tip of the injector.

wires went completely bad at once. If replacing the distributor cap and rotor does not cure the problem, replace the plug wires.

If you did not get a good spark from the coil wire, connect a test light to the negative terminal of the coil. Crank the engine. If the test

If the car is port injected, the task of verifying fuel to the engine is more difficult. Check the fuel pressure with a gauge; if the fuel pressure is correct, use a heater hose held to the ear or a mechanic's stethoscope to verify that the injectors are pulsing.

Ignition coils seldom fail while the engine is being rebuilt. If the fuel system is delivering, check the ignition system.

light blinks on and off as the engine is cranked, the problem is in the secondary side of the ignition system. Check the resistance of the coil wire. If the resistance is greater than 20,000 ohms, replace the coil wire. If the resistance is less than 20,000 ohms, replace the coil.

If the test light does not blink as the engine is cranked, the problem is in the primary. Move the test light to the positive terminal of the coil. Make sure the ignition key is on. If the test light does not light, a problem exists in the power supply side of the primary ignition system.

If the light does light, then the problem is in the ground side of the distributor.

If the problem was on the power side, crank the engine. If the test light illuminates while the engine is being cranked, check the resistance of the ballast resistor. The ballast resistor should have an extremely low resistance. Replace the ballast resistor if necessary. If the ballast resistor is good, repair the wiring in the bypass circuit. If the test light does not illuminate when the engine is cranked, check the circuit from the ignition switch up to where the current flow divides to go through the coil and the ballast resistor.

If the problem was on the distributor side, remove the distributor cap and inspect the points. If they appear to be pitted or burned, replace the points and condenser. Check again for a pulse at the negative terminal of the coil, with the test light. If the test light pulses when the engine is cranked, then the engine should now start. If the test light still does not pulse, check the distributor ground. If the distributor ground is good, repair the wire between the negative terminal of the coil and the distributor.

Failure to Keep Running When Key Is Released

In some cases, the engine starts but does not continue to run when the key is released. The most common cause of this classic point-condenser symptom is a defective ballast resistor. However, any open in the main 12-volt power supply to the ignition coil can produce the same failure.

Misfire at Idle

Although generally an ignition misfire is in the secondary side of the ignition system, problems with the ignition points can cause symptoms that are exactly the same as those of defective spark plugs.

Before troubleshooting any misfire, it is essential to verify that the engine is in good condition. A compression test is a good starting point. If the valves are adjustable, be sure they are properly adjusted.

With a pair of sissy pliers (insulated plier designed specifically for removing spark plug wires while the engine is running), remove and replace one plug wire at a time at the spark plugs. As

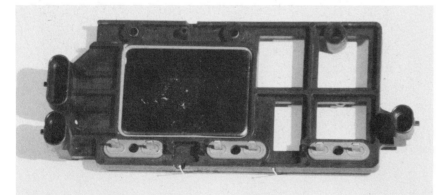

The ignition module can only be condemned by process of elimination. Verify that the spark plugs, distributor cap, rotor, plug wires, and pickup are in good condition; use an ohmmeter to check the condition of the ignition coil or coils.

each plug wire is removed, the engine rpm should drop. If one of the cylinders fails to produce as great a drop in rpm as the others, that cylinder is the source of the misfire.

Assuming the cylinder is in good condition and the valves are properly adjusted, remove the spark plug wire for that cylinder and check the resistance. The resistance should be less than 10,000 ohms per volt. If the resistance is correct, replace the spark plug. Unless the spark plugs are very new, replace them all. I was in an auto parts store in Fort Worth, Texas, several years ago when an elderly cowboy came in and asked for a single spark plug. After brief jibing from the counter people, the gentleman stated, "If you had a team of six horses and one broke his leg, you wouldn't shoot all six would you?" This rhetorical question is humorous but does not hold up well in the real world of troubleshooting.

Misfire Under a Load

Assuming the engine is in good condition, begin troubleshooting the problem of misfiring under a load by checking the spark plug gap. If they are gapped properly, replace the spark plugs. Even new spark plugs can misfire under a load.

If replacing the spark plugs does not solve the problem, remove the distributor cap. Inspect the wiring to the points. Frayed wiring can cause an intermittent open circuit as the vacuum advance moves the breaker plate. The intermittent open can cause a misfire.

Lack of Power

Many things can cause a lack of power, some related to the ignition system, some not. Begin checking this problem by confirming that the engine is in good condition and that the air and fuel filters are in good condition.

If a lack-of-power symptom is the result of problems in the ignition system, the problem is likely in the timing control system. To test the timing control system, connect a timing light to the engine. Disconnect the vacuum advance, and plug the hose. With the engine at idle speed, check the timing. Now, raise the engine speed to 2000rpm to 2500rpm. If the timing does not advance, the centrifugal advance

system is not working. Inspect the distributor weights. If they are free and move easily, replace the weight springs. If the springs are weak, they will allow the timing to advance all the way prematurely, even at idle. If the weights are frozen, use penetrating oil or whatever is necessary to free them. If

they are badly corroded, it may be necessary to replace the distributor.

When the centrifugal advance is working properly, with the engine still at 2000rpm to 2500rpm, reconnect the vacuum hose to the vacuum advance. When the vacuum hose is reconnected, the timing should advance several degrees.

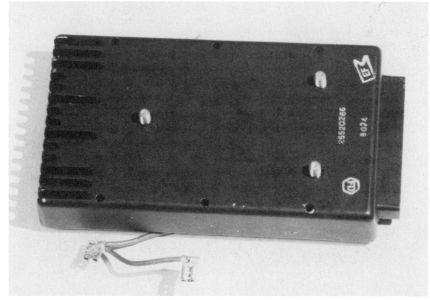

Some distributorless ignitions use a coil pack. If some of the spark plugs are receiving a spark and the plug wires are good, the coil pack is probably defective. If none of the coils fire, the coil pack is probably defective.

Troublesome Components and Systems

Hall Effect Sensor

The Hall effect sensor is often used as an alternative to the pickup coil. Many ignition systems, both distributorless and distributor type, use it. Its primary advantage over the pickup coil is that it is able to detect position and rotational speed from 0rpm to tens of thousands of rpm. Its primary disadvantage is that it is not as rugged as the pickup coil and is more sensitive to errant magnetic fields. An intense magnetic field can shut down the proper operation of a Hall effect sensor.

A Hall effect pickup sensor is a semiconductor carrying a current flow. When a magnetic field falls perpendicular to the direction of the current flow, part of that current is redirected perpendicular to the main current path. The semiconductor is placed near a permanent magnet. A set of metal blades, or armature, attached to a rotating shaft or other device passes between the Hall effect semiconductor and the permanent magnet. As the armature rotates, the magnetic field is alternately applied to the Hall effect sensor and interrupted. The result is a pulsing current perpendicular to the main current path. The frequency of this current is directly proportional to the speed of the armature rotation. Since the output is only dependent on the presence of the magnetic field, the Hall effect unit is capable of detecting armature position even when there is no rotational speed.

Testing

With an Ohmmeter

No valid test procedure using an ohmmeter is available for the Hall effect sensor.

With an Oscilloscope

Connect the oscilloscope to the Hall effect signal lead. Rotate the armature. Depending on the number of blades and the rotational speed of the armature, the scope pattern could appear either as a square wave or as a flat line that rises and falls with rotation.

With a Voltmeter

Connect a voltmeter to the Hall effect output lead. The voltmeter should display either a digital high (4 volts or more) or a digital low (around 0 volts). Slowly rotate the armature while observing the voltmeter. If the voltmeter initially read low, it should now read high; if the voltmeter initially read high, it should now read low. If the voltage fluctuates in this manner as the armature is rotated, then the Hall effect sensor is good.

With a Dwell Meter

Since the signal generated by the Hall effect sensor is a square wave, the dwell meter becomes a natural for testing. Connect the dwell meter between the Hall effect output and ground. Rotate the armature as fast as possible—for instance, crank the engine; the dwell meter should read something besides 0 and full-scale. If it does, the Hall effect sensor is good.

With a Tachometer

Like the dwell meter, the tachometer is also a good tool for detecting a square wave. Connect the tachometer between the Hall effect output and ground. With the armature rotating as described in the section on the dwell meter, the tachometer should read something other than 0 if the Hall effect sensor is good.

Specific Applications

Ford thick-film ignition used with electronic engine control (EEC) IV

Some General Motors (GM) HEIs

Computer-controlled coil ignition

Ford distributorless ignition system

Some Bosch ignition systems

Late-model Chrysler ignitions

Optical Sensor

The signal produced by the optical sensor is identical to the one produced by the Hall effect sensor. However, it is produced by an armature-interrupting light. A light-emitting diode (LED)—usually sending out an infrared, invisible light—sits opposite an optical receiving device such as a photodiode or a phototransistor. An armature is rotated between the LED and the receiver; unlike the armature in the Hall effect sensor, the one in the optical sensor can be metal, plastic, or any translucent material. As the armature rotates, light alternately falls on and is kept from falling on the receiver. As this occurs, the current flowing through the receiver is turned on and off, creating a square wave with a frequency directly proportional to armature rotation. In some cases, such as with many GM vehicle speed sensors, the light is

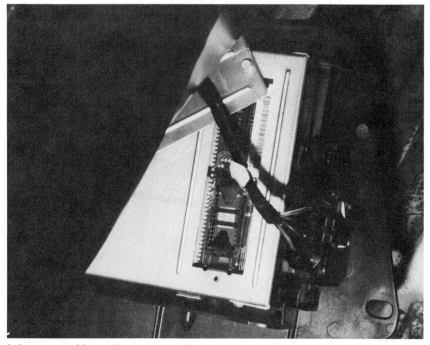

It is easy to blame the computer for being the cause of a problem. The fact is, if the fuel injection or ignition system or both performed properly before the rebuild, they are probably still in good condition.

reflected off rotating blades, rather than interrupted.

The main advantage of the optical rotational sensor over the pickup coil and the Hall effect sensor is its ability to produce extremely high frequencies. The 3-liter Chrysler distributor produces a frequency of 540,000 hertz (54 megahertz!) at just 3000rpm. The primary disadvantage is a sensitivity to dirt, oil, and grease, creating erroneous signals.

Testing
With an Ohmmeter
No valid test procedure using an ohmmeter is available for the optical sensor.
With an Oscilloscope
Connect the oscilloscope to the optical sensor signal lead. Rotate the armature. Depending on the number of blades and the rotational speed of the armature, the scope pattern could appear either as a square wave or as a flat line that rises and falls with rotation.
With a Voltmeter
Connect a voltmeter to the optical sensor output lead. The voltmeter should display either a digital high (4 volts or more) or a digital low (around 0 volts). Slowly rotate the armature while observing the voltmeter. If the voltmeter initially read low, it should now read high; if the voltmeter initially read high, it should now read low. If the voltage fluctuates in this manner as the armature is rotated, then the optical sensor is good.
With a Dwell Meter
Since the signal generated by the optical sensor is a square wave, the dwell meter becomes a natural for testing. Connect the dwell meter between the optical sensor output and ground. Rotate the armature as fast as possible—for instance, crank the engine; the dwell meter should read something besides 0 and full scale. If it does, the optical sensor is good.
With a Tachometer
Like the dwell meter, the tachometer is also a good tool for detecting a square wave. Connect the tachometer between the optical sensor output and ground. With the armature rotating as described in the section on the dwell meter, the tachometer should read something other than 0 if the optical sensor is good.

Specific Applications
GM vehicle speed sensors (many applications)
Some Hitachi ignition systems
Chrysler 3-liter ignition

Spark Plug Wires
Spark plug wires are tested in two ways. The first is with an engine analyzer oscilloscope. These scopes are very expensive and will typically only be found in an auto repair shop. I have been teaching the use of these engine analyzers to mechanics for over ten years. The result of the this teaching experience is the knowledge that very few mechanics know how to read an oscilloscope effectively. Ask around, ask mechanics if they know anyone really good at reading a scope. The second is with an ohmmeter. If you are using the second method, remove each plug wire and with your ohmmeter on the X1,000-ohm scale, measure its resistance end to end. A good plug wire will have less than 10,000 ohms but more than 1,000 ohms per foot.

You need to remember only a couple of important things when replacing secondary ignition wires. First, if the plug wires are installed in the incorrect order, a backfire may occur, resulting in damage to the airflow meter or air mass meter or the rubber tube that connects it to the throttle assembly. The original equipment plug wires have numbers on them indicating to which cylinder they should be connected. Aftermarket or replacement plug wires may not have these numbers. 3M and other companies make adhesive numbers that you can attach during installation or disassembly to ensure proper reinstallation.

Distributor Cap
Replacement of the distributor cap consists of simply releasing the attachment screws or clips and making sure the plug wires are installed in the correct order.

Whichever type of distributor you have on your car, it would be a good idea to replace the distributor

If the fuel injector or injectors do not pulse and the ignition system does not fire, the most likely cause is the distributor or crankshaft pickup. Two popular types are available. One is the alternating current (AC) pickup that has been used since the 1960s. Test the AC pickup with an AC voltmeter. The other type, shown here, is a direct current (DC) pickup known as a Hall effect sensor. Test this with a tachometer connected to the output wire, while cranking the engine. Any reading other than 0 will indicate that the Hall effect sensor is good.

cap and rotor together and to use the same brand. Pairing the caps and rotors of two different manufacturers can result in an incorrect rotor air gap. Excessive rotor air gap can cause excessively high spark initiation voltage and can result in incomplete combustion.

Air Filter

The real value of the air filter is significantly underestimated. It is the engine's only defense against sand, grit, and other hard-particle contamination. When these substances enter the combustion chamber, they can act like grinding compound on the cylinder walls, piston rings, and valves. Replace the air filter at least once a year or every 24,000 miles. In areas where sand blows around a lot, like West Texas or Arizona, the air filter should be replaced much more often.

On most carbureted cars, a restricted air filter will cause the engine to run rich. This is because the restriction causes a reduction of pressure in the venturi of the carburetor whereas the pressure in the fuel bowl remains constant at atmospheric. This increased pressure differential increases the flow of fuel into the venturi, and the mixture enriches.

On a fuel-injected engine, the engine control unit (ECU) uses the airflow meter to measure the exact volume of air entering the engine and delivers the correct amount of fuel for the measured amount of air. If the flow of incoming air is restricted, less air will be measured and less fuel will be metered into the engine.

In applications using a manifold absolute pressure (MAP) sensor, air measurement is not very precise and therefore the engine may run a little rich as a result of a restricted air filter.

Fuel Filter

The fuel filter is the most important service item among the components of the fuel injection system. In my seventeen years of experience with fuel-injected cars, I have replaced many original fuel filters on cars that were over ten years old. This lack of routine maintenance is just begging for trouble.

After removing the fuel filter, find a white ceramic container such as an old coffee cup, and drain the contents of the filter into it through the inlet fitting. Inspect the gasoline in the container for evidence of sand, rust, or other hard-particle contamination. Now, pour the gas into a clear container such as an old glass, and allow it to sit for about 30 minutes. If the fuel has a high water content, it will separate while sitting. The fuel will float on top of the water. If the tank contains excessive water or hard-particle contamination, it may have to be removed and professionally cleaned. For minor water contamination problems, additives can be purchased at your local parts house.

Should the fuel filter become excessively clogged, the following symptom might develop: You start the car in the morning, and it runs fine. As you drive several miles down the road, the car begins to buck a little or lose a little power, then suddenly, the engine quits, almost as though someone had shut off the key. After sitting on the side of the road for several minutes, the car can be restarted and driven for a couple of miles before the symptom recurs.

This could be caused by a severely restricted fuel filter. The car runs good initially because the bulk of what is causing the restriction has fallen to the bottom of the fuel filter as sediment. When the engine is started and the fuel begins to flow through the injection system, this sediment gets stirred up and pressed against the paper elements of the fuel filter. As it does, fuel volume to the injectors is decreased and the engine begins to run lean. Sooner or later, the engine leans out so much that it dies. The really bad news is that when the fuel filter becomes that restricted, some of the contaminants have forced their way through the filter and may contaminate the rest of the fuel system.

Fuel

Alcohol contamination can damage many of the fuel injection components. Use of gasohol can be one source of alcohol. If you suspect that excessive alcohol content has caused the failure of system components, then you might want to test a fuel sample for alcohol content.

Pour 200 milliliters (ml) of the sample fuel into a glass or clear plastic container along with 100ml of water. The two liquids will separate, and immediately after they are put in the container, the dividing line will be at the 100ml mark. Wait about 30 minutes. If the dividing line rises by more than 10 percent of the volume of the contents of the container, then the fuel con-

Professional engine analyzers such as this help pinpoint problems on the high-tech engines of the 1990s, but they are not necessary.

tains excessive alcohol. Drain the fuel from the tank and replace it with good fuel.

Many fuel additives on the market contain alcohol. The contents of a can of these additives is so small compared with the size of the typical fuel tank that it poses no threat to the fuel system. Nevertheless, use caution, ask around a little bit, and be selective when purchasing these products; some are much better than others.

Lambda Sensor

A rich running condition may be caused by a tricked Lambda sensor. A Lambda oxygen sensor can be tricked by

An exhaust leak
Low compression
A secondary ignition problem
Incorrect ignition timing
A defective air pump system
A defective component in the Lambda sensor itself

Testing for the "Dead Hole"

When a late-model fuel-injected engine has a cylinder with a misfire, the effects can go far beyond a rough idle or a loss of power. A cylinder that is still pulling in air but not burning that air will be pumping unburned oxygen past the Lambda sensor. This confuses the ECU, making it believe the engine is running lean. The ECU responds by enriching the mixture, and the gas mileage deteriorates dramatically.

Several effective methods can be used to isolate a dead cylinder, or "dead hole." All of these methods measure the power produced in each cylinder by killing the cylinders one at a time with the engine running a little above curb idle.

Back in the good old days, we used to take a test light, ground the alligator clip, and pierce through the insulation boot at the distributor cap end of the plug wire. This would ground out the spark for one cylinder, and an rpm drop would be noted. The greater the rpm drop, the more power that cylinder was contributing to the operation of the engine. Actually, this is a valid testing procedure; however, piercing the insulation boot is only asking for more problems than you started with.

Another "old days" method of performing a cylinder balance test was to isolate the dead hole by pulling off one plug wire at a time

and noting the rpm drops. The problem with this method is that you run the risk of damaging either yourself or the ignition module, with a high-voltage spark.

So, let's explore some alternatives.

Cylinder Inhibit Test

Several tool companies produce a cylinder-shorting tach—dwell meter. These devices electronically disable one cylinder at a time while displaying rpm. Engine speed drops can be noted. Unfortunately, these testers can cost $500 or more.

Another method does the old test light technique one better. Cut a piece of 1/8in vacuum hose into four, six, or eight sections–depending on the number of cylinders in the engine–each about 1in long. With the engine shut off and one at a time, so as not to confuse the firing order, remove the plug wires from the distributor cap, insert the segments of vacuum hose into the plug wire tower of the cap, and set the plug wires back on top of the hose segments. When you have installed all the segments, start the engine. Touching a vacuum hose "conductor" with a grounded test light will kill the corresponding cylinder so that you can note rpm drop. Again, the cylinder with the smallest drop in rpm is the weakest cylinder.

Whichever method you use, follow this procedure for the best results:

1. Adjust the engine speed to 1200rpm to 1400rpm by blocking the throttle open. Do not hold the throttle by hand; you just will not be steady enough. An old fashioned, spring type wooden clothes pin will serve this purpose very effectively. When the clothes pin is separated into its three base components you will have two wooden wedges and a spring. The wooden wedges provide a very effective tool for controlling throttle position.

2. Electrically disconnect the idle stabilizer motor, to prevent its affecting the idle speed.

3. Disconnect the Lambda sensor, to prevent it from altering the air-fuel ratio to compensate for the dead cylinder.

4. Perform the cylinder kill test. Rpm drops should be fairly equal between cylinders. Any cylinder that has an rpm drop that is considerably smaller than the rest is weak.

5. Introduce a little propane into the intake–just enough to provide the highest rpm. Repeat the cylinder kill test. If the rpm drop from the weak cylinder tends to equalize with the rest, then you have a vacuum leak to track down. If the car has an idle stabilizer, be

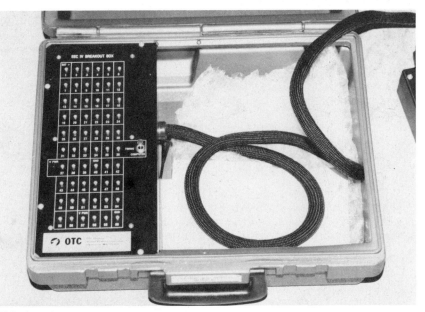

This breakout box for fuel-injected Fords makes the process of troubleshooting these cars easier.

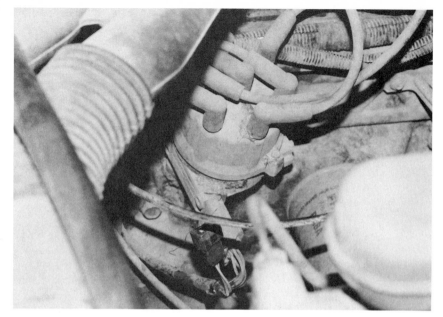

Rebuilding the engine without replacing ignition parts is penny-wise and dollar-foolish. Most running problems experienced after initial start-up relate to ignition parts that should have been replaced and were not.

sure to disable it so that it will not attempt to compensate for the lack of power input from the dead cylinder.

Point-Condenser Ignition System

The point-condenser ignition system served as the workhorse ignition system of the gasoline engine for over fifty years.

Components of the Primary Circuit

Coil

The heart of any spark ignition system is the coil. Basically, the ignition coil used in the point-condenser ignition system is a step-up transformer inside an oil-filled metal can. As there are many times more secondary windings than primary windings, the output of the secondary is potentially tens of thousands of volts.

Although the coil is relatively trouble free, both the primary and the secondary windings are subject to opens, shorts, grounds, and corrosion. When I was in trade school—and I confess, it was in the days when electronic ignition was viewed as a gimmick and aberration—my tune-up instructor pointed out the valid telltale sign of a coil defect. Most point-condenser ignitions have a recess in the bottom similar to that of an aluminum soda can. An internal problem in the coil can cause overheating, which can cause the oil intended to cool the coil to expand, pushing out the recessed area at the bottom of the coil. Although this evidence is not conclusive regarding coil condition, it can be one piece of the diagnostic puzzle.

Ignition Switch

The ignition switch is normally a key lock switch that serves as an on-off switch for primary current flow. The typical point-condenser ignition system has two circuit paths through the switch, for the primary side of the coil. The first path carries current to the ignition coil through a ballast resistor that reduces the voltage drop across the coil primary to about 9.6 volts and limits the current flow to about 2.5 amperes. The second path carries current directly to the ignition coil when the engine is being cranked for starting. Bypassing the ballast resistor increases the current flow and the available secondary power while starting the engine. This is especially important when the engine is being cold started.

The ignition switch is one component of the ignition system that is often overlooked during the troubleshooting procedure. Although it is seldom the cause of driveability problems, an intermittent open circuit in the ignition switch can cause stalling, power, and performance problems.

Battery

Most people, including most professional automotive technicians, do not think of the battery as part of the ignition system. Yet, the battery is the ultimate power source for every electrical and electronic component on the car. An intermittent open circuit in the battery can manifest itself in a wide variety of symptoms including intermittent coil operation. Intermittent coil operation can cause stalling and misfiring.

Ballast Resistor

The ballast resistor is a low-resistance, high-wattage resistor that is installed in the primary circuit to limit current flow. It also causes a reduction in the voltage drop across the ignition coil primary. The limiting of current and voltage reduces wear on the points by reducing their tendency to arc as they are opened to interrupt primary current flow.

The ballast resistor is located in the run circuit between the ignition switch and the coil. The bypass position of the ignition switch routes coil current around the ballast resistor while the engine is being cranked. This provides full coil power to the spark plugs while you are starting the engine. This is particularly important when you are trying to cold start the engine.

Well, if all this potential power can be created with full current flow to the ignition coil, why even have a ballast resistor? If the ballast resistor is eliminated from the system, then arcing and excessive wear can occur at the points.

Condenser

The ignition condenser is an electrolytic capacitor. This device is a small metal can. Inside the can are two thin foil strips separated by a thin insulating material. The condenser acts like an electrical shock absorber to the primary ignition system. When the points open, the primary current attempts to keep flowing. Without the condenser, the current would continue to flow across the opening points. This arcing would slow the collapse of the magnetic field and limit the potential power of the secondary ignition.

The condenser is seldom the cause of driveability problems. In fact, during the heyday of the point-condenser system, I worked for several repair shops that routinely did not replace the condenser during a routine tune-up. Yet, a defective condenser can cause poor idling and no-start misfiring.

Points

A point is little more than a cam-operated switch. It is the opening and closing of the points in a point-condenser ignition system that controls the current flow through the coil. As the crankshaft rotates, it drives the camshaft through gears or chains. A gear on the camshaft drives the shaft of the distributor. As the distributor shaft rotates, it turns a cam. This rotating cam opens and closes the point. Therefore, the opening and closing of the points is synchronized to the rotation of the crankshaft and the movement of the pistons.

The opening and closing of the points is an inadequate method of controlling the current, for several reasons. First, as the points open, the current tends to continue flowing. This tendency can cause an arc and slow the speed of collapse of the magnetic field around the primary windings of the coil. As the speed of collapse slows, the potential output of the coil is decreased. To control this tendency to arc, the current flow through the primary is kept low. This also limits the potential output of the system. Second, the points become pitted and worn over time. This increases the resistance across the points and limits the current flow. Third, the rubbing block can wear, which will alter the timing. Fourth, at extremely high engine rpm, the points will tend to bounce open when they close.

Several things were done over the years to decrease the effects of these problems. Special metals were used at the contact points to decrease the wear and resistance elements. Holes were drilled in the contact points to reduce the possibility of arcing. But most of these modifications only delayed the inevitable.

Since pitting and wear of the points can decrease the potential current flow through the primary, and since the current flow in the primary can affect the output of the secondary, points need routine

Alcohol contaminating the fuel can damage the fuel pump over time. Often, a fuel injection fuel pump will fail while sitting during the rebuild. This can result in low or no fuel pressure on initial start-up.

replacement. If the condenser is not perfectly matched to the rest of the primary ignition system, point pitting can be accelerated. Pitted points can cause erratic coil operation, which will result in misfiring, stalling, and difficulty in starting. The ignition points need to be replaced at least every 15,000 miles to ensure the dependability of the ignition system.

Components of the Secondary Ignition System

Coil

The ignition coil secondary consists of hundreds of windings of very thin wire. When current stops flowing through the primary, the magnetic field created by the primary current flow collapses. This collapsing magnetic field induces several thousand volts in the secondary. This is the voltage that is used to jump the gap of the spark plugs to fire the mixture in the cylinders.

Because of the relatively low current in this high-voltage side of the coil, few problems develop in the secondary side of the coil. The problems that do occur are usually in the form of open circuits.

Coil Wire

The secondary output coil wire carries the high-voltage current from the coil to the distributor cap. The coil wire is normally 6in to 12in long and has a resistance of a few thousand ohms. This relatively high resistance helps to reduce the intensity of the radio signal created by the secondary ignition.

All arcing generates a radio signal. In addition to the arcing that occurs at the spark plug, an arc is also created inside the distributor cap, between the cap and the rotor. All the secondary ignition wiring has a high resistance to reduce the effect of this arcing.

The coil wire can suffer from several possible problems. As it ages, its resistance tends to increase. In addition, the insulating quality of the jacket decreases, which makes it possible for the high voltages being carried by the wire to penetrate the jacket and arc to ground. Corrosion can also affect the current-carrying ability of the wire.

A defective coil wire can result in misfiring, a failure to start, and poor power.

Distributor Cap and Rotor

The distributor cap and rotor operate as a team. The coil wire delivers the high voltage to the center terminal of the distributor cap. The voltage is then carried by a carbon conductor to the center of the rotor. The rotor will have either a metal conductor or a carbon resistive conductor, which carries the voltage to the tip of the rotor. The rotor mounts on the top of the distributor shaft and is driven by the camshaft. As the rotor rotates, it approaches either copper or aluminum conductors on the inside of the distributor cap, and arcs to these conductors, which carry the voltage to the spark plug wires.

The distributor cap and rotor should be changed as a set. The cap is prone to cracking, corrosion, and carbon tracking. Carbon tracking occurs when a microscopic crack or dirt provides a current path to ground that is easier to follow than the current path along the plug wire. The rotor is subject to corrosion and perforation. Perforation occurs when the high voltage seeks and finds a ground through the rotor to the distributor shaft.

Routine replacement of the distributor cap and rotor can prevent unforeseen problems. It is not necessary to replace the cap and rotor at each tune-up, as many professional technicians recommend, but they should be replaced at every other tune-up. Do not assume that this means your mechanic has been ripping you off for the past ten years. It is no disservice to be charged $30 or $40 for a new cap and rotor at each tune-up to ensure that you have a lesser chance of developing premature problems.

The replacement distributor cap and rotor should also be built by the same manufacturer. I have had a mismatched cap and rotor cause the rotor air gap to be so large that the engine either would fail to start or would misfire.

Spark Plug Wires

Back in the late 1960s and the early 1970s, when I first got into the car repair business, we checked spark plug wires by starting the engine in a darkened shop. If sparks flew around under the hood, it meant that one or more of the plug wires had perforated and was arcing to ground.

For several years in the mid-1970s, I worked almost exclusively on fuel-injected imports. Upon returning to working on domestics in 1980, I was mystified at what I thought was the poor quality of the plug wires. I remembered very few

problems in the 1970s; now, I saw many problems. The difference was not the quality of the wires, but rather the leaner air-fuel ratios demanded in the early 1980s—and on into the 1990s. In the early 1970s, we unwittingly compensated for defective spark plug wires by turning the idle mixture screws on the carburetors to enrich the idle mixture. This option was not available on the sealed carburetors of the late 1970s. Therefore, technicians were forced to replace defective spark plug wires rather than simply masking the problem with a richer mixture.

When replacing spark plug wires, the old adage, "You get what you pay for," is true. A $50 set of spark plug wires can easily outlast four $12 sets. A marginal plug wire can cause a misfire when the engine is under an extreme load, and on a modern fuel-injected car, can make the engine run rich.

Spark Plugs

Every tune-up includes replacing the spark plugs. Many brands of spark plugs are on the market—some good, some bad. Asking for opinions on which is the best brand of spark plug is like asking which is the best soft drink: it is largely a matter of personal opinion. When I have a choice, I always use the brand the manufacturer installed at the factory. My thinking is that the manufacturer has a vested interest in choosing the spark plug that will provide the best driveability and that has the least chance of requiring replacement within 12,000 miles. This method has rarely failed to provide either myself or my customers with good service.

The spark plug consists of a pair of electrodes separated by an air gap of between 0.028in and 0.075in. As the spark from the coil travels down the plug wire seeking ground, it must arc across this air gap. If this arc is exposed to a properly preheated, well-atomized mixture of fuel and air, it will ignite the fuel.

As the spark plugs arc at a high frequency, in high temperatures, the electrode material will slowly vaporize. This causes the gap to widen. The wider the gap, the higher the voltage required to initiate the spark across the gap. Eventually, the voltage required to

initiate the spark across the gap will be greater than the voltage the coil is capable of generating, and a misfire will occur.

Common problems associated with the spark plugs are misfiring and difficulty in starting.

Timing Control

The ignition timing must change as the engine is running, to adjust to different engine speeds and loads. When the engine is running at an idle, the spark must begin at a point in the crankshaft rotation that will allow for the spark to extinguish when the crankshaft is about 10 degrees after top dead center. Since the length of time the spark is jumping the gap is a relative constant—about 2.5 milliseconds—the spark must start sooner as the engine speed increases.

For example, on a hypothetical engine, the spark occurs at 10 degrees before top dead center when the engine is running at 1000rpm. At this speed, the spark extinguishes at about 10 degrees after top dead center. This means the crankshaft has rotated 20 degrees since the initiation of the spark. As the engine speed increases, the crankshaft rotates more degrees in the 2.5 milliseconds that the spark is jumping the gap. At 2000rpm, the crankshaft will rotate twice as much. If the timing at 1000rpm should be 10 degrees before top dead center, then the timing at 2000rpm should be about 30 degrees before top dead center. As the engine speed continues to increase, the timing will need to continue to advance. The amount of total advance, or the upper limit of the advance, will vary depending on the design of the engine.

There are almost as many different procedures to follow in adjusting the initial timing in point-condenser ignition systems as there are different applications of point-condenser systems. The basic premise of adjusting or checking the initial timing is to disable the timing controls. Most point-condenser systems have a centrifugal advance system, which advances the timing as the speed of the engine increases. A second timing control system is the vacuum advance, which actually retards the timing when the engine is under a load.

With centrifugal advance, the change of timing in response to rpm is accomplished through a set of spring-loaded weights. As the speed of the engine increases, the weights swing out against spring tension. The cam that opens and closes the points, although it is mounted on the distributor shaft, is not part of the distributor shaft. The swinging weights cause the cam to rotate with respect to the distributor shaft. This advances the timing.

At first glance, *vacuum advance* is a misnomer. The vacuum advance actually retards the timing when the engine is under a load. In most applications, it is connected to ported vacuum. The advance unit receives no vacuum at an idle, but when the throttle is opened, the vacuum advances the timing. As the load on the engine increases, the vacuum drops. As the vacuum drops, the timing is not advanced as much—it retards. Retarding the timing lowers the combustion temperature, and therefore prevents detonation and decreases the potential of damage to the engine.

For most applications, to adjust the timing, disconnect and plug the vacuum advance hose and lower the engine idle speed as much as possible. Under these conditions, any vacuum that might be in the vacuum hose cannot affect the timing and the engine speed will be too low for the centrifugal weight to be advancing the timing.

Although essential to the control of emissions, the oxygen or Lambda sensor has little effect on the running of the engine during the initial start-up starting the engine. It is probably not at fault if the engine does not run right at initial start-up, but the oxygen sensor should be replaced as part of the rebuild because it is an essential part of the emission control system.

This procedure will usually work when the correct one for your application is not available. Be sure to follow the exact procedure for the application you are working on. This can be found on a decal under the hood.

If the vehicle is one of the late-model applications that have computerized control of ignition timing and the computer fails to control the ignition timing properly, refer to the Motorbooks International books such as *How to Repair and Modify Chevrolet Fuel Injection*, *How to Tune and Modify Ford Fuel Injection*, and *How to Tune and Modify Bosch Fuel Injection*, as appropriate. If these books do not cover the application you are working on, consult the factory service manuals.

Blueprinting and Balancing

15

When selecting an engine that will be blueprinted, the first consideration is whether the block and crank are in good condition. It is foolish to spend a great deal of money on a cracked or distorted block. Essentially, the engine should not require any special machining if a standard rebuild is being done.

The purpose of boring the block when blueprinting an engine is to increase the displacement and the compression ratio.

In a broad sense, every engine built is blueprinted and balanced. These processes can reap benefits in several areas. A blueprinted engine results in better combustion, which means better fuel economy and lower emissions. A balanced engine has fewer inertial anomalies to overcome as it runs. This means less power is lost to vibration and distortion. A smaller power loss means better fuel economy. Most balancing and blueprinting procedures do not conflict with, but rather enhance, EPA fuel economy and emissions standards.

It is not intended that this chapter turn you into a race car machinist. It is unrealistic for any single chapter or even any single book to strive for such a goal. The intent is to help you become literate and conversant so that you and your machinist might communicate better.

Blueprinting

Defining the concept of blueprinting is a lot like defining what makes a good film: it is difficult to do precisely, easy to do generally. In general, blueprinting means making sure an engine's tolerances are all within specs. When the term *blueprinted* is used in the performance sense, the distinction is a matter of precision.

Selecting a machinist to do your blueprinting is more difficult than selecting a good general automotive machinist to help you rebuild your engine. You want the kind of person who measures from the top of the *i* to the dot when signing a check. Precision is the order of business here.

Balancing and blueprinting can be broken up into seven categories:

Cylinder blocks
Crankshaft
Connecting rods
Pistons
Cylinder heads
Camshaft
Compression ratio

Cylinder Blocks

Is blueprinting worth it? Damaged and repaired blocks, engines being rebuilt for cars or trucks that have bent bodies and will be used to haul groceries home—these are examples where the extra benefits of blueprinting do not warrant the extra expense. Begin only with engine blocks that have had little previous machine work done on them since they left the factory. These blocks should have no cracks or warpage. Check them thoroughly as described earlier in this book. If your block checks out, go for it.

Line Boring

Line boring corrects for misalignment of the crankshaft journals in the block. Extreme heating and cooling of the engine block can cause warping. Even a slight misalignment of 0.0015in can cause a power loss and premature failure of the main bearings, and possibly break the crankshaft. The block should be line bored any time the engine is being rebuilt as a result of a broken crankshaft.

Line boring equipment is very large and very expensive. Many machine shops will opt to sublet this operation. The block is placed in a boring machine, and small amounts of metal are removed. As the metal is removed, the main journals are aligned. If too much metal is removed, the crankshaft is moved too far up in the block; this alters the compression ratio and slackens the timing chain. Even if the engine has a timing chain tensioner to compensate for the slack chain, cam timing will still be retarded. If the cam timing is controlled through meshing gears, special gears will have to be purchased, as the tooth penetration of a stock gear will be too deep. Excessive penetration can cause premature wear. Ask your machinist whether or not to replace the block.

Cylinder Boring

The repair of damaged cylinders by boring was discussed in chapter 10. Although excessive taper or out-of-round can be repaired by reboring the cylinders, the primary goal of doing so during the blueprinting of an engine is to increase performance. Since the procedure alters the diameter of the cylinder, boring increases engine displacement. A classic Ford 302 punched 0.03in over becomes a 306. At the same time, the compression ratio rises slightly. Boring the cylinders also removes from the cylinder walls metal that is an essential part in the removal of heat. Engines with cylinder walls that are too thin can run hot.

Before discussing with your machinist how much you are going to have the cylinders bored, check

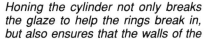

Honing the cylinder not only breaks the glaze to help the rings break in, but also ensures that the walls of the cylinder are vertical, parallel, and square.

the sizes of replacement pistons that are available. Typical replacement sizes are 0.02in, 0.03in, 0.04in, and sometimes 0.06in oversize. The most common rebore is 0.03in oversize.

Deburring

Deburring is an operation that can be performed by almost anyone. Anyone who has built a model car

Remove all the casting lines from (deburr) the crankshaft and the cylinder block.

Stock crankshafts have one oil port in each rod journal. As the crankshaft rotates, only one of the two bearing shells is lubricated at a time. Cross drilling the rod journals ensures an adequate oil supply to both bearing surfaces.

or a model airplane is familiar with the flashing that results from seepage of the plastic into the joints between the sections of the mold. When building a plastic model, you must remove this flashing to make the final product look neat.

In an engine block, flashing also marks the junction between the pieces of the mold. Removal of this flashing is for more than purely cosmetic purposes. The ridges formed by the flashing provide a starting point for cracks and stress fractures.

To remove the flashing, mount a rotary file in an electric drill motor. Air drills are acceptable if the motor has a variable speed. Most single-speed air drills spin so fast that the unwary hand could accidentally grind away the block and leave the flashing behind. Remove any flashing evident on the interior of the crankcase or the intake valley. Other places to look include the drain holes to the crankcase.

Do not get carried away with this procedure. The idea is to remove the flashing, not polish the inside of the block. Although a polished block may seem like a nice idea, in reality, the removal of all the little dimples reduces the surface area of the block and reduces heat transfer from the oil to the block.

The rotary file will not fit some places in the block. A flat-tipped punch will work well in those places. A file should be used to deburr the edges of the main bearing caps. The lifter holes can be deburred with a wheel cylinder abrasive ball hone. It is not advisable to use a wheel cylinder flat stone hone for this purpose.

Continue the deburring process until all the flashing is removed.

Decking

Decking the block makes sure the mating surface with the head is flat and even. It makes no sense, especially in a performance engine, to pay money to have the cylinder heads machined flat and then install them on a distorted cylinder block surface. Decking, when done properly, also ensures that the angle of the head mating surfaces is correct. For most V-engines, this angle is either 60 or 90 degrees. The accuracy of this angle is important to allow a proper fit of the intake manifold to the cylinder head.

For most individuals interested in performance, the purpose of decking the block is to provide the proper clearance between the piston at the top of the stroke, and the bottom of the cylinder head. Without giving it a great deal of thought, one might feel that the piston should be flush with the top of the block when it is at the top of its stroke. This would be true if the metal of the connecting rods were not slightly elastic. The piston is an inertial mass moving at approximately 2,000 feet per minute (nearly 23mph) as it travels up the cylin-

Although this main journal looks smooth to the eye, it is in need of polishing. Part of blueprinting any engine is polishing the crankshaft.

der. As the piston reaches the top of its travel, it must stop and reverse direction in as little as 3 milliseconds. During that time, tremendous forces are working on the connecting rod. This causes the connecting rod to stretch. When an engine is being built for street use, the static clearance between the top of the piston and the deck should be 0.035in. Owing to potentially much higher engine speeds, this clearance should be 0.045in on racing engines. If the engine is being reassembled with aluminum connecting rods, the clearance should be 0.06in.

When the deck-to-piston top clearance is being checked, you should consider the thickness of the head gasket. If you are building a stock street engine using a head gasket with a compressed thickness of 0.035in, a piston-to-deck clearance of 0in would be about right; 0.005in would be better. Keep in mind that a compression ratio loss will not occur at higher engine speeds, because of the stretch in the connecting rods.

Honing

When you are blueprinting an engine, honing serves two purposes. First, as in a standard overhaul, it is done to remove the glaze from the cylinder walls. As the engine is run over the years, the old piston rings polish the walls of the cylinders. Honing breaks up this glaze and allows the rings an abrasive surface to help seat them. Second, when blueprinting an engine, honing also serves to ensure that the cylinder walls are as round and straight as possible.

The berry ball hone discussed in chapter 3 is only used to break the glaze on the cylinder walls.

The correct honing technique will produce a crosshatch pattern on the cylinder walls. Only a flat stone hone can be used to true (smooth and even up) the cylinder walls. Although a flat stone hone mounted in a drill motor will do a reasonably good job for a stock engine, maximum precision for performance can only be achieved with your machinist's honing machine.

A "home" version of a precision honing machine does an excellent job. If you have a lot of time and a lot of money or if you are going to be building a lot of engines, then investing in this machine might be worthwhile. Proper performance honing requires that the block be submerged in oil during the process. Along with the honing machine, buy an old bathtub and several gallons of honing oil. Also, since you will likely need to remove 0.004in to 0.006in of metal from each cylinder, be sure nothing you want to see is on television for the next week.

If you are having the block bored, it is standard procedure for the machinist then to hone the cylinders. The boring machine will bore the cylinders 0.004in to

This port is stock on some connecting rods and can be added to those where it is not. The purpose of the port is to squirt oil on the cylinder walls as the crank rotates. This improves cylinder wall lubrication and decreases wear.

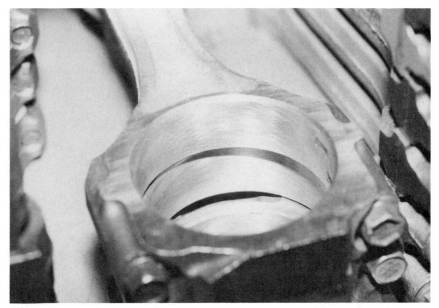

Start with good connecting rods, deburr them, and have them checked for straightness.

0.006in undersize. Honing is then used to remove the remaining metal for proper bore size. It would not hurt to confirm that honing will be part of the procedure, when you drop the block off with the machinist.

Rod-to-Block and Crankshaft-to-Block Clearance

When something other than the stock crankshaft or connecting rods is used, it may hit the inside of the block as the engine runs. The crankshaft and the rods should have a minimum clearance of 0.05in to all parts of the block.

Crankshaft

Deburring

Like the block, a stock crankshaft will have flashing that needs to be removed. Removal of this flashing is for more than purely cosmetic purposes. The ridges formed by the flashing provide a starting point for cracks and stress fractures.

Chamfering

Use a small, medium-grit grinding stone mounted in a drill motor to chamfer the opening of the crankshaft oil holes. Chamfering permits a smoother flow of oil to the journal. Once this procedure has been performed, the oil does not have to turn a sharp 90 degrees and the chamfer provides a reservoir. The result is better lubrication to the rod and main journals.

Counterweights

Work on the counterweights can be taken to several degrees. The crankcase is not a perfect environment in which to spin the crankshaft. A fine mist of oil impedes the movement of the crankshaft as the oil droplets contact it. The first, and simplest, step in solving this problem is to install a windage tray above the oil level in the oil pan. This is available commercially. The second step is to polish the rough surfaces on the counterweights, left behind by the casting process.

If the goal is a fire-breathing quarter-mile-gobbling, racing engine, three additional procedures may be advisable. A popular procedure for such engines is to knife-edge the counterweights. This involves removing metal to form a 45-degree leading edge to the counterweight. In much the same way that the sloped nose of a Chevy Lumina APV has better aerodynamics than does the front of a 1962 VW Microbus, a knife-edged counterweight slips through the air and oil mist of the crankcase much easier than does a blunt-edged counterweight. This procedure, of course, removes weight from the counterweights and should be done only if the crank, rod, and piston assemblies are to be balanced.

One of the most effective operations that can be done to the coun-terweights to improve performance is to reduce their radius. Removing metal to reduce the radius lightens the crank, making the engine more responsive to speed change requests from the driver, and reduces the wind resistance that results from the counterweight swinging through the air and oil mist in the block.

Anybody who remembers soft drinks in bottles has probably blown across the mouth of such a bottle. The sound that is created is evidence of wind resistance. When the factory and your machinist balanced the crankshaft, they did so

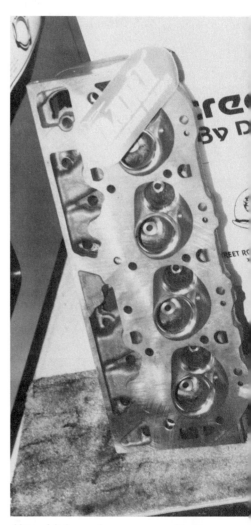

New high-performance cylinder heads can be purchased off the shelf. These are produced by many manufacturers and are available for a wide range of engines. Some of the engines they are available for are not commonly thought of as performance engines.

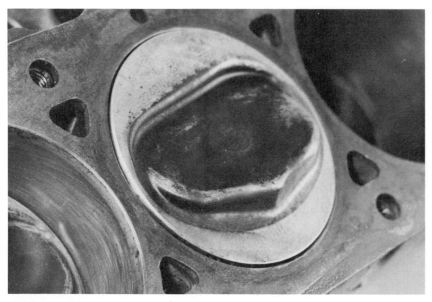

Domed pistons will need to be fitted into the combustion chamber. These modifications to the combustion chamber are called dome fitting and radiusing.

118

by drilling holes in the counterweights. These holes increase the wind resistance of the counterweight. During the final stages of balancing the crank, rod, and piston assemblies, these holes should be closed by welding special freeze plugs over them. After these plugs are welded in place, they are machined smooth. This process is called smooth balancing.

All the counterweight modifications you want to make should be done at the same time. Sit down with your machinist, and calculate how much each procedure will cost and how many meals your spouse and children can do without, before contracting what will be done.

Cross-drilling

In the typical crankshaft, each rod journal has only one hole to supply oil to the bearing. This means oil is only delivered to one of the bearing shells at a time. Each bearing shell will only receive oil once during each crankshaft revolution. Improved lubrication, and therefore bearing life, results from cross-drilling the rod journals. In this procedure, each oil supply hole in the rod journal is drilled straight through the journal.

Grinding

When the crankshaft has been damaged owing to spun bearings or extreme wear, it will need to be machined. Be sure to confirm the availability of undersize bearings. Common sizes for these are 0.01in, 0.02in, and 0.03in. If you are working on an import application, it is especially important to confirm availability, as the bearings do not always run in the standard sizes.

When the crankshaft is machined to 0.02in, the machinist will mount it in a lathe designed exclusively for that purpose. The machinist will then set the lathe to remove 0.01in of metal from each journal of the crankshaft. Since the same amount of metal is removed all the way around, the crank will end up being 0.02in undersize. After machining the crankshaft, the machinist will then use an attachment for the lathe to polish it.

So far, the procedure is the same as during a standard overhaul. For an additional fee, the machinist can index the crank journals. As an example, on a V-8 engine, the machinist would make

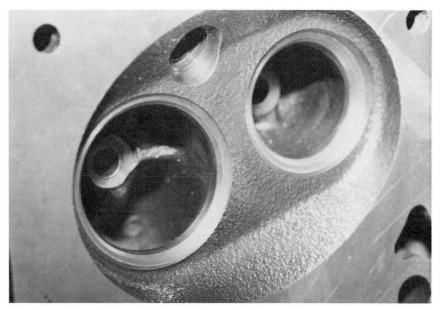

This head is cleaned, and the valve seats are ground and ready for porting and polishing. The valve pocket (the area immediately above the valve) is the area that requires the most attention on most cylinder heads.

sure the rod journal throws are exactly 90 degrees apart. Indexing is accomplished by offset grinding the rod journals. It ensures that the camshaft and the ignition system will be exactly phased to all the pistons, not just piston number one.

Tuftriding

Tuftriding is a hardening process that involves submerging the crankshaft in a molten salt. The crankshaft is thereby heat-treated and hardened.

Polishing

Industry specifications dictate that the crank journals should be polished to a smoothness of 5 to 10 microinches. Visual inspection of the crank journals to determine their need to be polished is wholly

As a last step of a valve grind, the valves should be lapped in; this ensures that they fit snugly and evenly into their seats.

inadequate. The human eye has an ability to see objects as small as 394 microinches. The smallest object you can see is therefore forty times larger than the minimum industry standard for smoothness.

Several methods are available for checking the smoothness of the crankshaft. The high-tech method is to use a profilometer. This is an electromechanical device that is sixty-two times more accurate than your fingernail.

The bottom line is have the crankshaft polished with each engine rebuild. Polishing should also be done after the crankshaft has been machined.

Shot-peening

The most common method of strengthening the crankshaft is through shot-peening. After the journals are masked to protect them, high-velocity shot is targeted at the other areas of the crank. Particular attention is paid to the fillet or radius areas of the main journals. The impact of the shot relieves stress in the metal that could cause microscopic cracks that could later lead to a broken crankshaft.

Straightening

If the crankshaft needs to be straightened, get a new one. However, if a lot of time, energy, or money has been put into a crankshaft, it can be straightened by a skilled technician.

Connecting Rods
Polishing

Using a stationary belt sander, grind the casting marks off the connecting rods. This operation denies cracks a place to start, making the rods more durable. If you are building this engine for racing, check with the sanctioning organization to make sure this procedure is legal for your class.

Rod-to-Camshaft Clearance

If non-stock connecting rods are used, sneak into your child's room an hour or so after you are sure he or she is asleep, and procure a lump of modeling clay. Mash a lump of the clay to each side of the connecting rods where you think there may be interference between the rods and the cam lobes. Tentatively install the pistons on the rods, the camshaft into the block, the crankshaft into the block, and the piston-rod assemblies onto the crankshaft. Torque the main bearing and rod caps in place. Rotate the crankshaft several times. Remove the piston-rod assemblies, and examine the clay on the connecting rods. Cut away part of the clay, and measure the minimal thickness; it should be at least 0.05in. If it is not, the sides of the rods will need to be clearanced while the crank-rod-piston assembly is being balanced.

Rod-to-Piston Skirt Clearance

Some non-stock piston-rod combinations do not work very well right out of the box. When the crank throw is at a 90-degree angle, the piston skirt can come in contact with the side of the rod. As the rod-to-cam clearance is being checked, rod-to-piston skirt clearance should be checked. It should be a minimum of 0.05in.

Sizing

The big end of the crankshaft can become stretched or machined oversize by spun rod bearings. Like so many other things, connecting rods are usually expendable and should simply be replaced. If the rod is rare, the machinist can machine the mating surfaces of the rod and the rod bearing cap. This makes the big end hole smaller top to bottom, but about the same diameter side to side. To adjust for this distortion, the machinist will now machine the proper diameter in the rod's big end.

Rod Bolts or Nuts

At the bottom end of the connecting rods is a surface where the nut or bolt must seat flat. In many cases, this surface has a chamfer that will put an angular stress on the bolt. Clearance should then be ground for the nut or bolt, and the mating surface for the nut or bolt machined, so that the fastener will receive no angular forces.

Shot-peening

Like the crankshaft, connecting rods are most commonly strengthened through shot-peening. High-velocity shot is targeted at the rod. Particular attention is paid to the fillet or radius areas. The impact of the shot relieves stress in the metal that could cause microscopic cracks, cracks that could later lead to a broken connecting rod.

Pistons
Dome Fitting

Overheard on a cruise through Fort Worth's 1849 Village in the late 1960s: "Yeah, Mike's got a new SS 396 with a race cam and pop-up pistons." Chances are, in Mike's street gas engine, the domes of his pop-up pistons did little more than disrupt the combustion chamber

The stock pushrods may cause the valve spring to bind if the cylinder heads and the block deck have been resurfaced. The problem can be resolved by selecting from different lengths of pushrods. As this is a trial-and-error procedure, it can be very time-consuming and expensive.

flame front. Engines that run on exotic racing fuels thrive on the kind of compression created by domed piston. The domes of the pistons may not fit properly into the cylinder head combustion chambers. Your machinist can remove metal from the domes of the pistons during the balancing process, to ensure proper fit.

Clearancing

High-powered engines also tend to run high-lift camshafts, which thrust the valve deep into the combustion chamber. Especially during the exhaust stroke, the exhaust valve and the intake valve may try to occupy the same space at the same time. Many pistons, even stock pistons, have notches cut in the top to accommodate the valves. Unfortunately, in too many cases, the person who designed the piston apparently never met the person who designed the head and the valvetrain. If you are building a fire breather, your machinist can notch the pistons to ensure proper valve-to-piston clearance.

Lightening

Metal can be removed from the inside of the piston to lighten it. The lighter the piston is, the less inertial mass it has and the faster it can change speeds and direction at top dead center and bottom dead center. Lightening should only be done as part of the balancing procedure.

Thickness

Whatever machining work is done on the pistons, a prime consideration should be the thickness of the piston. If the machine work results in the piston's being too thin, it will fail to absorb and dissipate the heat of combustion properly and will self-destruct.

Rings

Place each piston ring in the cylinder in which it is to be used. With a feeler gauge, measure the gap between the ends of the ring. Performance rings often have no end gap or will overlap when installed. K-D Tools makes a special filing tool, which can be used to file the rings to the perfect gap and yet ensure that the end surfaces of the rings are perfectly parallel. After the rings are filed with this special tool, the rough edges should be removed by hand filing.

The ring side clearance should also be checked. Place a feeler gauge in each of the ring grooves, with the ring that is destined for that groove installed. Insert progressively thicker feeler gauges until a snug fit is obtained. The ring side clearance should be 0.002in to 0.004in.

Gas Porting

Gas porting the piston involves precision drilling tiny holes in the top of the piston so that the gases that would otherwise be trapped between the top compression ring and the head of the piston can escape. Located at the back of the ring groove, these holes are typically 0.04in to 0.06in in diameter. The holes must be evenly spaced.

Only pistons destined for running a quarter-mile should be gas ported. In these engines, ring side clearance is often less than 0.002in. The gas ports are needed to prevent tremendous pressures from building and tearing the head off the piston at extreme rpm.

Skirt-to-Crankshaft Clearance

Performance piston, crankshaft, and rod combinations will sometimes create a condition where the piston skirt can come in contact with the crankshaft counterweight. This clearance should be checked with the modeling clay technique discussed in the section titled "Rod-to-Camshaft Clearance" earlier in this chapter.

Deburring

Deburr all the piston skirt edges.

Cylinder Heads
Valve Grinding

All valve grinds should be performance grinds. Three stones are used in a performance grind. The first stone, usually ground to a 45-degree angle, determines the seat angle. The second stone, usually ground to a 60-degree angle, narrows the seat from the bottom up. The third stone, usually ground to a 30-degree angle, narrows the seat from the top down.

The correct seat width is important in the proper transfer of heat from the valve to the valve seat to the cylinder head. When no specifications are available, the intake valve seat width should be no more than 0.0625in and the exhaust seat must be no less than 0.078in.

To begin a performance valve grind, insert a machined pilot into the valve guide from the combustion chamber side. This pilot ensures that the centerline of the grinding stone is perpendicular to the ground surface of the valve seat. Next, slip the grinding stone holder over the pilot. Then, lower a driver (a large electric motor, resembling a drill) onto the stone

The cylinder head can be resurfaced to flatten the mating surface with the block deck or to increase the combustion ratio for performance.

Remember that with 1990s fuels, high compression can cause detonation.

To cc a head, a graduated burette is the standard of the industry, but a graduated cylinder and a lot of patience work pretty well if the engine is not destined for Daytona or Indy.

holder. Power the driver briefly, and remove it from the stone holder while it is still spinning. Take extreme care not to allow the weight of the driver to rest on the stone holder at any time. The weight of the driver can seriously affect the quality of the grind as well as cause excess wear on the grinding stones.

After the initial 45-degree grind is made, try the valve to be used in that seat. Place a spot of Prussian blue on the valve face. Slip the valve into the guide. Using a lapping stick, rotate the valve against the seat at least twice. Remove the valve, and inspect its face. The Prussian blue should form a stripe roughly centered in the face of the valve. If the stripe is high on the valve, use a 30-degree stone on the seat to lower the contact point between the valve and the seat. If the stripe is too low, use a 60-degree stone on the seat to raise the contact point. If the contact stripe is too wide, use both a 30-degree stone and a 60-degree stone to narrow it. If the contact stripe is too narrow, use the 45-degree stone to widen it. Many manufacturers and machinists will recommend grinding the seats to 44 degrees. The valve faces are usually ground to 45 degrees. This provides an interference angle of 1 degree. This slight, deliberate mismatch of angles is intended to help the valves seat. After as few as 100 miles, the interference angle disappears.

Valve Guides

Although cast, the iron valve guides that are part of the cylinder head on most domestic engines work very well, and although knurling works very well when guides are worn, worn guides on performance engines should be repaired with bronze inserts. These inserts come in two forms: press-in and screw-in. Installation of both requires the skill of your friendly machinist.

Valve Lapping

Lapping valves was never in itself an effective method of ensuring an effective seal between the valve and the seat. In the days of the Model T, this was often done when the carbon was scraped from the cylinder head. Even in those days, it was unsatisfactory. Lapping is a valid procedure as a final step to ensure proper seating after a three-way valve grind is done.

Porting

Porting a cylinder head is not a job for mere mortals. Although considerable flow improvement can be achieved even by a neophyte, true high-performance porting requires the use of a flow bench. Racing teams sometimes spend $10,000 or more to have a set of heads prepared.

In porting a head for street use, three areas need attention. These are the valve bowl, the short side radius, and the intake ports. Use a carbide grinder to smooth the area immediately behind the valve, where the seat transitions into the intake port and around the bottom of the valve guide. When the head is manufactured, this area is left rough. The roughness disturbs the airflow into the cylinder. Try to remove as little metal as possible.

The short side radius is the bump in the floor of the intake port of the head. It is where the air has to turn the corner on its journey to the cylinder. Lower this hump, making the angle of the corner that has to be turned as shallow as possible.

Finally, use the carbide grinder to open the intake port to match the intake manifold gasket. Transition this enlargement smoothly into the valve bowl. Do not match the exhaust port to the exhaust manifold gasket. The misalignment normally found here is intentional; it forms a reversion dam, which keeps the exhaust gases from reentering the combustion chamber as the exhaust pressure pulses vary.

Pushrods

Decking the block, installing camshafts with non-stock base circles, and milling the cylinder heads can all affect rocker arm geometry. The problems created by these operations can be corrected by installing different-length pushrods. Pushrods are available in a variety of lengths; the correct length to cure the effect of these machining operations can only be found through trial and error.

Resurfacing

Constant changes of temperature coupled with inadequate maintenance such as routine retorquing of heads, or incorrect retorquing of heads, results in warpage.

Resurfacing the head involves milling off several thousandths of an inch of metal. In effect, this removes the high spots, making the head flat again.

Several things must be taken into account when the head is resurfaced. If the engine is an overhead cam design, removing several thousands of an inch of metal will cause the camshaft to be closer to the crankshaft. This can affect the tension or amount of slack in the timing chain or belt. Additionally, a warped bottom of the head may indicate that the top of the head is warped. If the top of the head is warped, the cam bearing alignment may be off. Misaligned cam bearings can bind, damage, and even break the camshaft.

Combustion Chamber Volume

Uneven-size combustion chambers result in uneven power from the cylinders. To measure the size of the chambers, use a graduated burette filled with mineral oil and a piece of Plexiglass with a small hole in it. With the valves installed, place the Plexiglass over one of the combustion chambers. The Plexiglass can be held in place with a little petroleum jelly. Meter the mineral oil out of the burette, through the hole in the Plexiglass, until the combustion chamber is full. The volume drained from the burette is the volume of that combustion chamber. Repeat this process for each combustion chamber. Then, use a carbide grinding bit to enlarge each smaller combustion chamber to match the largest.

Rocker Arms and Retainer-to-Guide Clearance

One inexpensive but easy and effective trick to increase valve lift is to use ratioed rocker arms. As the valve lift increases, whether through the use of a high-lift camshaft or through the use of ratioed rockers, the valve spring retainer gets closer and closer to the top of the valve guide.

Before the engine is fully assembled, insert the valves into the valve guides, holding them in place with a blob of modeling clay. Snug the cylinder in place with a head gasket installed. Rotate the crankshaft until the pushrod is at its highest point, then install and adjust the rocker. Install the retainer and valve keeper on the valve. Be careful not to drop the valve into the cylinder. The distance between the bottom of the valve keeper and the top of the valve guide should be a minimum of 0.06in. Repeat this procedure for each of the valves.

Spring Pressure

One important operation is to verify the correct tension in the valve spring. Heat for old springs and manufacturing inconsistencies for new springs can cause variations in spring rate. Your machinist can measure the spring rate with a device called a Rimac spring tension gauge machine, and balance the spring rates by adding shims.

Camshaft

To get maximum performance from an engine, it is necessary to synchronize precisely the camshaft and the crankshaft. This process is called phasing.

Attach a degree wheel to the front of the crankshaft. Rotate the crankshaft until the camshaft pushes the intake lifter for the number one cylinder to its highest point. The point of maximum lift should not be monitored visually; for accuracy, it should be checked with a dial indicator. Using the recommendations of the camshaft grinder, loosen the bolts in the cam sprocket holes that were previously slotted, and align the cam sprocket so that the intake centerline matches the recommended position on the crankshaft.

Valve lift can be modified by replacing these stock rocker arms with ratioed rocker arms.

Compression Ratio

To compute the compression ratio, first find the combustion chamber volume, using the method described in the section titled "Combustion Chamber Volume" earlier in this chapter. Then, use that volume to solve the following equation:

Compression ratio = $\{[(\pi / 4)(\text{bore}^2)(\text{stroke})] + \text{chamber volume}\} / \text{chamber volume}$.

With Domed Pistons

Domed pistons present a problem in calculating compression ratios. Install the rings on a piston, and slide the piston into its cylinder. Position the piston in the cylinder so that the flat part of the top of the piston is precisely 0.5in below the deck of the block. Pour mineral oil from a calibrated burette into the cylinder, on top of the piston, until the oil is level with the deck. Observe the amount of oil that was poured into the cylinder. Use the following formula to calculate the compression ratio:

Compression ratio = $[[(\pi / 4)(\text{bore}^2)(\text{stroke})] + \{\text{chamber volume} - [(\pi 4)(\text{bore}^2)(0.5)] - \text{cylinder oil volume}\}] / \{\text{chamber volume} - [(\pi / 4)(\text{bore}^2)(0.5)] - \text{cylinder oil volume}\}$

With Head Gasket and Valve Relief Area

If you wish or require absolute accuracy, measure the thickness of the head gasket and use the graduated burette to find the volume of the valve relief area in the pistons. Use this formula to find the compression ratio:

Compression ratio = $[[(\pi / 4)(\text{bore}^2)(\text{stroke})] + \{\text{chamber volume} - [(\pi / 4)(\text{bore}^2)(0.5)] - \text{cylinder oil volume}\} + \{[(\pi /4)(\text{bore}^2)(\text{head gasket thickness})] + \text{cylinder relief volume}\}] / [\{\text{chamber volume} - [(\pi / 4)(\text{bore}^2)(0.5)] - \text{cylinder oil volume}\} + \{[(\pi / 4)(\text{bore}^2)(\text{head gasket thickness})] + \text{cylinder relief volume}\}]$

Balancing

When you decide to balance your engine, be sure your pockets are deep enough. The process is slow, tedious work. Many good machinists will not even estimate the cost, short of guessing to the nearest thousand dollars. They have no way to predict how long a given engine will take.

Balancing involves making sure all the rotating and reciprocating masses exert even forces at all times. Reciprocating mass is the weight of the piston and wrist pin. Rotating mass includes the crankshaft, the harmonic balancer, the flywheel or flex plate, and the connecting rods. Metal is removed from the heavier areas to make them match the lighter areas. In some cases, it is necessary to add weight to the lighter components, if removing weight from the heavier ones would decrease their durability.

Performance Modifications

16

By the late 1980s, over ten years had passed since the golden age of the Detroit performance car. For over a decade nearly two decades, concerns about emissions, fuel economy, and safety had condemned the enthusiast either to running late-model slug-bait or to rebuilding wrecking yard refugees. However, in the late 1980s and heading into the 1990s, the late-model sleeper was again a realistic possibility. The manufacturers themselves had shown a renewed interest in performance, starting with the 1984 Buick Grand National. In 1987, Oldsmobile introduced the Quad 4 engine. This was a 2.3-liter four-cylinder with four valves for each cylinder, that produced 154 horsepower (hp) stock—over 1hp per cubic inch. Companies that were performance names in the 1960s, along with a whole basket of new companies, were hitting the market with performance parts.

One major difference distinguishes modifying engines from back in the 1960s and modifying engines today: emission laws. Different jurisdictions will have different mandates concerning emission control systems and what modifications are legal. As a whole, throughout the United States, it can be safely said that it is illegal to remove or modify any emission control device on a car that will be licensed for street use. A small amount of latitude is permitted, however, in some states, for the replacement of some components like intake manifolds, throttle bodies, and the camshaft, with specific tested and approved parts.

Performance modifications are therefore divided into two major categories: street and racing. Please keep in mind that regulations and approvals change frequently when it comes to emission controls, so be sure to ask your parts supplier if a given modification is street legal in your jurisdiction. Do not accept what this book describes as a legal modification to be necessarily legal in your jurisdiction.

Any real increase in performance has to begin with an improvement in the engine's ability to breathe. The improvement of engine breathing is divided into six categories:

Intake	Valve action
Camshaft	Exhaust
Cylinder heads	Mufflers

Intake

For street use, many of the modifications to the intake system that were traditional in the 1960s have already been done by the manufacturer when the engine was designed. Any meaningful modification is going to be found either in modifications to the air cleaner and ducting to the throttle body or in the complete rethinking and reworking of the intake side of the engine including throttle body, intake manifold, and valvetrain.

Begin by looking at what you already have on the car and what can be done to improve it. For example, examine the 5.7-liter Tuned Port Corvette, and explore the availability of over-the-counter performance-upgrading parts for the 5 and 2.5 as well.

First, let's look at the induction system, with a little mathematics relating to the air requirements of the engine. The air demands of the stock 5.7 Chevrolet 350 engine can be estimated with the following formula:

Cubic feet of displacement = cubic inches of displacement / cubic inches per cubic foot = 350 / 1,728 = 0.2025.

This formula converts cubic inches of displacement (cid) into cubic feet of displacement (cfd). This conversion changes the standard measurement for engine size (cubic inches) into the standard measurement for airflow (cubic feet). The result of 0.2025cfd describes the volumetric change of all the cylinders as the pistons move through one complete engine cycle. Since all the engines that Chevrolet uses are four-stroke engines, one engine cycle is represented by two revolutions of the crankshaft.

You can derive the cubic feet of air inhaled by the engine per minute (cfm), by multiplying the cubic feet of displacement by the maximum engine rpm you plan on running. You will then divide this number by two, since each cylinder inhales air only on every other crankshaft rotation. For the purpose of discussing airflow, limit the rpm to 5250.

Cubic feet of airflow per minute = [(cubic feet of displacement)(rpm)]/ 2 = [(0.2025)(5250)]/ 2 = 532.

At 5250rpm, the maximum amount of air that can be pumped through the 350 is 532 cubic feet (cf). This figure is not realistic, however, because it assumes 100 percent volumetric efficiency. In other words, it assumes that each cylinder at this speed is capable of being completely filled with air up to atmospheric pressure each time the intake valve opens. As you work to improve the performance of the engine, you will be working to increase the volumetric efficiency ever closer to 100 percent. Keep in mind, however, that in spite of "bolt-on" horsepower and product claims promising a power increase, it would violate some of the basic laws of physics to gain more than 100 percent volumetric efficiency without pressurizing the combustion chamber with a supercharger or turbocharger. This limits the ability to increase performance simply by improving the intake system.

For a stock 350, it would be fair to assume an 80 percent volumetric efficiency. This means that the actual amount of air inhaled by the example engine will be lower than 532cfm:

[(Ideal cubic feet per minute)(80 percent)]= [(532)(0.8)]= 426 estimated actual.

124

Since the expected airflow though the engine is 426cfm stock, we must be able to flow at least this much through all the intake components just to avoid reducing power.

Let's look at how the Corvette air induction system can be improved at a relatively low expense. The source for a lot of the following is flow bench research done by Tuned Port Induction Specialties (TPIS) of Chaska, Minnesota.

Air Cleaner Cover

The air cleaner on most cars is capable of flowing more than the actual airflow of the engine on which it is installed, during normal operation. If the car is to be used under circumstances where maximum performance is required, such as for racing or trailer towing, then the air cleaner assembly can become a restriction to airflow and therefore performance.

In the old days, people would flip the air cleaner lid upside-down. Although the effects of doing this were largely psychological, it did bypass the snorkel tube of the air cleaner and greatly increase the potential airflow. The design of fuel injection air cleaners does not make inverting the lid practical or desirable.

According to TPIS airflow studies, with a stock lid and a stock air filter, the air cleaner assembly is capable of flowing 648cfm. This seems to be a comfortable amount above the 426cfm estimated for the 350 Tuned Port engine, and indeed, modification on a stock engine would not be necessary. In fact, the stock air cleaner has enough airflow capability to handle 6400rpm at 100 percent volumetric efficiency. What this means to the average motorist is that modifying the air cleaner will only become worthwhile when there is a desire suddenly to change the pressure in the intake manifold.

When the throttle plates are opened, the first thing that occurs is a sudden increase in the mass velocity of the air entering the intake manifold. Cruising at 2000rpm, the sample 350 is only swallowing about 141cfm. When the throttle is matted, the demand suddenly jumps to a potential 434cfm, and as the rpm climb, so will the demand. The more open and free flowing the intake system

is ahead of the throttle plates, the faster the air mass will build and therefore the faster the torque will build.

TPIS and others make air cleaner housings for the 5.7 and 5 Tuned Port applications, that boast an increased capability to flow more cubic feet of air per minute and therefore an increased ability to make a sudden change in mass airflow rate. A crude but effective method of accomplishing the same thing is to trim the air filter lid so that all of the air filter is exposed and the airflow through the filter is totally unrestricted by the cover itself.

Air Filter

The air filter itself can severely impede airflow. TPIS, Hypertech, and others offer high-flow air filters for the 5 and 5.7. These filters cost about $50, but installing one is an easy and legal way of improving power. Hypertech also offers performance air filters for the V-6 and four-cylinder applications.

How do these performance air filters differ from a standard air filter to the extent that power can be noticeably improved? Begin with the premise that a stock air filter is designed to be easy and inexpensive to produce. The consumer who is not concerned about performance is interested in reducing the cost of maintenance, and these "stock"-style air filters are designed to meet that need.

A performance air filter sacrifices low price for improved airflow. The high-performance air filter consists of multiple layers of cotton "gauze" that has been treated with a light oil. The oil attracts the dirt and dust particles, allowing the gauze element to have a more open weave and still have good filtering capability. Typically, the filtering element will be layered across a metal grid, which holds the gauze in an accordion shape. As this accordion shape weaves its way back and forth, the frontal area for the passing of air into the engine is greatly increased.

High-performance filters can result in a 25 percent increase in airflow through the filter. Keep in mind that a filter capable of flowing 500cfm will not increase performance significantly if it is mounted in an air cleaner assembly that will flow only 200cfm.

Some of the sales literature concerning performance air filters states that they are not legal for use on California pollution-controlled cars. The 1990 Bureau of Auto Repair (BAR) *Smog Check* manual states in appendix K that the air filter is a Category 1 component. Category 1 replacement parts are not considered to be "of concern" as long as none of the emission control devices themselves are tampered with during the installation. Check with the shop that does your smog check about its interpretation of this rule, or contact your local BAR field office for a ruling.

These $50 dollar filters are designed to be a lifetime replacement. They do need to be serviced on a regular basis. A special solvent or cleaner removes road oil and dirt. The literature that comes with your new air filter will recommend the correct cleaners to use. After the filter is cleaned, the oil barrier must be replaced. Using the wrong oil–penetrating oil and so forth–even though the oil looks right, can reduce the efficiency of the air filter to the point where you would be better off with a stock filter. Again, follow the recommendations of the filter manufacturer. Plan on cleaning the air filter every time you change the oil; this may be a little more frequently than is really required, but it can't hurt.

MAF Sensor

One of the worst offenders in the restriction of airflow is one of the most necessary devices in the entire fuel injection system: the mass airflow (MAF) sensor. The one used on the Tuned Port Corvette was designed and built by Bosch. TPIS studies indicate that it is capable of flowing only 529cfm stock. Screens are located at each end of the sensor. These screens were put there to protect the delicate heated wire that is suspended across the main channel of airflow. Flow bench testing indicates that an increase of 182cfm, giving the sensor a very respectable flow rate of 711cfm, can be obtained by simply removing these screens.

The MAF sensor also has cooling fins for the electronic module on the side of the sensor, which sit across the main channel of airflow. These fins represent a restriction to airflow of about 39cfm. Although this is not nearly the restriction created by the screens, these cooling fins represent a possible loss of about 10 percent of the total horsepower potential of the engine.

Not only do you have these fins to contend with, but you also have the hot wire sensing element sitting across the main channel of airflow, seriously reducing the potential airflow as a result simply of doing its job. A rough estimate of the restriction created by the sensing element is about 20 percent.

You cannot do anything about the sensing element, but you can do something about the cooling fins. Legend has it that electronic failures of the MAF sensor occurred during Death Valley testing. These cooling fins were then added to increase the ability of the MAF sensor electronics to give up heat in high-temperature environments. The legend probably involves a certain amount of truth, since the Bosch fuel-injected applications such as Volvo and Porsche sport no such large fins.

If you are not going to be operating the car in a hot weather environment, then grab your hacksaw and your 200mph tape, and get busy. Cover each end of the sensing element venturi (the circle within the circle) with the tape, and ensure that the interior of the sensor is free of grease, oil, moisture, or anything else that might attract and hold the metal sawdust that is going to result from the removal of the cooling fins.

If you are like me, you may have something ranging from quiet trepidation to out-and-out fear about taking a hacksaw to a $400-plus electronic component. For people like me, TPIS sells a stock unit to replace the one I screw up, or one that is already modified, for less than dealer list. If you prefer, and can do without your car for a few days, your MAF sensor can be professionally modified for less than $150.

The Port Fuel Injection (PFI) applications use the Delco MAF sensor. The design of this unit does not lend itself to modification.

Oddly, Oldsmobile, on its 3800-series engines, uses a Japanese-designed MAF sensor. In this Hitachi version, the hot wire sensing element is located in a bypass tube outside the main channel of airflow. This technology eliminates not only the airflow restriction created by the cooling fins, but also the restriction of the sensing element itself–leaving, in effect, a big hollow tube for the air to pass through. Unfortunately for the performance enthusiast, this MAF sensor is not interchangeable with the Corvette MAF sensor–that is, unless you possess exceptional free time and a degree in electronics.

Throttle Body Assembly

The throttle body assembly holds possibly the most important potential for "bolt-on" improvement short of that provided by the intake manifold itself. Again, remember that Chevrolet spent much time and effort creating the Tuned Port system to be a good performer right off the showroom floor. As a result, any improvement in performance afforded by any of the techniques discussed here, including replacement of the throttle body, may be less likely to show up in the seat of the pants than on the quarter-mile. Even quarter-mile results might be disappointing to all but the most die-hard racer.

Several companies manufacture high-performance throttle assemblies, but let's begin our look at throttle body modifications by examining an inexpensive and clever approach. TPIS and Hypertech sell an airflow-directing device that helps to guide the incoming air through the throttle bore and into the intake manifold. Called an airfoil, this unit simply bolts onto the throttle assembly and provides an additional 8hp to 10hp. Documentation on the 350 'Vette engine shows an increase of up to 13 additional pounds-feet of torque at 4500rpm. Fine-tuning the flow of air through the throttle valve assembly with a device such as the airfoil increases the number of cubic feet flowed per minute in a flow bench test by 17.

Big-bore kits are available from Air Sensors and others. These kits consist of a complete throttle body assembly, which replaces the stock assembly. The Air Sensors version features a single large throttle plate replacing the pair of small throttle plates in the stock unit.

Holley markets a wide range of throttle body injection (TBI) replacement units. These fall into two general categories: stock emission-street legal performance and nonemission-legal street competition.

The emission-legal units are available in a 300cfm throttle body assembly for the 2- and 2.5-liter applications and in a 400cfm two-barrel version for the 2.8-liter V-6 TBI truck engines. These throttle bodies are direct-replacement bolt-on assemblies that come complete with the throttle position sensor (TPS) and the idle air control (IAC). Once they are installed, all that has to be done is to connect the vehicle wiring harness to the TPS, the IAC, and the injector; adjust the minimum air and the TPS closed-throttle voltage; and then drive the car away. These throttle body assemblies are for use on model years 1982 to 1986. Applications later than 1986 use a different throttle body assembly, which is not interchangeable with these units.

The nonemission-legal TBI units come with their own computer and wiring harnesses. These are covered in the chapter on aftermarket fuel injection.

When the installation of the airfoil, the big-bore kit, or the replacement TBI is complete, it may be necessary to adjust the minimum idle speed. Unless the installation instructions or the data supplied with other components that have been added to the engine specify otherwise, adjust the minimum idle speed to the specifications found in the minimum air adjustment charts.

Intake Manifolds

The stock tuned manifold is designed for peak performance; however, production tolerances are not such that perfection is always achieved. The Tuned Port manifold consists of a large central plenum box connected to the intake manifold base by individual tubes called runners. Some improvement in the airflow rate can be achieved by matching the sizes and alignment of the plenum, the runners, and the manifold base. Matching the alignment of the plenums can be achieved by applying a light film of Prussian blue to each end of the runner, installing and torquing down the runner, and then removing the runner and inspecting the Prussian blue contact point, which will show where the runners are misaligned. A more careful inspection will reveal where the runners are undersize or oversize compared with either the intake or the central plenum. A die grinder and an ample supply of patience will enlarge the undersize orifices to match the larger ones. Do not get carried away; the size and shape of the plenum, the runners, and the manifold are basically correct.

After painstaking hours of work, you will have gained only about 2hp or 3hp. You might say that it is hard to improve on what is basically a good design.

High-performance manifolds are available for the 5- and 5.7-liter engines from Edelbrock, TPIS, Air Sensors, and others. These manifolds offer a rethinking of the basic Chevrolet design and offer larger porting, improved runner matching, and improved runner flow angles. However, overall improvement in performance may be disappointing unless these manifolds are installed as a part of a complete performance upgrade.

For the TBI applications, performance improvements from intake manifold modifications may be more noticeable. The *General Motors Performance Parts Catalog* offers performance intake manifolds only for use with a two-barrel or four-barrel carburetor. Holley sells a performance manifold for the 2.5-liter TBI engines.

Summary

Back in the 1960s, massive and very noticeable improvements in performance could be effected through relatively minor and often not very expensive modifications. In those days, the large brute engines from Chevrolet had tremendous unlocked potential. The 396 had a flow rate potential of 458cfm, although factory equipped with about a 650cfm carburetor (depending on the year and exact application, this varied). Installation of a carburetor with a greater flow rate would instantly unlock horsepower and torque hidden by the inability of the stock carburetor to fill the manifold with air quickly enough when the throttle was matted.

The cars of the 1990s have evolved from the 1960s through a period in the 1970s where anything and everything was done to achieve an acceptable level of performance while maintaining a legal emission level. During the late 1970s and early 1980s, the manufacturers began a quiet mutual challenge back toward performance. This time, they did not have the luxury of simply bolting on a larger carburetor and dumping gallons of gas through the engine. As a result, the intake systems of the 1990s are highly refined when they roll off the assembly line. A lot of work on the manifold without considering other engine, computer, and sensor modifications may yield very disappointing results. Again, it's hard to improve on a good design.

Camshaft

The basic function of the camshaft is to open the intake valve as quickly, as smoothly, and as far as possible. The cam then leaves the valve open as long as possible to allow atmospheric pressure to push air and fuel into the combustion chamber. The camshaft must then begin—along with the assistance of the valve spring—to allow the intake valve to close in enough time for the combustion chamber to be sealed as the piston begins to move up on the compression stroke. Actually, the intake valve remains open for a short time as the piston begins to move upward on the compression stroke. This allows the velocity of the air traveling through the intake system to continue to cram air into the cylinder even as the piston begins to move upward. This effect is even more pronounced on engines equipped with a high-rise intake manifold such as on the tuned port fuel-injected (TPFI) applications. This is why increasing the airflow potential beyond the capability of the engine's volumetric displacement will result in improved performance. Less restriction in the intake system will increase the cylinder charging capability.

The camshaft must also open the exhaust valve as far, as fast, and as smoothly as possible. The opening of the exhaust valve begins as the piston nears bottom dead center on the crank power stroke. This ensures that the exhaust valve will be completely open when the piston begins to move upward on the exhaust stroke. The camshaft begins to close the exhaust valve near top dead center; however, the exhaust valve remains open for a short time, and the piston begins its downward travel. This does two things: (1) It takes advantage of the velocity of the exhaust gases exiting the combustion chamber to accelerate the incoming air-fuel charge. This increases the volumetric efficiency of the engine. (2) As the incoming charge is accelerated, it slows some of the outgoing exhaust gases, causing them to be left in the combustion chamber. From the perspective of performance, this is neither desirable nor efficient; however, it does produce an exhaust gas recirculation (EGR) effect, causing the combustion temperature to be lower and reducing the output of oxides of nitrogen.

Like the intake manifold, the TPFI camshaft was designed by Chevrolet with performance in mind. Multipoint injection minimizes the emission considerations in camshaft design, limiting the concerns to performance and driving comfort. As a result, a significant performance improvement will come at a cost of low-speed, low-load driveability.

Several companies offer off-the-shelf camshafts for performance and economy. For obvious reasons, these performance cams are pretty much restricted to the bigger engines—the 5.7, the 5, the 4.3, and the 60-degree V-6s. Designing a performance cam that will effectively increase torque and horsepower for an electronic fuel-injected engine is not a job for mere mortals. Changes in lift, duration, centerline, and timing that have been infallible in the past can cause a loss of power, underfueling, and overfueling in the 1990s. The reason is that changing the camshaft will change the intake manifold vacuum (pressure) and the airflow rates. These changes will affect the readings of the manifold absolute pressure (MAP) and MAF sensors. Changes in the MAP or MAF sensor readings at a given rpm or engine load may cause undesired changes in the air-fuel ratio and ignition timing.

Crane Cams and others have lines of camshafts that have been designed specifically for use with electronic fuel injection. Because of the research and development that has gone into these cams, it is unlikely that a custom-ground camshaft, unless it is ground by the best of the best, would work as well. Although a "local Joe, super racer" custom-ground camshaft may provide for a greater increase in performance, its added expense is not really justified for the typical performance enthusiast.

Several grinds are available from different camshaft manufacturers. A typical and effective grind for the 5.7 Corvette might be as follows:

Exhaust duration   262 Degrees
              (hydraulic flat tappet)
Intake duration   266 Degrees
              (hydraulic flat tappet)
Lift   451in
Intake centerline   104

This grind can provide an increase in horsepower of 6 at 2000rpm and up to 43 at 4500rpm, while maintaining very acceptable idle quality.

If you decide to perform a camshaft transplant, be sure to check with your supplier about how it will affect the street legality of your car. At the very least, consider that the increased valve overlap of a performance camshaft will tend to increase hydrocarbon emission at idle; since many states test emissions only at idle, installation may lead to emission test failure. The California BAR considers camshaft replacements–other than with a stock grind–to be unacceptable modifications.

Cylinder Heads

The stock 350 cylinder head may well be the single biggest candidate for performance improvement. The basic design of the 5.7-liter head dates back to the 1960s, and although improvements and upgrades have been made along the way, it still remains a rather old piece of technology when compared with the cylinder head of a Quad 4 or late-model Japanese engine.

To improve the cylinder head of the 5.7 Tuned Port engine, you have two good ways to go. The first option is to purchase an improved head. Many aftermarket companies make performance cylinder heads ready to be bolted on and driven away. These heads sell for $500 to $1,000 but can provide the most noticeable change in performance of anything yet discussed. In most jurisdictions, these cylinder heads meet emission requirements with ease.

The second option is to modify the existing cylinder heads. You may prefer to have a machinist do this, for it requires a minimum of manual skill but a maximum of knowing what to do. Let's take a look at some of the basics.

Most people who get involved in a "port-and-polish" job do not have a good understanding of flow dynamics. The result is that many performance modifiers end up paying a lot of money or spending a lot of time to accomplish very little or even to decrease performance. The typical port-and-polish job consists of enlarging the intake and exhaust ports of the cylinder head and then polishing the enlarged surface to a high gloss. Although this may look impressive, the original ports are basically large enough for the camshaft applications found in common street use, and often the high-gloss shine reduces turbulence, which can actually decrease the ability of the fuel to remain atomized in the air-fuel charge and therefore reduce performance. By the same token, for most "street" applications, big valves can have an adverse effect on airflow in and out of the combustion chamber.

The area that needs the most work or concentration is the valve pocket. This is the area just in front of the valve, in the cylinder head. The valve guide boss can restrict airflow; on the stock 350 head, this boss is much larger than it needs to be. Additionally, casting ridges can be removed. Flatten and enlarge the radius where the air passage turns down toward the valve.

Shop around a little for a qualified performance machinist if you decide not to do the work yourself. As you do, remember that the best may not always have the biggest reputation, and the person your buddy says is the best in town may not be. If performance is really your goal, spend a couple of days at the local drag strip or circle track, and ask who has the most consistently fast car. Some of the fastest cars may not be consistent performers; inconsistency may be a clue that the performance comes from "bells and whistles" rather than quality work. Once you have identified the consistent performers, find out who does their machine work; this is the person you want working for you.

Just pick up a copy of a popular hot rodding magazine, and you will be bombarded with advertisements offering custom-built small-block Chevy cylinder heads. These heads are just as valid for use on a TPFI engine as they are for use on a carbureted engine. Most of these heads are well engineered and professionally done, making them well worth the money.

Valve Action

Remember that we are talking about street performance, and although some tweaking can be done to items such as cylinder heads, camshafts, and intake components, modifications to other performance parts do not justify their expense on street applications by noticeably improving torque or horsepower. One area of questionable alterations is in the valvetrain. Although valvetrain modifications can provide an all-out race car with a 0.1-second improvement in the quarter-mile, this improvement would only be seen between the ears on a street rod.

Valvetrain modifications include ratioed rocker arms, high-tech pushrods, performance lifters, and heavy-duty valve springs. Engine rebuilders disagree on the necessity of replacing these components when the camshaft is replaced. When a new piece of metal rubs with a force of up to 300,000psi against another piece of metal, with only a thin film of oil in between, and we are going to expect it to do this for 100,000 to 150,000 miles, I would prefer that the piece of metal the new piece is rubbing against also be new.

The basic point of all this is that if you decide to replace the camshaft, then spending a few extra bucks on high-performance valvetrain parts that should be replaced anyway makes good sense; otherwise, put your money into areas where you can get more bang for the buck.

Exhaust

Looking back again to the 1960s, we saw a fascination among street enthusiasts, with bigger pipes and "freer" exhaust flow. The stock exhaust systems of the 1990s are a far cry from the stock systems of the 1960s. In spite of this, there is still room for improvement.

This improvement can begin with a set of headers bought over the counter, with threads and fittings for the oxygen sensor and the air pump devices. Catalytic converters with high flow rates are also available. Be sure to check with local automotive emission officials concerning the legality of any exhaust modifications you are planning.

Past those made to the catalytic converter, few modifications are illegal in any state. Mufflers, the connector, and exhaust pipes are all fair game for the performance enthusiast. The only restrictions are related to noise.

Mufflers

Exhaust systems and their technology have come a long way since the muscle car days of the 1960s. The high-performance mufflers of the 1990s exceed the flow potential of even open headers.

Two things travel down the piping from the exhaust manifold: these are exhaust gases and sonic vibrations, or frequencies. The movement of the frequencies through the exhaust system tends to pull the exhaust gases along in much the same way that ocean waves pull a surfer to shore. The effect of the exhaust gases being pulled through the exhaust system helps to scavenge the cylinder, improving the breathing of the engine.

Back in the 1960s, several companies marketed the turbo muffler. This muffler was developed by Chevrolet to be used on the Corvair Turbo applications. It consisted of a hollow tube with fiberglass pressed against the sides of the tube to deaden sound. The problem with this is that as the sound frequencies enter the muffler, they are killed by the fiberglass packing, negating the "surfer" effect.

The high-tech 1990s performance mufflers are able to reduce sound without eliminating the surfer effect. Imagine, for a moment, that you are setting up a stereo in your living room. The only place you can find to put one of the speakers is in the center of the north wall. The only place you can find to put the other speaker is directly opposite the first, on the south wall. The two speakers are facing each other squarely. The only place you can find to put your chair is exactly halfway between the two speakers. When the speakers are producing exactly the same sound, the frequencies being emitted from the speakers will collide and cancel one another, creating a dead zone. Modern high-performance mufflers take advantage of this phenomenon. As the frequencies and exhaust gases enter the muffler, they are divided and sent in two different directions, only to be brought back together as they

pass though the muffler. When they are brought back together, the identical frequencies that were split earlier collide and cancel each other like the frequencies from the two speakers described earlier. The end result is less sound without a loss of the surfer action.

Mufflers such as those described here are being used on everything from road racers to sprint cars.

H-pipe Installation

Most exhaust systems have an area where the exhaust sound frequencies we have been discussing tend to build up and eddy the exhaust gases. To reduce this build-up on dual exhaust systems, it helps to install an H-pipe between the two sides of the exhaust.

Installing an H-pipe in the wrong place does more harm than not installing one at all. To determine where an H-pipe is needed on your custom dual-pipe exhaust system, paint the area between the catalytic converters and the mufflers with black lacquer. Run the engine at 3200rpm for several minutes. Now, inspect the painted area. Where the lacquer has begun to burn, or has burned the worst, is where the H-pipe needs to be installed. Install the pipe between the indicated hot-spots in the two sides of the exhaust.

Legalities of Engine Modifications

17

Unlike most scientific regimens, the law has subtle twists, turns, and traps. This chapter is not intended as legal advice; it is intended to point out some of the issues involved in the high-performance modification of late-model cars. The bulk of the information that follows came from California's BAR and the California Air Research Board (ARB). The laws on the books in many states are very similar to those of California. California has the longest record of stringent enforcement, which is why I used its information.

Three categories of replacement parts are recognized by the ARB.

Category 1

Category 1 items are not considered by the BAR or the ARB to be of any concern as long as the required emission controls are not tampered with. Category 1 items include

PCV air bleeds
Air cleaner modifications
Air conditioner cutout systems
Antitheft systems
Blowby oil separators and filters
Electronic ignition systems retrofitted to vehicles originally fitted with point-condenser systems, as long as the original advance controls are maintained
Engine shutoff systems
Ignition bridges and coil modifications
Throttle lockout systems
Intercoolers for an original equipment of manufacturer (OEM) turbocharger
Undercarburetor screens
Vapor, steam, or water injectors

Category 2

Category 2 addresses allowable replacement parts.
Headers on cars that have no catalytic converter
Heat stoves for allowed headers
Intake manifolds for non-EGR vehicles, only if they allow for the installation and proper functioning of the OEM emission controls
Approved aftermarket catalytic converters
Carburetors marketed as "emission replacement"
Replacement fuel fill-pipe restrictors
Replacement gas caps

You can see from this list that for catalytic converter-equipped fuel-injected cars, no performance replacements are allowable without type approval from the ARB. The cars of the 1990s are EPA inspected as an integrated system; disturbing even the minutest portion of the emission control package would constitute a violation.

Category 3

Category 3 parts must have verification of acceptability. If you are replacing a part in Category 3, ask for and retain a copy of the verification of acceptability for that product; it may prove handy later on, even if you live in an area that is not currently strictly controlled. Category 3 modifications include
Carburetor conversions
Carburetors that replace OEM fuel injection
EGR system modifications
Replacement progammable read-only memories (computer chips)
Electronic ignition enhancements for computerized vehicles
Exhaust headers for catalytic converter-equipped vehicles
Fuel injection systems that replace OEM carburetors
Superchargers
Turbochargers

Engine Specifications

Note: Items marked "NA" means not applicable to this application or specification not available from manufacturer. Check the text in this book relating to that specification for guidelines.

1980—1984 American Motors (AMC) B151 Four-cylinder

Displacement	151ci
Volume	NA
Main journals	2.2988in
Main journal oil clearance	0.0005—0.0022in
Crankshaft end play	0.0035—0.0085in
Thrust journal length	5in
Rod journal diameter	2.000in
Rod oil clearance	0.0005—0.0026in
Rod side clearance	0.017in
Intake valve seat angle	46 degrees (deg)
Exhaust valve seat angle	46deg
Intake face angle	45deg
Exhaust face angle	45deg
Seat width	NA
Spring pressure	NA
Intake stem—to—guide clearance	0.0010—0.0027in
Exhaust stem—to—guide clearance	0.0010—0.0027in
Intake stem diameter	0.3423in
Exhaust stem diameter	0.3423in
Piston clearance	0.0025—0.0033in
Top compression (comp.) ring gap	0.010—0.022in
Bottom compression (comp.) ring gap	0.010—0.028in
Oil ring gap	0.015—0.055in
Top compression (comp.) side clearance	0.0030in
Bottom compression (comp.) side clearance	0.0030in
Oil side clearance	0.0000in

1977—1979 AMC G121 Four-cylinder

Displacement	121ci
Volume	NA
Main journals	2.5177—2.5185in
Main journal oil clearance	0.0010—0.0030in
Crankshaft end play	0.0040—0.0080in
Thrust journal length	3in
Rod journal diameter	1.8880—1.8890in
Rod oil clearance	0.0010—0.0020in
Rod side clearance	0.002—0.012in
Intake valve seat angle	45deg 45 minutes (min)
Exhaust valve seat angle	45deg min
Intake face angle	45deg 20min
Exhaust face angle	45deg 20min
Seat width	NA
Spring pressure	NA
Intake stem to guide clearance	0.0012—0.0026in
Exhaust stem to guide clearance	0.0015—0.0030in
Intake stem diameter	0.3529in
Exhaust stem diameter	0.3525in
Piston clearance	0.0009—0.0015in
Top comp. ring gap	0.010—0.020in
Bottom comp. ring gap	0.010—0.020in
Oil ring gap	0.010—0.016in
Top comp. side clearance	0.0012—0.0024in
Bottom comp. side clearance	0.0012—0.0024in
Oil side clearance	0.0012—0.0024in

1981—1984 AMC C258 Six-cylinder

Displacement	258ci
Volume	NA
Main journals	2.4986—2.5001in
Main journal oil clearance	0.0010—0.0030in
Crankshaft end play	0.0015—0.0065in
Thrust journal length	3in
Rod journal diameter	2.0934—2.0955in
Rod oil clearance	0.0010—0.0030in
Rod side clearance	0.005—0.014in
Intake valve seat angle	44deg 30min
Exhaust valve seat angle	44deg 30min
Intake face angle	44deg
Exhaust face angle	44deg
Seat width	NA
Spring pressure	NA
Intake stem to guide clearance	0.0010—0.0030in
Exhaust stem to guide clearance	0.0010—0.0030in
Intake stem diameter	0.3720in
Exhaust stem diameter	0.3720in
Piston clearance	0.0009—0.0017in
Top comp. ring gap	0.010—0.020in
Bottom comp. ring gap	0.010—0.020in
Oil ring gap	0.010—0.025in
Top comp. side clearance	0.0017—0.0032in
Bottom comp. side clearance	0.0017—0.0032in
Oil side clearance	0.0010—0.0080in

1980 AMC C258 Six-cylinder

Displacement	258ci
Volume	NA
Main journals	2.4986—2.5001in
Main journal oil clearance	0.0010—0.0030in
Crankshaft end play	0.0015—0.0065in
Thrust journal length	3in
Rod journal diameter	2.0934—2.0955in
Rod oil clearance	0.0010—0.0030in
Rod side clearance	0.005—0.014in
Intake valve seat angle	44deg 30min
Exhaust valve seat angle	44deg 30min
Intake face angle	44deg
Exhaust face angle	44deg
Seat width	NA
Spring pressure	NA
Intake stem to guide clearance	0.0010—0.0030in
Exhaust stem to guide clearance	0.0010—0.0030in
Intake stem diameter	0.3720in
Exhaust stem diameter	0.3720in
Piston clearance	0.0009—0.0017in
Top comp. ring gap	0.010—0.020in
Bottom comp. ring gap	0.010—0.020in
Oil ring gap	0.010—0.025in
Top comp. side clearance	0.0015—0.0030in
Bottom comp. side clearance	0.0015—0.0030in
Oil side clearance	0.0011—0.0080in

1979 AMC E232, A258, and C258 Six-cylinder

Displacement	232, 258ci
Volume	NA
Main journals	2.4986—2.5001in
Main journal oil clearance	0.0003—0.0024in
Crankshaft end play	0.0020—0.0070in
Thrust journal length	3in
Rod journal diameter	2.0934—2.0955in
Rod oil clearance	0.0010—0.0020in
Rod side clearance	0.005—0.014in
Intake valve seat angle	44deg 45min
Exhaust valve seat angle	44deg 45min
Intake face angle	44deg
Exhaust face angle	44deg
Seat width	NA
Spring pressure	NA
Intake stem to guide clearance	0.0010—0.0030in
Exhaust stem to guide clearance	0.0010—0.0027in
Intake stem diameter	0.3520in
Exhaust stem diameter	0.3722in
Piston clearance	0.0009—0.0017in
Top comp. ring gap	0.010—0.020in
Bottom comp. ring gap	0.010—0.020in

1978 AMC E232, A258, and C258 Six-cylinder

Displacement	232, 258ci
Volume	NA
Main journals	2.4986—2.5001in
Main journal oil clearance	0.0003—0.0004in
Crankshaft end play	0.0020—0.0070in
Thrust journal length	3in
Rod journal diameter	2.0934—2.0955in
Rod oil clearance	0.0010—0.0020in
Rod side clearance	0.005—0.014in
Intake valve seat angle	44deg 30min
Exhaust valve seat angle	44deg 30min
Intake face angle	44deg
Exhaust face angle	44deg
Seat width	NA
Spring pressure	NA
Intake stem to guide clearance	0.0010—0.0030in
Exhaust stem to guide clearance	0.0010—0.0020in
Intake stem diameter	0.3720in
Exhaust stem diameter	0.3722in
Piston clearance	0.0009—0.0017in
Top comp. ring gap	0.010—0.020in
Bottom comp. ring gap	0.010—0.020in
Oil ring gap	0.010—0.025in
Top comp. side clearance	0.0015—0.0030in
Bottom comp. side clearance	0.0015—0.0030in
Oil side clearance	0.0011—0.0080in

1977 AMC E232, A258, and C258 Six-cylinder

Displacement	232, 258ci
Volume	NA
Main journals	2.4986—2.5001in
Main journal oil clearance	0.0003—0.0004in
Crankshaft end play	0.0020—0.0070in
Thrust journal length	3in
Rod journal diameter	2.0934—2.0955in
Rod oil clearance	0.0010—0.0020in
Rod side clearance	0.005—0.014in
Intake valve seat angle	44deg 30min
Exhaust valve seat angle	44deg 30min
Intake face angle	44deg
Exhaust face angle	44deg
Seat width	NA
Spring pressure	NA
Intake stem to guide clearance	0.0010—0.0030in
Exhaust stem to guide clearance	0.0010—0.0017in
Intake stem diameter	0.3720in
Exhaust stem diameter	0.3722in
Piston clearance	0.0009—0.0017in
Top comp. ring gap	0.010—0.020in
Bottom comp. ring gap	0.010—0.020in
Oil ring gap	0.010—0.025in
Top comp. side clearance	0.0015—0.0030in
Bottom comp. side clearance	0.0015—0.0030in
Oil side clearance	0.0011—0.0080in

1977—1979 AMC H304 Eight-cylinder

Displacement	304ci
Volume	NA
Main journals	2.7474—2.7489; 2.7464—2.7479in (no. 5)
Main journal oil clearance	0.0010—0.0030in
Crankshaft end play	0.0030—0.0080in

Thrust journal length	3in
Rod journal diameter	2.0934—2.0955in
Rod oil clearance	0.0010—0.0030in
Rod side clearance	0.006—0.018in
Intake valve seat angle	44deg 30min
Exhaust valve seat angle	44deg 30min
Intake face angle	44deg
Exhaust face angle	44deg
Seat width	NA
Spring pressure	NA
Intake stem to guide clearance	0.0010—0.0030in
Exhaust stem to guide clearance	0.0010—0.0027in
Intake stem diameter	0.3720in
Exhaust stem diameter	0.3722in
Piston clearance	0.0010—0.0018in
Top comp. ring gap	0.010—0.020in
Bottom comp. ring gap	0.010—0.020in
Oil ring gap	0.010—0.025in
Top comp. side clearance	0.0015—0.0035in
Bottom comp. side clearance	0.0015—0.0030in
Oil side clearance	0.0011—0.0080in

1977—1978 AMC N360 Eight-cylinder

Displacement	360ci
Volume	NA
Main journals	2.7474—2.7489; 2.7464—2.7479in (no. 5)
Main journal oil clearance	0.0010—0.0030in
Crankshaft end play	0.0030—0.0080in
Thrust journal length	3in
Rod journal diameter	2.0934—2.0955in
Rod oil clearance	0.0010—0.0030in
Rod side clearance	0.006—0.018in
Intake valve seat angle	44deg 30min
Exhaust valve seat angle	44deg 30min
Intake face angle	44deg
Exhaust face angle	44deg
Seat width	NA
Spring pressure	NA
Intake stem to guide clearance	0.0010—0.0030in
Exhaust stem to guide clearance	0.0010—0.0027in
Intake stem diameter	0.3720in
Exhaust stem diameter	0.3722in
Piston clearance	0.0012—0.0020; 0.0016—0.0024in (police)
Top comp. ring gap	0.010—0.020in
Bottom comp. ring gap	0.010—0.020in
Oil ring gap	0.015—0.045in
Top comp. side clearance	0.0015—0.0030in
Bottom comp. side clearance	0.0015—0.00335in
Oil side clearance	0.0000—0.0070in

1983—1984 Audi 4000 Turbo D

Displacement	97ci
Volume	1.588
Main journals	1.8807in
Main journal oil clearance	0.001—0.003in
Crankshaft end play	0.003—0.007in
Thrust journal length	3in
Rod journal diameter	2.1248in
Rod oil clearance	0.0011—0.0034in
Rod side clearance	0.14in
Intake valve seat angle	45deg
Exhaust valve seat angle	45deg
Intake face angle	45deg
Exhaust face angle	45deg
Seat width	NA
Spring pressure	NA
Intake stem to guide clearance	0.039in
Exhaust stem to guide clearance	0.051in
Intake stem diameter	0.3140in
Exhaust stem diameter	0.3130in
Piston clearance	0.0011in
Top comp. ring gap	0.012—0.020in
Bottom comp. ring gap	0.012—0.020in
Oil ring gap	0.010—0.016in
Top comp. side clearance	0.002—0.004in
Bottom comp. side clearance	0.002—0.003in
Oil side clearance	0.001—0.002in

1982—1984 Audi 5000

Displacement	130.8ci
Volume	2.144
Main journals	1.8098in
Main journal oil clearance	0.0006—0.0030in
Crankshaft end play	0.003—0.007in
Thrust journal length	4in
Rod journal diameter	2.2822in
Rod oil clearance	0.0006—0.0020in
Rod side clearance	0.016in
Intake valve seat angle	45deg
Exhaust valve seat angle	45deg
Intake face angle	45deg
Exhaust face angle	45deg
Seat width	NA
Spring pressure	NA
Intake stem to guide clearance	0.039in
Exhaust stem to guide clearance	0.051in
Intake stem diameter	0.3140in
Exhaust stem diameter	0.3130in
Piston clearance	0.0011in
Top comp. ring gap	0.010—0.020in
Bottom comp. ring gap	0.010—0.020in
Oil ring gap	0.010—0.020in
Top comp. side clearance	0.0008—0.0030in
Bottom comp. side clearance	0.0008—0.0030in
Oil side clearance	0.0008—0.0030in

1982—1984 Audi 5000 Turbo D

Displacement	121ci
Volume	1.986
Main journals	1.9107in
Main journal oil clearance	0.0006—0.0030in
Crankshaft end play	0.003—0.007in
Thrust journal length	4in
Rod journal diameter	2.3187in
Rod oil clearance	0.0024—0.0050in
Rod side clearance	0.015in
Intake valve seat angle	45deg
Exhaust valve seat angle	45deg
Intake face angle	45deg
Exhaust face angle	45deg
Seat width	NA
Spring pressure	NA
Intake stem to guide clearance	0.039in
Exhaust stem to guide clearance	0.051in
Intake stem diameter	0.3140in
Exhaust stem diameter	0.3130in
Piston clearance	0.0011in
Top comp. ring gap	0.012—0.020in
Bottom comp. ring gap	0.012—0.020in
Oil ring gap	0.010—0.016in
Top comp. side clearance	0.0020—0.0035in
Bottom comp. side clearance	0.002—0.003in
Oil side clearance	0.001—0.002in

1982—1984 Audi Coupe 4000 5c

Displacement	130.8ci
Volume	2.144
Main journals	1.8098in
Main journal oil clearance	0.0006—0.0030in
Crankshaft end play	0.003—0.007in
Thrust journal length	4in
Rod journal diameter	2.2822in
Rod oil clearance	0.0006—0.0020in
Rod side clearance	0.016in
Intake valve seat angle	45deg
Exhaust valve seat angle	45deg
Intake face angle	45deg
Exhaust face angle	45deg
Seat width	NA
Spring pressure	NA
Intake stem to guide clearance	0.039in
Exhaust stem to guide clearance	0.051in
Intake stem diameter	0.3140in
Exhaust stem diameter	0.3130in
Piston clearance	0.0011in
Top comp. ring gap	0.010—0.020in
Bottom comp. ring gap	0.010—0.020in
Oil ring gap	0.010—0.020in
Top comp. side clearance	0.0008—0.0030in

Bottom comp. side clearance	0.0008—0.0030in
Oil side clearance	0.0008—0.0030in

1982—1984 Audi Quattro

Displacement	130.8ci
Volume	2.144
Main journals	1.8098in
Main journal oil clearance	0.0006—0.0030in
Crankshaft end play	0.003—0.007in
Thrust journal length	4in
Rod journal diameter	2.2822in
Rod oil clearance	0.0006—0.0020in
Rod side clearance	0.016in
Intake valve seat angle	45deg
Exhaust valve seat angle	45deg
Intake face angle	45deg
Exhaust face angle	45deg
Seat width	NA
Spring pressure	NA
Intake stem to guide clearance	0.039in
Exhaust stem to guide clearance	0.051in
Intake stem diameter	0.3140in
Exhaust stem diameter	0.03130in
Piston clearance	0.0011in
Top comp. ring gap	0.010—0.020in
Bottom comp. ring gap	0.010—0.020in
Oil ring gap	0.010—0.020in
Top comp. side clearance	0.0008—0.0030in
Bottom comp. side clearance	0.0008—0.0030in
Oil side clearance	0.0008—0.0030in

1982—1984 Audi Turbo

Displacement	130.8ci
Volume	2.144
Main journals	1.8098in
Main journal oil clearance	0.0006—0.0030in
Crankshaft end play	0.003—0.007in
Thrust journal length	4in
Rod journal diameter	2.2822in
Rod oil clearance	0.0006—0.0030in
Rod side clearance	0.016in
Intake valve seat angle	45deg
Exhaust valve seat angle	45deg
Intake face angle	45deg
Exhaust face angle	45deg
Seat width	NA
Spring pressure	NA
Intake stem to guide clearance	0.039in
Exhaust stem to guide clearance	0.051in
Intake stem diameter	0.3140in
Exhaust stem diameter	0.03130in
Piston clearance	0.0011in
Top comp. ring gap	0.010—0.020in
Bottom comp. ring gap	0.010—0.020in
Oil ring gap	0.010—0.020in
Top comp. side clearance	0.0008—0.0030in
Bottom comp. side clearance	0.0008—0.0030in
Oil side clearance	0.0008—0.0030in

1982—1983 Audi 4000 Diesel

Displacement	97ci
Volume	1.588
Main journals	1.8807in
Main journal oil clearance	0.001—0.003in
Crankshaft end play	0.003—0.007in
Thrust journal length	3in
Rod journal diameter	2.1248in
Rod oil clearance	0.0011—0.0034in
Rod side clearance	0.014in
Intake valve seat angle	45deg
Exhaust valve seat angle	45deg
Intake face angle	45deg
Exhaust face angle	45deg
Seat width	NA
Spring pressure	NA
Intake stem to guide clearance	0.039in
Exhaust stem to guide clearance	0.051in
Intake stem diameter	0.3140in
Exhaust stem diameter	0.3130in
Piston clearance	0.0011in
Top comp. ring gap	0.012—0.020in
Bottom comp. ring gap	0.012—0.020in

Oil ring gap 0.010—0.016in
Top comp. side clearance 0.002—0.004in
Bottom comp. side clearance 0.002—0.003in
Oil side clearance 0.001—0.002in

1981—1984 Audi 4000

Displacement 97ci
Volume 1.588
Main journals 1.8098in
Main journal oil clearance 0.001—0.003in
Crankshaft end play 0.003—0.007in
Thrust journal length 3in
Rod journal diameter 2.1247in
Rod oil clearance 0.0011—0.0034in
Rod side clearance 0.015in
Intake valve seat angle 45deg
Exhaust valve seat angle 45deg
Intake face angle 45deg
Exhaust face angle 45deg
Seat width NA
Spring pressure NA
Intake stem to guide clearance 0.039in
Exhaust stem to guide clearance 0.051in
Intake stem diameter 0.3140in
Exhaust stem diameter 0.3130in
Piston clearance 0.0011in
Top comp. ring gap 0.012—0.018in
Bottom comp. ring gap 0.012—0.018in
Oil ring gap 0.012—0.018in
Top comp. side clearance 0.0008—0.0020in
Bottom comp. side clearance 0.0008—0.0020in
Oil side clearance 0.0008—0.0020in

1980—1981 Audi Coupe 4000 5c

Displacement 130.8ci
Volume 2.144
Main journals 1.8110in
Main journal oil clearance 0.0006—0.0030in
Crankshaft end play 0.003—0.007in
Thrust journal length 4in
Rod journal diameter 2.2834in
Rod oil clearance 0.0006—0.0020in
Rod side clearance 0.016in
Intake valve seat angle 45deg
Exhaust valve seat angle 45deg
Intake face angle 45deg
Exhaust face angle 45deg
Seat width NA
Spring pressure NA
Intake stem to guide clearance 0.039in
Exhaust stem to guide clearance 0.051in
Intake stem diameter 0.3140in
Exhaust stem diameter 0.3130in
Piston clearance 0.0011in
Top comp. ring gap 0.010—0.020in
Bottom comp. ring gap 0.010—0.020in
Oil ring gap 0.010—0.020in
Top comp. side clearance 0.0008—0.0030in
Bottom comp. side clearance 0.0008—0.0030in
Oil side clearance 0.0008—0.0030in

1980—1981 Audi Turbo

Displacement 130.8ci
Volume 2.144
Main journals 1.8110in
Main journal oil clearance 0.0006—0.0030in
Crankshaft end play 0.003—0.007in
Thrust journal length 4in
Rod journal diameter 2.2834in
Rod oil clearance 0.0006—0.0020in
Rod side clearance 0.016in
Intake valve seat angle 45deg
Exhaust valve seat angle 45deg
Intake face angle 45deg
Exhaust face angle 45deg
Seat width NA
Spring pressure NA
Intake stem to guide clearance 0.039in
Exhaust stem to guide clearance 0.051in
Intake stem diameter 0.3140in
Exhaust stem diameter 0.3130in
Piston clearance 0.0011in

Top comp. ring gap 0.010—0.020in
Bottom comp. ring gap 0.010—0.020in
Oil ring gap 0.010—0.020in
Top comp. side clearance 0.0008—0.0030in
Bottom comp. side clearance 0.0008—0.0030in
Oil side clearance 0.0008—0.0030in

1980 Audi 4000

Displacement 97ci
Volume 1.588
Main journals 1.8387in
Main journal oil clearance 0.0010—0.0030in
Crankshaft end play 0.003—0.007in
Thrust journal length 3in
Rod journal diameter 2.1587in
Rod oil clearance 0.0011—0.0034in
Rod side clearance 0.015in
Intake valve seat angle 45deg
Exhaust valve seat angle 45deg
Intake face angle 45deg
Exhaust face angle 45deg
Seat width NA
Spring pressure NA
Intake stem to guide clearance 0.039in
Exhaust stem to guide clearance 0.051in
Intake stem diameter 0.3140in
Exhaust stem diameter 0.3130in
Piston clearance 0.0011in
Top comp. ring gap 0.012—0.018in
Bottom comp. ring gap 0.012—0.018in
Oil ring gap 0.012—0.018in
Top comp. side clearance 0.0008—0.0020in
Bottom comp. side clearance 0.0008—0.0020in
Oil side clearance 0.0008—0.0020in

1979—1981 Audi 5000 Diesel

Displacement 121ci
Volume 1.986
Main journals 1.9107in
Main journal oil clearance 0.0006—0.0030in
Crankshaft end play 0.003—0.007in
Thrust journal length 4in
Rod journal diameter 2.3187in
Rod oil clearance 0.0024—0.0050in
Rod side clearance 0.015in
Intake valve seat angle 45deg
Exhaust valve seat angle 45deg
Intake face angle 45deg
Exhaust face angle 45deg
Seat width NA
Spring pressure NA
Intake stem to guide clearance 0.051in
Exhaust stem to guide clearance 0.051in
Intake stem diameter 0.3140in
Exhaust stem diameter 0.03130in
Piston clearance 0.0011in
Top comp. ring gap 0.012—0.020in
Bottom comp. ring gap 0.012—0.020in
Oil ring gap 0.010—0.016in
Top comp. side clearance 0.0020—0.0035in
Bottom comp. side clearance 0.002—0.003in
Oil side clearance 0.001—0.002in

1978—1981 Audi 5000

Displacement 130.8ci
Volume 2.144
Main journals 1.8110in
Main journal oil clearance 0.0006—0.0030in
Crankshaft end play 0.003—0.007in
Thrust journal length 4in
Rod journal diameter 2.2834in
Rod oil clearance 0.0006—0.0020in
Rod side clearance 0.016in
Intake valve seat angle 45deg
Exhaust valve seat angle 45deg
Intake face angle 45deg
Exhaust face angle 45deg
Seat width NA
Spring pressure NA
Intake stem to guide clearance 0.039in
Exhaust stem to guide clearance 0.051in
Intake stem diameter 0.3140in

Exhaust stem diameter 0.3130in

Piston clearance 0.0011in
Top comp. ring gap 0.010—0.020in
Bottom comp. ring gap 0.010—0.020in
Oil ring gap 0.010—0.020in
Top comp. side clearance 0.0008—0.0030in
Bottom comp. side clearance 0.0008—0.0030in
Oil side clearance 0.0008—0.0030in

1977—1979 Audi Fox

Displacement 97ci
Volume 1.588
Main journals 1.8110in
Main journal oil clearance 0.0010—0.0030in
Crankshaft end play 0.003—0.007in
Thrust journal length 3in
Rod journal diameter 2.1260in
Rod oil clearance 0.0011—0.0034in
Rod side clearance 0.010in
Intake valve seat angle 45deg
Exhaust valve seat angle 45deg
Intake face angle 45deg
Exhaust face angle 45deg
Seat width NA
Spring pressure NA
Intake stem to guide clearance 0.039in
Exhaust stem to guide clearance 0.051in
Intake stem diameter 0.3140in
Exhaust stem diameter 0.3130in
Piston clearance 0.0011in
Top comp. ring gap 0.012—0.018in
Bottom comp. ring gap 0.012—0.018in
Oil ring gap 0.010—0.016in
Top comp. side clearance 0.0008—0.0020in
Bottom comp. side clearance 0.0008—0.0020in
Oil side clearance 0.0008—0.0020in

1977 Audi 100

Displacement 114.2ci
Volume 1.871
Main journals 1.8898in
Main journal oil clearance 0.0020—0.0040in
Crankshaft end play 0.003—0.007in
Thrust journal length 3in
Rod journal diameter 2.3622in
Rod oil clearance 0.001—0.003in
Rod side clearance 0.004—0.009in
Intake valve seat angle 45deg
Exhaust valve seat angle 45deg
Intake face angle 45deg 15min
Exhaust face angle 45deg 15min
Seat width NA
Spring pressure NA
Intake stem to guide clearance 0.001in
Exhaust stem to guide clearance 0.002in
Intake stem diameter 0.3507in
Exhaust stem diameter 0.3499in
Piston clearance 0.0010in
Top comp. ring gap 0.039in
Bottom comp. ring gap 0.039in
Oil ring gap 0.039in
Top comp. side clearance 0.0060in
Bottom comp. side clearance 0.0060in
Oil side clearance 0.0060in

1984 BMW 318i Four-cylinder

Displacement 108ci
Volume 1.766
Main journals 2.3622in
Main journal oil clearance 0.0012—0.0027in
Crankshaft end play 0.003—0.007in
Thrust journal length 3in
Rod journal diameter 1.8898in
Rod oil clearance 0.0009—0.0031in
Rod side clearance 0.0016in
Intake valve seat angle 45deg
Exhaust valve seat angle 45deg
Intake face angle 45deg 30min
Exhaust face angle 45deg 30min
Seat width NA
Spring pressure 64psi @ 1.48in Intake
stem to guide clearance 0.0010—0.0020in

Exhaust stem to guide clearance	0.0015—0.0030in
Intake stem diameter	0.3149in
Exhaust stem diameter	0.3149in
Piston clearance	0.0018in
Top comp. ring gap	0.012—0.018in
Bottom comp. ring gap	0.008—0.016in
Oil ring gap	0.010—0.020in
Top comp. side clearance	0.002—0.004in
Bottom comp. side clearance	0.002—0.003in
Oil side clearance	0.001—0.002in

1982—1984 BMW 528e Six-cylinder

Displacement	165ci
Volume	2.693
Main journals	2.3622in
Main journal oil clearance	0.0012—0.0027in
Crankshaft end play	0.003—0.007in
Thrust journal length	4in
Rod journal diameter	1.7717in
Rod oil clearance	0.0013—0.0027in
Rod side clearance	0.0016in
Intake valve seat angle	45deg
Exhaust valve seat angle	45deg
Intake face angle	45deg
Exhaust face angle	45deg
Seat width	NA
Spring pressure	NA
Intake stem to guide clearance	0.006in
Exhaust stem to guide clearance	0.006in
Intake stem diameter	0.276in
Exhaust stem diameter	0.276in
Piston clearance	0.0004—0.0015in
Top comp. ring gap	0.012—0.020in
Bottom comp. ring gap	0.012—0.020in
Oil ring gap	0.010—0.020in
Top comp. side clearance	0.0016—0.0028in
Bottom comp. side clearance	0.0012—0.0024in
Oil side clearance	0.0008—0.0017in

1982—1984 BMW 533i KS Six-cylinder

Displacement	196ci
Volume	3.210
Main journals	2.3622in
Main journal oil clearance	0.0012—0.0027in
Crankshaft end play	0.003—0.007in
Thrust journal length	4in
Rod journal diameter	1.8898in
Rod oil clearance	0.0009—0.0027in
Rod side clearance	0.0016in
Intake valve seat angle	45deg
Exhaust valve seat angle	45deg
Intake face angle	45deg 30min
Exhaust face angle	45deg 30min
Seat width	NA
Spring pressure	64psi @ 1.48in
Intake stem to guide clearance	0.0010—0.0020in
Exhaust stem to guide clearance	0.0015—0.0030in
Intake stem diameter	0.3149in
Exhaust stem diameter	0.3149in
Piston clearance	0.0018in
Top comp. ring gap	0.012—0.020in
Bottom comp. ring gap	0.008—0.016in
Oil ring gap	0.010—0.016in
Top comp. side clearance	0.0024—0.0036in
Bottom comp. side clearance	0.0016—0.0028in
Oil side clearance	0.0012—0.0024in

1982—1984 BMW 533i Mahle Six-cylinder

Displacement	196ci
Volume	3.210
Main journals	2.3622in
Main journal oil clearance	0.0012—0.0027in
Crankshaft end play	0.003—0.007in
Thrust journal length	4in
Rod journal diameter	1.8898in
Rod oil clearance	0.0009—0.0027in
Rod side clearance	0.0016in
Intake valve seat angle	45deg
Exhaust valve seat angle	45deg
Intake face angle	45deg 30min
Exhaust face angle	45deg 30min
Seat width	NA

Spring pressure	64psi @ 1.48in
Intake stem to guide clearance	0.0010—0.0020in
Exhaust stem to guide clearance	0.0015—0.0030in
Intake stem diameter	0.3149in
Exhaust stem diameter	0.3149in
Piston clearance	0.0018in
Top comp. ring gap	0.012—0.020in
Bottom comp. ring gap	0.008—0.016in
Oil ring gap	0.010—0.016in
Top comp. side clearance	0.0024—0.0036in
Bottom comp. side clearance	0.0020—0.0032in
Oil side clearance	0.0008—0.0020in

1982—1984 BMW 633CSi KS Six-cylinder

Displacement	196ci
Volume	3.210
Main journals	2.3622in
Main journal oil clearance	0.0012—0.0027in
Crankshaft end play	0.003—0.007in
Thrust journal length	4in
Rod journal diameter	1.8898in
Rod oil clearance	0.0009—0.0027in
Rod side clearance	0.0016in
Intake valve seat angle	45deg
Exhaust valve seat angle	45deg
Intake face angle	45deg 30min
Exhaust face angle	45deg 30min
Seat width	NA
Spring pressure	64psi @ 1.48in
Intake stem to guide clearance	0.0010—0.0020in
Exhaust stem to guide clearance	0.0015—0.0030in
Intake stem diameter	0.3149in
Exhaust stem diameter	0.3149in
Piston clearance	0.0018in
Top comp. ring gap	0.012—0.020in
Bottom comp. ring gap	0.008—0.016in
Oil ring gap	0.010—0.016in
Top comp. side clearance	0.0024—0.0036in
Bottom comp. side clearance	0.0016—0.0028in
Oil side clearance	0.0012—0.0024in

1982—1984 BMW 633CSi Mahle Six-cylinder

Displacement	196ci
Volume	3.210
Main journals	2.3622in
Main journal oil clearance	0.0012—0.0027in
Crankshaft end play	0.003—0.007in
Thrust journal length	4in
Rod journal diameter	1.8898in
Rod oil clearance	0.0009—0.0027in
Rod side clearance	0.0016in
Intake valve seat angle	45deg
Exhaust valve seat angle	45deg
Intake face angle	45deg 30min
Exhaust face angle	45deg 30min
Seat width	NA
Spring pressure	64psi @ 1.48in
Intake stem to guide clearance	0.0010—0.0020in
Exhaust stem to guide clearance	0.0015—0.0030in
Intake stem diameter	0.3149in
Exhaust stem diameter	0.3149in
Piston clearance	0.0018in
Top comp. ring gap	0.012—0.020in
Bottom comp. ring gap	0.008—0.016in
Oil ring gap	0.010—0.016in
Top comp. side clearance	0.0024—0.0036in
Bottom comp. side clearance	0.0020—0.0032in
Oil side clearance	0.0008—0.0020in

1982—1984 BMW 733i KS Six-cylinder

Displacement	196ci
Volume	3.210
Main journals	2.3622in
Main journal oil clearance	0.0012—0.0027in
Crankshaft end play	0.003—0.007in
Thrust journal length	4in
Rod journal diameter	1.8898in
Rod oil clearance	0.0009—0.0031in
Rod side clearance	0.0016in
Intake valve seat angle	45deg
Exhaust valve seat angle	45deg

Intake face angle	45deg 30min
Exhaust face angle	45deg 30min
Seat width	NA
Spring pressure	64psi @ 1.48in
Intake stem to guide clearance	0.0010—0.0020in
Exhaust stem to guide clearance	0.0015—0.0030in
Intake stem diameter	0.3149in
Exhaust stem diameter	0.3149in
Piston clearance	0.0018in
Top comp. ring gap	0.012—0.020in
Bottom comp. ring gap	0.008—0.016in
Oil ring gap	0.010—0.016in
Top comp. side clearance	0.0024—0.0036in
Bottom comp. side clearance	0.0016—0.0028in
Oil side clearance	0.0012—0.0024in

1982—1984 BMW 733i Mahle Six-cylinder

Displacement	196ci
Volume	3.210
Main journals	2.3622in
Main journal oil clearance	0.0012—0.0027in
Crankshaft end play	0.003—0.007in
Thrust journal length	4in
Rod journal diameter	1.8898in
Rod oil clearance	0.0009—0.0031in
Rod side clearance	0.0016in
Intake valve seat angle	45deg
Exhaust valve seat angle	45deg
Intake face angle	45deg 30min
Exhaust face angle	45deg 30min
Seat width	NA
Spring pressure	64psi @ 1.48in
Intake stem to guide clearance	0.0010—0.0020in
Exhaust stem to guide clearance	0.0015—0.0030in
Intake stem diameter	0.3149in
Exhaust stem diameter	0.3149in
Piston clearance	0.0018in
Top comp. ring gap	0.012—0.020in
Bottom comp. ring gap	0.008—0.016in
Oil ring gap	0.010—0.016in
Top comp. side clearance	0.0024—0.0036in
Bottom comp. side clearance	0.0020—0.0032in
Oil side clearance	0.0008—0.0020in

1980—1983 BMW 320i Four-cylinder

Displacement	108ci
Volume	1.766
Main journals	2.3622in
Main journal oil clearance	0.0012—0.0027in
Crankshaft end play	0.003—0.007in
Thrust journal length	3in
Rod journal diameter	1.8898in
Rod oil clearance	0.0009—0.0031in
Rod side clearance	0.0016in
Intake valve seat angle	45deg
Exhaust valve seat angle	45deg
Intake face angle	45deg 30min
Exhaust face angle	45deg 30min
Seat width	NA
Spring pressure	64psi @ 1.48in Intake
stem to guide clearance	0.0010—0.0020in
Exhaust stem to guide clearance	0.0015—0.0030in
Intake stem diameter	0.3149in
Exhaust stem diameter	0.3149in
Piston clearance	0.0018in
Top comp. ring gap	0.012—0.018in
Bottom comp. ring gap	0.008—0.016in
Oil ring gap	0.010—0.020in
Top comp. side clearance	0.002—0.004in
Bottom comp. side clearance	0.002—0.003in
Oil side clearance	0.001—0.002in

1980—1981 BMW 633CSi KS Six-cylinder

Displacement	196ci
Volume	3.210
Main journals	2.3622in
Main journal oil clearance	0.0012—0.0027in
Crankshaft end play	0.003—0.007in
Thrust journal length	4in
Rod journal diameter	1.8898in
Rod oil clearance	0.0009—0.0027in
Rod side clearance	0.0016in

Intake valve seat angle | 45deg
Exhaust valve seat angle | 45deg
Intake face angle | 45deg 30min
Exhaust face angle | 45deg 30min
Seat width | NA
Spring pressure | 64psi @ 1.48in
Intake stem to guide clearance | 0.0010—0.0020in
Exhaust stem to guide clearance | 0.0015—0.0030in
Intake stem diameter | 0.3149in
Exhaust stem diameter | 0.3149in
Piston clearance | 0.0018in
Top comp. ring gap | 0.012—0.020in
Bottom comp. ring gap | 0.008—0.016in
Oil ring gap | 0.010—0.016in
Top comp. side clearance | 0.0024—0.0036in
Bottom comp. side clearance | 0.0016—0.0028in
Oil side clearance | 0.0012—0.0024in

1980—1981 BMW 633CSi Mahle Six-cylinder

Displacement	196ci
Volume	3.210
Main journals	2.3622in
Main journal oil clearance	0.0012—0.0027in
Crankshaft end play	0.003—0.007in
Thrust journal length	4in
Rod journal diameter	1.8898in
Rod oil clearance	0.0009—0.0027in
Rod side clearance	0.0016in
Intake valve seat angle	45deg
Exhaust valve seat angle	45deg
Intake face angle	45deg 30min
Exhaust face angle	45deg 30min
Seat width	NA
Spring pressure	64psi @ 1.48in
Intake stem to guide clearance	0.0010—0.0020in
Exhaust stem to guide clearance	0.0015—0.0030in
Intake stem diameter	0.3149in
Exhaust stem diameter	0.3149in
Piston clearance	0.0018in
Top comp. ring gap	0.012—0.020in
Bottom comp. ring gap	0.008—0.016in
Oil ring gap	0.010—0.016in
Top comp. side clearance	0.0024—0.0036in
Bottom comp. side clearance	0.0020—0.0032in
Oil side clearance	0.0008—0.0020in

1980—1981 BMW 733i KS Six-cylinder

Displacement	196ci
Volume	3.210
Main journals	2.3622in
Main journal oil clearance	0.0012—0.0027in
Crankshaft end play	0.003—0.007in
Thrust journal length	4in
Rod journal diameter	1.8898in
Rod oil clearance	0.0009—0.0031in
Rod side clearance	0.0016in
Intake valve seat angle	45deg
Exhaust valve seat angle	45deg
Intake face angle	45deg 30min
Exhaust face angle	45deg 30min
Seat width	NA
Spring pressure	64psi @ 1.48in
Intake stem to guide clearance	0.0010—0.0020in
Exhaust stem to guide clearance	0.0015—0.0030in
Intake stem diameter	0.3149in
Exhaust stem diameter	0.3149in
Piston clearance	0.0018in
Top comp. ring gap	0.012—0.020in
Bottom comp. ring gap	0.008—0.016in
Oil ring gap	0.010—0.016in
Top comp. side clearance	0.0024—0.0036in
Bottom comp. side clearance	0.0016—0.0028in
Oil side clearance	0.0012—0.0024in

1980—1981 BMW 733i Mahle Six-cylinder

Displacement	196ci
Volume	3.210
Main journals	2.3622in
Main journal oil clearance	0.0012—0.0027in
Crankshaft end play	0.003—0.007in
Thrust journal length	4in

Rod journal diameter	1.8898in
Rod oil clearance	0.0009—0.0031in
Rod side clearance	0.0016in
Intake valve seat angle	45deg
Exhaust valve seat angle	45deg
Intake face angle	45deg 30min
Exhaust face angle	45deg 30min
Seat width	NA
Spring pressure	64psi @ 1.48in
Intake stem to guide clearance	0.0010—0.0020in
Exhaust stem to guide clearance	0.0015—0.0030in
Intake stem diameter	0.3149in
Exhaust stem diameter	0.3149in
Piston clearance	0.0018in
Top comp. ring gap	0.012—0.020in
Bottom comp. ring gap	0.008—0.016in
Oil ring gap	0.010—0.016in
Top comp. side clearance	0.0024—0.0036in
Bottom comp. side clearance	0.0020—0.0032in
Oil side clearance	0.0008—0.0020in

1979—1981 BMW 528i Six-cylinder

Displacement	170ci
Volume	2.788
Main journals	2.3622in
Main journal oil clearance	0.0012—0.0027in
Crankshaft end play	0.003—0.007in
Thrust journal length	4in
Rod journal diameter	1.8898in
Rod oil clearance	0.0009—0.0027in
Rod side clearance	0.0016in
Intake valve seat angle	45deg
Exhaust valve seat angle	45deg
Intake face angle	45deg 30min
Exhaust face angle	45deg 30min
Seat width	NA
Spring pressure	64psi @ 1.48in
Intake stem to guide clearance	0.0010—0.0020in
Exhaust stem to guide clearance	0.0015—0.0030in
Intake stem diameter	0.3149in
Exhaust stem diameter	0.3149in
Piston clearance	0.0018in
Top comp. ring gap	0.012—0.020in
Bottom comp. ring gap	0.012—0.020in
Oil ring gap	0.010—0.020in
Top comp. side clearance	0.0024—0.0036in
Bottom comp. side clearance	0.0012—0.0024in
Oil side clearance	0.0008—0.0020in

1978—1979 BMW 633CSi KS Six-cylinder

Displacement	196ci
Volume	3.210
Main journals	2.3622in
Main journal oil clearance	0.0012—0.0027in
Crankshaft end play	0.003—0.007in
Thrust journal length	4in
Rod journal diameter	1.8898in
Rod oil clearance	0.0009—0.0027in
Rod side clearance	0.0016in
Intake valve seat angle	45deg
Exhaust valve seat angle	45deg
Intake face angle	45deg 30min
Exhaust face angle	45deg 30min
Seat width	NA
Spring pressure	64psi @ 1.48in
Intake stem to guide clearance	0.0010—0.0020in
Exhaust stem to guide clearance	0.0015—0.0030in
Intake stem diameter	0.3149in
Exhaust stem diameter	0.3149in
Piston clearance	0.0018in
Top comp. ring gap	0.012—0.020in
Bottom comp. ring gap	0.008—0.016in
Oil ring gap	0.010—0.016in
Top comp. side clearance	0.0024—0.0036in
Bottom comp. side clearance	0.0016—0.0028in
Oil side clearance	0.0012—0.0024in

1978—1979 BMW 633CSi Mahle Six-cylinder

Displacement	196ci
Volume	3.210
Main journals	2.3622in

Main journal oil clearance	0.0012—0.0027in
Crankshaft end play	0.003—0.007in
Thrust journal length	4in
Rod journal diameter	1.8898in
Rod oil clearance	0.0009—0.0027in
Rod side clearance	0.0016in
Intake valve seat angle	45deg
Exhaust valve seat angle	45deg
Intake face angle	45deg 30min
Exhaust face angle	45deg 30min
Seat width	NA
Spring pressure	64psi @ 1.48in
Intake stem to guide clearance	0.0010—0.0020in
Exhaust stem to guide clearance	0.0015—0.0030in
Intake stem diameter	0.3149in
Exhaust stem diameter	0.3149in
Piston clearance	0.0018in
Top comp. ring gap	0.012—0.020in
Bottom comp. ring gap	0.008—0.016in
Oil ring gap	0.010—0.016in
Top comp. side clearance	0.0024—0.0036in
Bottom comp. side clearance	0.0020—0.0032in
Oil side clearance	0.0008—0.0020in

1978—1979 BMW 733i KS Six-cylinder

Displacement	196ci
Volume	3.210
Main journals	2.3622in
Main journal oil clearance	0.0012—0.0027in
Crankshaft end play	0.003—0.007in
Thrust journal length	4in
Rod journal diameter	1.8898in
Rod oil clearance	0.0009—0.0031in
Rod side clearance	0.0016in
Intake valve seat angle	45deg
Exhaust valve seat angle	45deg
Intake face angle	45deg 30min
Exhaust face angle	45deg 30min
Seat width	NA
Spring pressure	64psi @ 1.48in
Intake stem to guide clearance	0.0010—0.0020in
Exhaust stem to guide clearance	0.0015—0.0030in
Intake stem diameter	0.3149in
Exhaust stem diameter	0.3149in
Piston clearance	0.0018in
Top comp. ring gap	0.012—0.020in
Bottom comp. ring gap	0.008—0.016in
Oil ring gap	0.010—0.016in
Top comp. side clearance	0.0024—0.0036in
Bottom comp. side clearance	0.0016—0.0028in
Oil side clearance	0.0012—0.0024in

1978—1979 BMW 733i Mahle Six-cylinder

Displacement	196ci
Volume	3.210
Main journals	2.3622in
Main journal oil clearance	0.0012—0.0027in
Crankshaft end play	0.003—0.007in
Thrust journal length	4in
Rod journal diameter	1.8898in
Rod oil clearance	0.0009—0.0031in
Rod side clearance	0.0016in
Intake valve seat angle	45deg
Exhaust valve seat angle	45deg
Intake face angle	45deg 30min
Exhaust face angle	45deg 30min
Seat width	NA
Spring pressure	64psi @ 1.48in
Intake stem to guide clearance	0.0010—0.0020in
Exhaust stem to guide clearance	0.0015—0.0030in
Intake stem diameter	0.3149in
Exhaust stem diameter	0.3149in
Piston clearance	0.0018in
Top comp. ring gap	0.012—0.020in
Bottom comp. ring gap	0.008—0.016in
Oil ring gap	0.010—0.016in
Top comp. side clearance	0.0024—0.0036in
Bottom comp. side clearance	0.0020—0.0032in
Oil side clearance	0.0008—0.0020in

1977—1979 BMW 320i Four-cylinder

Displacement	121ci

Volume	1.990
Main journals	2.3622in
Main journal oil clearance	0.0012—0.0027in
Crankshaft end play	0.003—0.007in
Thrust journal length	3in
Rod journal diameter	1.8898in
Rod oil clearance	0.0009—0.0031in
Rod side clearance	0.0016in
Intake valve seat angle	45deg
Exhaust valve seat angle	45deg
Intake face angle	45deg 30min
Exhaust face angle	45deg 30min
Seat width	NA
Spring pressure	NA
Intake stem to guide clearance	0.0010—0.0020in
Exhaust stem to guide clearance	0.0015—0.0030in
Intake stem diameter	0.3149in
Exhaust stem diameter	0.3149in
Piston clearance	0.0018in
Top comp. ring gap	0.012—0.018in
Bottom comp. ring gap	0.008—0.016in
Oil ring gap	0.010—0.020in
Top comp. side clearance	0.002—0.004in
Bottom comp. side clearance	0.002—0.003in
Oil side clearance	0.001—0.002in

1977—1978 BMW 530i KS Six-cylinder

Displacement	182ci
Volume	2.985
Main journals	2.3622in
Main journal oil clearance	0.0012—0.0027in
Crankshaft end play	0.003—0.007in
Thrust journal length	4in
Rod journal diameter	1.8898in
Rod oil clearance	0.0009—0.0027in
Rod side clearance	0.0016in
Intake valve seat angle	45deg
Exhaust valve seat angle	45deg
Intake face angle	45deg 30min
Exhaust face angle	45deg 30min
Seat width	NA
Spring pressure	64psi @ 1.48in
Intake stem to guide clearance	0.0010—0.0020in
Exhaust stem to guide clearance	0.0015—0.0030in
Intake stem diameter	0.3149in
Exhaust stem diameter	0.3149in
Piston clearance	0.0018; 0.0016 (early)in
Top comp. ring gap	0.012—0.020in
Bottom comp. ring gap	0.008—0.016in
Oil ring gap	0.010—0.020 in
Top comp. side clearance	0.0024—0.0036in
Bottom comp. side clearance	0.0016—0.0028in
Oil side clearance	0.001—0.002in

1977—1978 BMW 530i Mahle Six-cylinder

Displacement	182ci
Volume	2.985
Main journals	2.3622in
Main journal oil clearance	0.0012—0.0027in
Crankshaft end play	0.003—0.007in
Thrust journal length	4in
Rod journal diameter	1.8898in
Rod oil clearance	0.0009—0.0027in
Rod side clearance	0.0016in
Intake valve seat angle	45deg
Exhaust valve seat angle	45deg
Intake face angle	45deg 30min
Exhaust face angle	45deg 30min
Seat width	NA
Spring pressure	64psi @ 1.48in
Intake stem to guide clearance	0.0010—0.0020in
Exhaust stem to guide clearance	0.0015—0.0030in
Intake stem diameter	0.3149in
Exhaust stem diameter	0.3149in
Piston clearance	0.0018; 0.0016 (early)in
Top comp. ring gap	0.012—0.020in
Bottom comp. ring gap	0.008—0.016in
Oil ring gap	0.010—0.020 in
Top comp. side clearance	0.0024—0.0036in
Bottom comp. side clearance	0.0012—0.0024in

Oil side clearance	0.001—0.002in

[1]1977 BMW 630CSi KS Six-cylinder

Displacement	182ci
Volume	2.985
Main journals	2.3622in
Main journal oil clearance	0.0012—0.0027in
Crankshaft end play	0.003—0.007in
Thrust journal length	4in
Rod journal diameter	1.8898in
Rod oil clearance	0.0009—0.0027in
Rod side clearance	0.0016in
Intake valve seat angle	45deg
Exhaust valve seat angle	45deg
Intake face angle	45deg 30min
Exhaust face angle	45deg 30min
Seat width	NA
Spring pressure	64psi @ 1.48in
Intake stem to guide clearance	0.0010—0.0020in
Exhaust stem to guide clearance	0.0015—0.0030in
Intake stem diameter	0.3149in
Exhaust stem diameter	0.3149in
Piston clearance	0.0018in
Top comp. ring gap	0.012—0.020in
Bottom comp. ring gap	0.008—0.016in
Oil ring gap	0.010—0.020in
Top comp. side clearance	0.0024—0.0036in
Bottom comp. side clearance	0.0016—0.0028in
Oil side clearance	0.0012—0.0024in

1977 BMW 630CSi Mahle Six-cylinder

Displacement	182ci
Volume	2.985
Main journals	2.3622in
Main journal oil clearance	0.0012—0.0027in
Crankshaft end play	0.003—0.007in
Thrust journal length	4in
Rod journal diameter	1.8898in
Rod oil clearance	0.0009—0.0027in
Rod side clearance	0.0016in
Intake valve seat angle	45deg
Exhaust valve seat angle	45deg
Intake face angle	45deg 30min
Exhaust face angle	45deg 30min
Seat width	NA
Spring pressure	64psi @ 1.48in
Intake stem to guide clearance	0.0010—0.0020in
Exhaust stem to guide clearance	0.0015—0.0030in
Intake stem diameter	0.3149in
Exhaust stem diameter	0.3149in
Piston clearance	0.0018in
Top comp. ring gap	0.012—0.020in
Bottom comp. ring gap	0.008—0.016in
Oil ring gap	0.010—0.020in
Top comp. side clearance	0.0024—0.0036in
Bottom comp. side clearance	0.0012—0.0024in
Oil side clearance	0.0008—0.0020in

1984 Chrysler Conquest

Displacement	155.9ci
Volume (liters)	2.6
Main journal diameter	2.3622in
Main journal oil clearance	0.0008—0.0020in
Crankshaft end play	0.002—0.007in
Thrust journal length	3in
Rod journal diameter	2.0866in
Rod oil clearance	0.0008—0.0024in
Rod side clearance	0.004—0.010in
Intake valve seat angle	45deg
Exhaust valve seat angle	45deg
Intake face angle	45deg
Exhaust face angle	45deg
Seat width	NA
Spring pressure	61psi @ 1.590in
Intake stem to guide clearance	0.0012—0.0024in
Exhaust stem to guide clearance	0.0020—0.0035in
Intake stem diameter	0.315in
Exhaust stem diameter	0.315in
Piston clearance	0.0008—0.0016in
Top comp. ring gap	0.012—0.020in
Bottom comp. ring gap	0.010—0.016in
Oil ring gap	0.012—0.031in

Top comp. side clearance	0.002—0.004in
Bottom comp. side clearance	0.001—0.002in
Oil side clearance	NA

1983—1984 Chrysler 1.4 Liter

Displacement	86.0ci
Volume (liters)	1.4
Main journal diameter	1.8898in
Main journal oil clearance	0.0008—0.0028in
Crankshaft end play	0.002—0.007in
Thrust journal length	3in
Rod journal diameter	1.6535in
Rod oil clearance	0.0004—0.0024in
Rod side clearance	0.004—0.010in
Intake valve seat angle	45deg
Exhaust valve seat angle	45deg
Intake face angle	45deg
Exhaust face angle	45deg
Seat width	NA
Spring pressure	69psi @ 1.417in
Intake stem to guide clearance	0.0012—0.0024in
Exhaust stem to guide clearance	0.0020—0.0035in
Intake stem diameter	0.315in
Exhaust stem diameter	0.315in
Piston clearance	0.0008—0.0016in
Top comp. ring gap	0.008—0.016in
Bottom comp. ring gap	0.008—0.016in
Oil ring gap	0.008—0.020in
Top comp. side clearance	0.0012—0.0028in
Bottom comp. side clearance	0.0008—0.0024in
Oil side clearance	NA

1983—1984 Chrysler 1.6 Liter

Displacement	97.5ci
Volume (liters)	1.6
Main journal diameter	2.2441in
Main journal oil clearance	0.0008—0.0028in
Crankshaft end play	0.002—0.007in
Thrust journal length	3in
Rod journal diameter	1.7717in
Rod oil clearance	0.0004—0.0028in
Rod side clearance	0.004—0.010in
Intake valve seat angle	45deg
Exhaust valve seat angle	45deg
Intake face angle	45deg
Exhaust face angle	45deg
Seat width	NA
Spring pressure	61psi @ 1.470in
Intake stem to guide clearance	0.0010—0.0022in
Exhaust stem to guide clearance	0.0020—0.0033in
Intake stem diameter	0.315in
Exhaust stem diameter	0.315in
Piston clearance	0.0008—0.0016in
Top comp. ring gap	0.008—0.016in
Bottom comp. ring gap	0.008—0.016in
Oil ring gap	0.008—0.020in
Top comp. side clearance	0.0012—0.0028in
Bottom comp. side clearance	0.0008—0.0024in
Oil side clearance	NA

1983—1984 Chrysler 2.6 Liter

Displacement	155.9ci
Volume (liters)	2.6
Main journal diameter	2.3622in
Main journal oil clearance	0.0008—0.0028in
Crankshaft end play	0.002—0.007in
Thrust journal length	3in
Rod journal diameter	2.0866in
Rod oil clearance	0.0008—0.0028in
Rod side clearance	0.004—0.010in
Intake valve seat angle	45deg
Exhaust valve seat angle	45deg
Intake face angle	45deg
Exhaust face angle	45deg
Seat width	NA
Spring pressure	61psi @ 1.590in
Intake stem to guide clearance	0.0012—0.0024in
Exhaust stem to guide clearance	0.0020—0.0035in
Intake stem diameter	0.315in
Exhaust stem diameter	0.315in
Piston clearance	0.0008—0.0016in
Top comp. ring gap	0.010—0.018in

Bottom comp. ring gap	0.010—0.018in
Oil ring gap	0.008—0.035in
Top comp. side clearance	0.0024—0.0039in
Bottom comp. side clearance	0.0008—0.0024in
Oil side clearance	NA

1983 Chrysler Conquest

Displacement	155.9ci
Volume (liters)	2.6
Main journal diameter	2.3622in
Main journal oil clearance	0.0008—0.0020in
Crankshaft end play	0.002—0.007in
Thrust journal length	3in
Rod journal diameter	2.0866in
Rod oil clearance	0.0008—0.0024in
Rod side clearance	0.004—0.010in
Intake valve seat angle	45deg
Exhaust valve seat angle	45deg
Intake face angle	45deg
Exhaust face angle	45deg
Seat width	NA
Spring pressure	61psi @ 1.590in
Intake stem to guide clearance	0.0012—0.0024in
Exhaust stem to guide clearance	0.0020—0.0035in
Intake stem diameter	0.315in
Exhaust stem diameter	0.315in
Piston clearance	0.0008—0.0016in
Top comp. ring gap	0.010—0.018in
Bottom comp. ring gap	0.010—0.018in
Oil ring gap	0.008—0.035in
Top comp. side clearance	0.0024—0.0039in
Bottom comp. side clearance	0.0008—0.0024in
Oil side clearance	NA

1981—1984 Chrysler 225 Six-cylinder

Displacement	225ci
Volume (liters)	NA
Main journal diameter	2.7495—2.7505in
Main journal oil clearance	0.0010—0.0025in
Crankshaft end play	0.0035—0.0095in
Thrust journal length	3in
Rod journal diameter	2.1865—2.1875in
Rod oil clearance	0.0010—0.0025in
Rod side clearance	0.007—0.013in
Intake valve seat angle	45deg
Exhaust valve seat angle	45deg
Intake face angle	45deg
Exhaust face angle	43deg
Seat width	NA
Spring pressure	NA
Intake stem to guide clearance	0.0010—0.0030in
Exhaust stem to guide clearance	0.0020—0.0040in
Intake stem diameter	0.3725in
Exhaust stem diameter	0.3715in
Piston clearance	0.0005—0.0015in
Top comp. ring gap	0.010—0.020in
Bottom comp. ring gap	0.010—0.020in
Oil ring gap	0.015—0.055in
Top comp. side clearance	0.0015—0.0030in
Bottom comp. side clearance	0.0015—0.0030in
Oil side clearance	0.0002—0.0050in

1980—1984 Chrysler 318 Eight-cylinder

Displacement	318ci
Volume (liters)	NA
Main journal diameter	2.4995—2.5005in
Main journal oil clearance	0.0005—0.0020; 0.0005—0.0015in (no. 1)
Crankshaft end play	0.002—0.009in
Thrust journal length	3in
Rod journal diameter	2.1240—2.1250in
Rod oil clearance	0.0005—0.0025in
Rod side clearance	0.006—0.014in
Intake valve seat angle	45deg
Exhaust valve seat angle	45deg
Intake face angle	45deg
Exhaust face angle	45deg
Seat width	NA
Spring pressure	NA
Intake stem to guide clearance	0.0010—0.0030in
Exhaust stem to guide clearance	0.0020—0.0040in

Intake stem diameter	0.3725in
Exhaust stem diameter	0.3715in
Piston clearance	0.0005—0.0015in
Top comp. ring gap	0.010—0.020in
Bottom comp. ring gap	0.010—0.020in
Oil ring gap	0.015—0.055in
Top comp. side clearance	0.0015—0.0040in
Bottom comp. side clearance	0.0015—0.0040in
Oil side clearance	0.0002—0.0050in

1980—1984 Chrysler 360 Eight-cylinder Four-barrel

Displacement	360ci
Volume (liters)	NA
Main journal diameter	2.8095—2.8105in
Main journal oil clearance	0.0005—0.0020; 0.0005—0.0015in (no. 1)
Crankshaft end play	0.002—0.009in
Thrust journal length	3in
Rod journal diameter	2.1240—2.1250in
Rod oil clearance	0.0005—0.0025in
Rod side clearance	0.006—0.014in
Intake valve seat angle	45deg
Exhaust valve seat angle	45deg
Intake face angle	45deg
Exhaust face angle	45deg
Seat width	NA
Spring pressure	NA
Intake stem to guide clearance	0.0010—0.0030in
Exhaust stem to guide clearance	0.0020—0.0040in
Intake stem diameter	0.3725in
Exhaust stem diameter	0.3715in
Piston clearance	0.0010—0.0020in
Top comp. ring gap	0.010—0.020in
Bottom comp. ring gap	0.010—0.020in
Oil ring gap	0.015—0.055in
Top comp. side clearance	0.0015—0.0040in
Bottom comp. side clearance	0.0015—0.0040in
Oil side clearance	0.0002—0.0050in

1980—1984 Chrysler 360 Eight-cylinder

Displacement	360ci
Volume (liters)	NA
Main journal diameter	2.8095—2.8105in
Main journal oil clearance	0.0005—0.0020; 0.0005—0.0015in (no. 1)
Crankshaft end play	0.002—0.009in
Thrust journal length	3in
Rod journal diameter	2.1240—2.1250in
Rod oil clearance	0.0005—0.0025in
Rod side clearance	0.006—0.014in
Intake valve seat angle	45deg
Exhaust valve seat angle	45deg
Intake face angle	45deg
Exhaust face angle	45deg
Seat width	NA
Spring pressure	NA
Intake stem to guide clearance	0.0010—0.0030in
Exhaust stem to guide clearance	0.0020—0.0040in
Intake stem diameter	0.3725in
Exhaust stem diameter	0.3715in
Piston clearance	0.0005—0.0015in
Top comp. ring gap	0.010—0.020in
Bottom comp. ring gap	0.010—0.020in
Oil ring gap	0.015—0.055in
Top comp. side clearance	0.0015—0.0040in
Bottom comp. side clearance	0.0015—0.0040in
Oil side clearance	0.0002—0.0050in

1979—1982 Chrysler 1.4 Liter

Displacement	86.0ci
Volume (liters)	1.4
Main journal diameter	1.8898in
Main journal oil clearance	0.0008—0.0028in
Crankshaft end play	0.002—0.007in
Thrust journal length	3in
Rod journal diameter	1.6535in
Rod oil clearance	0.0004—0.0024in
Rod side clearance	0.004—0.010in
Intake valve seat angle	45deg

Exhaust valve seat angle	45deg
Intake face angle	45deg
Exhaust face angle	45deg
Seat width	NA
Spring pressure	69psi @ 1.417in
Intake stem to guide clearance	0.0012—0.0024in
Exhaust stem to guide clearance	0.0020—0.0035in
Intake stem diameter	0.315in
Exhaust stem diameter	0.0315in
Piston clearance	0.0008—0.0016in
Top comp. ring gap	0.008—0.016in
Bottom comp. ring gap	0.008—0.016in
Oil ring gap	0.008—0.020in
Top comp. side clearance	0.0012—0.0028in
Bottom comp. side clearance	0.0008—0.0024in
Oil side clearance	NA

1979—1982 Chrysler 1.6 Liter [please supply engine name]

Displacement	97.5ci
Volume (liters)	1.6
Main journal diameter	2.2441in
Main journal oil clearance	0.0008—0.0028in
Crankshaft end play	0.002—0.007in
Thrust journal length	3in
Rod journal diameter	1.7717in
Rod oil clearance	0.0004—0.0028in
Rod side clearance	0.004—0.010in
Intake valve seat angle	45deg
Exhaust valve seat angle	45deg
Intake face angle	45deg
Exhaust face angle	45deg
Seat width	NA
Spring pressure	61psi @ 1.470in
Intake stem to guide clearance	0.0010—0.0022in
Exhaust stem to guide clearance	0.0020—0.0033in
Intake stem diameter	0.315in
Exhaust stem diameter	0.0315in
Piston clearance	0.0008—0.0016in
Top comp. ring gap	0.008—0.016in
Bottom comp. ring gap	0.008—0.016in
Oil ring gap	0.008—0.020in
Top comp. side clearance	0.0012—0.0028in
Bottom comp. side clearance	0.0008—0.0024in
Oil side clearance	NA

1979—1982 Chrysler 2.0 Liter

Displacement	121.7ci
Volume (liters)	2.0
Main journal diameter	2.5984in
Main journal oil clearance	0.0008—0.0028in
Crankshaft end play	0.002—0.007in
Thrust journal length	3in
Rod journal diameter	2.0866in
Rod oil clearance	0.0008—0.0028in
Rod side clearance	0.004—0.010in
Intake valve seat angle	45deg
Exhaust valve seat angle	45deg
Intake face angle	45deg
Exhaust face angle	45deg
Seat width	NA
Spring pressure	61psi @ 1.590in
Intake stem to guide clearance	0.0010—0.0022in
Exhaust stem to guide clearance	0.0020—0.0033in
Intake stem diameter	0.315in
Exhaust stem diameter	0.0315in
Piston clearance	0.0008—0.0016in
Top comp. ring gap	0.010—0.017in
Bottom comp. ring gap	0.010—0.017in
Oil ring gap	0.008—0.035in
Top comp. side clearance	0.0024—0.0039in
Bottom comp. side clearance	0.0008—0.0024in
Oil side clearance	NA

1979 Chrysler 318 Eight-cylinder

Displacement	318ci
Volume (liters)	NA
Main journal diameter	2.4995—2.5005in
Main journal oil clearance	0.0005—0.0020in
Crankshaft end play	0.002—0.009in
Thrust journal length	3in
Rod journal diameter	2.1240—2.1250in

Rod oil clearance	0.0005—0.0025in
Rod side clearance	0.006—0.014in
Intake valve seat angle	45deg
Exhaust valve seat angle	45deg
Intake face angle	45deg
Exhaust face angle	45deg
Seat width	NA
Spring pressure	NA
Intake stem to guide clearance	0.0010—0.0030in
Exhaust stem to guide clearance	0.0020—0.0040in
Intake stem diameter	0.3725in
Exhaust stem diameter	0.3715in
Piston clearance	0.0005—0.0015in
Top comp. ring gap	0.010—0.020in
Bottom comp. ring gap	0.010—0.020in
Oil ring gap	0.015—0.055in
Top comp. side clearance	0.0015—0.0040in
Bottom comp. side clearance	0.0015—0.0040in
Oil side clearance	0.0002—0.0050in

1979 Chrysler 360 Eight-cylinder Four-barrel

Displacement	360ci
Volume (liters)	NA
Main journal diameter	2.8095—2.8105in
Main journal oil clearance	0.0005—0.0020in
Crankshaft end play	0.002—0.009in
Thrust journal length	3in
Rod journal diameter	2.1240—2.1250in
Rod oil clearance	0.0005—0.0025in
Rod side clearance	0.006—0.014in
Intake valve seat angle	45deg
Exhaust valve seat angle	45deg
Intake face angle	45deg
Exhaust face angle	45deg
Seat width	NA
Spring pressure	NA
Intake stem to guide clearance	0.0010—0.0030in
Exhaust stem to guide clearance	0.0020—0.0040in
Intake stem diameter	0.3725in
Exhaust stem diameter	0.3715in
Piston clearance	0.0010—0.0020in
Top comp. ring gap	0.010—0.020in
Bottom comp. ring gap	0.010—0.020in
Oil ring gap	0.015—0.055in
Top comp. side clearance	0.0015—0.0040in
Bottom comp. side clearance	0.0015—0.0040in
Oil side clearance	0.0002—0.0050in

1979 Chrysler 360 Eight-cylinder

Displacement	360ci
Volume (liters)	NA
Main journal diameter	2.8095—2.8105in
Main journal oil clearance	0.0005—0.0020in
Crankshaft end play	0.002—0.009in
Thrust journal length	3in
Rod journal diameter	2.1240—2.1250in
Rod oil clearance	0.0005—0.0025in
Rod side clearance	0.006—0.014in
Intake valve seat angle	45deg
Exhaust valve seat angle	45deg
Intake face angle	45deg
Exhaust face angle	45deg
Seat width	NA
Spring pressure	NA
Intake stem to guide clearance	0.0010—0.0030in
Exhaust stem to guide clearance	0.0020—0.0040in
Intake stem diameter	0.3725in
Exhaust stem diameter	0.3715in
Piston clearance	0.0005—0.0015in
Top comp. ring gap	0.010—0.020in
Bottom comp. ring gap	0.010—0.020in
Oil ring gap	0.015—0.055in
Top comp. side clearance	0.0015—0.0040in
Bottom comp. side clearance	0.0015—0.0040in
Oil side clearance	0.0002—0.0050in

1979 Chrysler Conquest

Displacement	155.9ci
Volume (liters)	2.6
Main journal diameter	2.5984in
Main journal oil clearance	0.0008—0.0020in

Crankshaft end play	0.002—0.007in
Thrust journal length	3in
Rod journal diameter	2.0866in
Rod oil clearance	0.0008—0.0020in
Rod side clearance	0.004—0.010in
Intake valve seat angle	45deg
Exhaust valve seat angle	45deg
Intake face angle	45deg
Exhaust face angle	45deg
Seat width	NA
Spring pressure	61psi @ 1.590in
Intake stem to guide clearance	0.0012—0.0024in
Exhaust stem to guide clearance	0.0020—0.0035in
Intake stem diameter	0.315in
Exhaust stem diameter	0.315in
Piston clearance	0.0008—0.0016in
Top comp. ring gap	0.010—0.017in
Bottom comp. ring gap	0.010—0.017in
Oil ring gap	0.008—0.035in
Top comp. side clearance	0.0024—0.0039in
Bottom comp. side clearance	0.0008—0.0024in
Oil side clearance	NA

1978 Chrysler 440 Eight-cylinder

Displacement	440ci
Volume (liters)	NA
Main journal diameter	2.7495—2.7505in
Main journal oil clearance	0.0005—0.0020in
Crankshaft end play	0.002—0.009in
Thrust journal length	3in
Rod journal diameter	2.3750—2.3760in
Rod oil clearance	0.0005—0.0025in
Rod side clearance	0.009—0.017in
Intake valve seat angle	45deg
Exhaust valve seat angle	45deg
Intake face angle	45deg
Exhaust face angle	43deg
Seat width	NA
Spring pressure	NA
Intake stem to guide clearance	0.0011—0.0028in
Exhaust stem to guide clearance	0.0010—0.0027in
Intake stem diameter	0.3726in
Exhaust stem diameter	0.3722in
Piston clearance	0.0003—0.0013in
Top comp. ring gap	0.013—0.023in
Bottom comp. ring gap	0.013—0.023in
Oil ring gap	0.015—0.055in
Top comp. side clearance	0.0015—0.0030in
Bottom comp. side clearance	0.0015—0.0030in
Oil side clearance	0.0002—0.0050in

1977—1980 Chrysler 225 Six-cylinder

Displacement	225ci
Volume (liters)	NA
Main journal diameter	2.7495—2.7505in
Main journal oil clearance	0.0005—0.0020in
Crankshaft end play	0.002—0.009in
Thrust journal length	3in
Rod journal diameter	2.1865—2.1875in
Rod oil clearance	0.0005—0.0025in
Rod side clearance	0.006—0.025in
Intake valve seat angle	45deg
Exhaust valve seat angle	45deg
Intake face angle	45deg
Exhaust face angle	43deg
Seat width	NA
Spring pressure	NA
Intake stem to guide clearance	0.0010—0.0030in
Exhaust stem to guide clearance	0.0020—0.0040in
Intake stem diameter	0.3725in
Exhaust stem diameter	0.3715in
Piston clearance	0.0005—0.0015in
Top comp. ring gap	0.010—0.020in
Bottom comp. ring gap	0.010—0.020in
Oil ring gap	0.015—0.055in
Top comp. side clearance	0.0015—0.0030in
Bottom comp. side clearance	0.0015—0.0030in
Oil side clearance	0.0002—0.0050in

1977—1978 Chrysler 1.6 Liter

Displacement	97.5ci

Volume (liters)	1.600
Main journal diameter	2.2441in
Main journal oil clearance	0.0008—0.0028in
Crankshaft end play	0.002—0.007in
Thrust journal length	3in
Rod journal diameter	1.7717in
Rod oil clearance	0.0004—0.0028in
Rod side clearance	0.004—0.010in
Intake valve seat angle	45deg
Exhaust valve seat angle	45deg
Intake face angle	45deg
Exhaust face angle	45deg
Seat width	NA
Spring pressure	61psi @ 1.470in
Intake stem to guide clearance	0.0010—0.0022in
Exhaust stem to guide clearance	0.0020—0.0033in
Intake stem diameter	0.315in
Exhaust stem diameter	0.315in
Piston clearance	0.0008—0.0016in
Top comp. ring gap	0.008—0.016in
Bottom comp. ring gap	0.008—0.016in
Oil ring gap	0.008—0.020in
Top comp. side clearance	0.0012—0.0028in
Bottom comp. side clearance	0.0008—0.0024in
Oil side clearance	NA

1977—1978 Chrysler 2.0 Liter

Displacement	121.7ci
Volume (liters)	2.0
Main journal diameter	2.5984in
Main journal oil clearance	0.0008—0.0028in
Crankshaft end play	0.002—0.007in
Thrust journal length	3in
Rod journal diameter	2.0866in
Rod oil clearance	0.0008—0.0028in
Rod side clearance	0.004—0.010in
Intake valve seat angle	45deg
Exhaust valve seat angle	45deg
Intake face angle	45deg
Exhaust face angle	45deg
Seat width	NA
Spring pressure	61psi @ 1.590in
Intake stem to guide clearance	0.0010—0.0022in
Exhaust stem to guide clearance	0.0020—0.0033in
Intake stem diameter	0.315in
Exhaust stem diameter	0.315in
Piston clearance	0.0008—0.0016in
Top comp. ring gap	0.010—0.017in
Bottom comp. ring gap	0.010—0.017in
Oil ring gap	0.008—0.035in
Top comp. side clearance	0.0024—0.0039in
Bottom comp. side clearance	0.0008—0.0024in
Oil side clearance	NA

1977—1978 Chrysler 2.6 Liter

Displacement	155ci
Volume (liters)	2.6
Main journal diameter	2.5984in
Main journal oil clearance	0.0008—0.0028in
Crankshaft end play	0.002—0.007in
Thrust journal length	3in
Rod journal diameter	2.0866in
Rod oil clearance	0.008—0.028in
Rod side clearance	0.004—0.010in
Intake valve seat angle	45deg
Exhaust valve seat angle	45deg
Intake face angle	45deg
Exhaust face angle	45deg
Seat width	NA
Spring pressure	61psi @ 1.590in
Intake stem to guide clearance	0.0012—0.0024in
Exhaust stem to guide clearance	0.0020—0.0035in
Intake stem diameter	0.315in
Exhaust stem diameter	0.315in
Piston clearance	0.0008—0.0016in
Top comp. ring gap	0.012—0.020in
Bottom comp. ring gap	0.010—0.016in
Oil ring gap	0.012—0.031in
Top comp. side clearance	0.002—0.004in
Bottom comp. side clearance	0.001—0.002in
Oil side clearance	NA

1977—1978 Chrysler 318 Eight-cylinder

Displacement	318ci
Volume (liters)	NA
Main journal diameter	2.4995—2.5005in
Main journal oil clearance	0.0005—0.0020in
Crankshaft end play	0.002—0.009in
Thrust journal length	3in
Rod journal diameter	2.140—2.1250in
Rod oil clearance	0.0005—0.0025in
Rod side clearance	0.006—0.014in
Intake valve seat angle	45deg
Exhaust valve seat angle	45deg
Intake face angle	45deg
Exhaust face angle	43deg
Seat width	NA
Spring pressure	NA
Intake stem to guide clearance	0.0010—0.0030in
Exhaust stem to guide clearance	0.0020—0.0040in
Intake stem diameter	0.3725in
Exhaust stem diameter	0.3715in
Piston clearance	0.0005—0.0015in
Top comp. ring gap	0.010—0.020in
Bottom comp. ring gap	0.010—0.020in
Oil ring gap	0.015—0.055in
Top comp. side clearance	0.0015—0.0030in
Bottom comp. side clearance	0.0015—0.0030in
Oil side clearance	0.0002—0.0050in

1977—1978 Chrysler 360 Eight-cylinder Four-barrel

Displacement	360ci
Volume (liters)	NA
Main journal diameter	2.8095—2.8105in
Main journal oil clearance	0.0005—0.0020in
Crankshaft end play	0.002—0.009in
Thrust journal length	3in
Rod journal diameter	2.1240—2.1250in
Rod oil clearance	0.0005—0.0025in
Rod side clearance	0.006—0.014in
Intake valve seat angle	45deg
Exhaust valve seat angle	45deg
Intake face angle	45deg
Exhaust face angle	43deg
Seat width	NA
Spring pressure	NA
Intake stem to guide clearance	0.0010—0.0030in
Exhaust stem to guide clearance	0.0020—0.0040in
Intake stem diameter	0.3725in
Exhaust stem diameter	0.3715in
Piston clearance	0.0010—0.0020in
Top comp. ring gap	0.010—0.020in
Bottom comp. ring gap	0.010—0.020in
Oil ring gap	0.015—0.055in
Top comp. side clearance	0.0015—0.0040in
Bottom comp. side clearance	0.0015—0.0040in
Oil side clearance	0.0002—0.0050in

1977—1978 Chrysler 360 Eight-cylinder

Displacement	360ci
Volume (liters)	NA
Main journal diameter	2.8095—2.8105in
Main journal oil clearance	0.0005—0.0020in
Crankshaft end play	0.002—0.009in
Thrust journal length	3in
Rod journal diameter	2.1240—2.1250in
Rod oil clearance	0.0005—0.0025in
Rod side clearance	0.006—0.014in
Intake valve seat angle	45deg
Exhaust valve seat angle	45deg
Intake face angle	45deg
Exhaust face angle	43deg
Seat width	NA
Spring pressure	NA
Intake stem to guide clearance	0.0010—0.0030in
Exhaust stem to guide clearance	0.0020—0.0040in
Intake stem diameter	0.3725in
Exhaust stem diameter	0.3715in
Piston clearance	0.0005—0.0015in
Top comp. ring gap	0.010—0.020in
Bottom comp. ring gap	0.010—0.020in
Oil ring gap	0.015—0.055in

Top comp. side clearance	0.0015—0.0040in
Bottom comp. side clearance	0.0015—0.0040in
Oil side clearance	0.0002—0.0050in

1977—1978 Chrysler Conquest

Displacement	155.9ci
Volume (liters)	2.6
Main journal diameter	2.5984in
Main journal oil clearance	0.0008—0.0020in
Crankshaft end play	0.002—0.007in
Thrust journal length	3in
Rod journal diameter	2.0866in
Rod oil clearance	0.0008—0.0024in
Rod side clearance	0.004—0.010in
Intake valve seat angle	45deg
Exhaust valve seat angle	45deg
Intake face angle	45deg
Exhaust face angle	45deg
Seat width	NA
Spring pressure	61psi @ 1.590in
Intake stem to guide clearance	0.0012—0.0024in
Exhaust stem to guide clearance	0.0020—0.0035in
Intake stem diameter	0.315in
Exhaust stem diameter	0.315in
Piston clearance	0.0008—0.0016in
Top comp. ring gap	0.012—0.020in
Bottom comp. ring gap	0.010—0.016in
Oil ring gap	0.012—0.031in
Top comp. side clearance	0.002—0.004in
Bottom comp. side clearance	0.001—0.002in
Oil side clearance	NA

1977 Chrysler 400 Eight-cylinder

Displacement	400ci
Volume (liters)	NA
Main journal diameter	2.6245—2.6255in
Main journal oil clearance	0.0005—0.0020in
Crankshaft end play	0.002—0.009in
Thrust journal length	3in
Rod journal diameter	2.3750—2.3760in
Rod oil clearance	0.0005—0.0025in
Rod side clearance	0.009—0.017in
Intake valve seat angle	45deg
Exhaust valve seat angle	45deg
Intake face angle	45deg
Exhaust face angle	45deg
Seat width	NA
Spring pressure	NA
Intake stem to guide clearance	0.0011—0.0028in
Exhaust stem to guide clearance	0.0010—0.0027in
Intake stem diameter	0.3726in
Exhaust stem diameter	0.3722in
Piston clearance	0.0003—0.0013in
Top comp. ring gap	0.013—0.023in
Bottom comp. ring gap	0.013—0.023in
Oil ring gap	0.015—0.055in
Top comp. side clearance	0.0015—0.0030in
Bottom comp. side clearance	0.0015—0.0030in
Oil side clearance	0.000—0.005in

1978 Chrysler 400 Eight-cylinder

Displacement	400ci
Volume (liters)	NA
Main journal diameter	2.6245—2.6255in
Main journal oil clearance	0.0005—0.0020in
Crankshaft end play	0.002—0.009in
Thrust journal length	3in
Rod journal diameter	2.3750—2.3760in
Rod oil clearance	0.0005—0.0025in
Rod side clearance	0.009—0.017in
Intake valve seat angle	45deg
Exhaust valve seat angle	45deg
Intake face angle	45deg
Exhaust face angle	45deg
Seat width	NA
Spring pressure	NA
Intake stem to guide clearance	0.0011—0.0028in
Exhaust stem to guide clearance	0.0010—0.0027in
Intake stem diameter	0.3726in
Exhaust stem diameter	0.3722in
Piston clearance	0.0003—0.0013in
Top comp. ring gap	0.013—0.023in

Bottom comp. ring gap	0.013—0.023in
Oil ring gap	0.015—0.055in
Top comp. side clearance	0.0015—0.0030in
Bottom comp. side clearance	0.0015—0.0030in
Oil side clearance	0.0002—0.0050in

1977 Chrysler 440 Eight-cylinder

Displacement	440ci
Volume (liters)	NA
Main journal diameter	2.7495—2.7505in
Main journal oil clearance	0.0005—0.0020in
Crankshaft end play	0.002—0.009in
Thrust journal length	3in
Rod journal diameter	2.3750—2.3760in
Rod oil clearance	0.0005—0.0025in
Rod side clearance	0.009—0.017in
Intake valve seat angle	45deg
Exhaust valve seat angle	45deg
Intake face angle	45deg
Exhaust face angle	43deg
Seat width	NA
Spring pressure	NA
Intake stem to guide clearance	0.0011—0.0028in
Exhaust stem to guide clearance	0.0010—0.0027in
Intake stem diameter	0.3726in
Exhaust stem diameter	0.3722in
Piston clearance	0.0003—0.0013in
Top comp. ring gap	0.013—0.023in
Bottom comp. ring gap	0.013—0.023in
Oil ring gap	0.015—0.055in
Top comp. side clearance	0.0015—0.0030in
Bottom comp. side clearance	0.0015—0.0030in
Oil side clearance	0.000—0.005in

1982 Corvette 350

Displacement	359ci
Volume (liters)	NA
Main journal diameter	2.4484—2.4493in; 2.4479—2.4488in (no. 5); 2.4481—2.4490 (nos. 2, 3, & 4)
Main journal oil clearance	0.0008—0.0020in; 0.0017—0.0033in (no. 5); 0.0011—0.0023in (nos. 2, 3, & 4)
Crankshaft end play	0.002—0.006in
Thrust journal length	5in
Rod journal diameter	2.0988—2.0998in
Rod oil clearance	0.0013—0.0035in
Rod side clearance	0.008—0.014in
Intake valve seat angle	46deg
Exhaust valve seat angle	46deg
Intake face angle	45deg
Exhaust face angle	45deg
Seat width	NA
Spring pressure	NA
Intake stem to guide clearance	0.0010—0.0027in
Exhaust stem to guide clearance	0.0010—0.0027in
Intake stem diameter	0.3410—0.3417in
Exhaust stem diameter	0.3410—0.3417in
Piston clearance	0.0025—0.0045in
Top comp. ring gap	NA
Bottom comp. ring gap	NA
Oil ring gap	NA
Top comp. side clearance	NA
Bottom comp. side clearance	NA
Oil side clearance	NA

1981 Corvette 350

Displacement	350ci
Volume (liters)	NA
Main journal diameter	2.4484—2.4493; 2.4479—2.4488 (no. 5); 2.4481—2.4490 (nos. 2, 3, & 4)in
Main journal oil clearance	0.0008—0.0020; 0.0017—0.0033 (no. 5); 0.0011—0.0023 (nos. 2, 3, & 4)in
Crankshaft end play	0.002—0.006in
Thrust journal length	5in
Rod journal diameter	2.0988—2.0998in

Rod oil clearance | 0.0013—0.0035in
Rod side clearance | 0.008—0.014in
Intake valve seat angle | 46deg
Exhaust valve seat angle | 46deg
Intake face angle | 45deg
Exhaust face angle | 45deg
Seat width | NA
Spring pressure | NA
Intake stem to guide clearance | 0.0010—0.0027in
Exhaust stem to guide clearance | 0.0010—0.0027in
Intake stem diameter | 0.3410—0.3417in
Exhaust stem diameter | 0.3410—0.3417in
Piston clearance | 0.0046—0.0061in
Top comp. ring gap | NA
Bottom comp. ring gap | NA
Oil ring gap | NA
Top comp. side clearance | NA
Bottom comp. side clearance | NA
Oil side clearance | NA

1980—1981 Corvette 305

Displacement | 305ci
Volume (liters) | NA
Main journal diameter | 2.4484—2.4493; 2.4479—2.4466in (no. 5); 2.4481—2.4490in (nos. 2, 3, & 4)
Main journal oil clearance | 0.0008—0.0020; 0.0017—0.0033in (no. 5); 0.0011—0.0023in (nos. 2, 3, & 4)
Crankshaft end play | 0.002—0.006in
Thrust journal length | 5in
Rod journal diameter | 2.0988—2.0998in
Rod oil clearance | 0.0013—0.0035in
Rod side clearance | 0.008—0.014in
Intake valve seat angle | 46deg
Exhaust valve seat angle | 46deg
Intake face angle | 45deg
Exhaust face angle | 45deg
Seat width | NA
Spring pressure | NA
Intake stem to guide clearance | 0.0010—0.0027in
Exhaust stem to guide clearance | 0.0010—0.0027in
Intake stem diameter | 0.3410—0.3417in
Exhaust stem diameter | 0.3410—0.3417in
Piston clearance | 0.0007—0.0027in
Top comp. ring gap | NA
Bottom comp. ring gap | NA
Oil ring gap | NA
Top comp. side clearance | NA
Bottom comp. side clearance | NA
Oil side clearance | NA

1978—1980 Corvette 350

Displacement | 350ci
Volume (liters) | NA
Main journal diameter | 2.4484—2.4493; 2.4479—2.4488 (no. 5); 2.4481—2.4490in (nos. 2, 3, & 4)
Main journal oil clearance | 0.0008—0.0020; 0.0017—0.0033in (no. 5); 0.0011—0.0023in (nos. 2, 3, & 4)
Crankshaft end play | 0.002—0.006in
Thrust journal length | 5in
Rod journal diameter | 2.0988—2.0998in
Rod oil clearance | 0.0013—0.0035in
Rod side clearance | 0.008—0.014in
Intake valve seat angle | 46deg
Exhaust valve seat angle | 46deg
Intake face angle | 45deg
Exhaust face angle | 45deg
Seat width | NA
Spring pressure | NA
Intake stem to guide clearance | 0.0010—0.0027in
Exhaust stem to guide clearance | 0.0010—0.0027in
Intake stem diameter | 0.3410—0.3417in
Exhaust stem diameter | 0.3410—0.3417in
Piston clearance | 0.0036—0.0061in
Top comp. ring gap | NA

Bottom comp. ring gap | NA
Oil ring gap | NA
Top comp. side clearance | NA
Bottom comp. side clearance | NA
Oil side clearance | NA

1977 Corvette 350

Displacement | 350ci
Volume (liters) | NA
Main journal diameter | 2.4484—2.4493; 2.4479—2.4488in (no. 5); 2.4481—2.4490in (nos. 2, 3, &4)
Main journal oil clearance | 0.0008—0.0020; 0.0017—0.0033in (no. 5); 0.0011—0.0023in (nos. 2, 3, & 4)
Crankshaft end play | 0.002—0.006in
Thrust journal length | 5in
Rod journal diameter | 2.0988—2.0998in
Rod oil clearance | 0.0013—0.0035in
Rod side clearance | 0.008—0.014in
Intake valve seat angle | 46deg
Exhaust valve seat angle | 46deg
Intake face angle | 45deg
Exhaust face angle | 45deg
Seat width | NA
Spring pressure | NA
Intake stem to guide clearance | 0.0010—0.0027in
Exhaust stem to guide clearance | 0.0010—0.0027in
Intake stem diameter | 0.3410—0.3417in
Exhaust stem diameter | 0.3410—0.3417in
Piston clearance | 0.0007—0.0027in
Top comp. ring gap | NA
Bottom comp. ring gap | NA
Oil ring gap | NA
Top comp. side clearance | NA
Bottom comp. side clearance | NA
Oil side clearance | NA

1979—1982 Datsun A15

Displacement | 90.8ci
Volume (liters) | 1.488
Main journal diameter | 1.966—1.9671in
Main journal oil clearance | 0.0010—0.0035in
Crankshaft end play | 0.0020—0.0059in
Thrust journal length | 3in
Rod journal diameter | 1.7701—1.7706in
Rod oil clearance | 0.0012—0.0031in
Rod side clearance | 0.008—0.012in
Intake valve seat angle | 45deg 30min
Exhaust valve seat angle | 45deg 30min
Intake face angle | 45deg 30min
Exhaust face angle | 45deg 30min
Seat width | NA
Spring pressure | 52.7psi @ 1.19in
Intake stem to guide clearance | 0.0006—0.0018in
Exhaust stem to guide clearance | 0.0016—0.0028in
Intake stem diameter | 0.3138—0.3144in
Exhaust stem diameter | 0.3128—0.3134in
Piston clearance | 0.001—0.002in
Top comp. ring gap | 0.008—0.014in
Bottom comp. ring gap | 0.006—0.012in
Oil ring gap | 0.012—0.035in
Top comp. side clearance | 0.002—0.003in
Bottom comp. side clearance | 0.001—0.002in
Oil side clearance | Combination ring

1979—1982 Datsun A14

Displacement | 85.3ci
Volume (liters) | 1.397
Main journal diameter | 1.9666—1.9671in
Main journal oil clearance | 0.0010—0.0035in
Crankshaft end play | 0.0020—0.0059in
Thrust journal length | 3in
Rod journal diameter | 1.7701—1.7706in
Rod oil clearance | 0.0012—0.0031in
Rod side clearance | 0.008—0.012in
Intake valve seat angle | 45deg 30min
Exhaust valve seat angle | 45deg 30min
Intake face angle | 45deg 30min
Exhaust face angle | 45deg 30min

Seat width | NA
Spring pressure | 52.7psi @ 1.19in
Intake stem to guide clearance | 0.0006—0.0018in
Exhaust stem to guide clearance | 0.0016—0.0028in
Intake stem diameter | 0.3138—0.3144in
Exhaust stem diameter | 0.3128—0.3134in
Piston clearance | 0.001—0.002in
Top comp. ring gap | 0.008—0.014in
Bottom comp. ring gap | 0.006—0.012in
Oil ring gap | 0.012—0.035in
Top comp. side clearance | 0.002—0.003in
Bottom comp. side clearance | 0.001—0.002in
Oil side clearance | Combination ring

1982—1984 Datsun 200SX Z22 and Z22E

Displacement | 133.4ci
Volume (liters) | 2.181
Main journal diameter | 2.1631—2.1636in
Main journal oil clearance | 0.0008—0.0024in
Crankshaft end play | 0.0020—0.0071in
Thrust journal length | 3in
Rod journal diameter | 1.967—1.9675in
Rod oil clearance | 0.0010—0.0022in
Rod side clearance | 0.008—0.012in
Intake valve seat angle | 45deg
Exhaust valve seat angle | 45deg
Intake face angle | 45deg
Exhaust face angle | 45deg
Seat width | NA
Spring pressure | 155.3psi @ 1.16in
Intake stem to guide clearance | 0.0008—0.0021in
Exhaust stem to guide clearance | 0.0016—0.0029in
Intake stem diameter | 0.03136—0.3142in
Exhaust stem diameter | 0.3128—0.3134in
Piston clearance | 0.001—0.002in
Top comp. ring gap | 0.0098—0.0160in
Bottom comp. ring gap | 0.006—0.012in
Oil ring gap | 0.012—0.035in
Top comp. side clearance | 0.002—0.003in
Bottom comp. side clearance | 0.0010—0.0025in
Oil side clearance | NA

1981 Datsun 200SX Z20

Displacement | 119.1ci
Volume (liters) | 1.952
Main journal diameter | 2.1631—2.1636in
Main journal oil clearance | 0.0008—0.0024in
Crankshaft end play | 0.0020—0.0071in
Thrust journal length | 3in
Rod journal diameter | 1.9670—1.9675in
Rod oil clearance | 0.0010—0.0022in
Rod side clearance | 0.008—0.012in
Intake valve seat angle | 45deg
Exhaust valve seat angle | 45deg
Intake face angle | 45deg
Exhaust face angle | 45deg
Seat width | NA
Spring pressure | NA
Intake stem to guide clearance | 0.0008—0.0021in
Exhaust stem to guide clearance | 0.0016—0.0029in
Intake stem diameter | 0.3136—0.3142in
Exhaust stem diameter | 0.3128—0.3134in
Piston clearance | 0.001—0.002in
Top comp. ring gap | 0.0098—0.0160in
Bottom comp. ring gap | 0.006—0.012in
Oil ring gap | 0.012—0.035in
Top comp. side clearance | 0.002—0.003in
Bottom comp. side clearance | 0.0010—0.0025in
Oil side clearance | NA

1980 Datsun 200SX Z20E

Displacement | 119.1ci
Volume (liters) | 1.952
Main journal diameter | 2.1631—2.1636in
Main journal oil clearance | 0.0008—0.0024in
Crankshaft end play | 0.0020—0.0071in
Thrust journal length | 3in
Rod journal diameter | 1.9670—1.9675in
Rod oil clearance | 0.0010—0.0022in
Rod side clearance | 0.008—0.012in
Intake valve seat angle | 45deg
Exhaust valve seat angle | 45deg

Intake face angle	45deg
Exhaust face angle	45deg
Seat width	NA
Spring pressure	115.3psi @ 1.16in
Intake stem to guide clearance	0.0008—0.0021in
Exhaust stem to guide clearance	0.0016—0.0029in
Intake stem diameter	0.3136—0.3142in
Exhaust stem diameter	0.3128—0.3134in
Piston clearance	0.001—0.002in
Top comp. ring gap	0.0098—0.0160in
Bottom comp. ring gap	0.006—0.012in
Oil ring gap	0.012—0.035in
Top comp. side clearance	0.002—0.003in
Bottom comp. side clearance	0.0010—0.0025in
Oil side clearance	NA

1979 Datsun 200SX L20B

Displacement	119.1ci
Volume (liters)	1.952
Main journal diameter	2.3599—2.3600in
Main journal oil clearance	0.0008—0.0024in
Crankshaft end play	0.002—0.007in
Thrust journal length	3in
Rod journal diameter	1.9660—1.9670in
Rod oil clearance	0.001—0.002in
Rod side clearance	0.008—0.012in
Intake valve seat angle	45deg
Exhaust valve seat angle	45deg
Intake face angle	45deg
Exhaust face angle	45deg
Seat width	NA
Spring pressure	108psi @ 1.16in
Intake stem to guide clearance	0.008—0.0021in
Exhaust stem to guide clearance	0.0016—0.0029in
Intake stem diameter	0.3136—0.3142in
Exhaust stem diameter	0.3128—0.3134in
Piston clearance	0.001—0.002in
Top comp. ring gap	0.010—0.016in
Bottom comp. ring gap	0.012—0.020in
Oil ring gap	0.012—0.035in
Top comp. side clearance	0.002—0.003in
Bottom comp. side clearance	0.001—0.003in
Oil side clearance	NA

1977—1978 Datsun 200SX L20B

Displacement	119.1ci
Volume (liters)	1.952
Main journal diameter	2.3599—2.3600in
Main journal oil clearance	0.0008—0.0024in
Crankshaft end play	0.002—0.007in
Thrust journal length	3in
Rod journal diameter	1.9660—1.9670in
Rod oil clearance	0.001—0.002in
Rod side clearance	0.008—0.012in
Intake valve seat angle	45deg
Exhaust valve seat angle	45deg
Intake face angle	45deg
Exhaust face angle	45deg
Seat width	NA
Spring pressure	108psi @ 1.16in
Intake stem to guide clearance	0.008—0.0021in
Exhaust stem to guide clearance	0.0016—0.0029in
Intake stem diameter	0.3136—0.3142in
Exhaust stem diameter	0.3128—0.3134in
Piston clearance	0.001—0.002in
Top comp. ring gap	0.010—0.016in
Bottom comp. ring gap	0.012—0.020in
Oil ring gap	0.012—0.035in
Top comp. side clearance	0.002—0.003in
Bottom comp. side clearance	0.001—0.003in
Oil side clearance	NA

1979—1982 Datsun 210 A12A

Displacement	75.5ci
Volume (liters)	1.237
Main journal diameter	1.966—1.9671in
Main journal oil clearance	0.0010—0.0035in
Crankshaft end play	0.0020—0.0059in
Thrust journal length	3in
Rod journal diameter	1.7701—1.7706in
Rod oil clearance	0.0012—0.0031in
Rod side clearance	0.008—0.012in

Intake valve seat angle	45deg 30min
Exhaust valve seat angle	45deg 30min
Intake face angle	45deg 30min
Exhaust face angle	45deg 30min
Seat width	NA
Spring pressure	52.7psi @ 1.19in
Intake stem to guide clearance	0.0006—0.0018in
Exhaust stem to guide clearance	0.0016—0.0028in
Intake stem diameter	0.3138—0.3144in
Exhaust stem diameter	0.3128—0.3134in
Piston clearance	0.001—0.002in
Top comp. ring gap	0.008—0.014in
Bottom comp. ring gap	0.006—0.012in
Oil ring gap	0.012—0.035in
Top comp. side clearance	0.002—0.003in
Bottom comp. side clearance	0.001—0.002in
Oil side clearance	Combination ring

[1]1977—1978 Datsun 280Z L28

Displacement	168ci
Volume (liters)	2.753
Main journal diameter	2.1631—2.1636in
Main journal oil clearance	0.008—0.0028in
Crankshaft end play	0.002—0.007in
Thrust journal length	Centerin
Rod journal diameter	1.9670—1.9675in
Rod oil clearance	0.0010—0.0022in
Rod side clearance	0.0079—0.0118in
Intake valve seat angle	45deg
Exhaust valve seat angle	45deg
Intake face angle	45deg
Exhaust face angle	45deg
Seat width	NA
Spring pressure	108psi @ 1.16in
Intake stem to guide clearance	0.0008—0.0021in
Exhaust stem to guide clearance	0.0016—0.0029in
Intake stem diameter	0.3136—0.3142in
Exhaust stem diameter	0.3128—0.3134in
Piston clearance	0.0010—0.0018in
Top comp. ring gap	0.0098—0.0157in
Bottom comp. ring gap	0.0118—0.0197in
Oil ring gap	0.0118—0.0354in
Top comp. side clearance	0.0016—0.0019in
Bottom comp. side clearance	0.0012—0.0028in
Oil side clearance	NA

1981—1984 Datsun 280ZX L28E

Displacement	168ci
Volume (liters)	2.753
Main journal diameter	2.1631—2.1636in
Main journal oil clearance	0.0008—0.0026in
Crankshaft end play	0.002—0.007in
Thrust journal length	Centerin
Rod journal diameter	1.9670—1.9675in
Rod oil clearance	0.0009—0.0026in
Rod side clearance	0.0079—0.0118in
Intake valve seat angle	45deg 30min
Exhaust valve seat angle	45deg 30min
Intake face angle	45deg 30min
Exhaust face angle	45deg 30min
Seat width	NA
Spring pressure	108psi @ 1.16in
Intake stem to guide clearance	0.0008—0.0021in
Exhaust stem to guide clearance	0.0016—0.0029in
Intake stem diameter	0.3136—0.3142in
Exhaust stem diameter	0.3128—0.3134in
Piston clearance	0.0010—0.0018in
Top comp. ring gap	0.0098—0.0157in
Bottom comp. ring gap	0.0050—0.0118in
Oil ring gap	0.012—0.035in
Top comp. side clearance	0.0016—0.0029in
Bottom comp. side clearance	0.0012—0.0025in
Oil side clearance	NA

1979—1980 Datsun 280ZX L28

Displacement	168ci
Volume (liters)	2.753
Main journal diameter	2.1631—2.1636in
Main journal oil clearance	0.0008—0.0026in
Crankshaft end play	0.002—0.007in
Thrust journal length	Centerin
Rod journal diameter	1.9670—1.9675in

Rod oil clearance	0.0009—0.0026in
Rod side clearance	0.0079—0.0118in
Intake valve seat angle	45deg 30min
Exhaust valve seat angle	45deg 30min
Intake face angle	45deg 30min
Exhaust face angle	45deg 30min
Seat width	NA
Spring pressure	108psi @ 1.16in
Intake stem to guide clearance	0.0008—0.0021in
Exhaust stem to guide clearance	0.0016—0.0029in
Intake stem diameter	0.3136—0.3142in
Exhaust stem diameter	0.3128—0.3134in
Piston clearance	0.0010—0.0018in
Top comp. ring gap	0.0098—0.0157in
Bottom comp. ring gap	0.0118—0.0197in
Oil ring gap	0.0118—0.0354in
Top comp. side clearance	0.0016—0.0029in
Bottom comp. side clearance	0.0012—0.0025in
Oil side clearance	NA

1981—1984 Datsun 280ZX Turbo L28ET

Displacement	168ci
Volume (liters)	2.753
Main journal diameter	2.1631—2.1636in
Main journal oil clearance	0.0008—0.0026in
Crankshaft end play	0.002—0.007in
Thrust journal length	Centerin
Rod journal diameter	1.9670—1.9675in
Rod oil clearance	0.0009—0.0026in
Rod side clearance	0.0079—0.0118in
Intake valve seat angle	45deg 30min
Exhaust valve seat angle	45deg 30min
Intake face angle	45deg 30min
Exhaust face angle	45deg 30min
Seat width	NA
Spring pressure	108psi @ 1.16in
Intake stem to guide clearance	0.0008—0.0021in
Exhaust stem to guide clearance	0.0016—0.0029in
Intake stem diameter	0.3136—0.3142in
Exhaust stem diameter	0.3128—0.3134in
Piston clearance	0.0010—0.0018in
Top comp. ring gap	0.0075—0.0130in
Bottom comp. ring gap	0.0059—0.0118in
Oil ring gap	0.012—0.035in
Top comp. side clearance	0.0016—0.0029in
Bottom comp. side clearance	0.0012—0.0025in
Oil side clearance	0.0009—0.0028in

1981 Datsun 310 A15

Displacement	90.8ci
Volume (liters)	1.488
Main journal diameter	1.9666—1.9671in
Main journal oil clearance	0.0010—0.0035in
Crankshaft end play	0.0020—0.0059in
Thrust journal length	3in
Rod journal diameter	1.7701—1.7706in
Rod oil clearance	0.0012—0.0031in
Rod side clearance	0.008—0.012in
Intake valve seat angle	45deg 30min
Exhaust valve seat angle	45deg 30min
Intake face angle	45deg 30min
Exhaust face angle	45deg 30min
Seat width	NA
Spring pressure	52.7psi @ 1.19in
Intake stem to guide clearance	0.0006—0.0018in
Exhaust stem to guide clearance	0.0016—0.0028in
Intake stem diameter	0.3138—0.3144in
Exhaust stem diameter	0.3128—0.3134in
Piston clearance	0.001—0.002in
Top comp. ring gap	0.008—0.014in
Bottom comp. ring gap	0.006—0.012in
Oil ring gap	0.012—0.035in
Top comp. side clearance	0.002—0.003in
Bottom comp. side clearance	0.001—0.002in
Oil side clearance	Combination ring

1979—1980 Datsun 310 A14

Displacement	85.2ci
Volume (liters)	1.397
Main journal diameter	1.9666—1.9671in
Main journal oil clearance	0.0010—0.0035in

Crankshaft end play	0.0020—0.0059in
Thrust journal length	3in
Rod journal diameter	1.7701—1.7706in
Rod oil clearance	0.0012—0.0031in
Rod side clearance	0.008—0.012in
Intake valve seat angle	45deg 30min
Exhaust valve seat angle	45deg 30min
Intake face angle	45deg 30min
Exhaust face angle	45deg 30min
Seat width	NA
Spring pressure	52.7psi @ 1.19in
Intake stem to guide clearance	0.0006—0.0018in
Exhaust stem to guide clearance	0.0016—0.0028in
Intake stem diameter	0.3138—0.3144in
Exhaust stem diameter	0.3128—0.3134in
Piston clearance	0.001—0.002in
Top comp. ring gap	0.008—0.014in
Bottom comp. ring gap	0.006—0.012in
Oil ring gap	0.012—0.035in
Top comp. side clearance	0.002—0.003in
Bottom comp. side clearance	0.001—0.002in
Oil side clearance	Combination ring

1982—1984 Datsun 310 Sentra E15

Displacement	90.8ci
Volume (liters)	1.488
Main journal diameter	1.9663—1.9671in
Main journal oil clearance	0.0012—0.0030in (nos. 1 & 5); 0.0015-0.0030in (nos. 2, 3, & 4)
Crankshaft end play	0.002—0.007in
Thrust journal length	3in
Rod journal diameter	1.5730—1.5733in
Rod oil clearance	0.0012—0.0024in
Rod side clearance	0.0040—0.0146in
Intake valve seat angle	45deg 30min
Exhaust valve seat angle	45deg 30min
Intake face angle	45deg 30min
Exhaust face angle	45deg 30min
Seat width	NA
Spring pressure	128psi @ 1.19in
Intake stem to guide clearance	0.0008—0.0020in
Exhaust stem to guide clearance	0.0018—0.0030in
Intake stem diameter	0.2744—0.2750in
Exhaust stem diameter	0.2734—0.2740in
Piston clearance	0.0009—0.0017in
Top comp. ring gap	0.0079—0.0138in
Bottom comp. ring gap	0.0018—0.0059in
Oil ring gap	0.0118—0.0354in
Top comp. side clearance	0.0016—0.0029in
Bottom comp. side clearance	0.0012—0.0025in
Oil side clearance	0.0020—0.0057in

1981 Datsun 510 Z20

Displacement	119.1ci
Volume (liters)	1.952
Main journal diameter	2.1631—2.1636in
Main journal oil clearance	0.0008—0.0024in
Crankshaft end play	0.0020—0.0071in
Thrust journal length	3in
Rod journal diameter	1.9670—1.9675in
Rod oil clearance	0.0010—0.0022in
Rod side clearance	0.008—0.012in
Intake valve seat angle	45deg
Exhaust valve seat angle	45deg
Intake face angle	45deg
Exhaust face angle	45deg
Seat width	NA
Spring pressure	NA
Intake stem to guide clearance	0.0008—0.0021in
Exhaust stem to guide clearance	0.0016—0.0029in
Intake stem diameter	0.3136—0.3142in
Exhaust stem diameter	0.3128—0.3134in
Piston clearance	0.001—0.002in
Top comp. ring gap	0.0098—0.0160in
Bottom comp. ring gap	0.006—0.012in
Oil ring gap	0.012—0.035in
Top comp. side clearance	0.002—0.003in
Bottom comp. side clearance	0.0010—0.0025in
Oil side clearance	NA

1980 Datsun 510 Z20S

Displacement	119.1ci
Volume (liters)	1.952
Main journal diameter	2.1631—2.1636in
Main journal oil clearance	0.0008—0.0024in
Crankshaft end play	0.0020—0.0071in
Thrust journal length	3in
Rod journal diameter	1.9670—1.9675in
Rod oil clearance	0.0010—0.0022in
Rod side clearance	0.008—0.012in
Intake valve seat angle	45deg
Exhaust valve seat angle	45deg
Intake face angle	45deg
Exhaust face angle	45deg
Seat width	NA
Spring pressure	115.3psi @ 1.16in
Intake stem to guide clearance	0.0008—0.0021in
Exhaust stem to guide clearance	0.0016—0.0029in
Intake stem diameter	0.3136—0.3142in
Exhaust stem diameter	0.3128—0.3134in
Piston clearance	0.001—0.002in
Top comp. ring gap	0.0098—0.0160in
Bottom comp. ring gap	0.006—0.012in
Oil ring gap	0.012—0.035in
Top comp. side clearance	0.002—0.003in
Bottom comp. side clearance	0.0010—0.0025in
Oil side clearance	NA

1979 Datsun 510 L20B

Displacement	119.1ci
Volume (liters)	1.952
Main journal diameter	2.3599—2.3600in
Main journal oil clearance	0.0008—0.0024in
Crankshaft end play	0.002—0.007in
Thrust journal length	3in
Rod journal diameter	1.9660—1.9670in
Rod oil clearance	0.001—0.002in
Rod side clearance	0.008—0.012in
Intake valve seat angle	45deg
Exhaust valve seat angle	45deg
Intake face angle	45deg
Exhaust face angle	45deg
Seat width	NA
Spring pressure	108psi @ 1.16in
Intake stem to guide clearance	0.0021—0.0080in
Exhaust stem to guide clearance	0.0016—0.0029in
Intake stem diameter	0.3136—0.3142in
Exhaust stem diameter	0.3128—0.3134in
Piston clearance	0.001—0.002in
Top comp. ring gap	0.010—0.016in
Bottom comp. ring gap	0.012—0.020in
Oil ring gap	0.012—0.035in
Top comp. side clearance	0.002—0.003in
Bottom comp. side clearance	0.001—0.003in
Oil side clearance	NA

1978 Datsun 510 L20B

Displacement	119.1ci
Volume (liters)	1.952
Main journal diameter	2.3599—2.3600in
Main journal oil clearance	0.0008—0.0024in
Crankshaft end play	0.002—0.007in
Thrust journal length	3in
Rod journal diameter	1.9660—1.9670in
Rod oil clearance	0.001—0.002in
Rod side clearance	0.008—0.012in
Intake valve seat angle	45deg
Exhaust valve seat angle	45deg
Intake face angle	45deg
Exhaust face angle	45deg
Seat width	NA
Spring pressure	108psi @ 1.16in
Intake stem to guide clearance	0.0021—0.0080in
Exhaust stem to guide clearance	0.0016—0.0029in
Intake stem diameter	0.3136—0.3142in
Exhaust stem diameter	0.3128—0.3134in
Piston clearance	0.001—0.002in
Top comp. ring gap	0.010—0.016in
Bottom comp. ring gap	0.012—0.020in
Oil ring gap	0.012—0.035in
Top comp. side clearance	0.002—0.003in
Bottom comp. side clearance	0.001—0.003in

Oil side clearance	NA

1977 Datsun 710 L20B

Displacement	119.1ci
Volume (liters)	1.952
Main journal diameter	2.3599—2.3600in
Main journal oil clearance	0.0008—0.0024in
Crankshaft end play	0.002—0.007in
Thrust journal length	3in
Rod journal diameter	1.9660—1.9670in
Rod oil clearance	0.001—0.002in
Rod side clearance	0.008—0.012in
Intake valve seat angle	45deg
Exhaust valve seat angle	45deg
Intake face angle	45deg
Exhaust face angle	45deg
Seat width	NA
Spring pressure	108psi @ 1.16in
Intake stem to guide clearance	0.0021—0.0080in
Exhaust stem to guide clearance	0.0016—0.0029in
Intake stem diameter	0.3136—0.3142in
Exhaust stem diameter	0.3128—0.3134in
Piston clearance	0.001—0.002in
Top comp. ring gap	0.010—0.016in
Bottom comp. ring gap	0.012—0.020in
Oil ring gap	0.012—0.035in
Top comp. side clearance	0.002—0.003in
Bottom comp. side clearance	0.001—0.003in
Oil side clearance	NA

1979—1980 Datsun 810 L24

Displacement	146ci
Volume (liters)	2.393
Main journal diameter	2.1631—2.1636in
Main journal oil clearance	0.001—0.003in
Crankshaft end play	0.002—0.007in
Thrust journal length	Centerin
Rod journal diameter	1.9670—1.9675in
Rod oil clearance	0.001—0.003in
Rod side clearance	0.008—0.012in
Intake valve seat angle	45deg
Exhaust valve seat angle	45deg
Intake face angle	45deg
Exhaust face angle	45deg
Seat width	NA
Spring pressure	108psi @ 1.16in
Intake stem to guide clearance	0.001—0.002in
Exhaust stem to guide clearance	0.002—0.003in
Intake stem diameter	0.3136—0.3142in
Exhaust stem diameter	0.3128—0.3134in
Piston clearance	0.001—0.002in
Top comp. ring gap	0.009—0.015in
Bottom comp. ring gap	0.006—0.012in
Oil ring gap	0.012—0.035in
Top comp. side clearance	0.002—0.003in
Bottom comp. side clearance	0.001—0.003in
Oil side clearance	0.001—0.003in

1977—1978 Datsun 810 L24

Displacement	146ci
Volume (liters)	2.393
Main journal diameter	2.1631—2.1636in
Main journal oil clearance	0.001—0.003in
Crankshaft end play	0.002—0.007in
Thrust journal length	Centerin
Rod journal diameter	1.9670—1.9675in
Rod oil clearance	0.001—0.003in
Rod side clearance	0.008—0.012in
Intake valve seat angle	45deg
Exhaust valve seat angle	45deg
Intake face angle	45deg
Exhaust face angle	45deg
Seat width	NA
Spring pressure	108psi @ 1.16in
Intake stem to guide clearance	0.001—0.002in
Exhaust stem to guide clearance	0.002—0.003in
Intake stem diameter	0.3136—0.3142in
Exhaust stem diameter	0.3128—0.3134in
Piston clearance	0.001—0.002in
Top comp. ring gap	0.009—0.0145in
Bottom comp. ring gap	0.006—0.012in
Oil ring gap	0.012—0.035in

Top comp. side clearance 0.002—0.003in
Bottom comp. side clearance 0.001—0.003in
Oil side clearance 0.001—0.003in

1981—1984 Datsun 810 Maxima L24

Displacement	146ci
Volume (liters)	2.393
Main journal diameter	2.1631—2.1636in
Main journal oil clearance	0.001—0.003in
Crankshaft end play	0.002—0.007in
Thrust journal length	centerin
Rod journal diameter	1.9670—1.9675in
Rod oil clearance	0.001—0.003in
Rod side clearance	0.008—0.012in
Intake valve seat angle	45deg
Exhaust valve seat angle	45deg
Intake face angle	45deg
Exhaust face angle	45deg
Seat width	NA
Spring pressure	108psi @ 1.16in
Intake stem to guide clearance	0.001—0.002in
Exhaust stem to guide clearance	0.002—0.003in
Intake stem diameter	0.3136—0.3142in
Exhaust stem diameter	0.3128—0.3134in
Piston clearance	0.001—0.002in
Top comp. ring gap	0.009—0.015in
Bottom comp. ring gap	0.006—0.012in
Oil ring gap	0.012—0.035in
Top comp. side clearance	0.002—0.003in
Bottom comp. side clearance	0.001—0.003in
Oil side clearance	0.001—0.003in

1977—1978 Datsun B210 A14

Displacement	85.2ci
Volume (liters)	1.397
Main journal diameter	1.966—1.967in
Main journal oil clearance	0.0008—0.0020in
Crankshaft end play	0.002—0.006in
Thrust journal length	3in
Rod journal diameter	1.7701—1.7706in
Rod oil clearance	0.0008—0.0020in
Rod side clearance	0.008—0.012in
Intake valve seat angle	45deg
Exhaust valve seat angle	45deg
Intake face angle	45deg
Exhaust face angle	45deg
Seat width	NA
Spring pressure	52.9psi @ 1.52in
Intake stem to guide clearance	0.0006—0.0018in
Exhaust stem to guide clearance	0.0016—0.0028in
Intake stem diameter	0.3138—0.3144in
Exhaust stem diameter	0.3128—0.3134in
Piston clearance	0.0009—0.0020in
Top comp. ring gap	0.008—0.014in
Bottom comp. ring gap	0.006—0.012in
Oil ring gap	0.012—0.035in
Top comp. side clearance	0.002—0.003in
Bottom comp. side clearance	0.001—0.002in
Oil side clearance	Combination ring

1977—1978 Datsun F10 A14

Displacement	85.2ci
Volume (liters)	1.397
Main journal diameter	1.966—1.967in
Main journal oil clearance	0.0008—0.0020in
Crankshaft end play	0.002—0.006in
Thrust journal length	3in
Rod journal diameter	1.7701—1.7706in
Rod oil clearance	0.00058—0.0020in
Rod side clearance	0.008—0.012in
Intake valve seat angle	45deg
Exhaust valve seat angle	45deg
Intake face angle	45deg
Exhaust face angle	45deg
Seat width	NA
Spring pressure	52.9psi @ 1.52in
Intake stem to guide clearance	0.0006—0.0018in
Exhaust stem to guide clearance	0.0016—0.0028in
Intake stem diameter	0.3138—0.3144in
Exhaust stem diameter	0.3128—0.3134in
Piston clearance	0.0009—0.0020in
Top comp. ring gap	0.008—0.014in

Bottom comp. ring gap 0.006—0.012in
Oil ring gap 0.012—0.035in
Top comp. side clearance 0.002—0.003in
Bottom comp. side clearance 0.001—0.002in
Oil side clearance Combination ring

1983—1984 Datsun Sentra E16 and Pulsar E16

Displacement	97.6ci
Volume (liters)	1.597
Main journal diameter	1.9663—1.9671in
Main journal oil clearance	NA
Crankshaft end play	0.002—0.007in
Thrust journal length	3in
Rod journal diameter	1.5730—1.538in
Rod oil clearance	0.0012—0.0024in
Rod side clearance	0.0040—0.0146in
Intake valve seat angle	45deg 30min
Exhaust valve seat angle	45deg 30min
Intake face angle	45deg 30min
Exhaust face angle	45deg 30min
Seat width	NA
Spring pressure	128psi @ 1.19in
Intake stem to guide clearance	0.0008—0.0020in
Exhaust stem to guide clearance	0.0018—0.0030in
Intake stem diameter	0.2744—0.2750in
Exhaust stem diameter	0.2734—0.2740in
Piston clearance	0.0009—0.0017in
Top comp. ring gap	0.0079—0.0138in
Bottom comp. ring gap	0.0018—0.0059in
Oil ring gap	0.0118—0.0354in
Top comp. side clearance	0.0016—0.0029in
Bottom comp. side clearance	0.0012—0.0025in
Oil side clearance	0.0020—0.0057in

1982—1984 Datsun Stanza CA20

Displacement	120.4ci
Volume (liters)	1.974
Main journal diameter	2.0847—2.085in
Main journal oil clearance	0.0016—0.0024in
Crankshaft end play	0.002—0.007in
Thrust journal length	3in
Rod journal diameter	1.7701—1.7706in
Rod oil clearance	0.0008—0.0024in
Rod side clearance	0.008—0.012in
Intake valve seat angle	45deg 30min
Exhaust valve seat angle	45deg 30min
Intake face angle	45deg 30min
Exhaust face angle	45deg 30min
Seat width	NA
Spring pressure	47psi @ 1.575in
Intake stem to guide clearance	0.0008—0.0021in
Exhaust stem to guide clearance	0.0016—0.0029in
Intake stem diameter	0.2742—0.2748in
Exhaust stem diameter	0.2734—0.2740in
Piston clearance	0.0009—0.0017in
Top comp. ring gap	0.0079—0.0138in
Bottom comp. ring gap	0.0059—0.0118in
Oil ring gap	0.0118—0.0354in
Top comp. side clearance	0.0016—0.0029in
Bottom comp. side clearance	0.0012—0.0025in
Oil side clearance	0.0020—0.0057in

1982—1984 Fiat X 1.9

Displacement	1,498ci
Volume (liters)	1.498
Main journal diameter	1.9990—1.9997in
Main journal oil clearance	0.0019—0.0037in
Crankshaft end play	0.0021—0.0104in
Thrust journal length	NA
Rod journal diameter	2.1459—2.1465in
Rod oil clearance	0.0014—0.0034in
Rod side clearance	NA
Intake valve seat angle	45deg
Exhaust valve seat angle	45deg
Intake face angle	45deg 30min
Exhaust face angle	45deg 30min
Seat width	NA
Spring pressure	75.5psi @ 1.417in
Intake stem to guide clearance	0.0012—0.0026in
Exhaust stem to guide clearance	0.0012—0.0026in

Intake stem diameter 0.3139—0.3146in
Exhaust stem diameter 0.3139—0.3146in
Piston clearance 0.0011—0.0019in
Top comp. ring gap 0.0118—0.0177in
Bottom comp. ring gap 0.0118—0.0177in
Oil ring gap 0.0098—0.0157in
Top comp. side clearance 0.0018—0.0030in
Bottom comp. side clearance 0.0016—0.0028in
Oil side clearance 0.0011—0.0024in

1980 Fiat X 1.9

Displacement	1,498ci
Volume (liters)	1.498
Main journal diameter	1.9990—1.9997in
Main journal oil clearance	0.0019—0.0037in
Crankshaft end play	0.0021—0.0104in
Thrust journal length	NA
Rod journal diameter	2.2329—2.2334in
Rod oil clearance	0.0008—0.0025in
Rod side clearance	NA
Intake valve seat angle	45deg
Exhaust valve seat angle	45deg
Intake face angle	45deg 30min
Exhaust face angle	45deg 30min
Seat width	NA
Spring pressure	75psi @ 1.417in
Intake stem to guide clearance	0.0012—0.0026in
Exhaust stem to guide clearance	0.0012—0.0026in
Intake stem diameter	0.3139—0.3146in
Exhaust stem diameter	0.3139—0.3146in
Piston clearance	0.0011—0.0019in
Top comp. ring gap	0.0118—0.0177in
Bottom comp. ring gap	0.0118—0.0177in
Oil ring gap	0.0098—0.0157in
Top comp. side clearance	0.0018—0.0030in
Bottom comp. side clearance	0.0016—0.0028in
Oil side clearance	0.0011—0.0024in

1978 Fiat X 1.9 CC

Displacement	1,290ci
Volume (liters)	1.290
Main journal diameter	1.9994—2.0002in
Main journal oil clearance	0.0016—0.0033in
Crankshaft end play	0.0021—0.0104in
Thrust journal length	5in
Rod journal diameter	1.7913—1.7920in
Rod oil clearance	0.0014—0.0034in
Rod side clearance	NA
Intake valve seat angle	45deg
Exhaust valve seat angle	45deg
Intake face angle	45deg 30min
Exhaust face angle	45deg 30min
Seat width	NA
Spring pressure	75.5psi @ 1.417in
Intake stem to guide clearance	0.0012—0.0026in
Exhaust stem to guide clearance	0.0012—0.0026in
Intake stem diameter	0.3139—0.3146in
Exhaust stem diameter	0.3139—0.3146in
Piston clearance	0.0028—0.0035in
Top comp. ring gap	0.0118—0.0176in
Bottom comp. ring gap	0.0118—0.0176in
Oil ring gap	0.0098—0.0157in
Top comp. side clearance	0.0018—0.0030in
Bottom comp. side clearance	0.0016—0.0028in
Oil side clearance	0.0012—0.0024in

1978 Fiat X 1.9 SE

Displacement	1,290ci
Volume (liters)	1.290
Main journal diameter	1.9994—2.0002in
Main journal oil clearance	0.0016—0.0033in
Crankshaft end play	0.0021—0.0104in
Thrust journal length	5in
Rod journal diameter	1.7913—1.7920in
Rod oil clearance	0.0014—0.0034in
Rod side clearance	NA
Intake valve seat angle	45deg
Exhaust valve seat angle	45deg
Intake face angle	45deg 30min
Exhaust face angle	45deg 30min
Seat width	NA
Spring pressure	75.5psi @ 1.417in

Intake stem to guide clearance 0.0012—0.0026in
Exhaust stem to guide clearance 0.0012—0.0026in
Intake stem diameter 0.3139—0.3146in
Exhaust stem diameter 0.3139—0.3146in
Piston clearance 0.0028—0.0035in
Top comp. ring gap 0.0118—0.0176in
Bottom comp. ring gap 0.0118—0.0176in
Oil ring gap 0.0098—0.0157in
Top comp. side clearance 0.0018—0.0030in
Bottom comp. side clearance 0.0016—0.0028in
Oil side clearance 0.0012—0.0024in

1981 Fiat X 1.9

Displacement	1,498ci
Volume (liters)	1.498
Main journal diameter	1.9990—1.9997in
Main journal oil clearance	0.0019—0.0037in
Crankshaft end play	0.0021—0.0104in
Thrust journal length	NA
Rod journal diameter	2.1459—2.1465in
Rod oil clearance	0.0014—0.0034in
Rod side clearance	NA
Intake valve seat angle	45deg
Exhaust valve seat angle	45deg
Intake face angle	45deg 30min
Exhaust face angle	45deg 30min
Seat width	NA
Spring pressure	75.5psi @ 1.417in
Intake stem to guide clearance	0.0012—0.0026in
Exhaust stem to guide clearance	0.0012—0.0026in
Intake stem diameter	0.3139—0.3146in
Exhaust stem diameter	0.3139—0.3146in
Piston clearance	0.0011—0.0019in
Top comp. ring gap	0.0118—0.0177in
Bottom comp. ring gap	0.0118—0.0177in
Oil ring gap	0.0098—0.0157in
Top comp. side clearance	0.0018—0.0030in
Bottom comp. side clearance	0.0016—0.0028in
Oil side clearance	0.0011—0.0024in

1979 Fiat X 1.9

Displacement	1,498ci
Volume (liters)	1.498
Main journal diameter	1.9990—1.9997in
Main journal oil clearance	0.0019—0.0037in
Crankshaft end play	0.0021—0.0104in
Thrust journal length	NA
Rod journal diameter	2.1459—2.1465in
Rod oil clearance	0.0014—0.0034in
Rod side clearance	NA
Intake valve seat angle	45deg
Exhaust valve seat angle	45deg
Intake face angle	45deg 30min
Exhaust face angle	45deg 30min
Seat width	NA
Spring pressure	75.5psi @ 1.417in
Intake stem to guide clearance	0.0012—0.0026in
Exhaust stem to guide clearance	0.0012—0.0026in
Intake stem diameter	0.3139—0.3146in
Exhaust stem diameter	0.3139—0.3146in
Piston clearance	0.0011—0.0019in
Top comp. ring gap	0.0118—0.0177in
Bottom comp. ring gap	0.0118—0.0177in
Oil ring gap	0.0098—0.0157in
Top comp. side clearance	0.0018—0.0030in
Bottom comp. side clearance	0.0016—0.0028in
Oil side clearance	0.0011—0.0024in

1977 Fiat X 1.9

Displacement	1,290ci
Volume (liters)	1.290
Main journal diameter	1.9994—2.0002in
Main journal oil clearance	0.0016—0.0033in
Crankshaft end play	0.0021—0.0104in
Thrust journal length	5in
Rod journal diameter	1.7913—1.7920in
Rod oil clearance	0.0014—0.0034
Rod side clearance	NA
Intake valve seat angle	45deg
Exhaust valve seat angle	45deg
Intake face angle	45deg 30min
Exhaust face angle	45deg 30min

Seat width NA
Spring pressure 75.5psi @ 1.417in
Intake stem to guide clearance 0.0012—0.0026in
Exhaust stem to guide clearance 0.0012—0.0026in
Intake stem diameter 0.3139—0.3146in
Exhaust stem diameter 0.3139—0.3146in
Piston clearance 0.0028—0.0035in
Top comp. ring gap 0.0118—0.0176in
Bottom comp. ring gap 0.0118—0.0176in
Oil ring gap 0.0098—0.0157in
Top comp. side clearance 0.0018—0.0030in
Bottom comp. side clearance 0.0016—0.0028in
Oil side clearance 0.0012—0.0024in

1978 Fiat 124 CC A Class

Displacement	1,756ci
Volume (liters)	1.756
Main journal diameter	2.0860—2.0868in
Main journal oil clearance	0.0020—0.0037in
Crankshaft end play	0.0021—0.0120in
Thrust journal length	5in
Rod journal diameter	1.9997—2.001in
Rod oil clearance	0.0018—0.0032in
Rod side clearance	NA
Intake valve seat angle	45deg
Exhaust valve seat angle	45deg
Intake face angle	45deg 30min
Exhaust face angle	45deg 30min
Seat width	NA
Spring pressure	85.5psi @ 1.417in
Intake stem to guide clearance	0.0012—0.0026in
Exhaust stem to guide clearance	0.0012—0.0026in
Intake stem diameter	0.3139—0.3146in
Exhaust stem diameter	0.3139—0.3146in
Piston clearance	0.0016—0.0024in
Top comp. ring gap	0.0118—0.0176in
Bottom comp. ring gap	0.0079—0.0138in
Oil ring gap	0.0079—0.0138in
Top comp. side clearance	0.0018—0.0030in
Bottom comp. side clearance	0.0011—0.0027in
Oil side clearance	0.0011—0.0024in

1978 Fiat 124 CC B Class

Displacement	1,756ci
Volume (liters)	1.756
Main journal diameter	2.0860—2.0868in
Main journal oil clearance	0.0020—0.0037in
Crankshaft end play	0.0021—0.0120in
Thrust journal length	5in
Rod journal diameter	1.9993—1.9997in
Rod oil clearance	0.0018—0.0032in
Rod side clearance	NA
Intake valve seat angle	45deg
Exhaust valve seat angle	45deg
Intake face angle	45deg 30min
Exhaust face angle	45deg 30min
Seat width	NA
Spring pressure	85.5psi @ 1.417in
Intake stem to guide clearance	0.0012—0.0026in
Exhaust stem to guide clearance	0.0012—0.0026in
Intake stem diameter	0.3139—0.3146in
Exhaust stem diameter	0.3139—0.3146in
Piston clearance	0.0016—0.0024in
Top comp. ring gap	0.0118—0.0176in
Bottom comp. ring gap	0.0079—0.0138in
Oil ring gap	0.0079—0.0138in
Top comp. side clearance	0.0018—0.0030in
Bottom comp. side clearance	0.0011—0.0027in
Oil side clearance	0.0011—0.0024in

1978 Fiat 124 SE A Class

Displacement	1,756ci
Volume (liters)	1.756
Main journal diameter	2.0860—2.0868in
Main journal oil clearance	0.00020—0.0037in
Crankshaft end play	0.0021—0.0120in
Thrust journal length	5in
Rod journal diameter	1.9997—2.0001in
Rod oil clearance	0.0018—0.0032in
Rod side clearance	NA
Intake valve seat angle	45deg
Exhaust valve seat angle	45deg

Intake face angle 45deg 30min
Exhaust face angle 45deg 30min
Seat width NA
Spring pressure 85.5psi @ 1.417in
Intake stem to guide clearance 0.0012—0.0026in
Exhaust stem to guide clearance 0.0012—0.0026in
Intake stem diameter 0.3139—0.3146in
Exhaust stem diameter 0.3139—0.3146in
Piston clearance 0.0016—0.0024in
Top comp. ring gap 0.0118—0.0176in
Bottom comp. ring gap 0.0079—0.0138in
Oil ring gap 0.0079—0.0138in
Top comp. side clearance 0.0018—0.0030in
Bottom comp. side clearance 0.0011—0.0027in
Oil side clearance 0.0011—0.0024in

1978 Fiat 124 SE B Class

Displacement	1,756ci
Volume (liters)	1.756
Main journal diameter	2.0860—2.0868in
Main journal oil clearance	0.0020—0.0037in
Crankshaft end play	0.0021—0.0120in
Thrust journal length	5in
Rod journal diameter	1.9993—1.9997in
Rod oil clearance	0.0018—0.0032in
Rod side clearance	NA
Intake valve seat angle	45deg
Exhaust valve seat angle	45deg
Intake face angle	45deg 30min
Exhaust face angle	45deg 30min
Seat width	NA
Spring pressure	85.5psi @ 1.417in
Intake stem to guide clearance	0.0012—0.0026in
Exhaust stem to guide clearance	0.0012—0.0026in
Intake stem diameter	0.3139—0.3146in
Exhaust stem diameter	0.3139—0.3146in
Piston clearance	0.0016—0.0024in
Top comp. ring gap	0.0118—0.0176in
Bottom comp. ring gap	0.0079—0.0138in
Oil ring gap	0.0079—0.0138in
Top comp. side clearance	0.0018—0.0030in
Bottom comp. side clearance	0.0011—0.0027in
Oil side clearance	0.0011—0.0024in

1977 Fiat 124 B California

Displacement	1,756ci
Volume (liters)	1.756
Main journal diameter	2.0860—2.0868in
Main journal oil clearance	0.0020—0.0037in
Crankshaft end play	0.0021—0.0120in
Thrust journal length	5in
Rod journal diameter	1.9993—1.9997in
Rod oil clearance	0.0018—0.0032in
Rod side clearance	NA
Intake valve seat angle	45deg
Exhaust valve seat angle	45deg
Intake face angle	45deg 30min
Exhaust face angle	45deg 30min
Seat width	NA
Spring pressure	85.5psi @ 1.417in
Intake stem to guide clearance	0.0012—0.0026in
Exhaust stem to guide clearance	0.0012—0.0026in
Intake stem diameter	0.3139—0.3146in
Exhaust stem diameter	0.3139—0.3146in
Piston clearance	0.0016—0.0024in
Top comp. ring gap	0.0118—0.0176in
Bottom comp. ring gap	0.0079—0.0138in
Oil ring gap	0.0079—0.0138in
Top comp. side clearance	0.0018—0.0030in
Bottom comp. side clearance	0.0011—0.0027in
Oil side clearance	0.0011—0.0024in

1977 Fiat 124 A California

Displacement	1,756ci
Volume (liters)	1.756
Main journal diameter	2.0860—2.0868in
Main journal oil clearance	0.0020—0.0037in
Crankshaft end play	0.0021—0.0120in
Thrust journal length	5in
Rod journal diameter	1.9997—2.0001in
Rod oil clearance	0.0018—0.0032in
Rod side clearance	NA

Intake valve seat angle	45deg
Exhaust valve seat angle	45deg
Intake face angle	45deg 30min
Exhaust face angle	45deg 30min
Seat width	NA
Spring pressure	85.5psi @ 1.417in
Intake stem to guide clearance	0.0012—0.0026in
Exhaust stem to guide clearance	0.0012—0.0026in
Intake stem diameter	0.3139—0.3146in
Exhaust stem diameter	0.3139—0.3146
Piston clearance	0.0016—0.0024in
Top comp. ring gap	0.0118—0.0176in
Bottom comp. ring gap	0.0079—0.0138in
Oil ring gap	0.0079—0.0138in
Top comp. side clearance	0.0018—0.0030in
Bottom comp. side clearance	0.0011—0.0027in
Oil side clearance	0.0011—0.0024in

1977 Fiat 124 A Class

Displacement	1,756ci
Volume (liters)	1.756
Main journal diameter	2.0860—2.0868in
Main journal oil clearance	0.0020—0.0037in
Crankshaft end play	0.0021—0.0120in
Thrust journal length	5in
Rod journal diameter	1.9997—2.0001in
Rod oil clearance	0.0018—0.0032in
Rod side clearance	NA
Intake valve seat angle	45deg
Exhaust valve seat angle	45deg
Intake face angle	45deg 30min
Exhaust face angle	45deg 30min
Seat width	NA
Spring pressure	85.5psi @ 1.417in
Intake stem to guide clearance	0.0012—0.0026in
Exhaust stem to guide clearance	0.0012—0.0026in
Intake stem diameter	0.3139—0.3146in
Exhaust stem diameter	0.3139—0.3146in
Piston clearance	0.0016—0.0024in
Top comp. ring gap	0.0118—0.0176in
Bottom comp. ring gap	0.0079—0.0138in
Oil ring gap	0.0079—0.0138in
Top comp. side clearance	0.0018—0.0030in
Bottom comp. side clearance	0.0011—0.0027in
Oil side clearance	0.0011—0.0024in

1977 Fiat 124 B Class

Displacement	1,756ci
Volume (liters)	1.756
Main journal diameter	2.0860—2.0868in
Main journal oil clearance	0.0020—0.0037in
Crankshaft end play	0.0021—0.0120in
Thrust journal length	5in
Rod journal diameter	1.9993—1.9997in
Rod oil clearance	0.0018—0.0032in
Rod side clearance	NA
Intake valve seat angle	45deg
Exhaust valve seat angle	45deg
Intake face angle	45 deg 30min
Exhaust face angle	45deg 30min
Seat width	NA
Spring pressure	85.5psi @ 1.417in
Intake stem to guide clearance	0.0012—0.0026in
Exhaust stem to guide clearance	0.0012—0.0026in
Intake stem diameter	0.3139—0.3146in
Exhaust stem diameter	0.3139—0.3146in
Piston clearance	0.0016—0.0024in
Top comp. ring gap	0.0118—0.0176in
Bottom comp. ring gap	0.0079—0.0138in
Oil ring gap	0.0079—0.0138in
Top comp. side clearance	0.0018—0.0030in
Bottom comp. side clearance	0.0011—0.0027in
Oil side clearance	0.0011—0.0024in

1978 Fiat 128 CC

Displacement	1,290ci
Volume (liters)	1.290
Main journal diameter	1.9994—2.0002in
Main journal oil clearance	0.0016—0.0033in
Crankshaft end play	0.0021—0.0104in
Thrust journal length	5in
Rod journal diameter	1.7913—1.7920in

Rod oil clearance	0.0014—0.0034in
Rod side clearance	NA
Intake valve seat angle	45deg
Exhaust valve seat angle	45deg
Intake face angle	45deg 30min
Exhaust face angle	45deg 30min
Seat width	NA
Spring pressure	75.5psi @ 1.417in
Intake stem to guide clearance	0.0012—0.0026in
Exhaust stem to guide clearance	0.0012—0.0026in
Intake stem diameter	0.3139—0.3146in
Exhaust stem diameter	0.3139—0.3146in
Piston clearance	0.0028—0.0035in
Top comp. ring gap	0.0118—0.0176in
Bottom comp. ring gap	0.0118—0.0176in
Oil ring gap	0.0098—0.0157in
Top comp. side clearance	0.0018—0.0030in
Bottom comp. side clearance	0.0016—0.0028in
Oil side clearance	0.0012—0.0024in

1978 Fiat 128 SE

Displacement	1,290ci
Volume (liters)	1.290
Main journal diameter	1.9994—2.0002in
Main journal oil clearance	0.0016—0.0033in
Crankshaft end play	0.0021—0.0104in
Thrust journal length	5in
Rod journal diameter	1.7913—1.7920in
Rod oil clearance	0.0014—0.0034in
Rod side clearance	NA
Intake valve seat angle	45deg
Exhaust valve seat angle	45deg
Intake face angle	45deg 30min
Exhaust face angle	45deg 30min
Seat width	NA
Spring pressure	75.5psi @ 1.417in
Intake stem to guide clearance	0.0012—0.0026in
Exhaust stem to guide clearance	0.0012—0.0026in
Intake stem diameter	0.3139—0.3146in
Exhaust stem diameter	0.3139—0.3146in
Piston clearance	0.0028—0.0035in
Top comp. ring gap	0.0118—0.0176in
Bottom comp. ring gap	0.0118—0.0176in
Oil ring gap	0.0098—0.0157in
Top comp. side clearance	0.0018—0.0030in
Bottom comp. side clearance	0.0016—0.0028in
Oil side clearance	0.0012—0.0024in

1977 Fiat 128 California

Displacement	1,290ci
Volume (liters)	1.290
Main journal diameter	1.9994—2.0002in
Main journal oil clearance	0.0016—0.0033in
Crankshaft end play	0.0021—0.0104in
Thrust journal length	5in
Rod journal diameter	1.7913—1.7920in
Rod oil clearance	0.0014—0.0034in
Rod side clearance	NA
Intake valve seat angle	45deg
Exhaust valve seat angle	45deg
Intake face angle	45deg 30min
Exhaust face angle	45deg 30min
Seat width	NA
Spring pressure	75.5psi @ 1.417in
Intake stem to guide clearance	0.0012—0.0026in
Exhaust stem to guide clearance	0.0012—0.0026in
Intake stem diameter	0.3139—0.3146in
Exhaust stem diameter	0.3139—0.3146in
Piston clearance	0.0028—0.0035in
Top comp. ring gap	0.0118—0.0176in
Bottom comp. ring gap	0.0118—0.0176in
Oil ring gap	0.0098—0.0157in
Top comp. side clearance	0.0018—0.0030in
Bottom comp. side clearance	0.0016—0.0028in
Oil side clearance	0.0012—0.0024in

1977 Fiat 128

Displacement	1,290ci
Volume (liters)	1.290
Main journal diameter	1.9994—2.0002in
Main journal oil clearance	0.0016—0.0033in
Crankshaft end play	0.0021—0.0104in

Thrust journal length	5in
Rod journal diameter	1.7913—1.7920in
Rod oil clearance	0.0014—0.0034in
Rod side clearance	NA
Intake valve seat angle	45deg
Exhaust valve seat angle	45deg
Intake face angle	45deg 30min
Exhaust face angle	45deg 30min
Seat width	NA
Spring pressure	75.5psi @ 1.417in
Intake stem to guide clearance	0.0012—0.0026in
Exhaust stem to guide clearance	0.0012—0.0026in
Intake stem diameter	0.3139—0.3146in
Exhaust stem diameter	0.3139—0.3146in
Piston clearance	0.0028—0.0035in
Top comp. ring gap	0.0118—0.0176in
Bottom comp. ring gap	0.0118—0.0176in
Oil ring gap	0.0098—0.0157in
Top comp. side clearance	0.0018—0.0030in
Bottom comp. side clearance	0.0016—0.0028in
Oil side clearance	0.0012—0.0024in

1978 Fiat 131 B Class

Displacement	1,756ci
Volume (liters)	1.756
Main journal diameter	2.0860—2.0868in
Main journal oil clearance	0.0020—0.0037in
Crankshaft end play	0.0021—0.0120in
Thrust journal length	5in
Rod journal diameter	1.9993—1.9997in
Rod oil clearance	0.0018—0.0032in
Rod side clearance	NA
Intake valve seat angle	45deg
Exhaust valve seat angle	45deg
Intake face angle	45deg 30min
Exhaust face angle	45deg 30min
Seat width	NA
Spring pressure	85.5psi @ 1.417in
Intake stem to guide clearance	0.0012—0.0026in
Exhaust stem to guide clearance	0.0012—0.0026in
Intake stem diameter	0.3139—0.3146in
Exhaust stem diameter	0.3139—0.3146in
Piston clearance	0.0016—0.0024in
Top comp. ring gap	0.0118—0.0176in
Bottom comp. ring gap	0.0079—0.0138in
Oil ring gap	0.0079—0.0138in
Top comp. side clearance	0.0018—0.0030in
Bottom comp. side clearance	0.0011—0.0027in
Oil side clearance	0.0011—0.0024in

1977 Fiat 131 A California

Displacement	1,756ci
Volume (liters)	1.756
Main journal diameter	2.0860—2.0868in
Main journal oil clearance	0.0020—0.0037in
Crankshaft end play	0.0021—0.0120in
Thrust journal length	5in
Rod journal diameter	1.9997—2.0001in
Rod oil clearance	0.0018—0.0032in
Rod side clearance	NA
Intake valve seat angle	45deg
Exhaust valve seat angle	45deg
Intake face angle	45deg 30min
Exhaust face angle	45deg 30min
Seat width	NA
Spring pressure	85.5psi @ 1.417in
Intake stem to guide clearance	0.0012—0.0026in
Exhaust stem to guide clearance	0.0012—0.0026in
Intake stem diameter	0.3139—0.3146in
Exhaust stem diameter	0.3139—0.3146in
Piston clearance	0.0016—0.0024in
Top comp. ring gap	0.0118—0.0176in
Bottom comp. ring gap	0.0079—0.0138in
Oil ring gap	0.0079—0.0138in
Top comp. side clearance	0.0018—0.0030in
Bottom comp. side clearance	0.0011—0.0027in
Oil side clearance	0.0011—0.0024in

1977 Fiat 131 A Class

Displacement	1756ci
Volume (liters)	1.756
Main journal diameter	2.0860—2.0868in

Main journal oil clearance 0.0020—0.0037in
Crankshaft end play 0.0021—0.0120in
Thrust journal length 5in
Rod journal diameter 1.9997—2.0001in
Rod oil clearance 0.0018—0.0032in
Rod side clearance NA
Intake valve seat angle 45deg
Exhaust valve seat angle 45deg
Intake face angle 45deg 30min
Exhaust face angle 45deg 30min
Seat width NA
Spring pressure 85.5psi @ 1.417in
Intake stem to guide clearance 0.0012—0.0026in
Exhaust stem to guide clearance 0.0012—0.0026in
Intake stem diameter 0.3139—0.3146in
Exhaust stem diameter 0.3139—0.3146in
Piston clearance 0.0016—0.0024in
Top comp. ring gap 0.0118—0.0176in
Bottom comp. ring gap 0.0079—0.0138in
Oil ring gap 0.0079—0.0138in
Top comp. side clearance 0.0018—0.0030in
Bottom comp. side clearance 0.0011—0.0027in
Oil side clearance 0.0011—0.0024in

1978 Fiat 131 A Class

Displacement 1,756ci
Volume (liters) 1.756
Main journal diameter 2.0860—2.0868in
Main journal oil clearance 0.0020—0.0037in
Crankshaft end play 0.0021—0.0120in
Thrust journal length 5in
Rod journal diameter 1.9997—2.0001in
Rod oil clearance 0.0018—0.0032in
Rod side clearance NA
Intake valve seat angle 45deg
Exhaust valve seat angle 45deg
Intake face angle 45deg 30min
Exhaust face angle 45deg 30min
Seat width NA
Spring pressure 85.5psi @ 1.417in
Intake stem to guide clearance 0.0012—0.0026in
Exhaust stem to guide clearance 0.0012—0.0026in
Intake stem diameter 0.3139—0.3146in
Exhaust stem diameter 0.3139—0.3146in
Piston clearance 0.0016—0.0024in
Top comp. ring gap 0.0118—0.0176in
Bottom comp. ring gap 0.0079—0.0138in
Oil ring gap 0.0079—0.0138in
Top comp. side clearance 0.0018—0.0030in
Bottom comp. side clearance 0.0011—0.0027in
Oil side clearance 0.0011—0.0024in

1977 Fiat 131 B California

Displacement 1,756ci
Volume (liters) 1.756
Main journal diameter 2.0860—2.0868in
Main journal oil clearance 0.0020—0.0037in
Crankshaft end play 0.0021—0.0120in
Thrust journal length 5in
Rod journal diameter 1.9993—1.9997in
Rod oil clearance 0.0018—0.0032in
Rod side clearance NA
Intake valve seat angle 45deg
Exhaust valve seat angle 45deg
Intake face angle 45deg 30min
Exhaust face angle 45deg 30min
Seat width NA
Spring pressure 85.5psi @ 1.417in
Intake stem to guide clearance 0.0012—0.0026in
Exhaust stem to guide clearance 0.0012—0.0026in
Intake stem diameter 0.3139—0.3146in
Exhaust stem diameter 0.3139—0.3146in
Piston clearance 0.0016—0.0024in
Top comp. ring gap 0.0118—0.0176in
Bottom comp. ring gap 0.0079—0.0138in
Oil ring gap 0.0079—0.0138in
Top comp. side clearance 0.0018—0.0030in
Bottom comp. side clearance 0.0011—0.0027in
Oil side clearance 0.0011—0.0024in

1977 Fiat 131 B Class

Displacement 1,756ci

Volume (liters) 1.756
Main journal diameter 2.0860—2.0868in
Main journal oil clearance 0.0020—0.0037in
Crankshaft end play 0.0021—0.0120in
Thrust journal length 5in
Rod journal diameter 1.9993—1.9997in
Rod oil clearance 0.0018—0.0032in
Rod side clearance NA
Intake valve seat angle 45deg
Exhaust valve seat angle 45deg
Intake face angle 45deg 30min
Exhaust face angle 45deg 30min
Seat width NA
Spring pressure 85.5psi @ 1.417in
Intake stem to guide clearance 0.0012—0.0026in
Exhaust stem to guide clearance 0.0012—0.0026in
Intake stem diameter 0.3139—0.3146in
Exhaust stem diameter 0.3139—0.3146in
Piston clearance 0.0016—0.0024in
Top comp. ring gap 0.0118—0.0176in
Bottom comp. ring gap 0.0079—0.0138in
Oil ring gap 0.0079—0.0138in
Top comp. side clearance 0.0018—0.0030in
Bottom comp. side clearance 0.0011—0.0027in
Oil side clearance 0.0011—0.0024in

1981 Fiat Brava

Displacement 1,995ci
Volume (liters) 1.995
Main journal diameter 2.0860—2.0868in
Main journal oil clearance 0.0012—0.0030in
Crankshaft end play 0.0021—0.0120in
Thrust journal length NA
Rod journal diameter 2.2329—2.2334in
Rod oil clearance 0.0008—0.0025in
Rod side clearance NA
Intake valve seat angle 45deg
Exhaust valve seat angle 45deg
Intake face angle 45deg 30min
Exhaust face angle 45deg 30min
Seat width NA
Spring pressure 85.5psi @ 1.417in
Intake stem to guide clearance 0.0012—0.0026in
Exhaust stem to guide clearance 0.0012—0.0026in
Intake stem diameter 0.3139—0.3146in
Exhaust stem diameter 0.3139—0.3146in
Piston clearance 0.0016—0.0024in
Top comp. ring gap 0.0118—0.0177in
Bottom comp. ring gap 0.0118—0.0177in
Oil ring gap 0.0098—0.0157in
Top comp. side clearance 0.0018—0.0030in
Bottom comp. side clearance 0.0011—0.0027in
Oil side clearance 0.0011—0.0024in

1980 Fiat Brava

Displacement 1,995ci
Volume (liters) 1.995
Main journal diameter 2.0860—2.0868in
Main journal oil clearance 0.0012—0.0030in
Crankshaft end play 0.0021—0.0120in
Thrust journal length NA
Rod journal diameter 2.2329—2.2334in
Rod oil clearance 0.0008—0.0025in
Rod side clearance NA
Intake valve seat angle 45deg
Exhaust valve seat angle 45deg
Intake face angle 45deg 30min
Exhaust face angle 45deg 30min
Seat width NA
Spring pressure 85.5psi @ 1.417in
Intake stem to guide clearance 0.0012—0.0026in
Exhaust stem to guide clearance 0.0012—0.0026in
Intake stem diameter 0.3139—0.3146in
Exhaust stem diameter 0.3139—0.3146in
Piston clearance 0.0016—0.0024in
Top comp. ring gap 0.0118—0.0177in
Bottom comp. ring gap 0.0118—0.0177in
Oil ring gap 0.0098—0.0157in
Top comp. side clearance 0.0018—0.0030in
Bottom comp. side clearance 0.0011—0.0027in
Oil side clearance 0.0011—0.0024in

1979 Fiat Brava

Displacement 1,995ci
Volume (liters) 1.995
Main journal diameter 2.0860—2.0868in
Main journal oil clearance 0.0012—0.0030in
Crankshaft end play 0.0021—0.0120in
Thrust journal length NA
Rod journal diameter 2.2329—2.2334in
Rod oil clearance 0.0008—0.0025in
Rod side clearance NA
Intake valve seat angle 45deg
Exhaust valve seat angle 45deg
Intake face angle 45deg 30min
Exhaust face angle 45deg 30min
Seat width NA
Spring pressure 85.5psi @ 1.417in
Intake stem to guide clearance 0.0012—0.0026in
Exhaust stem to guide clearance 0.0012—0.0026in
Intake stem diameter 0.3139—0.3146in
Exhaust stem diameter 0.3139—0.3146
Piston clearance 0.0016—0.0024in
Top comp. ring gap 0.0118—0.0177in
Bottom comp. ring gap 0.0118—0.0177in
Oil ring gap 0.0098—0.0157in
Top comp. side clearance 0.0018—0.0030in
Bottom comp. side clearance 0.0011—0.0027in
Oil side clearance 0.0011—0.0024in

1978 Fiat Brava CC A Class

Displacement 1,756ci
Volume (liters) 1.756
Main journal diameter 2.0860—2.0868in
Main journal oil clearance 0.0020—0.0037in
Crankshaft end play 0.0021—0.0120in
Thrust journal length 5in
Rod journal diameter 1.9997—2.0001in
Rod oil clearance 0.0018—0.0032in
Rod side clearance NA
Intake valve seat angle 45deg
Exhaust valve seat angle 45deg
Intake face angle 45deg 30min
Exhaust face angle 45deg 30min
Seat width NA
Spring pressure 85.5psi @ 1.417in
Intake stem to guide clearance 0.0012—0.0026in
Exhaust stem to guide clearance 0.0012—0.0026in
Intake stem diameter 0.3139—0.3146in
Exhaust stem diameter 0.3139—0.3146in
Piston clearance 0.0016—0.0024in
Top comp. ring gap 0.0118—0.0176in
Bottom comp. ring gap 0.0079—0.0138in
Oil ring gap 0.0079—0.0138in
Top comp. side clearance 0.0018—0.0030in
Bottom comp. side clearance 0.0011—0.0027in
Oil side clearance 0.0011—0.0024in

1978 Fiat Brava CC B Class

Displacement 1,756ci
Volume (liters) 1.756
Main journal diameter 2.0860—2.0868in
Main journal oil clearance 0.0020—0.0037in
Crankshaft end play 0.0021—0.0120in
Thrust journal length 5in
Rod journal diameter 1.9993—1.9997in
Rod oil clearance 0.0018—0.0032in
Rod side clearance NA
Intake valve seat angle 45deg
Exhaust valve seat angle 45deg
Intake face angle 45deg 30min
Exhaust face angle 45deg 30min
Seat width NA
Spring pressure 85.5psi @ 1.417in
Intake stem to guide clearance 0.0012—0.0026in
Exhaust stem to guide clearance 0.0012—0.0026in
Intake stem diameter 0.3139—0.3146in
Exhaust stem diameter 0.3139—0.3146in
Piston clearance 0.0016—0.0024in
Top comp. ring gap 0.0118—0.0176in
Bottom comp. ring gap 0.0079—0.0138in
Oil ring gap 0.0079—0.0138in
Top comp. side clearance 0.0018—0.0030in

Bottom comp. side clearance 0.0011—0.0027in
Oil side clearance 0.0011—0.0024in

1978 Fiat Brava SE B Class
Displacement 1,756ci
Volume (liters) 1.756
Main journal diameter 2.0860—2.0868in
Main journal oil clearance 0.0020—0.0037in
Crankshaft end play 0.0021—0.0120in
Thrust journal length 5in
Rod journal diameter 1.9993—1.9997in
Rod oil clearance 0.0018—0.0032in
Rod side clearance NA
Intake valve seat angle 45deg
Exhaust valve seat angle 45deg
Intake face angle 45deg 30min
Exhaust face angle 45deg 30min
Seat width NA
Spring pressure 85.5psi @ 1.417in
Intake stem to guide clearance 0.0012—0.0026in
Exhaust stem to guide clearance 0.0012—0.0026in
Intake stem diameter 0.3139—0.3146in
Exhaust stem diameter 0.3139—0.3146in
Piston clearance 0.0016—0.0024in
Top comp. ring gap 0.0118—0.0176in
Bottom comp. ring gap 0.0079—0.0138in
Oil ring gap 0.0079—0.0138in
Top comp. side clearance 0.0018—0.0030in
Bottom comp. side clearance 0.0011—0.0027in
Oil side clearance 0.0011—0.0024in

1978 Fiat Brava SE A Class
Displacement 1,756ci
Volume (liters) 1.756
Main journal diameter 2.0860—2.0868in
Main journal oil clearance 0.0020—0.0037in
Crankshaft end play 0.0021—0.0120in
Thrust journal length 5in
Rod journal diameter 1.9997—2.0001in
Rod oil clearance 0.0018—0.0032in
Rod side clearance NA
Intake valve seat angle 45deg
Exhaust valve seat angle 45deg
Intake face angle 45deg 30min
Exhaust face angle 45deg 30min
Seat width NA
Spring pressure 85.5psi @ 1.417in
Intake stem to guide clearance 0.0012—0.0026in
Exhaust stem to guide clearance 0.0012—0.0026in
Intake stem diameter 0.3139—0.3146in
Exhaust stem diameter 0.3139—0.3146in
Piston clearance 0.0016—0.0024in
Top comp. ring gap 0.0118—0.0176in
Bottom comp. ring gap 0.0079—0.0138in
Oil ring gap 0.0079—0.0138in
Top comp. side clearance 0.0018—0.0030in
Bottom comp. side clearance 0.0011—0.0027in
Oil side clearance 0.0011—0.0024in

1979 Fiat Spider 2000
Displacement 1,995ci
Volume (liters) 1.995
Main journal diameter 2.0860—2.0868in
Main journal oil clearance 0.0012—0.0030in
Crankshaft end play 0.0021—0.0120in
Thrust journal length NA
Rod journal diameter 2.2329—2.2334in
Rod oil clearance 0.0008—0.0025in
Rod side clearance NA
Intake valve seat angle 45deg
Exhaust valve seat angle 45deg
Intake face angle 45deg 30min
Exhaust face angle 45deg 30min
Seat width NA
Spring pressure 85.5psi @ 1.417in
Intake stem to guide clearance 0.0012—0.0026in
Exhaust stem to guide clearance 0.0012—0.0026in
Intake stem diameter 0.3139—0.3146in
Exhaust stem diameter 0.3139—0.3146in
Piston clearance 0.0016—0.0024in
Top comp. ring gap 0.0118—0.0177in
Bottom comp. ring gap 0.0098—0.0177in

Oil ring gap 0.0118—0.0157in
Top comp. side clearance 0.0018—0.0030in
Bottom comp. side clearance 0.0011—0.0027in
Oil side clearance 0.0011—0.0024in

1982—1984 Fiat Spider 2000
Displacement 1,995ci
Volume (liters) 1.995
Main journal diameter 2.0860—2.0868in
Main journal oil clearance 0.0012—0.0030in
Crankshaft end play 0.0021—0.0120in
Thrust journal length NA
Rod journal diameter 2.2329—2.2334in
Rod oil clearance 0.0008—0.0025in
Rod side clearance NA
Intake valve seat angle 45deg
Exhaust valve seat angle 45deg
Intake face angle 45deg 30min
Exhaust face angle 45deg 30min
Seat width NA
Spring pressure 85.5psi @ 1.417in
Intake stem to guide clearance 0.0012—0.0026in
Exhaust stem to guide clearance 0.0012—0.0026in
Intake stem diameter 0.3139—0.3146in
Exhaust stem diameter 0.3139—0.3146in
Piston clearance 0.0016—0.0024in
Top comp. ring gap 0.0118—0.0177in
Bottom comp. ring gap 0.0118—0.0177in
Oil ring gap 0.0098—0.0157in
Top comp. side clearance 0.0018—0.0030in
Bottom comp. side clearance 0.0011—0.0027in
Oil side clearance 0.0011—0.0024in

1981 Fiat Spider 2000
Displacement 1,995ci
Volume (liters) 1.995
Main journal diameter 2.0860—2.0868in
Main journal oil clearance 0.0012—0.0030in
Crankshaft end play 0.0021—0.0120in
Thrust journal length NA
Rod journal diameter 2.2329—2.2334in
Rod oil clearance 0.0008—0.0025in
Rod side clearance NA
Intake valve seat angle 45deg
Exhaust valve seat angle 45deg
Intake face angle 45deg 30min
Exhaust face angle 45deg 30min
Seat width NA
Spring pressure 85.5psi @ 1.417in
Intake stem to guide clearance 0.0012—0.0026in
Exhaust stem to guide clearance 0.0012—0.0026in
Intake stem diameter 0.3139—0.3146in
Exhaust stem diameter 0.3139—0.3146in
Piston clearance 0.0016—0.0024in
Top comp. ring gap 0.0118—0.0177in
Bottom comp. ring gap 0.0118—0.0177in
Oil ring gap 0.0098—0.0157in
Top comp. side clearance 0.0018—0.0030in
Bottom comp. side clearance 0.0011—0.0027in
Oil side clearance 0.0011—0.0024in

1980 Fiat Spider 2000
Displacement 1,995ci
Volume (liters) 1.995
Main journal diameter 2.0860—2.0868in
Main journal oil clearance 0.012—0.0030in
Crankshaft end play 0.0021—0.0120in
Thrust journal length NA
Rod journal diameter 2.2329—2.2334in
Rod oil clearance 0.0008—0.0025in
Rod side clearance NA
Intake valve seat angle 45deg
Exhaust valve seat angle 45deg
Intake face angle 45deg 30min
Exhaust face angle 45deg 30min
Seat width NA
Spring pressure 85.5psi @ 1.417in
Intake stem to guide clearance 0.0012—0.0026in
Exhaust stem to guide clearance 0.0012—0.0026in
Intake stem diameter 0.3139—0.3146in
Exhaust stem diameter 0.3139—0.3146in
Piston clearance 0.0016—0.0024in

Top comp. ring gap 0.0118—0.0177in
Bottom comp. ring gap 0.0118—0.0177in
Oil ring gap 0.0098—0.0157in
Top comp. side clearance 0.0018—0.0030in
Bottom comp. side clearance 0.0011—0.0027in
Oil side clearance 0.0011—0.0024in

1982—1984 Fiat Spider Turbo
Displacement 1,995ci
Volume (liters) 1.995
Main journal diameter 2.0860—2.0868in
Main journal oil clearance 0.0012—0.0030in
Crankshaft end play 0.0021—0.0120in
Thrust journal length NA
Rod journal diameter 2.2329—2.2334in
Rod oil clearance 0.0008—0.0025in
Rod side clearance NA
Intake valve seat angle 45deg
Exhaust valve seat angle 45deg
Intake face angle 45deg 30min
Exhaust face angle 45deg 30min
Seat width NA
Spring pressure 85.5psi @ 1.417in
Intake stem to guide clearance 0.0012—0.0026in
Exhaust stem to guide clearance 0.0012—0.0026in
Intake stem diameter 0.3139—0.3146in
Exhaust stem diameter 0.3139—0.3146in
Piston clearance 0.0016—0.0024in
Top comp. ring gap 0.0118—0.0177in
Bottom comp. ring gap 0.0118—0.0177in
Oil ring gap 0.0098—0.0157in
Top comp. side clearance 0.0018—0.0030in
Bottom comp. side clearance 0.0011—0.0027in
Oil side clearance 0.0011—0.0024in

1982—1984 Fiat Strada
Displacement 1,498ci
Volume (liters) 1.498
Main journal diameter 1.9990—1.9997in
Main journal oil clearance 0.0019—0.0037in
Crankshaft end play 0.0021—0.0104in
Thrust journal length NA
Rod journal diameter 2.1459—2.1465in
Rod oil clearance 0.0014—0.0034in
Rod side clearance NA
Intake valve seat angle 45deg
Exhaust valve seat angle 45deg
Intake face angle 45deg 30min
Exhaust face angle 45deg 30min
Seat width NA
Spring pressure 75.5psi @ 1.417in
Intake stem to guide clearance 0.0012—0.0026in
Exhaust stem to guide clearance 0.0012—0.0026in
Intake stem diameter 0.3139—0.3146in
Exhaust stem diameter 0.3139—0.3146in
Piston clearance 0.0011—0.0019in
Top comp. ring gap 0.0118—0.0177in
Bottom comp. ring gap 0.0118—0.0177in
Oil ring gap 0.0098—0.0157in
Top comp. side clearance 0.0018—0.0030in
Bottom comp. side clearance 0.0016—0.0028in
Oil side clearance 0.0011—0.0024in

1981 Fiat Strada
Displacement 1,498ci
Volume (liters) 1.498
Main journal diameter 1.9990—1.9997in
Main journal oil clearance 0.0019—0.0037in
Crankshaft end play 0.0021—0.0104in
Thrust journal length NA
Rod journal diameter 2.1459—2.1465in
Rod oil clearance 0.0014—0.0034in
Rod side clearance NA
Intake valve seat angle 45deg
Exhaust valve seat angle 45deg
Intake face angle 45deg 30min
Exhaust face angle 45deg 30min
Seat width NA
Spring pressure 75.5psi @ 1.417in
Intake stem to guide clearance 0.0012—0.0026in
Exhaust stem to guide clearance 0.0012—0.0026in
Intake stem diameter 0.3139—0.3146in

Exhaust stem diameter 0.3139—0.3146in
Piston clearance 0.0011—0.0019in
Top comp. ring gap 0.0118—0.0177in
Bottom comp. ring gap 0.0118—0.0177in
Oil ring gap 0.0098—0.0157in
Top comp. side clearance 0.0018—0.0030in
Bottom comp. side clearance 0.0016—0.0028in
Oil side clearance 0.0011—0.0024in

1980 Fiat Strada

Displacement	1,498ci
Volume (liters)	1.498
Main journal diameter	1.9990—1.9997in
Main journal oil clearance	0.0019—0.0037in
Crankshaft end play	0.0021—0.0104in
Thrust journal length	NA
Rod journal diameter	2.1459—2.1465in
Rod oil clearance	0.0014—0.0034in
Rod side clearance	NA
Intake valve seat angle	45deg
Exhaust valve seat angle	45deg
Intake face angle	45deg 30min
Exhaust face angle	45deg 30min
Seat width	NA
Spring pressure	75.5psi @ 1.417in
Intake stem to guide clearance	0.0012—0.0026in
Exhaust stem to guide clearance	0.0012—0.0026in
Intake stem diameter	0.3139—0.3146in
Exhaust stem diameter	0.3139—0.3146in
Piston clearance	0.0011—0.0019in
Top comp. ring gap	0.0118—0.0177in
Bottom comp. ring gap	0.0118—0.0177in
Oil ring gap	0.0098—0.0157in
Top comp. side clearance	0.0018—0.0030in
Bottom comp. side clearance	0.0016—0.0028in
Oil side clearance	0.0011—0.0024in

1979 Fiat Strada

Displacement	1,498ci
Volume (liters)	1.498
Main journal diameter	1.9990—1.9997in
Main journal oil clearance	0.0019—0.0037in
Crankshaft end play	0.0021—0.0104in
Thrust journal length	NA
Rod journal diameter	2.1459—2.1465in
Rod oil clearance	0.0014—0.0034in
Rod side clearance	NA
Intake valve seat angle	45deg
Exhaust valve seat angle	45deg
Intake face angle	45deg 30min
Exhaust face angle	45deg 30min
Seat width	NA
Spring pressure	75.5psi @ 1.417in
Intake stem to guide clearance	0.0012—0.0026in
Exhaust stem to guide clearance	0.0012—0.0026in
Intake stem diameter	0.3139—0.3146in
Exhaust stem diameter	0.3139—0.3146in
Piston clearance	0.0011—0.0019in
Top comp. ring gap	0.0118—0.0177in
Bottom comp. ring gap	0.0098—0.0177in
Oil ring gap	0.0118—0.0157in
Top comp. side clearance	0.0018—0.0030in
Bottom comp. side clearance	0.0016—0.0028in
Oil side clearance	0.0011—0.0024in

1983—1984 Ford 1597 Four-cylinder

Displacement	NA
Volume (liters)	1.597
Main journal diameter	2.2826—2.2834in
Main journal oil clearance	0.0008—0.0015in
Crankshaft end play	0.004—0.008in
Thrust journal length	3in
Rod journal diameter	1.885—1.886in
Rod oil clearance	0.0002—0.0003in
Rod side clearance	0.004—0.011in
Intake valve seat angle	45deg
Exhaust valve seat angle	45deg
Intake face angle	45deg 30min
Exhaust face angle	45deg 30min
Seat width	NA
Spring pressure	NA
Intake stem to guide clearance	0.0008—0.0027in

Exhaust stem to guide clearance 0.0018—0.0037in
Intake stem diameter 0.316in
Exhaust stem diameter 0.315in
Piston clearance 0.0018—0.0026in
Top comp. ring gap 0.012—0.020in
Bottom comp. ring gap 0.012—0.020in
Oil ring gap 0.016—0.055in
Top comp. side clearance 0.001—0.003in
Bottom comp. side clearance 0.002—0.003in
Oil side clearance Snug

1982—1984 Ford 200 Six-cylinder

Displacement	200ci
Volume (liters)	3.3
Main journal diameter	2.2482—2.2490in
Main journal oil clearance	0.0005—0.0022in
Crankshaft end play	0.004—0.008in
Thrust journal length	5in
Rod journal diameter	2.1232—2.1240in
Rod oil clearance	0.0008—0.0015in
Rod side clearance	0.0035—0.105in
Intake valve seat angle	45deg
Exhaust valve seat angle	45deg
Intake face angle	44deg
Exhaust face angle	44deg
Seat width	NA
Spring pressure	NA
Intake stem to guide clearance	0.0008—0.0025in
Exhaust stem to guide clearance	0.0010—0.0027in
Intake stem diameter	0.3104in
Exhaust stem diameter	0.3102in
Piston clearance	0.0013—0.0021in
Top comp. ring gap	0.008—0.016in
Bottom comp. ring gap	0.008—0.016in
Oil ring gap	0.015—0.055in
Top comp. side clearance	0.002—0.004in
Bottom comp. side clearance	0.002—0.004in
Oil side clearance	Snug

1982 Ford 255 Eight-cylinder

Displacement	255ci
Volume (liters)	4.2
Main journal diameter	2.2482—2.2490in
Main journal oil clearance	0.0005—0.0015; 0.0001—0.0015in (no. 1)
Crankshaft end play	0.004—0.008in
Thrust journal length	3in
Rod journal diameter	2.1228—2.1236in
Rod oil clearance	0.0008—0.0026in
Rod side clearance	0.010—0.020in
Intake valve seat angle	44deg 30min—45deg
Exhaust valve seat angle	44deg 30min—45deg
Intake face angle	45deg 30min—45deg 45min
Exhaust face angle	45deg 30min—45deg 45min
Seat width	NA
Spring pressure	NA
Intake stem to guide clearance	0.0010—0.0027in
Exhaust stem to guide clearance	0.0015—0.0032in
Intake stem diameter	0.3420in
Exhaust stem diameter	0.3415in
Piston clearance	0.0018—0.0026in
Top comp. ring gap	0.010—0.020in
Bottom comp. ring gap	0.010—0.020in
Oil ring gap	0.015—0.055in
Top comp. side clearance	0.002—0.004in
Bottom comp. side clearance	0.002—0.004in
Oil side clearance	Snug

1982 Ford 302 Eight-cylinder

Displacement	302ci
Volume (liters)	5.0
Main journal diameter	2.2482—2.2390in
Main journal oil clearance	0.0005—0.0015; 0.0001—0.0015in (no. 1)
Crankshaft end play	0.004—0.008in
Thrust journal length	3in
Rod journal diameter	2.1228—2.1236in
Rod oil clearance	0.0008—0.0026in

Rod side clearance 0.010—0.020in
Intake valve seat angle 44deg 30min—45deg
Exhaust valve seat angle 44deg 30min—45deg
Intake face angle 45deg 30min—45deg 45min
Exhaust face angle 45deg 30min—45deg 45min
Seat width NA
Spring pressure NA
Intake stem to guide clearance 0.0010—0.0027in
Exhaust stem to guide clearance 0.0015—0.0032in
Intake stem diameter 0.3420in
Exhaust stem diameter 0.3415in
Piston clearance 0.0018—0.0026in
Top comp. ring gap 0.010—0.020in
Bottom comp. ring gap 0.010—0.020in
Oil ring gap 0.015—0.055in
Top comp. side clearance 0.002—0.004in
Bottom comp. side clearance 0.002—0.004in
Oil side clearance Snug

1982 Ford 1597 Four-cylinder

Displacement	NA
Volume (liters)	1.597
Main journal diameter	2.2826—2.2834in
Main journal oil clearance	0.0008—0.0015in
Crankshaft end play	0.004—0.008in
Thrust journal length	3in
Rod journal diameter	1.885—1.886in
Rod oil clearance	0.0002—0.0003in
Rod side clearance	0.004—0.011in
Intake valve seat angle	45deg
Exhaust valve seat angle	45deg
Intake face angle	45deg 30min
Exhaust face angle	45deg 30min
Seat width	NA
Spring pressure	NA
Intake stem to guide clearance	0.0010in
Exhaust stem to guide clearance	0.0021in
Intake stem diameter	0.320in
Exhaust stem diameter	0.310in
Piston clearance	0.0012—0.0020in
Top comp. ring gap	0.012—0.020in
Bottom comp. ring gap	0.012—0.020in
Oil ring gap	0.016—0.055in
Top comp. side clearance	0.001—0.003in
Bottom comp. side clearance	0.002—0.003in
Oil side clearance	Snug

1981 Ford 1597 Four-cylinder

Displacement	NA
Volume (liters)	1.597
Main journal diameter	2.2826—2.2834in
Main journal oil clearance	0.0008—0.0015in
Crankshaft end play	0.004—0.008in
Thrust journal length	3in
Rod journal diameter	1.885—1.886in
Rod oil clearance	0.0002—0.0003in
Rod side clearance	0.004—0.011in
Intake valve seat angle	45deg
Exhaust valve seat angle	45deg
Intake face angle	45deg 30min
Exhaust face angle	45deg 30min
Seat width	NA
Spring pressure	NA
Intake stem to guide clearance	0.0008—0.0027in
Exhaust stem to guide clearance	0.0015—0.0032in
Intake stem diameter	0.316in
Exhaust stem diameter	0.315in
Piston clearance	0.0008—0.0016in
Top comp. ring gap	0.012—0.020in
Bottom comp. ring gap	0.012—0.020in
Oil ring gap	0.016—0.055in
Top comp. side clearance	0.001—0.003in
Bottom comp. side clearance	0.002—0.003in
Oil side clearance	Snug

1980—1981 Ford 302 Eight-cylinder

Displacement	302ci
Volume (liters)	5.0
Main journal diameter	2.2482—2.2490in
Main journal oil clearance	0.0005—0.0015; 0.0001—0.0015in(no.1)

Crankshaft end play	0.004—0.008in
Thrust journal length	3in
Rod journal diameter	2.1228—2.1236in
Rod oil clearance	0.0008—0.0015in
Rod side clearance	0.010—0.020in
Intake valve seat angle	45deg
Exhaust valve seat angle	45deg
Intake face angle	44deg
Exhaust face angle	44deg
Seat width	NA
Spring pressure	NA
Intake stem to guide clearance	0.0010—0.0027in
Exhaust stem to guide clearance	0.0015—0.0032in
Intake stem diameter	0.3420in
Exhaust stem diameter	0.3415in
Piston clearance	0.0018—0.0026in
Top comp. ring gap	0.010—0.020in
Bottom comp. ring gap	0.010—0.020in
Oil ring gap	0.015—0.055in
Top comp. side clearance	0.002—0.004in
Bottom comp. side clearance	0.002—0.004in
Oil side clearance	Snug

1977—1983 Ford 140 Four-cylinder

Displacement	140ci
Volume (liters)	2.300
Main journal diameter	2.3982—2.3990in
Main journal oil clearance	0.0008—0.0015in
Crankshaft end play	0.004—0.008in
Thrust journal length	3in
Rod journal diameter	2.0464—2.0472in
Rod oil clearance	0.0008—0.0015in
Rod side clearance	0.0035—0.0105in
Intake valve seat angle	45deg
Exhaust valve seat angle	45deg
Intake face angle	44deg
Exhaust face angle	44deg
Seat width	NA
Spring pressure	NA
Intake stem to guide clearance	0.0010—0.0027in
Exhaust stem to guide clearance	0.0015—0.0032in
Intake stem diameter	0.3419in
Exhaust stem diameter	0.3415in
Piston clearance	0.0014—0.0022in
Top comp. ring gap	0.010—0.020in
Bottom comp. ring gap	0.010—0.020in
Oil ring gap	0.015—0.055in
Top comp. side clearance	0.0020—0.0040in
Bottom comp. side clearance	0.0020—0.0040in
Oil side clearance	Snug

1977—1981 Ford 200 Six-cylinder

Displacement	200ci
Volume (liters)	3.3
Main journal diameter	2.2482—2.2490in
Main journal oil clearance	0.0008—0.0015in
Crankshaft end play	0.004—0.008in
Thrust journal length	5in
Rod journal diameter	2.1232—2.1240in
Rod oil clearance	0.0008—0.0015in
Rod side clearance	0.0035—0.0105in
Intake valve seat angle	45deg
Exhaust valve seat angle	45deg
Intake face angle	44deg
Exhaust face angle	44deg
Seat width	NA
Spring pressure	NA
Intake stem to guide clearance	0.0008—0.0025in
Exhaust stem to guide clearance	0.0010—0.0027in
Intake stem diameter	0.3104in
Exhaust stem diameter	0.3102in
Piston clearance	0.0013—0.0021in
Top comp. ring gap	0.008—0.016in
Bottom comp. ring gap	0.008—0.016in
Oil ring gap	0.015—0.055in
Top comp. side clearance	0.002—0.004in
Bottom comp. side clearance	0.002—0.004in
Oil side clearance	Snug

1977—1980 Ford 250 Six-cylinder

Displacement	250ci

Volume (liters)	4.1
Main journal diameter	2.3982—2.3990in
Main journal oil clearance	0.0008—0.0015in
Crankshaft end play	0.004—0.008in
Thrust journal length	5in
Rod journal diameter	2.1232—2.1240in
Rod oil clearance	0.0008—0.0015in
Rod side clearance	0.0035—0.0105in
Intake valve seat angle	45deg
Exhaust valve seat angle	45deg
Intake face angle	44deg
Exhaust face angle	44deg
Seat width	NA
Spring pressure	NA
Intake stem to guide clearance	0.0008—0.0025in
Exhaust stem to guide clearance	0.0010—0.0027in
Intake stem diameter	0.3104in
Exhaust stem diameter	0.3102in
Piston clearance	0.0013—0.0021in
Top comp. ring gap	0.008—0.016in
Bottom comp. ring gap	0.008—0.016in
Oil ring gap	0.015—0.055in
Top comp. side clearance	0.002—0.004in
Bottom comp. side clearance	0.002—0.004in
Oil side clearance	Snug

1977—1979 Ford 171 Six-cylinder

Displacement	171ci
Volume (liters)	2.800
Main journal diameter	2.2433—2.2441in
Main journal oil clearance	0.0008—0.0015in
Crankshaft end play	0.004—0.008in
Thrust journal length	3in
Rod journal diameter	2.1252—2.1260in
Rod oil clearance	0.0006—0.0015in
Rod side clearance	0.004—0.011in
Intake valve seat angle	45deg
Exhaust valve seat angle	45deg
Intake face angle	44deg
Exhaust face angle	44deg
Seat width	NA
Spring pressure	NA
Intake stem to guide clearance	0.0008—0.0025in
Exhaust stem to guide clearance	0.0018—0.0035in
Intake stem diameter	0.3162in
Exhaust stem diameter	0.3153in
Piston clearance	0.0011—0.0019in
Top comp. ring gap	0.015—0.023in
Bottom comp. ring gap	0.015—0.023in
Oil ring gap	0.015—0.055in
Top comp. side clearance	0.0020—0.0033in
Bottom comp. side clearance	0.0020—0.0033in
Oil side clearance	Snug

1977—1979 Ford 400 Eight-cylinder

Displacement	400ci
Volume (liters)	6.6
Main journal diameter	2.9994—3.0002in
Main journal oil clearance	0.0008—0.0015in
Crankshaft end play	0.004—0.008in
Thrust journal length	3in
Rod journal diameter	3.3103—2.3111in
Rod oil clearance	0.0008—0.0015in
Rod side clearance	0.010—0.020in
Intake valve seat angle	45deg
Exhaust valve seat angle	45deg
Intake face angle	44deg
Exhaust face angle	44deg
Seat width	NA
Spring pressure	NA
Intake stem to guide clearance	0.0010—0.0027in
Exhaust stem to guide clearance	0.0015—0.0032in
Intake stem diameter	0.3420in
Exhaust stem diameter	0.3415in
Piston clearance	0.0014—0.0022in
Top comp. ring gap	0.010—0.020in
Bottom comp. ring gap	0.010—0.020in
Oil ring gap	0.015—0.055in
Top comp. side clearance	0.002—0.004in
Bottom comp. side clearance	0.002—0.004in
Oil side clearance	Snug

1977—1978 Ford 302 Eight-cylinder

Displacement	302ci
Volume (liters)	5.0
Main journal diameter	2.2482—2.2490in
Main journal oil clearance	0.0005—0.0015; 0.0001—0.0015in (no. 1)
Crankshaft end play	0.004—0.008in
Thrust journal length	3in
Rod journal diameter	2.1228—2.1236in
Rod oil clearance	0.0008—0.0015in
Rod side clearance	0.010—0.020in
Intake valve seat angle	45deg
Exhaust valve seat angle	45deg
Intake face angle	44deg
Exhaust face angle	44deg
Seat width	NA
Spring pressure	NA
Intake stem to guide clearance	0.0010—0.0027in
Exhaust stem to guide clearance	0.0015—0.0032in
Intake stem diameter	0.3420in
Exhaust stem diameter	0.3415in
Piston clearance	0.0018—0.0026in
Top comp. ring gap	0.010—0.020in
Bottom comp. ring gap	0.010—0.020in
Oil ring gap	0.015—0.055in
Top comp. side clearance	0.0020—0.0040in
Bottom comp. side clearance	0.0020—0.0040in
Oil side clearance	Snug

1977—1978 Ford 351M Eight-cylinder

Displacement	351ci
Volume (liters)	5.8
Main journal diameter	2.9994—3.0002in
Main journal oil clearance	0.0008—0.0015in
Crankshaft end play	0.004—0.008in
Thrust journal length	3in
Rod journal diameter	2.3103—2.3111in
Rod oil clearance	0.0008—0.0015in
Rod side clearance	0.010—0.020in
Intake valve seat angle	45deg
Exhaust valve seat angle	45deg
Intake face angle	44deg
Exhaust face angle	44deg
Seat width	NA
Spring pressure	NA
Intake stem to guide clearance	0.0010—0.0027in
Exhaust stem to guide clearance	0.0015—0.0032in
Intake stem diameter	0.3420in
Exhaust stem diameter	0.3415in
Piston clearance	0.0014—0.0022in
Top comp. ring gap	0.010—0.020in
Bottom comp. ring gap	0.010—0.020in
Oil ring gap	0.015—0.055in
Top comp. side clearance	0.002—0.004in
Bottom comp. side clearance	0.002—0.004in
Oil side clearance	Snug

1977—1978 Ford 351M Eight-cylinder Four-barrel

Displacement	351ci
Volume (liters)	5.8
Main journal diameter	2.9994—3.0002in
Main journal oil clearance	0.0011—0.0015in
Crankshaft end play	0.004—0.008in
Thrust journal length	3in
Rod journal diameter	2.3103—2.3111in
Rod oil clearance	0.0011—0.0015in
Rod side clearance	0.010—0.020in
Intake valve seat angle	45deg
Exhaust valve seat angle	45deg
Intake face angle	44deg
Exhaust face angle	44deg
Seat width	NA
Spring pressure	NA
Intake stem to guide clearance	0.0010—0.0027in
Exhaust stem to guide clearance	0.0015—0.0032in
Intake stem diameter	0.3420in
Exhaust stem diameter	0.3415in
Piston clearance	0.0014—0.0022in
Top comp. ring gap	0.010—0.020in

<table>
<tbody>
<tr><td>Bottom comp. ring gap</td><td>0.010—0.020in</td></tr>
<tr><td>Oil ring gap</td><td>0.015—0.055in</td></tr>
<tr><td>Top comp. side clearance</td><td>0.002—0.004in</td></tr>
<tr><td>Bottom comp. side clearance</td><td>0.002—0.004in</td></tr>
<tr><td>Oil side clearance</td><td>Snug</td></tr>
</tbody>
</table>

1977—1978 Ford 460 Eight-cylinder

Displacement	460ci
Volume (liters)	7.5
Main journal diameter	2.9994—3.0002in
Main journal oil clearance	0.0008—0.0015in
Crankshaft end play	0.004—0.008in
Thrust journal length	3in
Rod journal diameter	2.4992—2.500in
Rod oil clearance	0.0008—0.0015in
Rod side clearance	0.010—0.020in
Intake valve seat angle	44deg 30min—45deg
Exhaust valve seat angle	44deg 30min—45deg
Intake face angle	45deg 30min—45deg 45min
Exhaust face angle	45deg 30min—45deg 45min
Seat width	NA
Spring pressure	NA
Intake stem to guide clearance	0.0010—0.0027in
Exhaust stem to guide clearance	0.0010—0.0027in
Intake stem diameter	0.3420in
Exhaust stem diameter	0.3420in
Piston clearance	0.0014—0.0022in
Top comp. ring gap	0.010—0.020in
Bottom comp. ring gap	0.010—0.020in
Oil ring gap	0.015—0.055in
Top comp. side clearance	0.0025—0.0045in
Bottom comp. side clearance	0.0025—0.0045in
Oil side clearance	Snug

1980—1981 Ford 255 Eight-cylinder

Displacement	255ci
Volume (liters)	4.2
Main journal diameter	2.2482—2.2490in
Main journal oil clearance	0.0005—0.0015; 0.0001—0.0015in (no. 1)
Crankshaft end play	0.004—0.008in
Thrust journal length	3in
Rod journal diameter	2.1228—2.1236in
Rod oil clearance	0.0008—0.0015in
Rod side clearance	0.010—0.020in
Intake valve seat angle	45deg
Exhaust valve seat angle	45deg
Intake face angle	44deg
Exhaust face angle	44deg
Seat width	NA
Spring pressure	NA
Intake stem to guide clearance	0.0010—0.0027in
Exhaust stem to guide clearance	0.0015—0.0032in
Intake stem diameter	0.3420in
Exhaust stem diameter	0.3415in
Piston clearance	0.0018—0.0026in
Top comp. ring gap	0.010—0.020in
Bottom comp. ring gap	0.010—0.020in
Oil ring gap	0.015—0.055in
Top comp. side clearance	0.002—0.004in
Bottom comp. side clearance	0.002—0.004in
Oil side clearance	Snug

1980 Ford 351W Eight-cylinder

Displacement	351ci
Volume (liters)	5.8
Main journal diameter	2.9994—3.0002in
Main journal oil clearance	0.0008—0.0015; 0.0001—0.0015in (no. 1)
Crankshaft end play	0.004—0.008in
Thrust journal length	3in
Rod journal diameter	2.3103—2.3111in
Rod oil clearance	0.0008—0.0015in
Rod side clearance	0.010—0.020in
Intake valve seat angle	45deg
Exhaust valve seat angle	45deg
Intake face angle	44deg
Exhaust face angle	44deg

Seat width	NA
Spring pressure	NA
Intake stem to guide clearance	0.0010—0.0027in
Exhaust stem to guide clearance	0.0015—0.0032in
Intake stem diameter	0.3420in
Exhaust stem diameter	0.3415in
Piston clearance	0.0018—0.0026in
Top comp. ring gap	0.010—0.020in
Bottom comp. ring gap	0.010—0.020in
Oil ring gap	0.015—0.055in
Top comp. side clearance	0.002—0.004in
Bottom comp. side clearance	0.002—0.004in
Oil side clearance	Snug

1977—1979 Ford 302 Eight-cylinder

Displacement	302ci
Volume (liters)	5.0
Main journal diameter	2.2482—2.2490in
Main journal oil clearance	0.0005—0.0015; 0.0001—0.0015in (no. 1)
Crankshaft end play	0.004—0.008in
Thrust journal length	3in
Rod journal diameter	2.1228—2.1236in
Rod oil clearance	0.0008—0.0015in
Rod side clearance	0.010—0.020in
Intake valve seat angle	45deg
Exhaust valve seat angle	45deg
Intake face angle	44deg
Exhaust face angle	44deg
Seat width	NA
Spring pressure	NA
Intake stem to guide clearance	0.0010—0.0027in
Exhaust stem to guide clearance	0.0015—0.0032in
Intake stem diameter	0.3420in
Exhaust stem diameter	0.3415in
Piston clearance	0.0018—0.0026in
Top comp. ring gap	0.010—0.020in
Bottom comp. ring gap	0.010—0.020in
Oil ring gap	0.015—0.055in
Top comp. side clearance	0.002—0.004in
Bottom comp. side clearance	0.002—0.004in
Oil side clearance	Snug

1977—1979 Ford 351W Eight-cylinder

Displacement	351ci
Volume (liters)	5.8
Main journal diameter	2.9994—3.0002in
Main journal oil clearance	0.0008—0.0015; 0.0001—0.00015in (no. 1)
Crankshaft end play	0.004—0.008in
Thrust journal length	3in
Rod journal diameter	3.3103—2.3111in
Rod oil clearance	0.0008—0.0015in
Rod side clearance	0.010—0.020in
Intake valve seat angle	45deg
Exhaust valve seat angle	45deg
Intake face angle	44deg
Exhaust face angle	44deg
Seat width	NA
Spring pressure	NA
Intake stem to guide clearance	0.0010—0.0027in
Exhaust stem to guide clearance	0.0015—0.0032in
Intake stem diameter	0.3420in
Exhaust stem diameter	0.3415in
Piston clearance	0.0018—0.0026in
Top comp. ring gap	0.010—0.020in
Bottom comp. ring gap	0.010—0.020in
Oil ring gap	0.015—0.055in
Top comp. side clearance	0.002—0.004in
Bottom comp. side clearance	0.002—0.004in
Oil side clearance	Snug

1984 Ford Four-Wheel-Drive 2300 Four-cylinder

Displacement	NA
Volume (liters)	2.300
Main journal diameter	2.2489—2.2490in
Main journal oil clearance	0.0008—0.0024in
Crankshaft end play	0.004—0.008in

Thrust journal length	3in
Rod journal diameter	2.1232—2.1240
Rod oil clearance	0.0008—0.0015in
Rod side clearance	0.0035—0.0105in
Intake valve seat angle	45deg
Exhaust valve seat angle	45deg
Intake face angle	45deg 30min
Exhaust face angle	45deg 30min
Seat width	NA
Spring pressure	NA
Intake stem to guide clearance	0.0018in
Exhaust stem to guide clearance	0.0023in
Intake stem diameter	0.3415in
Exhaust stem diameter	0.3411in
Piston clearance	0.0013—0.0021in
Top comp. ring gap	0.008—0.016in
Bottom comp. ring gap	0.008—0.16in
Oil ring gap	0.015—0.055in
Top comp. side clearance	0.002—0.004in
Bottom comp. side clearance	0.002—0.004in
Oil side clearance	Snug

1979—1980 GM 231 Six-cylinder

Displacement	231ci
Volume (liters)	NA
Main journal diameter	2.4995in
Main journal oil clearance	0.0003—0.0017in
Crankshaft end play	0.004—0.008in
Thrust journal length	2in
Rod journal diameter	2.2487—2.2495in
Rod oil clearance	0.0005—0.0026in
Rod side clearance	0.006—0.023in
Intake valve seat angle	45deg
Exhaust valve seat angle	45deg
Intake face angle	45deg
Exhaust face angle	45deg
Seat width	NA
Spring pressure	NA
Intake stem to guide clearance	0.0015—0.0032in
Exhaust stem to guide clearance	0.0015—0.0032in
Intake stem diameter	0.3408in
Exhaust stem diameter	0.3408in
Piston clearance	0.0008—0.0020in
Top comp. ring gap	0.013—0.023in
Bottom comp. ring gap	0.013—0.023in
Oil ring gap	0.015—0.035in
Top comp. side clearance	0.0030—0.0050in
Bottom comp. side clearance	0.0030—0.0050in
Oil side clearance	0.0035in maximum (max.)

1979 GM 305 Eight-cylinder

Displacement	305ci
Volume (liters)	NA
Main journal diameter	2.4484—2.4493 (no. 1); 2.4481—2.4490in (nos. 2, 3, & 4); 2.4479—2.4488in (no. 5)
Main journal oil clearance	0.0008—0.0020in (no. 1); 0.0011—0.0023 (nos. 2, 3, & 4); 0.0017—0.0033in (no. 5)
Crankshaft end play	0.002—0.006in
Thrust journal length	5in
Rod journal diameter	2.0988—2.0998in
Rod oil clearance	0.0013—0.0035in
Rod side clearance	0.008—0.014in
Intake valve seat angle	45deg
Exhaust valve seat angle	45deg
Intake face angle	45deg
Exhaust face angle	45deg
Seat width	NA
Spring pressure	NA
Intake stem to guide clearance	0.0015—0.0032in
Exhaust stem to guide clearance	0.0015—0.0032in
Intake stem diameter	0.3408in
Exhaust stem diameter	0.3408in
Piston clearance	0.0007—0.0017in
Top comp. ring gap	0.010—0.020in

Bottom comp. ring gap	0.010—0.025in
Oil ring gap	0.010—0.035in
Top comp. side clearance	0.0012—0.0032in
Bottom comp. side clearance	0.0012—0.0032in
Oil side clearance	0.002—0.007in

1978 GM 196 Six-cylinder

Displacement	196ci
Volume (liters)	NA
Main journal diameter	2.4995in
Main journal oil clearance	0.0003—0.0017in
Crankshaft end play	0.004—0.008in
Thrust journal length	2in
Rod journal diameter	2.2487—2.2495in
Rod oil clearance	0.0005—0.0026in
Rod side clearance	0.006—0.027in
Intake valve seat angle	45deg
Exhaust valve seat angle	45deg
Intake face angle	45deg
Exhaust face angle	45deg
Seat width	NA
Spring pressure	NA
Intake stem to guide clearance	0.0015—0.0032in
Exhaust stem to guide clearance	0.0015—0.0032in
Intake stem diameter	0.3408in
Exhaust stem diameter	0.3408in
Piston clearance	0.0008—0.0020in
Top comp. ring gap	0.010—0.020in
Bottom comp. ring gap	0.010—0.020in
Oil ring gap	0.015—0.035in
Top comp. side clearance	0.0030—0.0050in
Bottom comp. side clearance	0.0030—0.0050in
Oil side clearance	0.0035in max.

1978 GM 231 Six-cylinder

Displacement	231ci
Volume (liters)	NA
Main journal diameter	2.4995in
Main journal oil clearance	0.0003—0.0017in
Crankshaft end play	0.004—0.008in
Thrust journal length	2in
Rod journal diameter	2.2487—2.2495in
Rod oil clearance	0.0005—0.0026in
Rod side clearance	0.006—0.027in
Intake valve seat angle	45deg
Exhaust valve seat angle	45deg
Intake face angle	45deg
Exhaust face angle	45deg
Seat width	NA
Spring pressure	NA
Intake stem to guide clearance	0.0015—0.0032in
Exhaust stem to guide clearance	0.0015—0.0032in
Intake stem diameter	0.3408in
Exhaust stem diameter	0.3408in
Piston clearance	0.0008—0.0020in
Top comp. ring gap	0.010—0.020in
Bottom comp. ring gap	0.010—0.020in
Oil ring gap	0.015—0.035in
Top comp. side clearance	0.0030—0.0050in
Bottom comp. side clearance	0.0030—0.0050in
Oil side clearance	0.0035in max.

1978 GM 305 Eight-cylinder

Displacement	305ci
Volume (liters)	NA
Main journal diameter	2.4484—2.4493in (no. 1); 2.4481—2.4490 (nos. 2, 3, & 4); 2.4479—2.4488in (no. 5)
Main journal oil clearance	0.0008—0.0020in (no. 1); 0.0011—0.0023 (nos. 2, 3, & 4); 0.0017—0.0033in (no. 5)
Crankshaft end play	0.002—0.006in
Thrust journal length	5in
Rod journal diameter	2.0988—2.0998in
Rod oil clearance	0.0013—0.0035in
Rod side clearance	0.008—0.014in
Intake valve seat angle	46deg
Exhaust valve seat angle	46deg

Intake face angle	45deg
Exhaust face angle	45deg
Seat width	NA
Spring pressure	NA
Intake stem to guide clearance	0.0010—0.0027in
Exhaust stem to guide clearance	0.0010—0.0027in
Intake stem diameter	0.3414in
Exhaust stem diameter	0.3414in
Piston clearance	0.0007—0.0017in
Top comp. ring gap	0.010—0.020in
Bottom comp. ring gap	0.010—0.025in
Oil ring gap	0.015—0.055in
Top comp. side clearance	0.0012—0.0032in
Bottom comp. side clearance	0.0012—0.0032in
Oil side clearance	0.002—0.007in

1977—1978 GM 151 Four-cylinder

Displacement	151ci
Volume (liters)	NA
Main journal diameter	2.3000in
Main journal oil clearance	0.0002—0.0022in
Crankshaft end play	0.0035—0.0085in
Thrust journal length	5in
Rod journal diameter	2.0000in
Rod oil clearance	0.0005—0.0026in
Rod side clearance	0.006—0.022in
Intake valve seat angle	46deg
Exhaust valve seat angle	46deg
Intake face angle	45deg
Exhaust face angle	45deg
Seat width	NA
Spring pressure	NA
Intake stem to guide clearance	0.0010—0.0027in
Exhaust stem to guide clearance	0.0010—0.0027; 0.0020—0.0037in (bottom)
Intake stem diameter	0.3400in
Exhaust stem diameter	0.3400in
Piston clearance	0.0025—0.0033in
Top comp. ring gap	0.010—0.020in
Bottom comp. ring gap	0.010—0.020in
Oil ring gap	0.015—0.035in
Top comp. side clearance	0.0015—0.0035in
Bottom comp. side clearance	0.0015—0.0035in
Oil side clearance	0.0015—0.0035in

1977 GM 140 Four-cylinder

Displacement	140ci
Volume (liters)	NA
Main journal diameter	2.3004in
Main journal oil clearance	0.0003—0.0029in
Crankshaft end play	0.002—0.008in
Thrust journal length	4in
Rod journal diameter	1.999—2.000in
Rod oil clearance	0.0007—0.0027in
Rod side clearance	0.0009—0.0013in
Intake valve seat angle	46deg
Exhaust valve seat angle	46deg
Intake face angle	45deg
Exhaust face angle	45deg
Seat width	NA
Spring pressure	NA
Intake stem to guide clearance	0.0010—0.0027in
Exhaust stem to guide clearance	0.0010—0.0027in
Intake stem diameter	0.3414in
Exhaust stem diameter	0.3414in
Piston clearance	0.0018—0.0028in
Top comp. ring gap	0.015—0.025in
Bottom comp. ring gap	0.009—0.019in
Oil ring gap	0.010—0.030in
Top comp. side clearance	0.0012—0.0027in
Bottom comp. side clearance	0.0012—0.0027in
Oil side clearance	0.000—0.005in

1977 GM 231 Six-cylinder

Displacement	231ci
Volume (liters)	NA
Main journal diameter	2.4995in
Main journal oil clearance	0.0004—0.0015in
Crankshaft end play	0.004—0.008in
Thrust journal length	2in
Rod journal diameter	2.0000in

Rod oil clearance	0.0005—0.0026in
Rod side clearance	0.006—0.014in
Intake valve seat angle	45deg
Exhaust valve seat angle	45deg
Intake face angle	45deg
Exhaust face angle	45deg
Seat width	NA
Spring pressure	NA
Intake stem to guide clearance	0.0015—0.0035in
Exhaust stem to guide clearance	0.0015—0.0035in
Intake stem diameter	0.3414in
Exhaust stem diameter	0.3414in
Piston clearance	0.0008—0.0020in
Top comp. ring gap	0.010—0.020in
Bottom comp. ring gap	0.010—0.020in
Oil ring gap	0.015—0.035in
Top comp. side clearance	0.0030—0.0050in
Bottom comp. side clearance	0.0030—0.0050in
Oil side clearance	0.0035in max.

1977 GM 305

Displacement	305ci
Volume (liters)	NA
Main journal diameter	2.4502; 2.4508in (no. 5)
Main journal oil clearance	0.0008—0.0020 (no. 1); 0.0011—0.0023 (nos. 2, 3, & 4); 0.0017—0.0033 (no. 5)
Crankshaft end play	0.002—0.007in
Thrust journal length	5in
Rod journal diameter	2.098—2.099in
Rod oil clearance	0.0013—0.0035in
Rod side clearance	0.008—0.014in
Intake valve seat angle	46deg
Exhaust valve seat angle	46deg
Intake face angle	45deg
Exhaust face angle	45deg
Seat width	NA
Spring pressure	NA
Intake stem to guide clearance	0.0010—0.0027in
Exhaust stem to guide clearance	0.0010—0.0027in
Intake stem diameter	0.3414in
Exhaust stem diameter	0.3414in
Piston clearance	0.0007—0.0017in
Top comp. ring gap	0.010—0.020in
Bottom comp. ring gap	0.010—0.025in
Oil ring gap	0.015—0.055in
Top comp. side clearance	0.0012—0.0032in
Bottom comp. side clearance	0.0012—0.0032in
Oil side clearance	0.000—0.001in

1979—1980 GM 151 Four-cylinder

Displacement	151ci
Volume (liters)	NA
Main journal diameter	2.2988in
Main journal oil clearance	0.0002—0.0022in
Crankshaft end play	0.0035—0.0085in
Thrust journal length	5in
Rod journal diameter	2.0000in
Rod oil clearance	0.0005—0.0026in
Rod side clearance	0.006—0.022in
Intake valve seat angle	46deg
Exhaust valve seat angle	46deg
Intake face angle	45deg
Exhaust face angle	45deg
Seat width	NA
Spring pressure	NA
Intake stem to guide clearance	0.0010—0.0027in
Exhaust stem to guide clearance	0.0010—0.0027; 0.0020—0.0037in (bottom)
Intake stem diameter	0.3400in
Exhaust stem diameter	0.3400in
Piston clearance	0.0025—0.0033in
Top comp. ring gap	0.016—0.026in
Bottom comp. ring gap	0.009—0.019in
Oil ring gap	0.015—0.055in
Top comp. side clearance	0.0015—0.0035in
Bottom comp. side clearance	0.0015—0.0035in
Oil side clearance	0.0015—0.0035in

1979 GM 196 Six-cylinder

Displacement	196ci
Volume (liters)	NA
Main journal diameter	2.4995in
Main journal oil clearance	0.0003—0.0017in
Crankshaft end play	0.004—0.008in
Thrust journal length	2in
Rod journal diameter	2.2487—2.2495in
Rod oil clearance	0.0005—0.0026in
Rod side clearance	0.006—0.023in
Intake valve seat angle	45deg
Exhaust valve seat angle	45deg
Intake face angle	45deg
Exhaust face angle	45deg
Seat width	NA
Spring pressure	NA
Intake stem to guide clearance	0.0015—0.0032in
Exhaust stem to guide clearance	0.0015—0.0032in
Intake stem diameter	0.3408in
Exhaust stem diameter	0.3408in
Piston clearance	0.0008—0.0020in
Top comp. ring gap	0.013—0.023in
Bottom comp. ring gap	0.013—0.023in
Oil ring gap	0.015—0.035in
Top comp. side clearance	0.0030—0.0050in
Bottom comp. side clearance	0.0030—0.0050in
Oil side clearance	0.0035in max.

1979—1984 GM T-body 1.6-Liter Four-cylinder

Displacement	NA
Volume (liters)	1.6
Main journal diameter	2.0078—2.0088in
Main journal oil clearance	0.0005—0.0019; 0.0009—0.0026in (no. 5)
Crankshaft end play	0.004—0.008in
Thrust journal length	4in
Rod journal diameter	1.809—1.810in
Rod oil clearance	0.0014—0.0031in
Rod side clearance	0.004—0.012in
Intake valve seat angle	45deg
Exhaust valve seat angle	45deg
Intake face angle	45deg
Exhaust face angle	45deg
Seat width	NA
Spring pressure	NA
Intake stem to guide clearance	0.0015—0.0028in
Exhaust stem to guide clearance	0.0018—0.0030in
Intake stem diameter	0.3128—0.3134in
Exhaust stem diameter	0.3126—0.3132in
Piston clearance	0.0008—0.0016in
Top comp. ring gap	0.009—0.019in
Bottom comp. ring gap	0.008—0.018in
Oil ring gap	0.015—0.055in
Top comp. side clearance	0.0012—0.0027in
Bottom comp. side clearance	0.0012—0.0032in
Oil side clearance	0.0000—0.0050in

1978 GM T-body 1.6-Liter Four-cylinder

Displacement	NA
Volume (liters)	1.6
Main journal diameter	2.0078—2.0088in
Main journal oil clearance	0.0009—0.0026in
Crankshaft end play	0.004—0.008in
Thrust journal length	4in
Rod journal diameter	1.809—1.810in
Rod oil clearance	0.0014—0.0031in
Rod side clearance	0.004—0.012in
Intake valve seat angle	45deg
Exhaust valve seat angle	45deg
Intake face angle	46deg
Exhaust face angle	46deg
Seat width	NA
Spring pressure	NA
Intake stem to guide clearance	0.0006—0.0017in
Exhaust stem to guide clearance	0.0014—0.0025in
Intake stem diameter	0.3141in
Exhaust stem diameter	0.3133in
Piston clearance	0.0008—0.0016in
Top comp. ring gap	0.009—0.019in
Bottom comp. ring gap	0.008—0.018in
Oil ring gap	0.015—0.055in
Top comp. side clearance	0.0012—0.0027in
Bottom comp. side clearance	0.0012—0.0032in
Oil side clearance	0.0000—0.0050in

1977 GM T-body 1.4-Liter Four-cylinder

Displacement	NA
Volume (liters)	1.4
Main journal diameter	2.0078—2.0088in
Main journal oil clearance	0.0009—0.0026in
Crankshaft end play	0.004—0.008in
Thrust journal length	4in
Rod journal diameter	1.809—1.810in
Rod oil clearance	0.0014—0.0031in
Rod side clearance	0.004—0.012in
Intake valve seat angle	46deg
Exhaust valve seat angle	46deg
Intake face angle	45deg
Exhaust face angle	45deg
Seat width	NA
Spring pressure	NA
Intake stem to guide clearance	0.0006—0.0017in
Exhaust stem to guide clearance	0.0014—0.0025in
Intake stem diameter	0.3141in
Exhaust stem diameter	0.3133in
Piston clearance	0.0008—0.0016in
Top comp. ring gap	0.009—0.019in
Bottom comp. ring gap	0.008—0.018in
Oil ring gap	0.015—0.055in
Top comp. side clearance	0.0012—0.0027in
Bottom comp. side clearance	0.0012—0.0032in
Oil side clearance	0.0000—0.0050in

1977 GM T-body 1.6-Liter Four-cylinder

Displacement	NA
Volume (liters)	1.6
Main journal diameter	2.0078—2.0088in
Main journal oil clearance	0.0009—0.0026in
Crankshaft end play	0.004—0.008in
Thrust journal length	4in
Rod journal diameter	1.809—1.810in
Rod oil clearance	0.0014—0.0031in
Rod side clearance	0.004—0.012in
Intake valve seat angle	46deg
Exhaust valve seat angle	46deg
Intake face angle	45deg
Exhaust face angle	45deg
Seat width	NA
Spring pressure	NA
Intake stem to guide clearance	0.0006—0.0017in
Exhaust stem to guide clearance	0.0014—0.0025in
Intake stem diameter	0.3141in
Exhaust stem diameter	0.3133in
Piston clearance	0.0008—0.0016in
Top comp. ring gap	0.009—0.019in
Bottom comp. ring gap	0.008—0.018in
Oil ring gap	0.015—0.055in
Top comp. side clearance	0.0012—0.0027in
Bottom comp. side clearance	0.0012—0.0032in
Oil side clearance	0.0000—0.0050in

1979—1981 Mazda 626

Displacement	120.2ci
Volume (liters)	1.970
Main journal diameter	2.4804in
Main journal oil clearance	0.0012—0.0020in
Crankshaft end play	0.003—0.009in
Thrust journal length	5in
Rod journal diameter	2.0866in
Rod oil clearance	0.001—0.003in
Rod side clearance	0.004—0.008in
Intake valve seat angle	45deg
Exhaust valve seat angle	45deg
Intake face angle	45deg
Exhaust face angle	45deg
Seat width	NA
Spring pressure	31.4psi @ 1.339in
Intake stem to guide clearance	0.0007—0.0021in
Exhaust stem to guide clearance	0.0007—0.0021in
Intake stem diameter	0.3150in
Exhaust stem diameter	0.3150in

1983—1984 Mazda 626

Displacement	121.9ci
Volume (liters)	1.998
Main journal diameter	2.359in
Main journal oil clearance	0.0012—0.0019in
Crankshaft end play	0.0031—0.0071in
Thrust journal length	NA
Rod journal diameter	2.005—2.006in
Rod oil clearance	0.0010—0.0026in
Rod side clearance	0.004—0.010in
Intake valve seat angle	45deg
Exhaust valve seat angle	45deg
Intake face angle	45deg
Exhaust face angle	45deg
Seat width	NA
Spring pressure	NA
Intake stem to guide clearance	0.0010—0.0024in
Exhaust stem to guide clearance	0.0010—0.0024in
Intake stem diameter	0.3177—0.3185in
Exhaust stem diameter	0.3159—0.3165in
Piston clearance	0.0014—0.0030in
Top comp. ring gap	0.0012—0.0028in
Bottom comp. ring gap	0.0012—0.0028in
Oil ring gap	NA
Top comp. side clearance	0.008—0.014in
Bottom comp. side clearance	0.006—0.012in
Oil side clearance	0.012—0.035in

1982 Mazda 626

Displacement	120.2ci
Volume (liters)	1.970
Main journal diameter	2.4804in
Main journal oil clearance	0.0012—0.0020in
Crankshaft end play	0.003—0.009in
Thrust journal length	5in
Rod journal diameter	2.0866in
Rod oil clearance	0.001—0.003in
Rod side clearance	0.004—0.008in
Intake valve seat angle	45deg
Exhaust valve seat angle	45deg
Intake face angle	45deg
Exhaust face angle	45deg
Seat width	NA
Spring pressure	31.4psi @ 1.339in
Intake stem to guide clearance	0.0007—0.0021in
Exhaust stem to guide clearance	0.0007—0.0021in
Intake stem diameter	0.3150in
Exhaust stem diameter	0.3150in
Piston clearance	0.0019—0.0025in
Top comp. ring gap	0.0012—0.0028in
Bottom comp. ring gap	0.0012—0.0025in
Oil ring gap	0.008—0.016in
Top comp. side clearance	0.008—0.016in
Bottom comp. side clearance	0.008—0.016in
Oil side clearance	0.012—0.035in

1981—1984 Mazda GLC

Displacement	90.9ci
Volume (liters)	1.490
Main journal diameter	1.9664in
Main journal oil clearance	0.0009—0.0017in
Crankshaft end play	0.004—0.006in
Thrust journal length	5in
Rod journal diameter	1.5729in
Rod oil clearance	0.0009—0.0019in
Rod side clearance	0.004—0.010in
Intake valve seat angle	45deg
Exhaust valve seat angle	45deg
Intake face angle	45deg
Exhaust face angle	45deg
Seat width	NA
Spring pressure	NA
Intake stem to guide clearance	0.0007—0.0021in
Exhaust stem to guide clearance	0.0007—0.0021in

Intake stem diameter | 0.3164in
Exhaust stem diameter | 0.3163in
Piston clearance | 0.0010—0.0026in
Top comp. ring gap | 0.0012—0.0028in
Bottom comp. ring gap | 0.0012—0.0028in
Oil ring gap | 0.008—0.016in
Top comp. side clearance | 0.008—0.016in
Bottom comp. side clearance | 0.008—0.016in
Oil side clearance | 0.012—0.035in

1979—1980 Mazda GLC

Displacement	86.4ci
Volume (liters)	1.415
Main journal diameter	1.9685in
Main journal oil clearance	0.0009—0.0017in
Crankshaft end play	0.004—0.006in
Thrust journal length	5in
Rod journal diameter	1.5748in
Rod oil clearance	0.0009—0.0019in
Rod side clearance	0.004—0.008in
Intake valve seat angle	45deg
Exhaust valve seat angle	45deg
Intake face angle	45deg
Exhaust face angle	45deg
Seat width	NA
Spring pressure	36.6psi @ 1.319in
Intake stem to guide clearance	0.0007—0.0021in
Exhaust stem to guide clearance	0.0007—0.0021in
Intake stem diameter	0.3150in
Exhaust stem diameter	0.3150in
Piston clearance	0.0021—0.0026in
Top comp. ring gap	0.0012—0.0025in
Bottom comp. ring gap	0.0012—0.0025in
Oil ring gap	0.008—0.016in
Top comp. side clearance	0.008—0.016in
Bottom comp. side clearance	0.008—0.016in
Oil side clearance	0.012—0.035in

1977—1978 Mazda 808

Displacement	77.6ci
Volume (liters)	1.272
Main journal diameter	2.4804in
Main journal oil clearance	0.0012—0.0024in
Crankshaft end play	0.003—0.009in
Thrust journal length	5in
Rod journal diameter	1.7717in
Rod oil clearance	0.0011—0.0029in
Rod side clearance	0.004—0.008in
Intake valve seat angle	45deg
Exhaust valve seat angle	45deg
Intake face angle	45deg
Exhaust face angle	45deg
Seat width	NA
Spring pressure	43.7psi @ 1.1319in
Intake stem to guide clearance	0.0007—0.0021in
Exhaust stem to guide clearance	0.0007—0.0023in
Intake stem diameter	0.3150in
Exhaust stem diameter	0.3150in
Piston clearance	0.0021—0.0026in
Top comp. ring gap	0.0014—0.0028in
Bottom comp. ring gap	0.0012—0.0025in
Oil ring gap	0.008—0.016in
Top comp. side clearance	0.008—0.016in
Bottom comp. side clearance	0.008—0.016in
Oil side clearance	0.008—0.016in

1977—1978 Mazda 808

Displacement	96.8ci
Volume (liters)	1.586
Main journal diameter	2.4804in
Main journal oil clearance	0.001—0.002in
Crankshaft end play	0.003—0.009in
Thrust journal length	5in
Rod journal diameter	2.0866in
Rod oil clearance	0.001—0.003in
Rod side clearance	0.004—0.008in
Intake valve seat angle	45deg
Exhaust valve seat angle	45deg
Intake face angle	45deg
Exhaust face angle	45deg
Seat width	NA
Spring pressure	31.4psi @ 1.339in

1977—1978 Mazda GLC

Intake stem to guide clearance	0.0007—0.0021in
Exhaust stem to guide clearance	0.0007—0.0021in
Intake stem diameter	0.3150in
Exhaust stem diameter	0.3150in
Piston clearance	0.0022—0.0028in
Top comp. ring gap	0.0014—0.0028in
Bottom comp. ring gap	0.0012—0.0025in
Oil ring gap	0.008—0.016in
Top comp. side clearance	0.008—0.016in
Bottom comp. side clearance	0.008—0.016in
Oil side clearance	0.008—0.016in

Displacement	77.6ci
Volume (liters)	1.272
Main journal diameter	2.4804in
Main journal oil clearance	0.0012—0.0024in
Crankshaft end play	0.003—0.009in
Thrust journal length	5in
Rod journal diameter	1.7717in
Rod oil clearance	0.0011—0.0029in
Rod side clearance	0.004—0.008in
Intake valve seat angle	45deg
Exhaust valve seat angle	45deg
Intake face angle	45deg
Exhaust face angle	45deg
Seat width	NA
Spring pressure	43.7psi @ 1.319in
Intake stem to guide clearance	0.0007—0.0021in
Exhaust stem to guide clearance	0.0007—0.0023in
Intake stem diameter	0.3150in
Exhaust stem diameter	0.3150in
Piston clearance	0.0021—0.0026in
Top comp. ring gap	0.0014—0.0028in
Bottom comp. ring gap	0.0012—0.0025in
Oil ring gap	0.008—0.016in
Top comp. side clearance	0.008—0.016in
Bottom comp. side clearance	0.008—0.016in
Oil side clearance	0.008—0.016in

1977—1984 Saab (All)

Displacement	121.0ci
Volume (liters)	1.985
Main journal diameter	2.283—2.284in
Main journal oil clearance	0.0008—0.0025in
Crankshaft end play	0.003—0.011in
Thrust journal length	3in
Rod journal diameter	2.0465—2.0472in
Rod oil clearance	0.0010—0.0025in
Rod side clearance	NA
Intake valve seat angle	45deg
Exhaust valve seat angle	45deg
Intake face angle	44deg 30min
Exhaust face angle	44deg 30min
Seat width	NA
Spring pressure	178—198psi @ 1.16in
Intake stem to guide clearance	0.020in
Exhaust stem to guide clearance	0.020in
Intake stem diameter	0.03134—0.0319in
Exhaust stem diameter	0.03132—0.3142in
Piston clearance	3.5425—3.5428in
Top comp. ring gap	0.014—0.022in
Bottom comp. ring gap	0.012—0.018in
Oil ring gap	0.015—0.055in
Top comp. side clearance	0.002—0.003in
Bottom comp. side clearance	0.002—0.003in
Oil side clearance	NA

1983—1984 Subaru Horizontally Opposed Four-cylinder

Displacement	97ci
Volume (liters)	1.6
Main journal diameter	1.9673—1.9677in (center [ctr])
Main oil clearance	0.0004—0.0014; 0.0004—0.0010in ctr
Crankshaft end play	0.0016—0.0054in
Thrust journal length	2in
Rod journal diameter	1.7715—1.7720in
Rod oil clearance	0.0008—0.0028in
Rod side clearance	0.0028—0.0130in

Intake valve seat angle | 45deg
Exhaust valve seat angle | 45deg
Intake face angle | 45deg
Exhaust face angle | 45deg
Seat width | NA
Spring pressure | NA
Intake stem to guide clearance | 0.0014—0.0026in
Exhaust stem to guide clearance | 0.0016—0.0028in
Intake stem diameter | 0.3130—0.3136in
Exhaust stem diameter | 0.3128—0.3134in
Piston clearance | 0.001—0.002in
Top comp. ring gap | 0.008—0.013in
Bottom comp. ring gap | 0.008—0.013in
Oil ring gap | 0.008—0.035in
Top comp. side clearance | 0.001—0.003in
Bottom comp. side clearance | 0.001—0.003in
Oil side clearance | None

1983—1984 Subaru Horizontally Opposed Four-cylinder

Displacement	109ci
Volume (liters)	1.8
Main journal diameter	2.1636—2.1642in
Main oil clearance	0.0004—0.0012in; 0.0004—0.0010in (center)
Crankshaft end play	0.0004—0.0037in
Thrust journal length	2in
Rod journal diameter	1.7715—1.7720in
Rod oil clearance	0.0008—0.0028in
Rod side clearance	0.0028—0.0130in
Intake valve seat angle	45deg
Exhaust valve seat angle	45deg
Intake face angle	45deg
Exhaust face angle	45deg
Seat width	NA
Spring pressure	NA
Intake stem to guide clearance	0.0014—0.0026in
Exhaust stem to guide clearance	0.0016—0.0028in
Intake stem diameter	0.3130—0.3136in
Exhaust stem diameter	0.3128—0.3134in
Piston clearance	0.001—0.002in
Top comp. ring gap	0.008—0.013in
Bottom comp. ring gap	0.008—0.013in
Oil ring gap	0.008—0.035in
Top comp. side clearance	0.001—0.003in
Bottom comp. side clearance	0.001—0.003in
Oil side clearance	None

1980—1982 Subaru Horizontally Opposed Four-cylinder

Displacement	97ci
Volume (liters)	1.6
Main journal diameter	1.9673—1.9677in (center)
Main oil clearance	0.0004—0.0014; 0.0004—0.0010in (center)
Crankshaft end play	0.00016—0.0054in
Thrust journal length	2in
Rod journal diameter	1.7715—1.7720in
Rod oil clearance	0.008—0.0028in
Rod side clearance	0.0028—0.0130in
Intake valve seat angle	45deg
Exhaust valve seat angle	45deg
Intake face angle	45deg
Exhaust face angle	45deg
Seat width	NA
Spring pressure	NA
Intake stem to guide clearance	0.0014—0.0026in
Exhaust stem to guide clearance	0.0016—0.0028in
Intake stem diameter	0.3130—0.0136in
Exhaust stem diameter	0.3128—0.3134in
Piston clearance	0.001—0.002in
Top comp. ring gap	0.008—0.013in
Bottom comp. ring gap	0.008—0.013in
Oil ring gap	0.008—0.035in
Top comp. side clearance	0.001—0.003in
Bottom comp. side clearance	0.001—0.003in
Oil side clearance	None

1980—1982 Subaru-Horizontally Opposed Four-cylinder

Displacement	109ci
Volume (liters)	1.8
Main journal diameter	2.1636—2.1642in
Main oil clearance	0.004—0.0012in; 0.0004—0.0010in ctr
Crankshaft end play	0.0016—0.0054in
Thrust journal length	2in
Rod journal diameter	1.7715—1.7720in
Rod oil clearance	0.008—0.0028in
Rod side clearance	0.0028—0.0130in
Intake valve seat angle	45deg
Exhaust valve seat angle	45deg
Intake face angle	45deg
Exhaust face angle	45deg
Seat width	NA
Spring pressure	NA
Intake stem to guide clearance	0.0014—0.0026in
Exhaust stem to guide clearance	0.0016—0.0028in
Intake stem diameter	0.3130—0.3136in
Exhaust stem diameter	0.3128—0.3134in
Piston clearance	0.001—0.002in
Top comp. ring gap	0.008—0.013in
Bottom comp. ring gap	0.008—0.013in
Oil ring gap	0.008—0.035in
Top comp. side clearance	0.001—0.003in
Bottom comp. side clearance	0.001—0.003in
Oil side clearance	None

1977—1979 Subaru Horizontally Opposed Four-cylinder

Displacement	97ci
Volume (liters)	1.6
Main journal diameter	1.9673—1.9677in ctr
Main oil clearance	0.0004—0.0016; 0.0018 ctr.
Crankshaft end play	0.0016—0.0054in
Thrust journal length	2in
Rod journal diameter	1.7715—1.7720in
Rod oil clearance	0.0008—0.0028in
Rod side clearance	0.0028—0.0130in
Intake valve seat angle	45deg
Exhaust valve seat angle	45deg
Intake face angle	45deg
Exhaust face angle	45deg
Seat width	NA
Spring pressure	NA
Intake stem to guide clearance	0.0015—0.0026in
Exhaust stem to guide clearance	0.0016—0.0028in
Intake stem diameter	0.3130—0.3136
Exhaust stem diameter	0.3128—0.3134in
Piston clearance	0.001—0.002in
Top comp. ring gap	0.012—0.020in
Bottom comp. ring gap	0.012—0.020in
Oil ring gap	0.012—0.035in
Top comp. side clearance	0.001—0.003in
Bottom comp. side clearance	0.001—0.003in
Oil side clearance	None

1983—1984 Toyota Corolla 4A-C

Displacement	97ci
Volume (liters)	1.587
Main journal diameter	1.8892—1.8898in
Main oil clearance	0.0005—0.0019in
Crankshaft end play	0.0008—0.0073in
Thrust journal length	3in
Rod journal diameter	1.5742—1.5748in
Rod oil clearance	0.0008—0.0020in
Rod side clearance	0.0059—0.0098in
Intake valve seat angle	45deg
Exhaust valve seat angle	45deg
Intake face angle	44deg 30min
Exhaust face angle	44deg 30min
Seat width	NA
Spring pressure	NA
Intake stem to guide clearance	0.0010—0.0024in
Exhaust stem to guide clearance	0.0012—0.0026in
Intake stem diameter	0.2747in
Exhaust stem diameter	0.2745in
Piston clearance	0.0039—0.0047in

Top comp. ring gap	0.0098—0.0138 in
Bottom comp. ring gap	0.0059—0.0118in
Oil ring gap	0.0079—0.0276TPin
Top comp. side clearance	0.0016—0.0031in
Bottom comp. side clearance	0.0012—0.0028in
Oil side clearance	NA

1983—1984 Toyota Cressida 5M-GE

Displacement	168.4ci
Volume (liters)	2.759
Main journal diameter	2.3617—2.3627in
Main oil clearance	0.0013—0.0023in
Crankshaft end play	0.0020—0.0098in
Thrust journal length	4in
Rod journal diameter	2.0463—2.0472in
Rod oil clearance	0.0008—0.0021in
Rod side clearance	0.0063—0.01117in
Intake valve seat angle	45deg
Exhaust valve seat angle	45deg
Intake face angle	44deg 30min
Exhaust face angle	44deg 30min
Seat width	NA
Spring pressure	NA
Intake stem to guide clearance	0.0010—0.0024in
Exhaust stem to guide clearance	0.0012—0.0026in
Intake stem diameter	0.3138—0.3144in
Exhaust stem diameter	0.3136—0.3142in
Piston clearance	0.0020—0.0028in
Top comp. ring gap	0.0083—0.0146in
Bottom comp. ring gap	0.0067—0.0209in
Oil ring gap	0.0079—0.0276in
Top comp. side clearance	0.0012—0.0028in
Bottom comp. side clearance	0.0008—0.0024in
Oil side clearance	Snug

1983—1984 Toyota Starlet 4K-E

Displacement	79ci
Volume (liters)	1.290
Main journal diameter	1.9676—1.9685in
Main oil clearance	0.0006—0.0016in
Crankshaft end play	0.0016—0.0095in
Thrust journal length	3in
Rod journal diameter	1.6526—1.6535in
Rod oil clearance	0.0006—0.0016in
Rod side clearance	0.0079—0.0150in
Intake valve seat angle	45deg
Exhaust valve seat angle	45deg
Intake face angle	44deg 30min
Exhaust face angle	44deg 30min
Seat width	NA
Spring pressure	NA
Intake stem to guide clearance	0.0012—0.0026in
Exhaust stem to guide clearance	0.0014—0.0028in
Intake stem diameter	0.3136—0.3142in
Exhaust stem diameter	0.3134—0.3140in
Piston clearance	0.0012—0.0020in
Top comp. ring gap	0.0063—0.0118in
Bottom comp. ring gap	0.0059—0.0118in
Oil ring gap	0.0080—0.0350in
Top comp. side clearance	0.0012—0.0028in
Bottom comp. side clearance	0.0008—0.0024in
Oil side clearance	Snug

1981—1984 Toyota Celica 22R and 22R-E

Displacement	144.4ci
Volume (liters)	2.367
Main journal diameter	2.3614—2.3622in
Main oil clearance	0.006—0.0020in
Crankshaft end play	0.0008—0.0087in
Thrust journal length	3in
Rod journal diameter	2.0862—2.0866in
Rod oil clearance	0.0010—0.0022in
Rod side clearance	0.0063—0.0102in
Intake valve seat angle	45deg
Exhaust valve seat angle	45deg
Intake face angle	44deg 30min
Exhaust face angle	44deg 30min
Seat width	NA
Spring pressure	NA
Intake stem to guide clearance	0.0008—0.0024in
Exhaust stem to guide clearance	0.0012—0.0028in
Intake stem diameter	0.3145—0.3188 in

Exhaust stem diameter	0.3136—0.3142in
Piston clearance	0.0020—0.0028in
Top comp. ring gap	0.0094—0.0142in
Bottom comp. ring gap	0.0071—0.0154in
Oil ring gap	Snug
Top comp. side clearance	0.0080 max.in
Bottom comp. side clearance	0.0080 max.in
Oil side clearance	Snug

1981—1982 Toyota Corona 22R

Displacement	144.4ci
Volume (liters)	2.367
Main journal diameter	2.3614—2.3622in
Main oil clearance	0.0006—0.0020in
Crankshaft end play	0.0008—0.0087in
Thrust journal length	3in
Rod journal diameter	2.0862—2.0866in
Rod oil clearance	0.0010—0.0022in
Rod side clearance	0.0063—0.0102in
Intake valve seat angle	45deg
Exhaust valve seat angle	45deg
Intake face angle	44deg 30min
Exhaust face angle	44deg 30min
Seat width	NA
Spring pressure	NA
Intake stem to guide clearance	0.0008—0.0024in
Exhaust stem to guide clearance	0.0012—0.0028in
Intake stem diameter	0.3145—0.3188 in
Exhaust stem diameter	0.3136—0.3142in
Piston clearance	0.0020—0.0028in
Top comp. ring gap	0.0094—0.0142in
Bottom comp. ring gap	0.0071—0.0154in
Oil ring gap	Snug
Top comp. side clearance	0.0080 max.in
Bottom comp. side clearance	0.0080 max.in
Oil side clearance	Snug

1981—1982 Toyota Cressida 5M-E

Displacement	168.4ci
Volume (liters)	2.759
Main journal diameter	2.3617—2.3627in
Main oil clearance	0.0013—0.0023in
Crankshaft end play	0.0020—0.0098in
Thrust journal length	4in
Rod journal diameter	2.0463—2.0472in
Rod oil clearance	0.0008—0.0021in
Rod side clearance	0.0063—0.0117in
Intake valve seat angle	45deg
Exhaust valve seat angle	45deg
Intake face angle	44deg 30min
Exhaust face angle	44deg 30min
Seat width	NA
Spring pressure	NA
Intake stem to guide clearance	0.0010—0.0024in
Exhaust stem to guide clearance	0.0014—0.0028in
Intake stem diameter	0.3138—0.3144in
Exhaust stem diameter	0.3134—0.3140in
Piston clearance	0.0020—0.0028in
Top comp. ring gap	0.0039—0.0110in
Bottom comp. ring gap	0.0039—0.0110in
Oil ring gap	0.0079—0.0200in
Top comp. side clearance	0.0012—0.0028in
Bottom comp. side clearance	0.0008—0.0024in
Oil side clearance	Snug

1981 Toyota Supra 5M-E

Displacement	168.4ci
Volume (liters)	2.759
Main journal diameter	2.3617—2.3627in
Main oil clearance	0.0013—0.0023in
Crankshaft end play	0.0020—0.0098in
Thrust journal length	4in
Rod journal diameter	2.0463—2.0472in
Rod oil clearance	0.0008—0.0021in
Rod side clearance	0.0063—0.0117in
Intake valve seat angle	45deg
Exhaust valve seat angle	45deg
Intake face angle	44deg 30min
Exhaust face angle	44deg 30min
Seat width	NA
Spring pressure	NA
Intake stem to guide clearance	0.0010—0.0024in

Exhaust stem to guide clearance	0.0014—0.0028in
Intake stem diameter	0.3138—0.3144in
Exhaust stem diameter	0.3134—0.3142in
Piston clearance	0.0020—0.0028in
Top comp. ring gap	0.0039—0.0110in
Bottom comp. ring gap	0.0039—0.0110in
Oil ring gap	0.0079—0.0200in
Top comp. side clearance	0.0012—0.0028in
Bottom comp. side clearance	0.0008—0.0024in
Oil side clearance	Snug

1980—1984 Toyota Tercel 1A-C, 3A, and 3A-C

Displacement	88.6ci
Volume (liters)	1.452
Main journal diameter	1.8892—1.8898in
Main oil clearance	0.0005—0.0019in
Crankshaft end play	0.0008—0.0073in
Thrust journal length	3in
Rod journal diameter	1.5742—1.5748in
Rod oil clearance	0.0008—0.0020in
Rod side clearance	0.0059—0.0098in
Intake valve seat angle	45deg
Exhaust valve seat angle	45deg
Intake face angle	44deg 30min
Exhaust face angle	44deg 30min
Seat width	NA
Spring pressure	NA
Intake stem to guide clearance	0.0010—0.0024in
Exhaust stem to guide clearance	0.0012—0.0026in
Intake stem diameter	0.2747in
Exhaust stem diameter	0.2745in
Piston clearance	0.0039—0.0047in
Top comp. ring gap	0.0079—0.0157in
Bottom comp. ring gap	0.0059—0.0138in
Oil ring gap	0.0039—0.0236in
Top comp. side clearance	0.0016—0.0031in
Bottom comp. side clearance	0.0012—0.0028in
Oil side clearance	NA

1980—1982 Toyota Corolla 3T-C

Displacement	108.0ci
Volume (liters)	1.800
Main journal diameter	2.2825—2.2835in
Main oil clearance	0.0009—0.0019in
Crankshaft end play	0.0008—0.0087in
Thrust journal length	3in
Rod journal diameter	1.8889—1.8897in
Rod oil clearance	0.0009—0.0019in
Rod side clearance	0.0012—0.0063in
Intake valve seat angle	45deg
Exhaust valve seat angle	45deg
Intake face angle	44deg 30min
Exhaust face angle	44deg 30min
Seat width	NA
Spring pressure	NA
Intake stem to guide clearance	0.0010—0.0024in
Exhaust stem to guide clearance	0.0012—0.0026in
Intake stem diameter	0.3139in
Exhaust stem diameter	0.3139in
Piston clearance	0.0020—0.0028in
Top comp. ring gap	0.0039—0.0098in
Bottom comp. ring gap	0.0059—0.0118in
Oil ring gap	0.0079—0.0276in
Top comp. side clearance	0.0008—0.0024in
Bottom comp. side clearance	0.0006—0.0022in
Oil side clearance	NA

1980 Toyota Cressida 4M-E

Displacement	156.4ci
Volume (liters)	2.563
Main journal diameter	2.3617—2.3627in
Main oil clearance	0.0013—0.0023in
Crankshaft end play	0.0020—0.0098in
Thrust journal length	4in
Rod journal diameter	2.0463—2.0472in
Rod oil clearance	0.0008—0.0021in
Rod side clearance	0.0063—0.0117in
Intake valve seat angle	45deg
Exhaust valve seat angle	45deg
Intake face angle	44deg 30min
Exhaust face angle	44deg 30min

Seat width	NA
Spring pressure	NA
Intake stem to guide clearance	0.0010—0.0024in
Exhaust stem to guide clearance	0.0014—0.0028in
Intake stem diameter	0.3141in
Exhaust stem diameter	0.3137in
Piston clearance	0.0020—0.0028in
Top comp. ring gap	0.0039—0.0110in
Bottom comp. ring gap	0.0039—0.0110in
Oil ring gap	0.0079—0.0200in
Top comp. side clearance	0.0012—0.0028in
Bottom comp. side clearance	0.0008—0.0024in
Oil side clearance	NA

1978—1980 Toyota Celica 20R

Displacement	133.6ci
Volume (liters)	2.189
Main journal diameter	2.3614—2.3622in
Main oil clearance	0.0010—0.0022in
Crankshaft end play	0.0010—0.0080in
Thrust journal length	3in
Rod journal diameter	2.0862—2.0866in
Rod oil clearance	0.0010—0.0022in
Rod side clearance	0.0063—0.0102in
Intake valve seat angle	45deg
Exhaust valve seat angle	45deg
Intake face angle	44deg 30min
Exhaust face angle	44deg 30min
Seat width	NA
Spring pressure	NA
Intake stem to guide clearance	0.0006—0.0024in
Exhaust stem to guide clearance	0.0012—0.0026in
Intake stem diameter	0.3141in
Exhaust stem diameter	0.3140in
Piston clearance	0.0012—0.0020in
Top comp. ring gap	0.0004—0.0012in
Bottom comp. ring gap	0.0004—0.0012in
Oil ring gap	Snug
Top comp. side clearance	0.0008in
Bottom comp. side clearance	0.0008in
Oil side clearance	Snug

1978—1980 Toyota Corona 20R

Displacement	133.6ci
Volume (liters)	2.189
Main journal diameter	2.3614—2.3622in
Main oil clearance	0.0010—0.0022in
Crankshaft end play	0.0010—0.0080in
Thrust journal length	3in
Rod journal diameter	2.0862—2.0866in
Rod oil clearance	0.0010—0.0022in
Rod side clearance	0.0063—0.0102in
Intake valve seat angle	45deg
Exhaust valve seat angle	45deg
Intake face angle	44deg 30min
Exhaust face angle	44deg 30min
Seat width	NA
Spring pressure	NA
Intake stem to guide clearance	0.0006—0.0024in
Exhaust stem to guide clearance	0.0012—0.0026in
Intake stem diameter	0.3141in
Exhaust stem diameter	0.3140in
Piston clearance	0.0012—0.0020in
Top comp. ring gap	0.0004—0.0012in
Bottom comp. ring gap	0.0004—0.0012in
Oil ring gap	Snug
Top comp. side clearance	0.0008in
Bottom comp. side clearance	0.0008in
Oil side clearance	Snug

1978—1979 Toyota Corolla 3K-C

Displacement	71.2ci
Volume (liters)	1.166
Main journal diameter	1.9675—1.9685in
Main oil clearance	0.0005—0.0015in
Crankshaft end play	0.0016—0.0087in
Thrust journal length	3in
Rod journal diameter	1.6525—1.6535in
Rod oil clearance	0.0009—0.0019in
Rod side clearance	0.0043—0.0080in
Intake valve seat angle	45deg
Exhaust valve seat angle	45deg

Intake face angle	44deg 30min
Exhaust face angle	44deg 30min
Seat width	NA
Spring pressure	NA
Intake stem to guide clearance	0.0012—0.0026in
Exhaust stem to guide clearance	0.0014—0.0028in
Intake stem diameter	0.3140in
Exhaust stem diameter	0.3140in
Piston clearance	0.0010—0.0020in
Top comp. ring gap	0.004—0.011in
Bottom comp. ring gap	0.004—0.011in
Oil ring gap	0.008—0.035in
Top comp. side clearance	0.0011—0.0027in
Bottom comp. side clearance	0.001—0.003in
Oil side clearance	0.0006—0.0023in

1978—1979 Toyota Cressida 4M

Displacement	156.4ci
Volume (liters)	2.563
Main journal diameter	2.3617—2.3627in
Main oil clearance	0.0012—0.0021in
Crankshaft end play	0.0020—0.0100in
Thrust journal length	4in
Rod journal diameter	2.0463—2.0472in
Rod oil clearance	0.0008—0.0021in
Rod side clearance	0.0063—0.0117in
Intake valve seat angle	45deg
Exhaust valve seat angle	45deg
Intake face angle	44deg 30min
Exhaust face angle	44deg 30min
Seat width	NA
Spring pressure	NA
Intake stem to guide clearance	0.0006—0.0018in
Exhaust stem to guide clearance	0.0010—0.0024in
Intake stem diameter	0.3146in
Exhaust stem diameter	0.3140in
Piston clearance	0.0020—0.0030in
Top comp. ring gap	0.0039—0.0110in
Bottom comp. ring gap	0.0059—0.0110in
Oil ring gap	0.0008—0.0200in
Top comp. side clearance	0.001—0.003in
Bottom comp. side clearance	0.0008—0.0035in
Oil side clearance	Snug

1977 Toyota Celica 20R

Displacement	133.6ci
Volume (liters)	2.189
Main journal diameter	2.3614—2.3622in
Main oil clearance	0.0010—0.0022in
Crankshaft end play	0.0008—0.0079in
Thrust journal length	3in
Rod journal diameter	2.0862—2.0866in
Rod oil clearance	0.0010—0.0022in
Rod side clearance	0.0063—0.0102in
Intake valve seat angle	45deg
Exhaust valve seat angle	45deg
Intake face angle	44deg 30min
Exhaust face angle	44deg 30min
Seat width	NA
Spring pressure	NA
Intake stem to guide clearance	0.0006—0.0024in
Exhaust stem to guide clearance	0.0012—0.0026in
Intake stem diameter	0.3141in
Exhaust stem diameter	0.3140in
Piston clearance	0.0012—0.0020in
Top comp. ring gap	0.0004—0.0012in
Bottom comp. ring gap	0.0004—0.0012in
Oil ring gap	Snug
Top comp. side clearance	0.0008in
Bottom comp. side clearance	0.0008in
Oil side clearance	Snug

1977 Toyota Corolla 2T-C

Displacement	96.9ci
Volume (liters)	1.588
Main journal diameter	2.2827—2.2834in
Main oil clearance	0.0012—0.0024in
Crankshaft end play	0.0030—0.0070in
Thrust journal length	3in
Rod journal diameter	1.8889—1.8897in
Rod oil clearance	0.0008—0.0020in
Rod side clearance	0.0063—0.0102in

Intake valve seat angle	45deg
Exhaust valve seat angle	45deg
Intake face angle	44deg 30min
Exhaust face angle	44deg 30min
Seat width	NA
Spring pressure	NA
Intake stem to guide clearance	0.0012—0.0020in
Exhaust stem to guide clearance	0.0012—0.0024in
Intake stem diameter	0.3140in
Exhaust stem diameter	0.3140in
Piston clearance	0.0024—0.0031in
Top comp. ring gap	0.0008—0.0016in
Bottom comp. ring gap	0.0004—0.0012in
Oil ring gap	0.0004—0.0012in
Top comp. side clearance	0.0008—0.0024in
Bottom comp. side clearance	0.0008—0.0024in
Oil side clearance	0.0008—0.0024in

1977 Toyota Corolla 3K-C

Displacement	71.2ci
Volume (liters)	1.166
Main journal diameter	1.9675—1.9685in
Main oil clearance	0.0005—0.0015in
Crankshaft end play	0.0020—0.0090in
Thrust journal length	3in
Rod journal diameter	1.6525—1.6535in
Rod oil clearance	0.0006—0.0015in
Rod side clearance	0.0040—0.0080in
Intake valve seat angle	45deg
Exhaust valve seat angle	45deg
Intake face angle	44deg 30min
Exhaust face angle	44deg 30min
Seat width	NA
Spring pressure	NA
Intake stem to guide clearance	0.0010—0.0020in
Exhaust stem to guide clearance	0.0020—0.0030in
Intake stem diameter	0.3140in
Exhaust stem diameter	0.3140in
Piston clearance	0.0010—0.0020in
Top comp. ring gap	0.0006—0.0014in
Bottom comp. ring gap	0.0006—0.0014in
Oil ring gap	0.0006—0.0014in
Top comp. side clearance	0.0011—0.0027in
Bottom comp. side clearance	0.0007—0.0023in
Oil side clearance	0.0006—0.0023in

1977 Toyota Corona 20R

Displacement	133.6ci
Volume (liters)	2.189
Main journal diameter	2.3614—2.3622in
Main oil clearance	0.0010—0.0022in
Crankshaft end play	0.0008—0.0079in
Thrust journal length	3in
Rod journal diameter	2.0862—2.0866in
Rod oil clearance	0.0010—0.0022in
Rod side clearance	0.0063—0.0102in
Intake valve seat angle	45deg
Exhaust valve seat angle	45deg
Intake face angle	44deg 30min
Exhaust face angle	44deg 30min
Seat width	NA
Spring pressure	NA
Intake stem to guide clearance	0.0006—0.0024in
Exhaust stem to guide clearance	0.0012—0.0026in
Intake stem diameter	0.3141in
Exhaust stem diameter	0.3140in
Piston clearance	0.0012—0.0020in
Top comp. ring gap	0.0004—0.0012in
Bottom comp. ring gap	0.0004—0.0012in
Oil ring gap	Snug
Top comp. side clearance	0.0008in
Bottom comp. side clearance	0.0008in
Oil side clearance	Snug

1982—1984 Toyota Supra 5M-GE

Displacement	168.4ci
Volume (liters)	2.759
Main journal diameter	2.3617—2.3627in
Main oil clearance	0.0013—0.0023in
Crankshaft end play	0.0020—0.0098in
Thrust journal length	4in
Rod journal diameter	2.0463—2.0472in

Rod oil clearance	0.0008—0.0021in
Rod side clearance	0.0063—0.0117in
Intake valve seat angle	45deg
Exhaust valve seat angle	45deg
Intake face angle	44deg 30min
Exhaust face angle	44deg 30min
Seat width	NA
Spring pressure	NA
Intake stem to guide clearance	0.0010—0.0024in
Exhaust stem to guide clearance	0.0012—0.0026in
Intake stem diameter	0.3138—0.3144in
Exhaust stem diameter	0.3136—0.3142in
Piston clearance	0.0020—0.0028in
Top comp. ring gap	0.0083—0.0146in
Bottom comp. ring gap	0.0067—0.0209in
Oil ring gap	0.0079—0.0276in
Top comp. side clearance	0.0012—0.0028in
Bottom comp. side clearance	0.0008—0.0024in
Oil side clearance	Snug

1981—1982 Toyota Starlet 4K-C

Displacement	78.7ci
Volume (liters)	1.290
Main journal diameter	1.9676—1.9685in
Main oil clearance	0.0006—0.0016in
Crankshaft end play	0.0016—0.0095in
Thrust journal length	3in
Rod journal diameter	1.6526—1.6535in
Rod oil clearance	0.0006—0.0016in
Rod side clearance	0.0079—0.0150in
Intake valve seat angle	45deg
Exhaust valve seat angle	45deg
Intake face angle	44deg 30min
Exhaust face angle	44deg 30min
Seat width	NA
Spring pressure	NA
Intake stem to guide clearance	0.0012—0.0026in
Exhaust stem to guide clearance	0.0014—0.0028in
Intake stem diameter	0.3136—0.3142in
Exhaust stem diameter	0.3134—0.3140in
Piston clearance	0.0012—0.0020in
Top comp. ring gap	0.0039—0.0110in
Bottom comp. ring gap	0.0039—0.0118in
Oil ring gap	0.0080—0.0350in
Top comp. side clearance	0.0012—0.0028in
Bottom comp. side clearance	0.0008—0.0024in
Oil side clearance	Snug

1979-1/2—1980 Toyota Supra 4M-E

Displacement	156.4ci
Volume (liters)	2.563
Main journal diameter	2.3617—2.3627in
Main oil clearance	0.0013—0.0023in
Crankshaft end play	0.0020—0.0098in
Thrust journal length	4in
Rod journal diameter	2.0463—2.0472in
Rod oil clearance	0.0008—0.0021in
Rod side clearance	0.0063—0.0117in
Intake valve seat angle	45deg
Exhaust valve seat angle	45deg
Intake face angle	44deg 30min
Exhaust face angle	44deg 30min
Seat width	NA
Spring pressure	NA
Intake stem to guide clearance	0.0010—0.0024in
Exhaust stem to guide clearance	0.0014—0.0028in
Intake stem diameter	0.3141in
Exhaust stem diameter	0.3137in
Piston clearance	0.0020—0.0028in
Top comp. ring gap	0.0039—0.0110in
Bottom comp. ring gap	0.0039—0.0110in
Oil ring gap	0.0079—0.0200in
Top comp. side clearance	0.0012—0.0028in
Bottom comp. side clearance	0.0008—0.0024in
Oil side clearance	NA

1978—1979 Toyota Corolla 2T-C

Displacement	96.9ci
Volume (liters)	1.588
Main journal diameter	2.2827—2.2834in
Main oil clearance	0.0009—0.0019in
Crankshaft end play	0.0010—0.0090in

Thrust journal length	3in
Rod journal diameter	1.8889—1.8897in
Rod oil clearance	0.0008—0.0020in
Rod side clearance	0.0063—0.0102in
Intake valve seat angle	45deg
Exhaust valve seat angle	45deg
Intake face angle	44deg 30min
Exhaust face angle	44deg 30min
Seat width	NA
Spring pressure	NA
Intake stem to guide clearance	0.0012—0.0020in
Exhaust stem to guide clearance	0.0012—0.0024in
Intake stem diameter	0.3140in
Exhaust stem diameter	0.3140in
Piston clearance	0.0024—0.0031in
Top comp. ring gap	0.006—0.011in
Bottom comp. ring gap	0.008—0.013in
Oil ring gap	0.008—0.028in
Top comp. side clearance	0.0008—0.0024in
Bottom comp. side clearance	0.0006—0.0022in
Oil side clearance	0.008—0.035in

1983—1984 Volvo 240s B21

Displacement	130ci
Volume (liters)	2.217
Main journal diameter	2.4981—2.4986in
Main journal oil clearance	0.0011—0.0033in
Crankshaft end play	0.0015—0.0058in
Thrust journal length	5in
Rod journal diameter	2.1255—2.1260in
Rod oil clearance	0.0009—0.0028in
Rod side clearance	0.006—0.014in
Intake valve seat angle	44deg 45min
Exhaust valve seat angle	44deg 45min
Intake face angle	45deg 30min
Exhaust face angle	45deg 30min
Seat width	NA
Spring pressure	NA
Intake stem to guide clearance	0.0012—0.0024in
Exhaust stem to guide clearance	0.0024—0.0035in
Intake stem diameter	0.3132—0.3135in
Exhaust stem diameter	0.3126—0.3138in
Piston clearance	0.0004—0.0016in
Top comp. ring gap	0.014—0.026in
Bottom comp. ring gap	0.014—0.022in
Oil ring gap	0.010—0.024in
Top comp. side clearance	0.0016—0.0028in
Bottom comp. side clearance	0.0016—0.0028in
Oil side clearance	0.0012—0.0024in

1983—1984 Volvo 240s B23 v1

Displacement	140ci
Volume (liters)	2.230
Main journal diameter	2.4981—2.4986in
Main journal oil clearance	0.0011—0.0033in
Crankshaft end play	0.0015—0.0058in
Thrust journal length	5in
Rod journal diameter	2.1255—2.1260in
Rod oil clearance	0.0009—0.0028in
Rod side clearance	0.006—0.014in
Intake valve seat angle	45deg
Exhaust valve seat angle	45deg
Intake face angle	44deg 30min
Exhaust face angle	44deg 30min
Seat width	NA
Spring pressure	NA
Intake stem to guide clearance	0.0012—0.0024in
Exhaust stem to guide clearance	0.0024—0.0035in
Intake stem diameter	0.3132—0.3138in
Exhaust stem diameter	0.3124—0.3128in
Piston clearance	0.0020—0.0028in
Top comp. ring gap	0.014—0.026in
Bottom comp. ring gap	0.014—0.022in
Oil ring gap	0.0010—0.0024in
Top comp. side clearance	0.0015—0.0028in
Bottom comp. side clearance	0.0015—0.0028in
Oil side clearance	0.0012—0.0024in

1983—1984 Volvo 240s B23 v2

Displacement	140ci
Volume (liters)	2.230
Main journal diameter	2.4981—2.4986in

Main journal oil clearance 0.0011—0.0033in
Crankshaft end play 0.0015—0.0058in
Thrust journal length 5in
Rod journal diameter 2.1255—2.1260in
Rod oil clearance 0.0009—0.0028in
Rod side clearance 0.006—0.014in
Intake valve seat angle 45deg
Exhaust valve seat angle 45deg
Intake face angle 44deg 30min
Exhaust face angle 44deg 30min
Seat width NA
Spring pressure NA
Intake stem to guide clearance 0.0012—0.0024in
Exhaust stem to guide clearance 0.0024—0.0035in
Intake stem diameter 0.3132—0.3138in
Exhaust stem diameter 0.3124—0.3128in
Piston clearance 0.0016—0.0040in
Top comp. ring gap 0.014—0.026in
Bottom comp. ring gap 0.014—0.022in
Oil ring gap 0.0010—0.0024in
Top comp. side clearance 0.0015—0.0028in
Bottom comp. side clearance 0.0015—0.0028in
Oil side clearance 0.0012—0.0024in

1977—1982 Volvo 240s B21

Displacement 130ci
Volume (liters) 2.217
Main journal diameter 2.4981—2.4986in
Main journal oil clearance 0.0011—0.0033in
Crankshaft end play 0.0015—0.0058in
Thrust journal length 5in
Rod journal diameter 2.1255—2.1260in
Rod oil clearance 0.0009—0.0028in
Rod side clearance 0.006—0.014in
Intake valve seat angle 44deg 45min
Exhaust valve seat angle 44deg 45min

Intake face angle 45deg 30min
Exhaust face angle 45deg 30min
Seat width NA
Spring pressure NA
Intake stem to guide clearance 0.0012—0.0024in
Exhaust stem to guide clearance 0.0024—0.0035in
Intake stem diameter 0.3132—0.3135in
Exhaust stem diameter 0.3126—0.3128in
Piston clearance 0.0004—0.0012in
Top comp. ring gap 0.0138—0.0217in
Bottom comp. ring gap 0.0138—0.0217in
Oil ring gap 0.010—0.016in
Top comp. side clearance 0.0016—0.0028in
Bottom comp. side clearance 0.0016—0.0028in
Oil side clearance 0.0016—0.0028in

1980—1984 Volvo 260s B28

Displacement 174ci
Volume (liters) 2.849
Main journal diameter 2.7583in
Main journal oil clearance 0.0035in
Crankshaft end play 0.0106in
Thrust journal length 4in
Rod journal diameter 2.0585in
Rod oil clearance 0.0031in
Rod side clearance 0.015in
Intake valve seat angle 29deg 30min
Exhaust valve seat angle 30deg
Intake face angle 29deg 30min
Exhaust face angle 30deg
Seat width NA
Spring pressure NA
Intake stem to guide clearance 0.3150—0.3158
tapered
Exhaust stem to guide clearance 0.3150—0.3158
tapered
Intake stem diameter 0.3140—0.3146in
Exhaust stem diameter 0.3136—0.3142in

Piston clearance 0.0008—0.0016in
Top comp. ring gap 0.016—0.022in
Bottom comp. ring gap 0.016—0.022in
Oil ring gap 0.015—0.055in
Top comp. side clearance 0.0018—0.0029in
Bottom comp. side clearance 0.0010—0.0021in
Oil side clearance 0.0004—0.0092in

1977—1979 Volvo 260s B27

Displacement 162ci
Volume (liters) 2.660
Main journal diameter 2.7576in
Main journal oil clearance 0.0015in
Crankshaft end play 0.0028in
Thrust journal length 4in
Rod journal diameter 2.0578in
Rod oil clearance 0.0012in
Rod side clearance 0.008in
Intake valve seat angle 29deg 30min
Exhaust valve seat angle 30deg
Intake face angle 29deg 30min
Exhaust face angle 30deg
Seat width NA
Spring pressure NA
Intake stem to guide clearance 0.3150—0.3158
tapered
Exhaust stem to guide clearance 0.3150—0.3158
tapered
Intake stem diameter 0.3136—0.3142in
Exhaust stem diameter 0.3128—0.3134in
Piston clearance 0.0008—0.0016in
Top comp. ring gap 0.016—0.022in
Bottom comp. ring gap 0.016—0.022in
Oil ring gap 0.015—0.055in
Top comp. side clearance 0.0018—0.0029in
Bottom comp. side clearance 0.0010—0.0021in
Oil side clearance 0.0004—0.0092

Drill Sizes for Taps

Nominal drill sizes for taps, American threads

Nominal size	Tap drill, inches	Tap drill, mm
1/16-64	3/64	1.2
3/32-48	#49	1.85
1/8-40	#38	2.6
5/32-32	1/8	3.2
5/32-36	#30	3.25
3/16-24	#26	3.75
3/16-32	5/32	4
7/32-24	#16	4.5
7/32-32	3/16	4.8
1/4-20	13/64	5.1
1/4-24	#4	5.3
1/4-28	7/32	5.5
1/4-32	7/32	5.6
5/16-18	F	6.5
5/16-24	I	6.9
5/16-32	9/32	7.2
3/8-16	5/16	8
3/8-24	Q	8.5
7/16-14	3/8	9.3
7/16-20	25/64	9.9
1/2-12	27/64	10.75
1/2-13	27/64	10.75
1/2-20	29/64	11.5
9/16-12	31/64	12
9/16-18	33/64	13
5/8-11	17/32	13.5
5/8-18	37/64	14.5
11/16-11	19/32	15
11/16-16	5/8	16
3/4-10	21/32	16.5
3/4-16	11/16	17.5

Nominal drill sizes for taps, metric

Nominal size	Pitch, m/m	Tap drill, m/m
1.5	0.35	1.1
2	0.40	1.6
2	0.45	1.5
2	0.50	1.5
2.3	0.40	1.9
2.5	0.45	2
2.6	0.45	2.1
3	0.50	2.5
3	0.60	2.4
3	0.75	2.25
3.5	0.60	2.9
4	0.70	3.3
4	0.75	3.25
4.5	0.75	3.75
5	0.75	4.25
5	0.80	4.2
5	0.90	4.1
5	1.00	4
5.5	0.75	4.75
5.5	0.90	4.6
6	1.00	5
6	1.25	4.8
7	1.00	6
7	1.25	5.8
8	1.00	7
8	1.25	6.8
9	1.00	8
9	1.25	7.8
10	1.25	8.8
10	1.5	8.6
11	1.5	9.6
12	1.25	11
12	1.50	10.5
12	1.75	10.5
13	1.50	11.5
13	1.75	11.5
13	2.00	11
14	1.25	13
14	1.75	12.5
14	2.00	12
15	1.75	13.5
15	2.00	13
16	2.00	14
17	2.00	15
18	1.5	16.5
18	2.00	16
18	2.50	15.5
19	2.50	16.5
20	2.00	18
20	2.50	17.5
22	2.50	19.5
24	3.00	21
26	3.00	23
27	3.00	24
28	3.00	25
30	3.50	26.5

Tapping Lubricants

Sulphur bases oil	DryLight oil	Kerosene & lard oil
Cast steel	Hard rubberBrass	Aluminum
Stainless steel	FiberBronze	Duralumin
Machinery steel	Cast ironCopper	Die castings
Tool steel	Synthetic resins	Mangenese
Chromium steel	Bronze	
Moly steel		
Nickel steel		
Vanadium steel		
Mangenese steel		
Malleable iron		

Index